A collector's guide to
SEASHELLS
of the WORLD

A collector's guide to
SEASHELLS
of the WORLD

by

Jerome M. Eisenberg

Consulting Editor: William E. Old, Jr.

with photographs and drawings by the author

McGraw-Hill Book Company
NEW YORK · LONDON
St. Louis · San Francisco · Auckland · Johannesburg
Mexico · Sydney · Tokyo · Toronto

First published in the United States of America, 1981,
by McGraw-Hill Book Company
1221 Avenue of the Americas, New York

First published in the United Kingdom, 1981,
by McGraw-Hill Book Company (UK) Limited,
Maidenhead, Berkshire, England

Library of Congress Cataloging in Publication Data

Eisenberg, Jerome M.
  A collector's guide to seashells of the world.

  Includes index.
  1. Shells. 2. Shells – Identification.
I. Old, William E. II. Title.
QL403.E35   594'.0471   80–14886
ISBN 0–07–019140–9

This book was designed and produced by John Calmann and Cooper Ltd., London
Typeset by Composing Operations Limited, Tunbridge Wells, Kent

Printed in Hong Kong

**1. (*Frontispiece*) XENOPHORA
PALLIDULA Reeve, with shells
and sponge attached. Philippine
Islands. *See* pl. 39, no. 8. (2/3).**

Contents

Introduction

Numerous books on seashells are available: why produce another? Since I began actively collecting seashells, ten years ago, I have felt the strong need for a single, comprehensive volume to identify most worldwide seashells, rather than having to rely on a variety of publications.

In my opinion there are perhaps no more than 1,000 species that are outstanding for their aesthetic appeal, and another thousand or so species that are also commonly collected, traded or sold. Thus the contents of this book were first visualized as an ideal 2,000-species collection. To reach this goal I then began actively collecting, exchanging or buying the needed shells to add to my existing collection. By cross-indexing all the species included in previous popular publications, I came up with more than 2,000 shells that appeared over and over again. Then, in order to give a better overall picture of the vast seashell kingdom, by adding shells that were being currently listed by the leading shell dealers, as well as many examples of species from the more obscure families that are rarely offered for sale or illustrated, I ended up with over 2,600 species. All of the specimens illustrated in this book – more than 4,000 – are in my collection.

There are several features in this book which should aid the collector in identification. Whenever possible, more than one example has been illustrated to demonstrate the remarkable range of colors, patterns and even forms of many species, which can lead to confusion in their identification. The members of a family are illustrated as far as possible in the same scale.

Emphasized, of course, are the most popular families, especially the cowries, cones, murex, volutes, olives and pectens. The representation of these families in this book is the most comprehensive of any publication to date, monographs excepted. Those monographs dealing with the individual families are listed in the bibliography.

In addition to the minimum and maximum sizes, which apply in most cases for adult specimens, the range of average sizes normally collected is also indicated whenever possible. The relative rarity of shells can be difficult to assess. A shell can be prolific in one location and rare in another. I have indicated the relative rarity by taking the world average for the entire geographic distribution of each shell. Also taken into consideration are the abundance in the principal collecting areas and the number being offered for sale.

2. (*Top*) STELLARIA SOLARIS Linne. Taiwan. *See* pl. 40, no. 7. (3/2).

3. (*Bottom*) STROMBUS GALLUS Linne. Martinique. See listing on pl. 33. (3/2).

Shell Names

At first glance the scientific names of seashells appear quite complicated to the novice or amateur collector, who would be delighted to use just the popular or common names. However, these common names may vary in different areas, even different parts of the same country, or the same name may be used for two or more species.

A binomial system, with names in Latin, established by Carl Linné (or Linnaeus) in 1758, is accepted worldwide and used for all forms of animal and plant life, including the fossil forms. The first name, always with an initial capital, refers to the genus. The second name, not capitalized, refers to the species. The name of the author who first described and named the species is placed after it. The date of publication may follow the name in more formal publications. Example: *Cypraea tigris* Linné, 1758. When a subgenus is used, it is placed in parentheses after the generic name and is also capitalized. Example: *Conus (Cylinder) textile* Linné, 1758. When the subspecies is named, it is placed after the species name, also not capitalized, and the author of the subspecies is placed after it, eliminating the name of the author of the species. Example: *Cypraea tigris schilderiana* Cate, 1961. The name of the genus, subgenus, species, subspecies and form should be italicized. As an example of the confusion in names, the subspecies used above as an example is now considered to be just a geographic form. Thus it should properly be described as *Cypraea tigris forma schilderiana* Cate, 1961. The abbreviation for forma (f.) or variety (var.) may be used, also in italics.

When a genus or species name is repeated in the text, it may be abbreviated by its initials. Examples: *C. tigris* or *C. t. schilderiana*. Another usage, not employed in this and most other popular publications, is the placing of the author's name and date in parentheses if the species has been reclassified under another genus. Example: *Murex regius* Swainson is now *Hexaplex regius* (Swainson, 1821).

As more is learned about the anatomy and physiology of the many families and genera of shells, there is a great deal of reclassification and reassignment of species. This is especially true of the larger and more complicated families. Thus a multitude of names have been discarded for new ones. Names used later for a species that has already been described are normally judged redundant and are discarded, then being known as synonyms. Those popular names and synonyms most often encountered are included in the descriptive section of this book to help the collector in identifying and reattributing shells.

For comparison, the systematic classification of two common species of animals are listed below. The prefixes "super-" and "sub-" are used for further degrees of division, especially in the phylum Mollusca.

Phylum:	Mollusca	Chordata
Class:	Gastropoda	Mammalia
Subclass:	Prosobranchia	
Order:	Mesogastropoda	Primates
Suborder:	Taenioglossa	
Superfamily:	Cypraeacea	
Family:	Cypraeidae	Hominidae
Subfamily:	Cypraeinae	
Genus:	*Cypraea*	*Homo*
Subgenus:	*Cypraea*	
Species:	*tigris*	*sapiens*
Subspecies:		
Form:	*schilderiana*	

Life History and Characteristics

The phylum Mollusca contains about 50,000 living species, or perhaps as many as 100,000 according to some authorities, divided into seven classes. All have a soft body, mostly covered by an exoskeleton or external calcareous shell, which is secreted by a fleshy mantle.

Some are hermaphroditic, with both sex organs in the same shell. A few even change from male to female as they mature. In most species the female lays eggs, often enclosed in capsules, and the male sheds sperm. The egg passes through several larval stages, generally changing into a free-swimming veliger, which soon produces a shell. Some develop completely within the egg capsule. Some species are also live-bearing.

Most shells have a life-span varying from two to about fifteen years. Some larger shells may live for far longer periods of time, perhaps even as much as seventy-five years or more.

The color of the shell is produced by pigments made by the glands in the mantle and deposited in the uppermost calcareous layer of the shell. The color may be affected by the animal's food, the pattern by variations in the production of the pigments.

The shape and color of the shell is often affected by the turbulence, temperature and depth of the water. Rough, shallow waters will generally produce a smoother, thicker, less sculptured shell with a larger aperture. The most colorful shells are usually found in shallow, warm waters, while virtually all Arctic and deep-sea shells are drab or white. Rapid growth will generally produce a less patterned shell. The periods of growth are reflected in the growth lines that run parallel to the edge or margin.

4. (*Overleaf, left*) **CYPRAEA VALENTIA Perry. Philippine Islands.** *See listing on* pl. 54. (2/1).

5. (*Overleaf, right*) **MUREX PHYLLOPTERUS Lamarck. Martinique.** *See* pl. 74, no. 3. (5/2).

The Classes of Seashells

Class GASTROPODA. The gastropod, also known as a snail or univalve, has a head with tentacles, eyes and a rasping tongue or radula. The distinct foot often produces a cover or operculum to close the shell. Practically all have a single coiled or cap-shaped shell. Some, such as the nudibranchs, lack shells. This class also includes slugs and freshwater snails. There are perhaps 40,000 living species.

Class BIVALVIA. The bivalve or pelecypod has basically two interlocking calcareous valves held together by one or two adductor muscles. Some have a wedge-shaped foot; others may be attached to the substrate by the byssus, secreted by the foot, or cemented by one of the valves.

They are headless and lack radula and tentacles. The Pectinidae and Spondylidae have eye-spots on their mantle edge. There are 7,500 or more bivalve species, about one-third of which are freshwater.

Class POLYPLACOPHORA. The polyplacophorans or chitons have an elongate soft body covered by eight overlapping shelly plates, surrounded by a leathery girdle. They are headless, with no eyes, radula or tentacles. Usually attached to rocks in shallow water, they move slowly with a broad creeping foot, feeding mainly on algae. There are about 600 or more species. See pages 206–7 and plates 157–8.

Class APLACOPHERA. The aplacopherans or solenogasters are rare, wormlike, deepwater mollusks, lacking a shell but covered with tiny calcareous spicules. They are without a head or foot, but do have a slit-like mouth with a radula. All are hermaphroditic. They were once combined with the Polyplacophora as the class "Amphineura". About 250 species are known.

Class MONOPLACOPHORA. The monoplacophorans or gastroverms are the most primitive mollusks and so rare that the first living forms were only discovered in 1957. They have a small cap-like shell, with paired internal organs. They lack eyes and a foot, but have a radula in the mouth. About ten species are known, all in very deep water.

Class SCAPHOPODA. The scaphopod or tusk shell has a hollow, calcareous, tube-like shell. It has a mouth with radula, eyeless tentacles and a conical foot. They number about 350 species. See page 207 and plate 158.

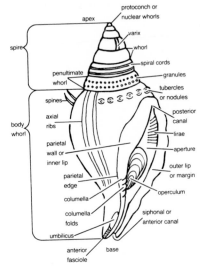

Parts of a gastropod

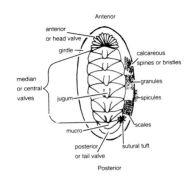

Parts of a chiton

6. (*Overleaf, left*) OLIVA
RUBROLABIATA H. Fischer.
New Hebrides. *See* pl. 105, no. 12.
(9/2).

7. (*Overleaf, right*) CONUS
CROCATUS Lamarck. Thailand.
See pl. 118, no. 13. (4/1).

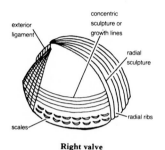

**Right valve
of a bivalve (exterior)**

Class CEPHALOPODA. The cephalopods are the most advanced mollusks, having a highly developed head with large eyes, beak and radula. All possess eight or more arms with suckers. Most members of this class, including the squid, octopus and cuttlefish, lack an external shell. They number about 800 species. See pages 207–8 and plate 158.

Distribution in Depth

Most seashells are found in intertidal to shallow waters, on sand, mud or rocky bottoms. Most of the more colorful species are found in warm waters, near coral reefs.

Pelagic mollusks are those that live at or near the surface of the water.

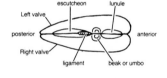

Dorsal view of a bivalve

Intertidal or *littoral* species are found between the high- and low-tide lines of the seashore. Some are found above the high-tide line in the so-called splash zone. Many species thrive in areas such as mangrove swamps, where fresh water meets sea water.

Shallow-water shells include those found from either the high-tide line, including the intertidal zone, or low-tide line to a depth of from 80 to 200 feet. The interpretation of both boundaries varies with different authors.

Deep-water or *abyssal* specimens are those found in either 200 feet or, according to some, 400 feet or more of water. In fact, the term "moderately deep" has been used for only 80 feet or more, and our term "deep-water" follows this usage.

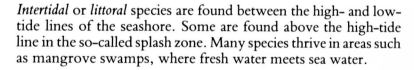

**Left valve
of a bivalve (interior)**

Geographical Distribution

The marine faunal or zoogeographical provinces are somewhat loosely defined areas of the world's major bodies of water which possess conditions favorable to a specific group of mollusks. A species may live in part or all of this province and may also occasionally range beyond it.

Arctic: Circumpolar or north polar seas, including N.Canada south to the Gulf of St. Lawrence, Greenland, N.Siberia, N. Alaska.

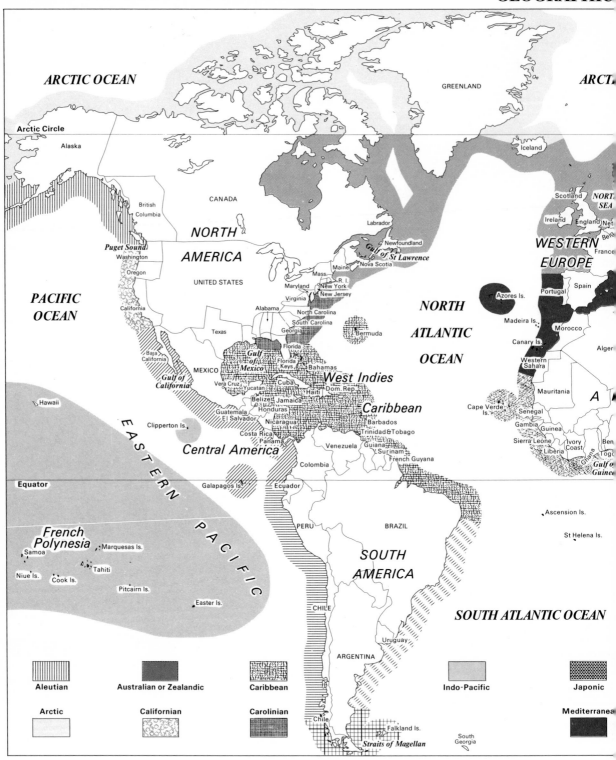

ARCTIC OCEAN

Arctic Circle

Alaska

British Columbia

CANADA

NORTH AMERICA

UNITED STATES

Puget Sound
Washington

Oregon

PACIFIC OCEAN

California

Baja California

MEXICO

Gulf of California

Hawaii

Vera Cruz

Yucatan

Gulf of Mexico

Florida
Florida Keys

Cuba

Belize
Guatemala
El Salvador
Honduras
Nicaragua
Costa Rica
Panama

Central America

Clipperton Is.

EASTERN PACIFIC

Equator

French Polynesia
Samoa
Marquesas Is.
Niue Is.
Cook Is.
Tahiti
Pitcairn Is.
Easter Is.

Galapagos Is.

Ecuador

PERU

Colombia

Venezuela

Guiana
Surinam
French Guyana

CHILE

BRAZIL

SOUTH AMERICA

Uruguay

ARGENTINA

Chile

Falkland Is.

South Georgia

Straits of Magellan

GREENLAND

Labrador

Newfoundland
Gulf of St Lawrence
Nova Scotia

Maine
Mass.
R. I.
New York
New Jersey

Maryland

Virginia

North Carolina
South Carolina
Georgia

Alabama

Texas

Bermuda

Bahamas

Haiti
Dom. Rep.

Jamaica

West Indies

Caribbean

Barbados
Trinidad&Tobago

Iceland

NORTH ATLANTIC OCEAN

Azores Is.

Madeira Is.

Canary Is.

Cape Verde Is.

Scotland

Ireland

NORTH SEA

England
Net

Belg
France

WESTERN EUROPE

Spain

Portugal

Morocco

Western Sahara

Algeri

Mauritania

A

Senegal
Gambia
Guinea
Sierra Leone
Liberia
Ivory Coast
Ben

Gulf of Guinea

Ascension Is.

St Helena Is.

SOUTH ATLANTIC OCEAN

Legend

	Aleutian
	Arctic
	Australian or Zealandic
	Californian
	Caribbean
	Carolinian
	Indo-Pacific
	Japonic
	Mediterranea

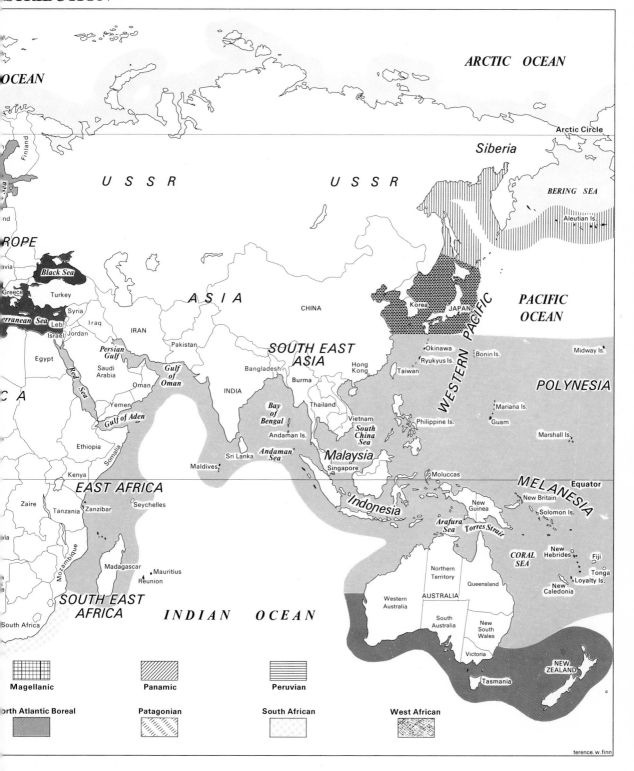

Magellanic

Panamic

Peruvian

orth Atlantic Boreal

Patagonian

South African

West African

terence. w. finn

Aleutian or *North Pacific Boreal*: A subprovince including the N.Pacific from Siberia and Alaska to the Bering Sea and south to British Columbia. Cold waters.

Japonic or *Japanese*: Japan to Korea, not including S.Japan and the Ryukyu Islands. Temperate to subtropical waters.

Indo-Pacific: The most extensive and prolific province, including the Red Sea, the entire coast of E.Africa south to Natal, S.Africa, the Indian Ocean, Indonesia, north to S.Japan and the China Seas, south to the north and east coasts of Australia, and the tropical Pacific east to Hawaii and Polynesia, even including Easter and Clipperton Islands in the E.Pacific. Warm, tropical waters.

Australian or *Zealandic*: Southern Australia, Tasmania and New Zealand. Subtropical to temperate waters.

California: British Columbia to northern Baja California. May be divided into two subprovinces: *Oregonian*, from British Columbia to Central California, and *Californian*, now referring to Central California to northern Baja California.

Panamic or *Panamanian*: Southern Baja California and the Gulf of California south to Ecuador, including the Galàpagos Islands. Mainly warm, tropical waters.

Peruvian: Ecuador to Chile. Subtropical to temperate waters.

Magellanic: S.Chile, S.Argentina, Falkland Islands, south to Antarctica. Cold waters.

North Atlantic Boreal: A subprovince including the N. Atlantic from the Gulf of St. Lawrence to northern Cape Cod, S. Iceland, and W.Europe south of the Arctic Circle, including the North Sea and Baltic Sea, south to the English Channel. Cool waters.

Carolinian or *Transatlantic*: Southern Cape Cod to the east and west coasts of the northern half of Florida and Texas in the Gulf of Mexico. May be divided into two subprovinces: *Virginian*, from Cape Cod to North Carolina, and *Carolinian*, now referring to the region from North Carolina southward.

Caribbean: Southern half of Florida, Gulf of Mexico, Bermuda, West Indies, Caribbean Sea to the north coast of South America, south to Bahia, Brazil. Warm, tropical waters.

8. (*Previous page, left*) CHLAMYS (Mimachlamys) AUSTRALIS Sowerby. Australia. *See* pl. 140, no. 15. (3/2).

9. (*Previous page, right*) CHLAMYS (Mimachlamys) NOBILIS Reeve. Japan. *See* pl. 142, no. 12. (1/1).

Patagonian: Bahia, Brazil to Central Argentina. Subtropical to temperate waters.

Mediterranean or **Lusitanian**: Includes the Bay of Biscay, Mediterranean Sea, south to Cape Verde Islands and Western Sahara, including the Azores and the Canary Islands; also the Black Sea. Temperate waters.

West African: Western Sahara to central S.W.Africa, including the Cape Verde Islands. Tropical waters.

South African: S.W.Africa to Natal on the east coast. Cool, temperate waters.

Collecting Seashells

Beachcombing can be a very pleasant pastime, and indeed I am one of its devotees. Often, especially following storms, live or freshly dead seashells may be found on the beach, in particular under seaweed and other ocean debris, but usually few good specimens are found in this manner – they are generally chipped, scratched or faded. A number of species live in the wet intertidal sands. Tide pools are often the haven for many interesting species.

Most live shells can be found in just a few feet of water, many under rocks or in seaweed. Always replace overturned stones and coral, otherwise you may destroy many forms of sealife. Small shells may be found by sifting sand or mud through a sieve. A glass-bottomed box or pail placed on the water's surface affords a clear vision of the life below. The face mask and snorkel are of great assistance in searching out specimens and are indispensable to the serious collector. A mesh bag or plastic bucket, tied by string to the body to allow for freedom of movement, is used to hold the live animals while collecting. Do not use a mesh bag when collecting possibly venomous cones. Sneakers or underwater footgear should be worn to avoid such hazards as coral cuts and sea-urchin spines. Gloves are also helpful, but remember that they will not protect against the stings and bites of venomous animals.

The best collecting is done at night at low tide, when the mollusks are searching for food; otherwise they tend to avoid the light. Some species leave identifiable trails when burrowing in and on the sandy or muddy bottom.

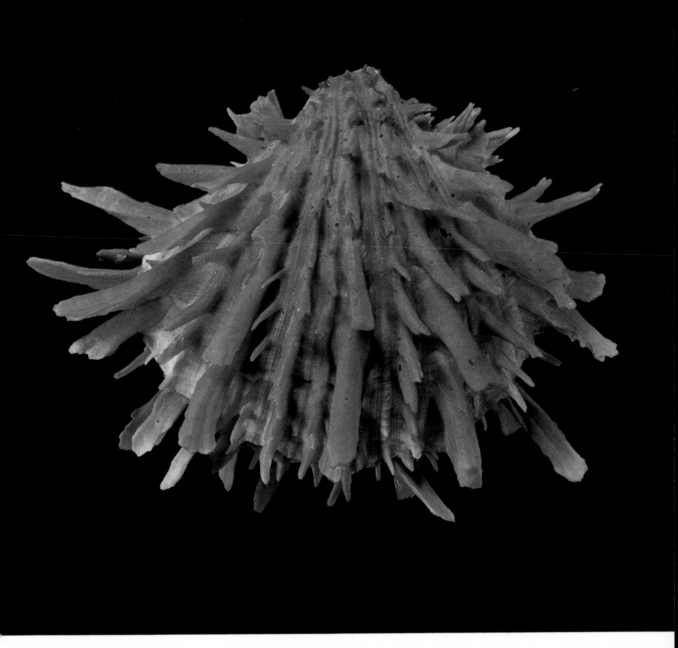

11. (*Above*) SPONDYLUS PRINCEPS Broderip. West Mexico. See pl. 145, no. 14. (3/2).

Those able to participate in scuba-diving have an unlimited field for collecting, but it is not recommended to the novice collector. Never dive alone. Shells can be collected in deeper water by employing wire-mesh dredges. Some carnivorous mollusks can be obtained by baiting fish-traps or even using bait on fishing-lines.

Do *not* overcollect. Take only those live shells you wish to add to your collection or several more for future exchanges. Do not collect immature or juvenile shells. Be aware that removing much animal life from the ocean has an effect on the immediate environment. Observe the local wildlife and fishery laws. Many areas require a license to collect certain species of shells in order to protect the interests of the commercial fishermen, or else prohibit the collecting of certain species or even all forms of life in a specific area to preserve an endangered ecological system.

One can often obtain excellent specimens from local fishermen or fish-markets. There are a number of professional shell dealers who publish periodical lists of select, properly classified

10. (*Left*) SPONDYLUS AMERICANUS Hermann. Florida. See pl. 145, no. 1. (3/2).

specimens with correct locality data. They advertise in the popular periodicals listed in the bibliography on page 217. Exchanging with other collectors, shell clubs, museums and dealers is an excellent way to augment your collection at little expense.

As much information as possible should be recorded about each shell collected. Shells in a collection may be numbered in an inconspicuous spot, such as inside the lip of a gastropod, with black India ink. This eliminates the possibility of mixing up specimens. A proper label should include the scientific name, the exact location, depth of water, type of bottom, date collected and the name of the collector. Example:

> *Conus californicus* Hinds.
> Collected in 6 feet, sand bottom,
> among seaweeds. Shell Beach,
> La Jolla, California, 6/30/80. J. Eisenberg,
> collector.

Cleaning Shells

Most shells can be cleaned by placing them in just-boiled water for several minutes, then cooling them slowly to avoid cracking. The dead animal may then be extracted. Small shells may be cleaned overnight in alcohol; larger shells in a solution of 70% alcohol for several days. To remove most surface growths such as coral and algae, place the specimen overnight in equal quantities of water and household (chlorine) bleach. Remove the operculum first, as it will be damaged or dissolved by the bleach. Use rubber gloves and, when mixing, pour the bleach into the water. Use a toothbrush to help clean the surface. Heavy encrustations may be scraped off with a wire brush or the dull edge of a knife.

A weak solution of hydrochloric acid or caustic soda is sometimes used to help stubborn shells, but this method is best left to professionals, as both the surface of the shell and your skin could be damaged. You can also employ the time-honored method of burying the shells in the ground or near an anthill and feeding the local insect population. Shells should not be left in the sunlight as they tend to dry out and fade. Shells should be rinsed thoroughly after cleaning. A very light coating of mineral oil or baby oil may be used to protect the surface and bring out the color.

A multi-drawered cabinet is the best method of housing a shell collection. The individual shells may be kept in small open cardboard boxes or trays, each with a proper label. Small shells may be kept in vials.

For further information on collecting and cleaning seashells see the bibliography on pages 214-17.

Systematic Classification of Mollusks

The classification used in this book is primarily that of J. Thiele's *Handbuch der Systematischen Weichtierkunde* (1929–1935), R.C. Moore's *Treatise on Invertebrate Paleontology,* Parts I, N: Mollusca (1960–1971), R.T. Abbott's *Indo-Pacific Mollusca* (1959–1976), and A.M. Keen & E. Coan's *Marine Molluscan Genera of Western North America* (1974). A number of rare minor families are not included. For a description of the individual families and listing of the principal genera see pages 177–208.

Class: GASTROPODA

SUBCLASS: PROSOBRANCHIA
(or Streptoneura)

ORDER: ARCHAEOGASTROPODA
(or Diotocardia)

Superfamily	Family
Pleurotomariacea	Pleurotomariidae
	Haliotidae
	Scissurellidae
Fissurellacea	Fissurellidae
Patellacea	Patellidae
	Acmaeidae
	Lepetidae
Trochacea	Trochidae
	Angariidae
	Stomatellidae
	Liotiidae
	Cyclostrematidae
	Skeneidae
	Turbinidae
	Orbitestellidae
	Phasianellidae
Neritacea	Neritopsidae
	Neritidae
	Phenacolepadidae
Cocculinacea	Cocculinidae
	Lepetellidae

ORDER: MESOGASTROPODA
(or Monotocardia)

Superfamily	Family
Seguenziacea	Seguenziidae
Littorinacea	Littorinidae
	Lacunidae
Rissoacea	Rissoidae (and several minor families)
Architectonicacea	*Architectonicidae
Turritellacea	Orectospiridae
	Turritellidae
	Caecidae
	*Mathildidae
	Modulidae
	Vermetidae
Cerithiacea	Cerithiidae
	Planaxidae
	Potamididae
Strombacea	Aporrhaidae
	Struthiolariidae
	Strombidae
Triphoracea	*Triphoridae
Epitoniacea	*Epitoniidae
	*Janthinidae
Eulimacea	Eulimidae
	Aclididae
	Stiliferidae
Hipponicacea	Hipponicidae
	Fossaridae
	Vanikoridae
Calyptraeacea	Calyptraeidae
	Capulidae
	Trichotropidae
	Xenophoridae
Lamellariacea	Lamellariidae
Triviacea	Triviidae
Cypraeacea	Cypraeidae
	Ovulidae
Atlantacea	Atlantidae
	Carinariidae
	Pterotracheidae (lack shell)
Naticacea	Naticidae
Tonnacea	Tonnidae
	Cassididae
	Oocorythidae
	Ficidae
Cymatiacea	Cymatiidae
	Bursidae
	Colubrariidae

ORDER: NEOGASTROPODA
(or Stenoglossa)

Superfamily	Family
Muricacea	Muricidae
	Coralliophilidae
	Rapanidae
	Thaididae
	Columbariidae

*These five families have also been grouped together under a fourth Prosobranchia order following the Neogastropoda: order HETEROGASTROPODA.

25

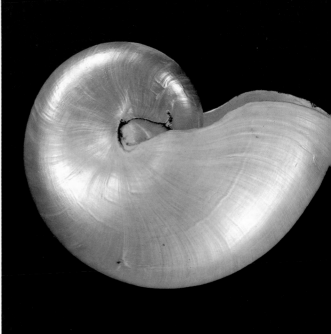

12. (*Top, left*) NAUTILUS POMPILIUS Lamarck. Philippine Islands. *See* pl. 158, no. 20. (1/2).

(*Top, right*) NAUTILUS POMPILIUS Lamarck. Philippine Islands. A pearled specimen. (1/2).

(*Bottom, left*) Above – NAUTILUS MACROMPHALUS Sowerby. New Caledonia. Below – NAUTILUS SCROBICULATUS Lightfoot. Solomon Islands. See listings on pl. 158. (1/2).

(*Bottom, right*) Above – ARGONAUTA ARGO Linné. Taiwan. Below, left – ARGONAUTA HIANS Lightfoot. Philippine Islands. Below, right – ARGONAUTA NODUSA Lightfoot. Philippine Islands. See listings on pl. 158. (1/2).

Buccinacea	Buccinidae
	Neptuneidae
	Columbellidae
	Melongenidae
	Nassariidae
	Fasciolariidae
Volutacea	Volutidae
	Volutomitridae
	Harpidae
	Turbinellidae
	Olividae
	Vasidae
	Marginellidae
Mitracea	Mitridae
Cancellariacea	Cancellariidae
Conacea	Conidae
	Terebridae
	Turridae

SUBCLASS: OPISTHOBRANCHIA (or Euthyneura)

ORDER: PYRAMIDELLIDA (or Entomotaeniata)

Superfamily	*Family*
Pyramidellacea	Pyramidellidae

ORDER: PARASITA (or Entoconchida)

Superfamily	*Family*
	Enteroxenidae (larval shells)
	Entoconchidae (larval shells)

ORDER: CEPHALASPIDEA (or Tectibranchia)

Superfamily	*Family*
Acteonacea	Acteonidae
	Acteocinidae
	Ringiculidae
	Hydatinidae
Bullacea	Bullidae
	Atyidae
	Retusidae
Diaphanacea	Diaphanidae
	Notodiaphanidae
Philinacea	Philinidae
	Aglajidae
	Gastropteridae
	Scaphandridae
	Runcinidae (lack shell)

ORDER: THECOSOMATA (or Pteropoda, in part)

Superfamily	*Family*
	Cavoliniidae
	Limacinidae (and several other minor families)

ORDER: ANASPIDEA

Superfamily	*Family*
Aplysiacea	Aplysiidae
	Akeridae
	Dolabellidae
	Dolabriferidae

ORDER: GYMNOSOMATA (or Pteropoda, in part) (lack shell)

ORDER: NOTASPIDEA

Superfamily	*Family*
Pleurobranchacea	Pleurobranchidae
Umbraculacea	Umbraculidae
	Tylodinidae

ORDER: SACOGLOSSA

Superfamily	*Family*
Juliacea	Juliidae (bivalved gastropods)
Oxynoacea	Oxynoidae
Plakobranchacea	Plakobranchidae (and several other minor families; all lack shell)

ORDER: ACOCHLIDIOIDEA (Sand Nudibranchs; lack shell)

ORDER: NUDIBRANCHIA (Nudibranchs and Sea slugs; lack shell)

ORDER: GYMNOPHILA (or Onchidiata; lack shell)

SUBCLASS: PULMONATA

Superfamily	*Family*
Amphibolacea	Amphibolidae
Melampacea	Melampidae
Siphonariacea	Siphonariidae
	Trimusculidae

Class: PELECYPODA (or Bivalvia)

ORDER: SOLEMYOIDA

Superfamily	Family
Solemyacea	Solemyidae

ORDER: NUCULOIDA

Superfamily	Family
Nuculacea	Nuculidae
Malletiacea	Malletiidae
Nuculanacea	Nuculanidae

ORDER: ARCOIDA

Superfamily	Family
Arcacea	Arcidae
	Noetiidae
	Cucullaeidae
Limopsacea	Glycymerididae
	Limopsidae
	Nucinellidae
	Philobryidae

ORDER: MYTILOIDA

Superfamily	Family
Mytilacea	Mytilidae
Pinnacea	Pinnidae

ORDER: PTERIOIDA

Superfamily	Family
Pteriacea	Pteriidae
	Isognomonidae
	Malleidae
Ostreacea	Ostreidae
Pectinacea	Plicatulidae
	Pectinidae
	Dimyidae
	Spondylidae
Limacea	Limidae
Anomiacea	Anomiidae

ORDER: VENEROIDA

Superfamily	Family
Crassatellacea	Crassatellidae
	Cardiniidae
Astartacea	Astartidae
Trigoniacea	Trigoniidae
Carditacea	Carditidae
	Condylocardiidae
Corbiculacea	Corbiculidae
Dreissenacea	Dreissenidae
Glossacea	Glossidae
	Vesicomyidae
Arcticacea	Arcticidae
	Bernardinidae
Trapeziacea	Trapeziidae
Cyrenoidacea	Cyrenoididae
Lucinacea	Lucinidae
	Thyasiridae
	Ungulinidae
Galeommatacea (or Leptonacea, etc.)	Erycinidae
	Kelliidae
	Leptonidae
	Montacutidae
	Galeommatidae
Chlamydoconchacea	Chlamydoconchidae
Cyamiacea	Sportellidae
	Turtoniidae (or Cyamiidae)
	Neoleptonidae
Chamacea	Chamidae
Cardiacea	Cardiidae
Veneracea	Veneridae
	Petricolidae
	Cooperellidae
Tridacnacea	Tridacnidae
Mactracea	Mactridae
	Cardiliidae
	Mesodesmatidae
	Anatinellidae
Tellinacea	Tellinidae
	Donacidae
	Psammobiidae
	Solecurtidae
	Scrobiculariidae
	Semelidae
Gaimardiacea	Gaimardiidae

ORDER: MYOIDA

Superfamily	Family
Myacea	Myidae
	Corbulidae
	Spheniopsidae
Gastrochaenacea	Gastrochaenidae
Hiatellacea	Hiatellidae
Pholadacea	Pholadidae
	Teredinidae
	Xylophaginidae

ORDER: PHOLADOMYOIDA

Superfamily	*Family*
Pholadomyacea	Pholadomyidae
Pandoracea	Pandoridae
	Cleidothaeridae
	Laternulidae
	Lyonsiidae
	Myochamidae
	Periplomatidae
	Thraciidae
	Pholadomyidae
Poromyacea	Poromyidae
	Cuspidariidae
	Verticordiidae

Class: POLYPLACOPHORA
(or Amphineura, in part)

ORDER: NEOLORICATA

Suborder: ACANTHOCHITONINA

Family
Acanthochitonidae

Suborder: ISCHNOCHITONINA

Family
Ischnochitonidae
Callistoplacidae
Callochitonidae
Chaetopleuridae
Chitonidae
Mopaliidae
Schizochitonidae
Schizoplacidae

Suborder: LEPIDOPLEURINA

Family
Lepidopleuridae
Hanleyidae
Chloriplacidae

Class: APLACOPHORA (or Amphineura, in part)

ORDER: NEOMENIIDA

Family
Neomeniidae (and
several other minor
families)

ORDER: CHAETODERMATIDA

Family
Chaetodermatidae

Class: MONOPLACOPHORA
ORDER: TRYBLIDIOIDEA

Family
Tryblidiidae

Class: SCAPHOPODA

Family
Dentaliidae
Siphonodentaliidae

Class: CEPHALOPODA
SUBCLASS: NAUTILOIDEA

Family
Nautilidae

SUBCLASS: COLEOIDEA
ORDER: SEPIOIDEA

Family
Spirulidae (other
families lack shell)

ORDER: TEUTHOIDEA (lack shell)
ORDER: OCTOPODA

Family
Argonautidae (other
families lack shell)

ORDER: VAMPYROMORPHA (lack shell)

Use of the Color Plates and Descriptions of Species

The color plates are organized according to the proper systematic classification of the Mollusca. A progressive spectrum of colors has been used for the backgrounds, the color changing for nearly every family, to assist in their quick location and identification. The specific characteristics of each family are described in detail in the chapter on the Identification of Families, pages 177–208, each family being keyed to the appropriate color plates so that use of the index is not necessary.

The following information is included in the descriptions of species accompanying the color plates:

SCIENTIFIC NAME and AUTHOR

POPULAR NAME

GEOGRAPHICAL DISTRIBUTION (A hyphen between two place names, for example, E.Afr.-Poly., indicates that the species occurs over this entire range, but perhaps only sporadically.)

SIZE (Minimum, average and maximum sizes.)

RARITY (Sequence used: very common (VC), common (C), uncommon (UC), scarce (S), very scarce (VS), rare (R), very rare (VR), extremely rare (Ext. R), unique.)

DESCRIPTION

SUBSPECIES and FORMS

COMPARISON TO SIMILAR SPECIES

SYNONYMS (Only those most commonly encountered.)

The genera of the various families are listed in proper taxonomic order, unless still in dispute, in which cases they are listed alphabetically. All species within a family are listed alphabetically unless their identification had been reassigned after the plates were photographed.

With very few exceptions, the members of each family are illustrated in the same scale to assist in the comparison of the various species. The amount of reduction is indicated by the fraction at the bottom of each plate (1/3, 1/2, 2/3, 1/1).

Abbreviations used in Text

Afr.	Africa	N.G.	New Guinea
Am.	America	New Heb.	New Hebrides
And.	Andaman Is.	N.S.W.	New South
Ant.	Antilles		Wales,
Atl.	Atlantic		Australia
Aust.	Australia	N.T.	Northern
avg.	average		Territory,
			Australia
Bah.	Bahamas	N.Z.	New Zealand
Barb.	Barbados	No.	North,
Berm.	Bermuda		Northern
Br.	British		
		Oc.	Ocean,
C	common		Oceania
C.	Central	operc.	operculum
ca.	about	Ore.	Oregon
Cal.	California		
Carib.	Caribbean	Pac.	Pacific
cm.	centimeters	Pak.	Pakistan
Col.	Columbia	Pan.	Panama
cp.	compare	per.	periostracum
C.R.	Costa Rica	Per.	Persian
C.V.	Cape Verde Is.	P.I.	Philippine Is.
		Poly.	Polynesia
E.	East		
Ecu.	Ecuador	Qld.	Queensland,
esp.	especially		Australia
Eur.	Europe	q.v.	quite variable
excl.	excluding		
ext.	extremely	R	rare
ext.v.	extremely variable		
		S	scarce
Fla.	Florida	S.	South
Fr.	French	S.Afr.	South Africa
Fr.Oc.	French Oceania	S.Am.	South America
Fr.Poly.	French Polynesia	S.E.Afr.	South Africa to Mozambique
		sep.sp.	separate species
G.	Gulf	Sey.	Seychelles Is.
Galap.	Galapagos	Sing.	Singapore
Guat.	Guatemala	sm.	small
		So.	South, Southern
Haw.	Hawaii	Sol.	Solomon Is.
imp.	imperfect	sp.	species
illus.	illustrated	spec.	specimen(s)
incl.	including	subsp.	subspecies
Ind.	Indian	syn.	synonym
Indon.	Indonesia		
I-P	Indo-Pacific	Tai.	Taiwan
		Tas.	Tasmania
lge.	large		
		UC	uncommon
Mad.	Madagascar		
Mal.	Maldive Is.	v., V.	very
Marq.	Marquesas Is.	var.	variety
Maur.	Mauritius	Venez.	Venezuela
med.	medium	Vic.	Victoria,
Med.	Mediterranean		Australia
Mex.	Mexico		
mm.	millimeters	VR	very rare
Moz.	Mozambique	VS	very scarce
N.	North, Northern, New	W.	West, Western
		W.I.	West Indies
N.Am.	North America		
N.C.	North Carolina	Zan.	Zanzibar
New Cal.	New Caledonia	<	less than
		>	more than

Abbreviations of Authors' Names

B., H.& S.	Baker, Hanna & Strong	Lam.	Lamarck
		Midff.	Middendorff
Blain.	Blainville	Mont.	Montfort
Brug.	Bruguiere	Muhl.	Mühlfeld
Cern.	Cernohorsky	Nutt.	Nuttall
Cpr.	Carpenter	Old.	Oldroyd
D., B.& R.	Dall, Bartsch & Rehder	Ols.	Olsson
		Orb.	Orbigny
Dautz.	Dautzenberg	Payr.	Payraudeau
Desh.	Deshayes	Phil.	Philippi
Em.	Emerson	Pils.	Pilsbry
Esch.	Eschscholtz	Q.& G.	Quoy & Gaimard
G.& P.	Griffith & Pidgeon		
		R.& D.	Radwin & D'Attilio
Gm.	Gmelin	Röd.	Röding
Helb.	Helbling	S.& S.	Schilder & Schilder
Hert.	Hertlein		
Ire.	Iredale	Swain.	Swainson
Jous.	Jousseaume	Val.	Valenciennes
L.	Linné or Linnaeus		

1. AMBLYCHILEPAS JAVANICENSIS Lam. S.W.Aust.-N.S.W., Tas. Avg.20–25mm. C.

2. MEGATEBENNUS SCUTELLUM Gm. S.Afr. Avg.22–28mm. C.

3. FISSURELLA BARBADENSIS Gm. **Barbados Keyhole Limpet.** S.E.Fla.-W.I.-Brazil, Berm. 25–28–32–40mm. VC.

4. FISSURELLA CRASSA Lam. Chile. Avg. 40–50mm. UC.

5. FISSURELLA MAXIMA Sow. **Maximum Keyhole Limpet.** Chile. 60–70–90–110mm. UC.

6. FISSURELLA NODOSA Born. **Knobby Keyhole Limpet.** Fla.Keys-W.I. 20–25–35–38mm. VC. (Fla.: R).

7. FISSURELLA PICTA Gm. Chile. Avg. 50–65mm. UC.

8. FISSURELLIDEA APERTA Sow. S.W.Afr.-S.Afr. 20–25–35–50mm. C.

9. FISSURELLIDEA HIANTULA Lam. Argentina. Avg.20–25mm. S.

10. MACROSCHISMA AFRICANA Tomlin. S.Afr. Avg.17–22mm. UC.

11. MACROSCHISMA COMPRESSA Adams. S.Afr. Avg.17–20mm. UC.

12. MONTFORTULA CONOIDEA Reeve. **Cap-shaped False Limpet.** Qld.-N.S.W., Tas. 12–19mm. C.

13. NOTOMELLA HEDLEYI Thiele. **Notched False Limpet.** Qld.-N.S.W.-S.Aust. Avg.6–8mm. C. Has been sold under genus *Emarginula.*

14. SCUTUS ANTIPODES Montfort. **Duck-bill, Roman Shield** or **Elephant Fish.** S.W. Aust.-N.S.W., Tas., N.Z. 60–80–100–125mm. C. Heavy. Syn.: *S.anatinus* Donovan.

15. SCUTUS SINENSIS Blainville. Japan. 16–20–30–48mm. C. Syn.: *S.scapha* Gm.

16. DIODORA ASPERA Eschscholtz. **Rough Keyhole Limpet.** Alaska-Baja Cal. 30–40–50–75mm. VC.

17. DIODORA CAYENENSIS Lam. **Cayenne Keyhole Limpet.** N.J.-Fla.-Carib.-Brazil, Berm. 22–25–35–50mm. VC.

18. DIODORA LISTERI Orbigny. **Lister's Keyhole Limpet.** Fla.-W.I.-Brazil, Berm. 25–30–40–44mm. C.

19. MEGATHURA CRENULATA Sow. **Great Keyhole Limpet.** C.Cal.-Mex. 65–75–100–132mm. C.

20. PATELLA BARBARA L. S.W.Afr.-S.E. Afr. 50–70–85–100mm. C. Variable form.

21. PATELLA CAERULEA L. Med., Spain-Morocco, Canary Is. 33–40–60–72mm. C.

22. PATELLA COCHLEAR Born. **Pear Limpet** or **Tent Shell.** S.Afr. 25–30–55–70mm. C. Heavy. Often has scars of juveniles.

23. PATELLA COMPRESSA L. **Compressed Limpet.** S.W.Afr.-S.Afr. 40–60–80–110mm. UC.

24. PATELLA GRANATINA L. S.W.Afr.-S.Afr. Avg.70–90mm. C.

25. PATELLA GRANULARIS L. Angola-S.Afr. 19–35–45–60mm. C.

Plate 16 | Patellidae

1. *PATELLA LONGICOSTA* Lam. **Spiked Limpet.** S.Afr. 50–60–80–95mm. C. Heavy.

2. *PATELLA MINIATA* Born. S.W.Afr.-S.Afr. 45–55–70–85mm. UC. Beach spec. fade to pink. Usually encrusted.

3. *PATELLA OCULUS* Born. S.Afr. <60–70–80–90mm. C.

4. *PATELLA SAFIANA* Lam. Algeria-S.W.Afr. 42–50–80–110mm. C. Form and color variable.

5. *PATELLA TABULARIS* Krauss. S.Afr. 75–95–120–140mm. C. Largest S.African limpet.

6. *PATELLA VULGATA* L. **Common Limpet.** W.Eur.-Med. 20–30–50–60mm. VC. Form and color q.v.

7. *ANCISTROMESUS MEXICANA* Brod. & Sow. **Giant Mexican Limpet.** G. of Cal.-Peru. 100–120–150–>250mm. UC. World's largest limpet. Being over-collected for food. Illus. spec. has barnacles attached. Syn.: *Patella maxima* Orbigny.

8. *HELCION PECTUNCULUS* Gm. S.W. Afr.-S.Afr. Avg.20–30mm. C.

9. *PATIONIGERA DEAURATA* Gm. Argentina-Chile, Falkland Is. Avg.50–60mm. UC.

10. *CELLANA CAPENSIS* Gm. S.Afr.-Moz. Avg.30–40mm. C. Pattern variable.

11. *CELLANA EXARATA* Reeve. **Black Limpet** or **Opihi.** Hawaii. 35–40–60–?80mm. C. Edible.

12. *CELLANA GRATA* Gould. Japan. 22–25–30–32mm. VC. Syn.: *C.eucosmia* Pilsbry.

13. *CELLANA NIGROLINEATA* Reeve. Japan. 30–40–60–70mm. VC.

14. *CELLANA ORNATA* Dillwyn. **Ornate Limpet.** N.Z. 25–30–40–44mm. VC. Apex often quite eroded.

15. *CELLANA RADIANS* Gm. **Radiate Limpet.** N.Z. 36–50mm. VC.

16. *CELLANA STELLIFERA* Gm. **Star Limpet.** N.Z. <30–35–50–57mm. C. Usually heavily encrusted.

17. *CELLANA TALCOSA* Gould. **Kneecap Shell.** Haw. <65–70–85–95mm. UC. Syn.: *Patella argentata* Sow.

1. CELLANA TESTUDINARIA L. **Tortoise Shell.** W.Pac. 35–50–60–65mm. VC. Pattern variable. Polished spec. (2B, C, D) used for jewelry. Often misplaced under genus **Patella**.

2. CELLANA TOREUMA Reeve. W.Pac., esp. Japan. 25–28–35–>55mm. VC. Pattern variable.

3. CELLANA TRAMOSERICA Holten. S.Qld.-S.Aust., Tas. 30–40–50–60mm. VC. Color and pattern variable. Syn.: **C.variegata** Blainville.

4. ACMAEA (Patelloida) ALTICOSTATA Angas. **Ridged** or **Tall-ribbed Limpet.** S.W. Aust.-S.Qld., Tas. 30–35–40–42mm. C.

5. ACMAEA (Notoacmaea) CONCINNA Lischke. Japan. ca.16–24mm. C. Spec. illus. is subsp. **A.c.fuscoviridis** Teramachi (10–15mm., with blue-green interior).

6. ACMAEA (Collisella) DALLIANA Pilsbry. **Dall's Limpet.** G. of Cal. 20–30–45–54mm. UC.

7. ACMAEA (Collisella) DIGITALIS Eschscholtz. **Finger(ed) Limpet,** Aleutians-Mex. ca. 25–35mm. VC. Syn.: for **Collisella: Nomaeopelta.**

8. ACMAEA (Notoacmaea) GLORIOSA Habe. Japan. Avg.20–22mm. UC.

9. ACMAEA (Collisella) LIMATULA Carpenter. **File Limpet.** Puget Sound-Baja Cal. 25–30–40–53mm. C.

10. ACMAEA (Scurria) MESOLEUCA Menke. **Half-white Limpet.** S.Baja Cal.-Ecu.-Galáp. <20–22–28–35mm. C.

11. ACMAEA (Patelloida) PALLIDA Gould. **Snowy Limpet.** W.Pac., esp. Japan. 40–45–50–60mm. C.

12. ACMAEA (Collisella) PELTA Rathke. **Shield Limpet.** Alaska-Baja Cal. 25–30–40–54mm. C.

13. ACMAEA (Patelloida) SACCHARINA L. **Sweet Limpet.** W.Pac., esp. Japan. 15–20–35–40mm. VC.

14. ACMAEA (Collisella) STANFORDIANA Berry. **Stanford's Limpet.** G. of Cal. 20–22–26–30mm. C.

15. ACMAEA (Collisella) TESTUDINALIS Müller. **Atlantic Plate** or **Tortoise Shell Limpet.** Arctic-N.Y. 25–43mm. C. Also, subsp. **A.t.scutum** Eschscholtz, **Pacific Plate Limpet,** Alaska-Baja C., to 69mm.

16. LOTTIA GIGANTEA Sow. **Giant Owl Limpet.** C.Cal.-Baja Cal. 38–50–75–121mm. VC.

17. PECTINODONTA ORIENTALIS Schepman. Indon.-Japan. 12–18mm. C.

18. LEPETA ALBA Dall. Alaska-Wash. Avg. 11–14mm. C.

19. LEPETA CONCENTRICA Middendorff. Arctic Oc.-Alaska. Avg.11–14mm. C.

Plate 18 | Trochidae

1. *MARGARITES PUPILLUS* Gould. **Puppet Margarite.** Bering Sea-No.Cal. 8–14mm. C.

2. *LISCHKEIA (CIDARINA) CIDARIS* Carpenter. **Spiny Top, Diadem Shell.** Alaska-Baja Cal. 22–25–30–38mm. C.

3. *LISCHKEIA ALWINAE* Lischke. Japan-Tai. 35–40–45–50mm. C.

4. *MONODONTA CANALIFERA* Lam. W.Pac. Avg.25–30mm. C.

5. *MONODONTA LABIO* L. **Labio** or **Thick-lipped Monodonta.** W.Pac. 15–16–20–25mm. VC. Color and pattern ext.v.

6. *MONODONTA TURBINATA* Born. Med. 20–25–35–?60mm. C.

7. *AUSTROCOCHLEA CONCAMERATA* Wood. **Speckled, Squat** or **Wavy Periwinkle.** S.W.Aust.-S.Qld., Tas. 19–25mm. C.

8. *AUSTROCOCHLEA CONSTRICTA*
Lam. **Southern Periwinkle.** W.Aust.-N.S.W., Tas. 19–25mm. VC. Color and pattern q.v. Syn.: *A.obtusa* Dillwyn.

9. *BANKIVIA FASCIATUS* Menke. **Banded** or **Silver Kelp.** S.Aust.-N.S.W., Tas. 14–25mm. VC. Fragile. Color and pattern ext.v. Syn.: *B.varians* Beck.

10. *BATHYBEMBIX AEOLA* Watson. Japan. Avg.40–50mm. S. Thin greenish-yellow per.

11. *BATHYBEMBIX ARGENTEONITENS* Lischke. Japan. Avg.38–50mm. C. Silvery surface beneath thin brownish per.

12. *BATHYBEMBIX BAIRDII* Dall. Bering Sea-G. of Cal. Avg.38–50mm. UC. Thin greenish-yellow per. Also placed under *Lischkeia*.

13. *BATHYBEMBIX CRUMPII* Pilsbry. Japan. 25–30–40–45mm. UC.

14. *CANTHARIDUS INFUSCATUS* Gould. Japan. Avg.14–16mm. C.

15. *CANTHARIDUS IRIS* Gm. **Opal Top Shell.** N.Z. Avg.40–45mm. UC. Syn.: *C. opalus* Martyn.

16. *CANTHARIDUS PURPUREUS* Gm. **Pink Top Shell.** N.Z. 20–32mm. C.

17. *CANTHARIDUS (PHASIANO-TROCHUS) BELLULUS* Dunker. **Necklace Shell** or **Elegant Kelp.** S.Aust.-Vic.-Tas. Avg. 12–14mm. VC.

18. *CANTHARIDUS (PHASIANO-TROCHUS) EXIMIUS* Perry. **Choice Seaweed Shell** or **True Kelp.** S.W.Aust.-N.S.W., Tas. 23–30–38–40mm. C. Variable pattern.

19. *CANTHARIDUS (PHASIANO-TROCHUS) IRISODONTIS* Q. & G. **Rainbow Kelp.** W.Aust.-Vic. Avg.10–13mm.VC.

20. *CHRYSOSTOMA PARADOXUM* Born. **Orange-mouthed Top-shell.** W.Pac. 15–17–22–25mm. VC.

21. *DILOMA SUBROSTRATA* Gray. **Mud-flat Top-shell.** N.Z. 11–19mm. VC.

22. *OXYSTELE SINENSIS* Gm. S.Afr. 18–25–35–51mm. VC.

23. *OXYSTELE TABULARIS* Krauss. S.E.Afr. 14–20mm. C.

24. *OXYSTELE "TIGRINA".* S.Afr. 25–28–35–43mm. VC.

Plate 19

1. *TEGULA BRUNNEA* Philippi. **Brown Tegula** or **Top.** No.-C.Cal. 20–25–35–45mm. C. Eroded areas exhibit pearly luster.

2. *TEGULA FUNEBRALIS* A.Adams. **Black Tegula** or **Top.** Br.Col.-Baja Cal. 20–25–35–40mm. C. Purplish-black per. Eroded areas exhibit pearly luster.

3. *TEGULA GALLINA* Forbes. **Speckled Tegula** or **Top.** C.Cal.-Baja Cal.-G.of Cal. 20–25–35–38mm. C.

4. *TEGULA MONTEREYI* Kiener. **Monterey Tegula** or **Top.** Cal. 25–38mm. UC.

5. *TEGULA PELLISSERPENTIS* Wood. **Snake-skin Top-shell.** El Salvador-Col. 15–20–35–45mm. C.

6. *TEGULA REGINA* Stearns. **Queen Tegula** or **Top.** S.Cal.-G. of Cal. 38–45–55–64mm. UC (becoming S). Heavy.

7. *TEGULA RUBROFLAMMULATA* Koch & Philippi. G. of Cal.-Col. Avg.15–18mm. C.

8. *TEGULA RUGOSA* A.Adams. **Rough Top.** G. of Cal. 20–25–30–50mm. VC.

9. *TEGULA VIRIDULA* Gm. Brazil. Avg. 25mm. C.

10. *TEGULA (Chlorostoma) XANTHOSTIGMA* A.Adams. Japan. 22–33mm. C.

11. *THALOTIA CONICA* Gray. **Conical** or **Hoop Top-shell.** S.W.Aust.-N.S.W., Tas. 15–19mm. C.

12. *THALOTIA ELONGATUS* Wood. W.Pac. Avg.25–30mm. C.

13. *PROTHALOTIA PULCHERRIMA* Angas. N.S.W. Avg.15–17mm. C.

14. *GIBBULA CINERARIA* L. **Gray Top-shell.** W.Eur.-Med.Sea-Adriatic Sea. Avg.12–18mm. C.

15. *GIBBULA MAGUS* L. **Great Top-shell.** Med., England-Senegal, Azores. 20–32mm. C.

16. *CITTARIUM PICA* L. **West Indian Top.** W.I. 40–50–90–136mm. VC.

17. *GAZA SERICATA* Kuroda. Japan. Avg. 15–18mm. UC.

18. *GAZA SUPERBA* Dall. **Superb Gaza.** No. G.of Mex.-W.I. 25–38mm. S.

19. *NORRISIA NORRISII* Sow. **Norris Top.** C.Cal.-Baja Cal. 30–35–50–67mm. UC (was VC). 19A has spec. of *Crepidula norrisianum* Williamson attached.

37

Plate 20 | Trochidae

1. *CALLIOSTOMA ADELAE* Schwengel. **Adele's Top-shell.** S.E.Fla. 15–19mm. C.

2. *CALLIOSTOMA AEQUISCULPTUM* Carpenter. W.Mex.-Pan. Avg.20–25mm. C.

3. *CALLIOSTOMA ANNULATUM* Light-foot. Alaska-S.Cal. **Pacific Ringed Top-shell.** 20–22–30–35mm. UC.

4. *CALLIOSTOMA ANTONII* Koch. ?Baja Cal., El Salvador-Peru. 10–15–20–24mm. C.

5. *CALLIOSTOMA BAIRDII* Verrill & Smith. Mass.-Fla.-G.of Mex. 20–23–28–32mm. UC. Illus. is lighter, pearlier subsp. *C.b.psyche* Dall.

6. *CALLIOSTOMA BONITA* Strong, Hanna & Hertlein. W.Mex. 18–24mm. C. Cp. *C. palmeri* (higher spire; stronger color).

7. *CALLIOSTOMA CANALICULATUM* Lightfoot. **Channeled Top-shell.** Alaska-S.Cal. 20–25–35–39mm. C.

8. *CALLIOSTOMA CONULUS* L. Med. 15–20–25–35mm. C.

9. *CALLIOSTOMA COPPINGERI* Smith.

Brazil-Argentina. Avg.13–15mm. S.

10. *CALLIOSTOMA EUCOSMIA* Bartsch. S.Afr.-E.Afr. 13–18–20–23mm. C.

11. *CALLIOSTOMA EXIMIUM* Reeve. Baja Cal.-G.of Cal.-Ecu. 15–18–22–25mm. C.

12. *CALLIOSTOMA FORMOSENSE* Smith. **Formosan Top.** Tai. 50–52–60–63mm. C.

13. *CALLIOSTOMA GRANULATUM* Born. Med. Avg.25–30mm. UC.

14. *CALLIOSTOMA HALIARCHUS* Melvill. Japan. Avg.40–46mm. S.

15. *CALLIOSTOMA JAVANICUM* Lam. **Javanese** or **Chocolate-lined Top-shell.** S.Fla.-W.I. 19–22–26–35mm. S.

16. *CALLIOSTOMA JUJUBINUM* Gm. **Jujube Top-shell.** N.C.-Texas, W.I.-Brazil. 13–20–25–34mm. C.

17. *CALLIOSTOMA KIIENSIS* Ikebe. Japan-Tai. 18–20–25–27mm. C.

18. *CALLIOSTOMA LIGATUM* Gould. **Costate** or **Western Ribbed Top-shell.** Alaska-

S.Cal. 15–18–22–33mm. VC. Syn.: *C.costatum* Martyn.

19. *CALLIOSTOMA MONILE* Reeve. **Monile Top.** Aust. 15–25mm. C.

20. *CALLIOSTOMA PALMERI* Dall. G.of Cal.-W.Mex. 20–22–26–30mm. C.

21. *CALLIOSTOMA SHINAGAWENSIS* Tokunaga. Japan. 12–21mm. C.

22. *CALLIOSTOMA SOYOAE* Ikeba. Japan. 12–22mm. UC.

23. *CALLIOSTOMA SPECIOSUM* A.Adams. **Beautiful Top.** Qld.-N.S.W. Avg. 25–30mm. C.

24. *CALLIOSTOMA UNICUM* Dunker. Japan-Tai. 13–15–20–23mm. VC.

25. *CALLIOSTOMA VICENTAE* Rutllant. Morocco-Angola. 13–18–25–32mm. C.

26. *CALLIOSTOMA ZIZYPHINUS* L. **Painted** or **Common Top-shell.** Med. 15–20–30–40mm. C.

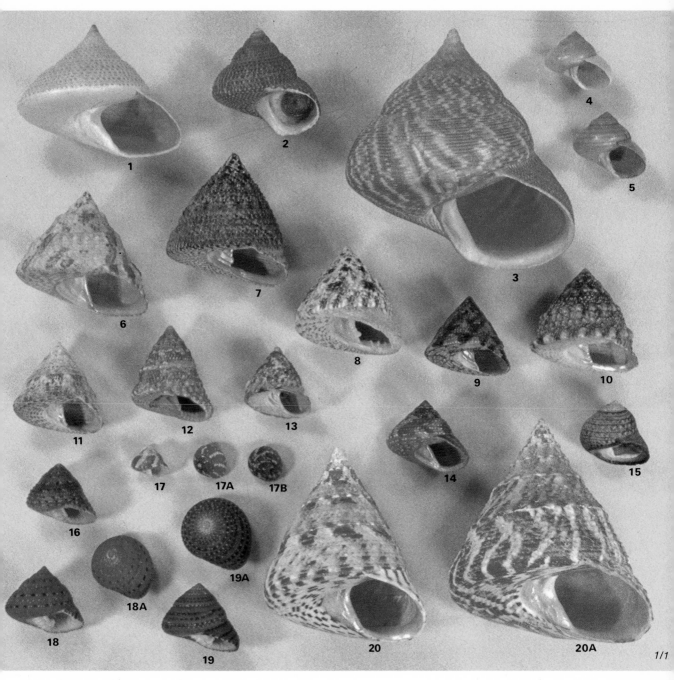

1. *MAUREA CUNNINGHAMI* Griffith & Pidgeon. **Pale Tiger Shell** or **Cunningham's Top.** N.Z. 35–40–48–50mm. C.

2. *MAUREA PUNCTULATA* Martyn. **Spotted Tiger Shell.** N.Z. ca.15–20–35–40mm. C.

3. *MAUREA TIGRIS* Martyn. **Tiger Shell.** N.Z. Avg.55–70mm. S.

4–5. *PHOTINULA TAENIATA* Wood. Argentina, Falkland Is. 12–22mm. C.

6. *TROCHUS ERYTHRAEUS* Brocchi. Red Sea, E.Afr.-Ind.Oc. Avg.30–38mm. C.

7. *TROCHUS LINEATUS* Lam. **Lined Top.** W.Pac. 32–35–45–50mm. VC.

8. *TROCHUS MACULATUS* L. **Maculated Top.** E.Afr.-W.Pac. 25–30–40–60mm. VC. Heavy. Form, color and pattern q.v.

9. *TROCHUS NIGROPUNCTATUS* Reeve. S.E.Afr. 20–30mm. C.

10. *TROCHUS SACELLUM* Philippi. W.Pac. 20–30mm. UC.

11. *TROCHUS (HISTRIO) INTEXTUS* Kiener. W.Pac.-Haw. 20–30mm. C. Syn.: *T. sandwichiensis* Souleyet Eydolet.

12. *TECTUS VIRGATUS* Gm. Red Sea-Per. Gulf, E.Afr.-Ind.Oc. 30–45–60–68mm. C.

13. *TROCHUS VIRIDUS* Gm. **Green Top Shell.** N.Z. 16–25mm. C.

14. *TROCHUS (Infundibulops) CARINIFERUS* Beck. Ind.Oc. Avg.25–30mm. UC.

15. *TROCHUS (Thoristella) OPPRESSA* Hutton. N.Z. Avg.20mm. C.

16. *CLANCULUS GUINEENSIS* Gm. W.Afr. Avg.15–20mm. UC.

17. *CLANCULUS KRAUSSI* Philippi. Morocco-W.Afr. 9–16mm. C.

18. *CLANCULUS PUNICEUS* Philippi. S.E. Afr.-E.Afr. 13–22mm. C.

19. *CLANCULUS PHARAONIUS* L. **Strawberry Top.** Red Sea, G.of Oman. 13–22mm. C.

20. *TECTUS CONUS* Gm. W.Pac. 45–50–60–>70mm. C. 20A is *T.c.hirasei* Pilsbry from Bonin Is. (off Japan).

Plate 22 | Trochidae

1. *TECTUS FENESTRATUS* Gm. **Fene-strated** or **Latticed Top.** W.-C.Pac. 24–26–32–40mm. C.

2. *TECTUS FOVEOLATUS* Gm. Red Sea-Ind.Oc. 45–50–60–>70mm.

3. *TECTUS NILOTICUS* L. **Button, Commercial** or **Pearly Top.** W.Pac. 50–75–100–138mm. VC. Heavy. Pearled for buttons and decorative use. Form or syn.: *T.maximus* Philippi.

4. *TECTUS PYRAMIS* Born. **Pyramid Top.** W.Pac. 50–55–65–70mm. C. Often pearled for decorative use (4A).

– – *TECTUS VIRGATUS* Gm. – See no. 12.

5. *UMBONIUM COSTATUM* Val. W.Pac. 12–14–18–24mm. C.

6. *UMBONIUM ELEGANS* Kiener. W.Pac. Avg.12–17mm. UC.

7. *UMBONIUM GIGANTEUM* Lesson. **Giant Button Top.** W.Pac. 22–25–35–45mm. VC. Color and pattern q.v.

8. *UMBONIUM MONILIFERUM* Lam. Japan. 10–12–15–18mm. C. Color and pattern q.v.

9. *UMBONIUM VESTIARIUM* L. **Vesta's Button Top.** S.E.Afr.-Ind.Oc. 7–10–13–15mm. VC. Color and pattern ext.v.

10. *UMBONIUM ZELANDICUM* A.Adams. **Wheel Shell.** N.Z. 15–18mm. VC.

11. *MONILEA CALLIFERA* Lam. Indon.-Aust. 15–20mm. UC.

12. *MONILEA SMITHI* Dunker. Japan. 15–20mm. UC.

13. *SOLARIELLA PERMABILIS* Cpr. **Lovely Top.** Alaska-S.Cal. 6–13mm. UC. Iridescent interior.

2/3

1. ANGARIA DELPHINUS L. **Common Delphinula** or **Dolphin Shell.** I-P to Fiji. 40–50–75–80mm. VC. Color and form q.v. 1B is form **A.d.atrata** Reeve from Japan (20–45mm.). 1C is **A.d.melanacantha** Reeve (Syn.: **A.imperialis** Reeve).

2. ANGARIA SPHAERULA Kiener. W.Pac., esp. P.I. ca.30–40–55–65mm. VR. ?Form of **A. delphinus.**

3. ANGARIA TYRIA Reeve. Aust. Avg.42–50mm. UC.

4. PSEUDOSTOMATELLA PAPYRACEA Gm. **Beautiful Wide-mouthed Shell.** P.I. Avg. 30–33mm. C.

5. GRANATA IMBRICATA Lam. **True Wide-mouthed Shell** or **Imbricated Pearl Shell.** P.I., N.Aust. 19–25–32–38mm. VC. Often confused with genus **Stomatella.**

6. LIOTINA PERONII Kiener. **Large Liotina.** S.W.-C.Pac. 10–12–16–20mm. C. Concave granulose operc. Often confused with genus **Liotia.**

7. ASTRAEA (Lithopoma) TECTA AMERICANA Gm. **American Star-shell.** S.E.Fla. 18–22–30–41mm. C. ?Subsp. of **A.tecta.**

8. ASTRAEA (Cookia or Bolma) AUREOLUM Hedley. **Scaled Star-shell.** Qld. 60–65–75–90mm. UC. Heavy flesh-colored operc.

9. ASTRAEA (Astralium) BREVISPINA Lam. W.I. Avg.40–50mm. C.

10. ASTRAEA (Uvanilla) BUSCHII Philippi. **Busch's Turban.** W.Mex.-Peru. 20–22–32–50mm. C.

11. ASTRAEA (Lithopoma) CAELATA Gm. **Carved** or **Engraved Star-shell.** S.E.Fla.-W.I. 40–45–60–75mm. C. Granulate white operc.

12. ASTRAEA (Astralium) CALCAR L. **Calcar** or **Wheel-like Star.** W.Pac., esp. P.I. 20–25–35–43mm. C. White or pale green operc.

13. ASTRAEA (Pomaulax) GIBBEROSA Dillwyn. **Red Turban.** Br.Col.-Baja Cal. 40–50–60–80mm. C. Base variable. Smooth white operc.

14. ASTRAEA (Astralium) HEIMBURGI Dunker. Japan. Avg.21–24mm. C.

15. ASTRAEA HELIOTROPIUM Martyn. **Sunburst Star-shell** or **Circular Saw.** N.Z. 70–90–100–115mm. UC. Thick creamy operc.

16. ASTRAEA (Bolma) MILLEGRANOSA Kuroda & Habe. Japan-Tai. Avg.35–40mm. S.

17. ASTRAEA (Bolma) MODESTA Reeve. Japan. 33–38–50–>55mm. C. Thick white granular operc.

41

Plate 24 | Turbinidae

1. *ASTRAEA (Astralium) OKAMOTOI* Kuroda & Habe. Japan. Avg.15–20mm. UC.

2. *ASTRAEA (Uvanilla) OLIVACEA* Wood. **Olive Turban.** Baja Cal.-W.Mex. 30–40–50–75mm. UC. Fibrous greenish per.

3. *ASTRAEA (Astralium) PHOEBIA* Röd. **Long-spined Star-shell.** S.E.Fla.-W.I.-Brazil, Berm. 20–35–50–78mm. C. Thick white operc. Syn.: *A.longispina* Lam.

4. *ASTRAEA PILEOLA* Reeve. **Frilled Star-shell.** N.W.Aust. 32–35–45–>50mm. C. Purplish-brown operc.

5. *ASTRAEA (Astralium) ROTULARIA* Lam. **Rotary** or **Knob Star-shell.** W.Aust. 25–30–40–50mm. C. Purplish-brown or deep green operc.

6. *ASTRAEA (Bolma) RUGOSA* L. S.W.Eur.-Med. 25–35–50–60mm. C. Thick glossy cream to orange operc.

7. *ASTRAEA (Bellastraea) SIRIUS* Gould. **Tent Star-shell.** N.S.W.-Vic. 25–30–40–50mm. VC. Oval spiral operc.

8. *ASTRAEA STELLARE* Gm. **Northern Star.** S.W.Pac. 25–30–40–50mm. C. Blue operc. 8A is form *A.s.asteriscus* Reeve.

9. *ASTRAEA (Cookia) SULCATA* Martyn. **Cook's Turban.** N.Z. ca.50–75–85–90mm. C. Usually with limey encrustation. Thick reddish-brown per. Rib on operc.

10. *ASTRAEA (Bolma) TAYLORIANA* Smith. S.Afr. 65–75–85–90mm. S. Thick white operc.

11. *ASTRAEA (Lithopoma) TECTA* Light-foot. **Imbricated Star-shell.** Fla.-W.I.-Brazil. 20–25–35–40mm. C.

12. *ASTRAEA (Lithopoma) TUBER* L. **Green Star-shell** or **Stone Apple.** S.E.Fla.-W.I. 25–30–40–50mm. C. Thick ridge on operc.

13. *ASTRAEA (Pomaulax) UNDOSA* Wood. **Wavy Turban.** S.Cal.-Baja Cal. <40–60–80–142mm. C. Spiny ridged white operc.

14. *ASTRAEA UNGUIS* Wood. G.of Cal.-Peru. 30–35–45–63mm. VC.

15. *GALEOASTRAEA* SPECIES. P.I. 40mm. VR. New, unnamed sp.

16. *GUILDFORDIA ABYSSORUM* Schepman. **Deep Sea Star-shell.** Indon., Japan. 12–15–20–25mm. UC.

17. *GUILDFORDIA TRIUMPHANS* Philippi. **Triumphant Star-shell.** Japan. 35–40–50–>60mm. C.

18. *GUILDFORDIA YOKA* Jousseaume. **Yoca Star-shell.** Japan. 70–75–95–100mm. UC.

2/3

1. TURBO (Ma.) ARGYROSTOMUS L. **Silver-mouth Turban.** E.Afr.-W.Pac. 45–55–75–90mm. VC. Color and pattern variable. Scabrous or foliated spiral cords. Silvery aperture. Thick white, greenish or orange-stained pustulose operc. Cp. *T.setosus.*

2. TURBO (Ma.) BRUNEUS Röd. W.Pac. 30–35–45–50mm. C. Purplish granular operc.

3. TURBO (Ta.) CANALICULATUS Hermann. **Channeled Turban.** S.E.Fla.-W.I.-Brazil. 50–70–80–91mm. UC.

4. TURBO (Ma.) CASTANEA Gm. **Chestnut Turban.** N.C.-Fla.-Texas-W.I.-Brazil. 25–30–35–40mm. C. Thick white convex operc.

5. TURBO (Ma.) CHRYSOSTOMUS L. **Gold-** or **Yellow-mouth Turban.** S.E.Afr.-W.Pac. 40–45–60–80mm. VC. Color and pattern variable. Aperture golden-orange. Brown or green area on smooth operc.

6. TURBO (Oc.) CIDARIS Gm. Angola-S.Afr. 25–30–40–?58mm. C. Granular operc.

7. TURBO (Lu.) CINEREUS Born. **Lunella** or **Smoothed Turban.** W.Pac. 20–25–30–35mm. C. Color variable. Operc. pustulose.

8. TURBO CIRCULARIS Reeve. Malaysia-Aust. Avg.30–35mm. UC.

9. TURBO (Ba.) CORNUTUS Lightfoot. **Horned** or **Spiny Turban.** W.Pac. 65–70–85–103mm. C. Granular ribbed white operc.

10. TURBO CORONATUS Gm. S.E.Afr.-W.Pac. 25–30–35–40mm. C. Thick olive-brown per. Thick greenish-white operc.

11. TURBO CRASSUS Wood. **Heavy Turban.** W.Pac. 50–80mm. UC. Col. and patt. var. Brown operc. Cp. *T.sparverius.*

12. TURBO EXCELLENS Sow. Japan. Avg.18–22mm. UC. Spiral-ridged white operc. Cp. *T.stenogyrus.*

13. TURBO (Ca.) FLUCTUOSUS Wood. **Fluctuating Turban.** Baja Cal.-G.of Cal.-Peru. 25–40–55–86mm. VC. Smooth to rough surface. Knobby, spiny operc. Also orange form.

14. TURBO (Ma.) LAJONKAIRII Deshayes. Ind.Oc.-W.Pac. 50–65–80–100mm. UC. Dull orange-stained operc.

15. TURBO (Lt.) MARMORATUS L. **Green Turban.** E.Afr.-Fiji. 100–125–150–>210mm. C. Pattern variable. Heavy dull white operc. Shell carved or pearled for decorative use. Juveniles are rounder, without spines (15A).

16. TURBO MILITARIUS Reeve. **Military Turban.** N.Qld.-N.S.W. 60–65–85–100mm. UC. Dull white operc.

17. TURBO (Tu.) PETHOLATUS L. **Cat's Eye Turban.** Moz.-W.Pac. 38–40–50–80mm. VC. Pattern q.v. Columella yellowish-green. Bluish-green "cat's eye" operc. has burnt orange-brown rim. Cp. *T.reevei.*

43

Plate 26 | Turbinidae – Phasianellidae

1. *TURBO PULCHER* Reeve. **Beautiful Turban.** W.-N.Aust. 40–50–60–>80mm. C. Pustulose white operc.

2. *TURBO REEVEI* Philippi. **Tapestry** or **Reeve's Turban.** W.Pac. 32–35–50–80mm. C. Columella white. Smooth white operc. Orange and green color forms. ?Form of *T.petholatus*.

3. *TURBO (Sa.) SARMATICUS* L. **South African Turban** or **Turk's Cap.** S.Afr. 40–50–75–>110mm. C. Greenish per. Solid pustulose white operc.

4. *TURBO SAXOSUS* Wood. Nicaragua-Peru. 20–30–45–54mm. C. Knobby, spiny operc.

5. *TURBO (Ma.) SETOSUS* Gm. **Setose Turban.** S.W.Pac. 50–55–70–80mm. C. Thick white operc., striated on edge. Cp. *T.argyrostomus*, *T.sparverius*.

6. *TURBO (Lu.) SMARAGDUS* Gm. N.Z. Avg.45–50mm. VC. White operc. stained dark green.

7. *TURBO SPARVERIUS* Gm. W.Pac. Avg. 70–80mm. UC. Purplish-brown operc. is green and white on edges.

8. *TURBO SPECIOSUS* Reeve. Aust. Avg. 37–45mm. C. Brown-stained granulose operc.

9. *TURBO (Ma.) SQUAMOSA* Gray. **Squamose Turban.** S.W.Pac., esp. W.Aust. 20–25–35–>50mm. C. ?Syn. for *T.bruneus*.

10. *TURBO STENOGYRUS* Fischer. Japan-Tai. 20–22–25–32mm. C. Granular operc. Cp. *T.excellens*.

11. *TURBO (Ni.) TORQUATUS* Gm. **Heavy Turban.** S.W.Aust.-N.S.W. 45–75–100–110mm. C. A subsp., *T.t.whitleyi* Iredale, with a strong ridge on body whorl, is the S.W.Aust. form. Thick granulose white operc. with spiral ridges (11a). Syn.: *T.stamineus* Martyn.

12. *TURBO (Su.) UNDULATUS* Lightfoot. **Wavy Turbo** or **Common Warrener.** Aust.-Tas. 40–45–65–75mm. C. Smooth thick operc. Edible.

13. *PHASIANELLA AETHIOPICUS* Philippi. Ind.Oc. 12–15–18–23mm. C. Pattern q.v.

14. *PHASIANELLA AUSTRALIS* Gm. **Painted Lady** or **Australian Pheasant Shell.** W.-S.Aust.-Tas. 50–60–75–100mm. C. Thin. Color and pattern ext.v. White operc.

15. *PHASIANELLA KOCHI* Philippi. S.Afr. Avg.12–13mm. C. Variable pattern.

16. *PHASIANELLA VENTRICOSUS* Swainson. **Common** or **Swollen Pheasant.** Aust. ca.25–32–40–45mm. VC. Color and pattern ext.v. Thick white operc.

1. *NERITOPSIS RADULA* L. **Trap-door Nerite.** Ind.Oc.-W.Pac., Haw. (R) 16–25–30–33mm. C. Calcareous operc.

2. *NERITA ALBICILLA* L. **Ox-palate** or **Tubercular Nerite.** S.E.Afr.-W.Pac., Haw. 20–25–30–33mm. VC. Color and pattern q.v. Greenish per. Pustulose, pink-tinged operc.

3. *NAVICELLA BORBONICA* Bory. Maur., Reunion. Avg.20–25mm. UC.

4. *NERITA CHAMAELEON* L. **Chamaeleon Nerite.** W.Pac. Avg.25–30mm. C. Color q.v. Deep green or purplish-green pustulose operc.

5. *NERITA EXUVIA* L. **Snake-skin Nerite.** Ind.Oc.-W.Pac. Avg.25–30mm. C.

6. *NERITA FULGURANS* Gm. **Lightning** or **Antillean Nerite.** S.E.Fla.-Texas, W.I.-Brazil, Berm. 20–25mm. C. Bluish-white operc.

7. *NERITA FUNICULATA* Menke. Baja Cal.-G.of Cal.-Peru, Galáp. 15–22mm. C.

8. *NERITA LINEATA* Gm. **Lineated Nerite.** W.Pac., Haw. 30–45mm. VC. Thin. Finely granulose purplish operc.

9. *NERITA PELORONTA* L. **Bleeding Tooth.** S.E.Fla.-W.I., Berm. 20–25–38–49mm.

VC. Color and pattern q.v. Shiny orange-brown operc.

10. *NERITA PICEA* Récluz. **Pica Nerite.** Indon.-W.Pac., Haw. 12–20mm. VC.

11. *NERITA PLICATA* L. **Plicate Nerite.** S.E.Afr.-W.Pac., Haw. 20–30mm. C. Color and pattern variable. Smooth grayish operc.

12. *NERITA POLITA* L. **Polita** or **Polished Nerite.** S.E.Afr.-W.Pac., Haw. 20–25–35–40mm. VC. Color and pattern q.v. Smooth brownish-green operc. Orange-mouthed form (12B) is *N.p.antiquata* Récluz (?Sep.sp.).

13. *NERITA SCABRICOSTA* Lam. **Rough-ribbed Nerite.** Baja Cal.-Ecu. 20–25–45–51mm. C.

14. *NERITA SENEGALENSIS* Gm. Senegal-Angola. 15–25mm. VC.

15. *NERITA TESSELATA* Gm. **Tessellate Nerite.** Fla.-W.I.-Brazil, Berm. Avg.15–20mm. VC. Black operc.

16. *NERITA TEXTILIS* Gm. **Plexa Nerite.** S.E.Afr.-W.Pac. Avg.35–40mm. UC. Bluish-black pustulose operc. Syn.: *N.plexita* Dillwyn.

17. *NERITA UNDATA* L. **Undate Nerite.**

E.Afr.-W.Pac. Avg.30–40mm. VC. Syn.: *N. undulata* Gm.

18. *NERITA VERSICOLOR* Gm. **Variegated** or **Four-toothed Nerite.** S.Fla.-W.I., Berm. Avg.20–25mm. C. Granular brownish-gray operc.

19. *PUPERITA JAPONICA* Dunker. W.Pac. Avg.15–18mm. C.

20. *PUPERITA PUPA* L. **Zebra Nerite.** S.E.Fla.(R)-W.I., Berm. 8–15mm. C. Smooth cream-colored operc.

21. *THEODOXUS LUTEOFASCIATUS* Miller. G.of Cal.-Peru. Avg.11–13mm. C. Syn.: *Neritina picta* Sow.

22. *CLITHON SOWERBIANUS* Récluz. Japan. Avg.14–17mm. VC. Spire often eroded.

Plate 28 | Neritidae – Littorinidae

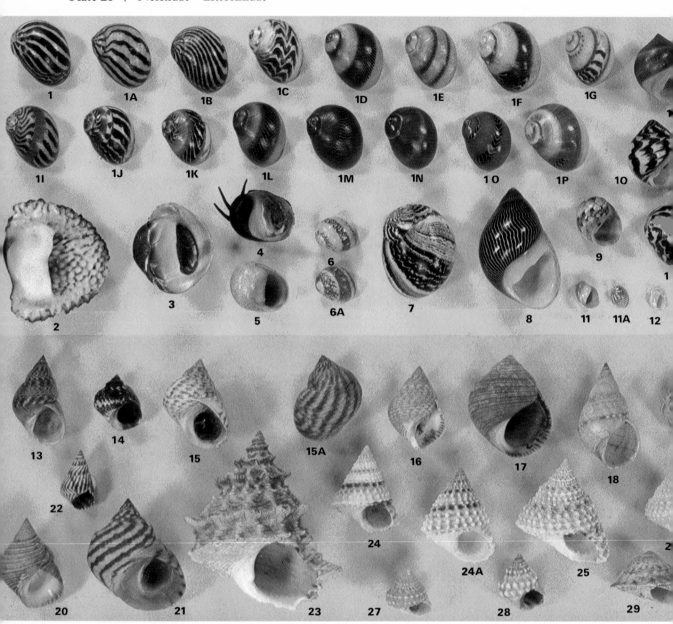

1. NERITINA COMMUNIS Q. & G. **Common Nerite.** W.Pac., esp. P.I. Avg.15–20mm. VC. Color and pattern ext.v. Also placed under genus **Theodoxus.**

2. NERITINA GRANOSA Sow. **Black Nerite.** Haw.(S). 25–30–40–50mm. C. A brackish shell. White. Black per.

3. NERITINA LATISSIMA Brod. W.Mex.-Ecu. 20–25–32–38mm. UC.

4. NERITINA LONGISPINA Récluz. Maur. Avg.20–25mm. UC.

5. NERITINA MELEAGRIS Lam. **Scaly Nerite.** Ant.-C.Am.-Brazil. Avg.10–15mm. C.

6. NERITINA OULANENSIS Lam. Ind.Oc.-W.Pac. Avg.8–11mm. C. Color and pattern q.v.

7. NERITINA SMITHI Gray. India. Avg.20–25mm. VS.

8. NERITINA TURRITA Gm. W.Pac., esp. P.I. 20–30mm. C. Color and pattern q.v.

9. NERITINA VIRGINEA L. **Virgin Nerite.** Fla.-Texas, W.I.-Brazil, Berm. Avg.13–18mm. VC. Color q.v.

10. NERITINA ZICZAC Lam. W.Pac. Avg. 20–25mm. C.

11. SMARAGDIA RANGIANA Récluz. **Rang's Neritina.** Moz.-W.Pac. 5–9mm. C. Green to rose.

12. SMARAGDIA VIRIDIS L. **Emerald Nerite.** Fla.(R)Carib., Med., Mauritania-Senegal. 3–5–7–10mm. C. Pattern variable.

13. LITTORINA ANGULIFERA Lam. **Angulate Periwinkle.** S.Fla.-Texas, W.I.-Brazil, Berm.; W.Pan. 13–20–30–38mm. C. Color and pattern q.v.

14. LITTORINA BREVICULA Philippi. Japan. Avg.13–16mm. C.

15. LITTORINA FASCIATA Gray. Baja Cal.-G.of Cal.-Ecu. 15–18–25–30mm. C.

16. LITTORINA IRRORATA Say. **Marsh Periwinkle.** N.Y.-Fla.-Texas. 15–25mm. C.

17. LITTORINA LITTOREA L. **Common** or **Shore Periwinkle.** Labrador-Md.; W.Eur. 20–25–35–53mm. VC. Edible.

18. LITTORINA SCABRA L. **Rough** or **Variegated Periwinkle.** S.E.Afr.-W.Pac., Haw. 15–20–30–35mm. C. Color and pattern q.v.

19. LITTORINA UNDULATA Gray. N.Ind. Oc.-Samoa, Haw. 10–15–22–25mm. C. Color

and pattern variable.

20. LITTORINA VARIA Sow. **Varied Periwinkle.** Pan.-Ecu.-?Peru. 20–30mm. C.

21. LITTORINA ZEBRA Donovan. C.R.-Col. 20–22–28–32mm. UC.

22. LITTORINA ZICZAC Gm. **Zigzag Periwinkle.** S.E.Fla.-W.I.-Brazil, Berm. 13–19mm. VC.

23. TECTARIUS PAGODUS L. **Pagoda** or **Giant Periwinkle.** Ind.Oc.-W.Pac. ca.30–40–55–65mm. C. Horny operc.

24. ECHINELLA CORONATUS Val. W.Pac. Avg.20–25mm. C.

25. ECHINELLA GRANDINATUS Gm. W.Pac. Avg.25–30mm. C.

26. TECTARIUS MURICATUS L. **Beaded Periwinkle.** S.Fla.-W.I., Berm. 13–15–20–30mm. VC. Horny brown operc.

27. ECHINUS CUMINGII Philippi. W.Pac. 12–14–20–25mm. C. Spec. illus. is subsp. **E.c. luchuanus** Pilsbry from Japan.

28. NODILITTORINA PYRAMIDALIS Q. & G. W.Pac. Avg.12–15mm. C. Horny operc.

29. BEMBICIUM AURATUM Q. & G.

Gold-mouthed Conniwink. S.Aust.-S.Qld., Tas. Avg.15–20mm. C. Color and pattern q.v. Horny operc.

Plate 29

1. *ARCHITECTONICA ACUTISSIMA* Sow. W.Pac. Avg.25–30mm. UC. Thin, horny operc. Old syn. for genus: *Solarium*.

2. *ARCHITECTONICA MAXIMA* Philippi. **Great Sundial.** S.Afr.; W.Pac., Haw. 30–35–45–?80mm. C. Fawn tone. Cp. *A.trochlearis*.

3. *ARCHITECTONICA NOBILIS* Röd. **Common, Noble** or **Granulated Sundial.** N.C.-Fla.-Texas, W.I.-Brazil; also Baja Cal.-Peru. 20–25–40–50mm. C. Pinkish tone. Thin brown operc. Syn.: *A.granulata* Lam.

4. *ARCHITECTONICA PERDIX* Hinds. **Partridge Sundial.** Sri Lanka-W.Pac. Avg.25–32mm. C.

5. *ARCHITECTONICA PERSPECTIVA* L. **Perspective** or **Oriental Sundial.** E.Afr.-W.Pac., Haw. <30–32–45–72mm. C.

6. *ARCHITECTONICA TROCHLEARIS* Hinds. **Pacific Sundial.** W.Pac. 35–40–60–71mm. C. Horny operc.

7. *HELIACUS STRAMINEUS* Gm. India-W.Pac. **Yellow-brown Sundial.** Avg.22–25mm. C. Genus also called *Torinia*.

8. *HELIACUS VARIEGATUS* Gm. **Variegated Sundial.** S.E.Afr.-Marq., Haw. 12–20mm. C.

9. *PHILIPPIA HYBRIDA* L. **Hybrid Sundial.** E.Afr.-W.Pac. Avg.22–25mm. UC.

10. *PHILIPPIA LUTEA* Lam. S.Aust.-N.S.W., Tas., N.Z. Avg.10–13mm. UC. Horny operc.

11. *PHILIPPIA RADIATA* Röd. S.E.Afr.-Marq. 18–25mm. C. Color and pattern variable. Thin yellowish-brown concave operc.

12. *ORECTOSPIRA TECTIFORMIS* Watson. Japan. 18–27mm. UC.

13. *TURRITELLA ANACTOR* Berry. No. G.of Cal. 100–105–120–145mm. C.

14. *TURRITELLA BANKSI* Reeve. G.of Cal.-Ecu. 20–30–50–86mm. C.

15. *TURRITELLA BICINGULATA* Lam. Senegal-Angola, C.V. <50–55–65–70mm. C.

16. *TURRITELLA CARINIFERA* Lam. S.Afr. 38–50–70–87mm. C.

17. *TURRITELLA CINGULATA* Sow. **Girdled Screw Shell.** Ecu.-Chile-Argentina. 40–45–55–?70mm. C.

18. *TURRITELLA COMMUNIS* Risso. **Common** or **European Screw Shell.** N.W. Eur.-Med., Black Sea. 38–40–55–60mm. C.

19. *TURRITELLA COOPERI* Cpr. C.Cal.-Baja Cal. 35–50mm. C.

20. *TURRITELLA GONIOSTOMA* Val. G.of Cal.-Ecu. <90–95–115–163mm. C. Also, dark color form.

21. *TURRITELLA LEUCOSTOMA* Val. **Tiger Turret.** Baja Cal.-G.of Cal.-Pan. 70–75–100–123mm. UC. Syn.: *T.tigrina* Kiener.

22. *TURRITELLA LIGAR* Deshayes. Senegal. 80–90–115–123mm. C. Syn.: *T.flammulata* Kiener.

Plate 30 | Turritellidae – Modulidae – Vermetidae

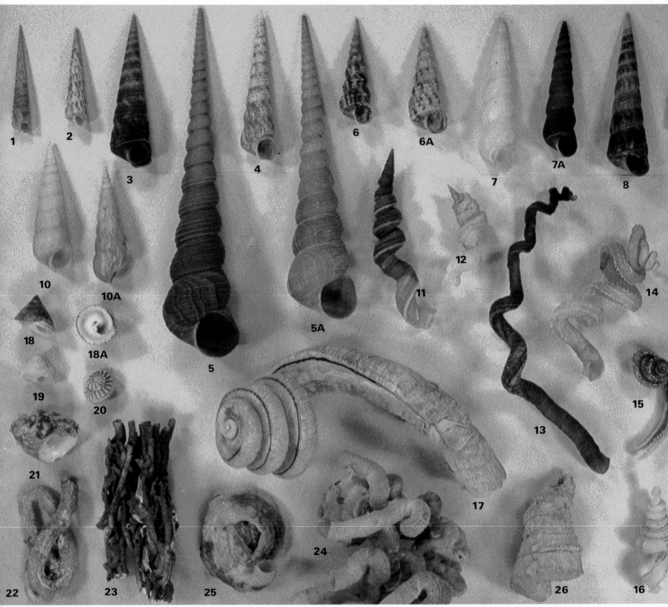

1. TURRITELLA MARIANA Dall. **Maria's Turret.** Baja Cal.-Col. <35–40–55–63mm. UC. ?Syn.: *T.radula* Kiener.

2. TURRITELLA NODULOSA King & Brod. **Nodular Turret.** Baja Cal.-Ecu. <25–30–40–50mm. C.

3. TURRITELLA ROSEUS Q. & G. N.Z. Avg.60–75mm. VC.

4. TURRITELLA SANGUINEA Reeve. S.Afr. 55–70–85–106mm. UC. Syn.: *T.natalensis* Smith.

5. TURRITELLA TEREBRA L. **Augur** or **Great Screw Shell.** E.Afr.-W.Pac. 60–70–110–159mm. VC.

6. TURRITELLA TORULOSA Kiener. Mauritania-Senegal. 40–50–70–100mm. C.

7. TURRITELLA UNGULINA L. Senegal-Congo. 50–55–65–80mm. C. Variable color.

8. TURRITELLA VARIEGATA L. **Variegated Turret.** W.I., So.G.of Mex. 63–80–100–114mm. C.

9. TURRITELLA WILLETTI McLean. W.Mex. 34–40–55–61mm. UC.

10. MESALIA BREVIALIS Lam. Portugal-Senegal. 43–45–55–65mm. C.

11. VERMICULARIA FARGOI Olsson. **Fargo's Worm Shell.** S.E.Fla.-Texas. Avg.70–80mm. C. ?Form of *V.spirata*.

12. VERMICULARIA PELLUCIDA Brod. & Sow. S.Cal.-G.of Cal.-Pan. 35–40–55–60mm. C.

13. VERMICULARIA SPIRATA Philippi. **Common** or **West Indian Worm Shell.** Mass.-S.E.Fla.-Gulf Coast-W.I., Berm. Avg. 70–80mm. C. Coiled stage dark brown. *V. knorri* Deshayes is similar, but coiled stage is white.

14. SILIQUARIA ANGUINA L. **Squamous Worm Shell** or **Pod Shell.** W.Pac. Avg.45–65mm. UC.

15. SILIQUARIA ARMATA Habe & Kuroda. Japan-Tai. Avg.35–50mm. UC.

16. SILIQUARIA CUMINGI Mörch. Japan-New Britain. 25–30–55–75mm. C.

17. SILIQUARIA PONDEROSA Mörch. **Ponderous Worm Shell.** Tai., N.Aust. 125–150–250–467mm. UC.

18. MODULUS CATENULATUS Philippi. G.of Cal.-Ecu. 15–22mm. VC.

19. MODULUS CARCHEDONIUS Lam.

Angled Modulus. W.I.-N.coast of S.Am. Avg. 15mm. UC.

20. MODULUS MODULUS L. **Atlantic Modulus.** N.C.-Fla.-Texas, W.I.-Brazil, Berm. 10–16mm. VC.

21. MODULUS TECTUM Gm. **Knobby Snail.** E.Afr.-W.Pac., Haw. Avg.25–30mm. C.

22. VERMETUS ADANSONI Daudin. Mauritania-Gabon. Avg.40–50mm. C.

23. PETALOCONCHUS VARIANS Orbigny. **Variable Worm Shell.** S.Fla.-W.I.-Brazil, Berm. 50–60–80–100mm. C. Irregularly coiled.

24. SERPULORBIS SQUAMIGERUS Carpenter. **Western Scaled Worm Shell.** Calif.-?Peru. Avg.95–115mm. VC. Grows in twisted masses.

25. SERPULORBIS XENOPHORUS Habe. Japan. Avg.38–44mm. C.

26. TRIPSYCHA TRIPSYCHA Pilsbry & Lowe. G.of Cal.-W.Mex. ca.40–50–70–80mm. UC.

1. CERITHIUM ADUSTUM Kiener. W.Mex.-Ecu., Galáp. 30–35–45–50mm. C.

2. CERITHIUM (Aluco) ALUCO L. W.Pac. 45–50–65–>75mm. C.

3. CERITHIUM (Rhinoclavis) ARTICULATUS Adams & Reeve. E.Afr.-W.Pac., Haw. 35–50mm. C.

4. CERITHIUM (Rhinoclavis) ASPER L. **Rough Creeper.** E.Afr.-W.Pac. 35–38–50–60mm. VC.

5. CERITHIUM CARBONARIUM Philippi. I-P. 25–40mm. C.

6. CERITHIUM CHEMNITZIANUS Pilsbry. W.Pac. Avg.25–30mm. C.

7. CERITHIUM CLAVA Gm. Tahiti. ca.100–129mm. S.

8. CERITHIUM (Aluco) CUMINGI Adams. W.Pac. 60–70–80–90mm. C.

9. CERITHIUM (Rhinoclavis) FASCIATUS Brug. **Banded Creeper.** E.Afr.-W.Pac., Haw. 48–55–70–80mm. VC. Pattern q.v. Cp. **C. pharos.**

10. CERITHIUM LITTERATUM Born. **Stocky** or **Lettered Horn Shell.** S.E.Fla.-W.I.-Brazil, Berm. 20–30mm. C.

11. CERITHIUM MACULOSUM Kiener. Baja Cal.-G.of Cal. 35–40–50–55mm. C.

12. CERITHIUM NODULOSUM Brug. **Giant Knobbed Cerith.** E.Afr.-W.Pac. 70–75–100–130mm. C. Heavy.

13. CERITHIUM (Rhinoclavis) PHAROS Hinds. Ind.Oc.-Fiji, Haw. ca.50–75mm. UC. ?Syn. for **C.fasciatus.**

14. CERITHIUM SOWERBYI Kiener. Ind. Oc.-W.Pac. 70–90mm. C. Cp. **C.aluco.**

15. CERITHIUM STERCUSMUSCARUM Val. Baja Cal.-G.of Cal.-Peru. 25–35mm. C.

16. CERITHIUM (Rhinoclavis) VERTAGUS L. **Common (Pacific) Cerith.** W.Pac. 40–45–55–63mm. VC. Brown bands or all white.

17. CERITHIUM VULGATUS Brug. **Common (Atlantic) Cerith.** W.Eur., Med. 40–50–60–>70mm. C. Pattern q.v.

18. CERITHIUM ZONATUS Wood. W.Pac. to Fiji. 20–25–40–57mm. UC. Syn.: **C. lemniscatum** Q. & G.

19. CAMPANILE SYMBOLICUM Iredale. S.W.Aust. <150–160–200–215mm. UC. Heavy. Usually eroded.

20. PLANAXIS (Quoyia) DECOLLATUS
Q. & G. **Decollated Clusterwink.** N.Aust.-N.G. 25–30mm. C. Reddish-brown per.

21. PLANAXIS SULCATUS Born. **Ribbed Clusterwink.** S.E.Afr.-S.W.Pac. 15–20–25–30mm. C.

22. CERITHIDEA MONTAGNEI Orbigny. Baja Cal.-G.of Cal.-Ecu. Avg.30–38mm. VC.

23. PYRAZUS EBENINUS Brug. **Club Mud Whelk** or **Hercules Club.** Qld.-Vic. 70–75–90–100mm. VC. Edible.

24. TELESCOPIUM TELESCOPIUM L. **Telescopic Creeper.** Ind.Oc.-W.Pac. 48–70–90–100mm. C. Edible.

25. TEREBRALIA PALUSTRIS L. **Northern Mud Creeper.** S.E.Afr.-W.Pac. 75–80–100–120mm. C. Chestnut brown per. Edible.

26. TEREBRALIA SULCATA Born. **Sulcate Creeper.** Vietnam-W.Pac. 40–45–55–63mm. VC. Spire often broken.

27. TYMPANOTONUS FUSCATUS L. Senegal-Angola, C.V. 40–45–60–70mm. VC. Form **T.f.radula** has no spines.

28. RHINOCORYNE HUMBOLDTI Val. G.of Cal.-Chile. 25–30–35–38mm. C.

Plate 32 | Aporrhaidae – Struthiolariidae – Strombidae

1. APORRHAIS ELEGANTISSIMUS Parenzan. Med.-Senegal. 30–38mm. S.

2. APORRHAIS OCCIDENTALIS Beck. **American Pelican's Foot.** Labrador–N.C. ca. 40–50–65–75mm. UC.

3. APORRHAIS PESPELICANI L. **Pelican's Foot.** Iceland-W.Med. 25–30–45–55mm. C.

4. APORRHAIS SENEGALENSIS Gray. Senegal-Angola, C.V. 18–25mm. UC.

5. APORRHAIS SERRESIANUS Michaud. W.Med. Avg.40–50mm. UC.

6. STRUTHIOLARIA PAPULOSA Martyn. **Large Ostrich Foot.** N.Z. 70–88mm. C.

7. STRUTHIOLARIA (Tylospira) SCUTU- LATA Martyn. N.S.W. Avg.30–35mm. UC. Claw-shaped operc.

8. STRUTHIOLARIA VERMIS Martyn.

N.Z. **Small Ostrich Foot.** 30–50mm. C.

9. TEREBELLUM TEREBELLUM L. **Common Little Augur** or **Terebellum.** E.Afr.-Samoa. ca.30–35–45–67mm. C. Very thin. Color and pattern q.v.

10. TIBIA (Rostellariella) DELICATULA Nevill. **Delicate Tibia.** E.Afr.-Per.G.-Sri Lanka. 45–50–65–75mm. R. Dwarf form, <50mm. Syn. for genus: *Rostellaria*.

11. TIBIA FUSUS L. **Shinbone** or **Spindle Tibia.** Tai.-P.I. 160–190–230–308mm. UC. Horny brown operc.

12. TIBIA INSULAECHORAB Röd. **Arabian Tibia.** Red Sea-No.Ind.Oc. Heavy. Also, yellow-mouthed and albino forms. Syn.: *T.curvirostris* Lam.

13. TIBIA MARTINII Marrat. Tai.-P.I. <50–100–120–>125mm. S (was R). Thin.

14. TIBIA POWISI Petit. S.W.Pac. 32–40–50–65mm. UC.

15. VARICOSPIRA (Rimella) CANCELLATA Lam. **Dwarf Tibia** or **Cancelled Beak Shell.** P.I., N.G. 13–16–25–32mm. UC.

16. VARICOSPIRA CRISPATA Sow. P.I., Melanesia. 20–25mm. S.

Plate 33

1. STROMBUS ALATUS Gm. **Florida Fighting Conch.** N.C.-E.& W.Fla.-Texas-Yucatan. <70–80–95–117mm. VC. Aperture color q.v. Also, albino form. Cp. *S.pugilis*.

2. STROMBUS AURISDIANAE L. **Diana's Ear** or **Imperial.** E.Afr.-Sol. 48–50–60–96mm. VC. Cp. *S.bulla.* Not illus.: *S.a.aratrum* Röd., **Black-mouthed Conch,** from Indon.-N.G.-N. Qld.(?Sep.sp.).

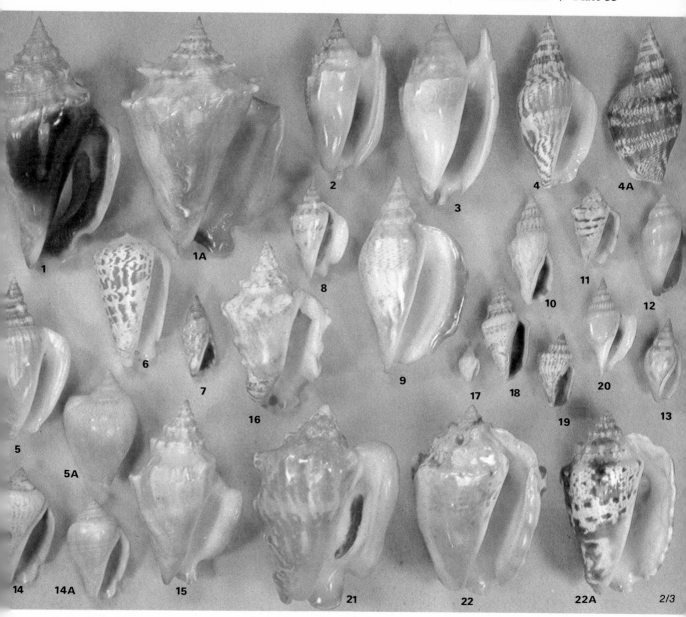

2/3

3. STROMBUS BULLA Röd. **Bubble Conch.** W.Pac. to Samoa. ca.48–55–70–>75mm. C. Cp. *S.aurisdianae.*

4. STROMBUS CAMPBELLI Griffith & Pidgeon. N.W.Aust.-Qld.-N.S.W. ca.42–45–55–>60mm. C. ?Subsp. of *S.vittatus.*

5. STROMBUS CANARIUM L. **Dog** or **Yellow Conch, Pacific** or **Partridge-wing Stromb.** India-New Heb. <35–40–55–102mm. VC. Heavy. Also, albino and dwarf forms.

– – *STROMBUS COSTATUS* Gm. – See pl. 35, no. 1.

6. STROMBUS DECORUS Röd. **Mauritius Conch.** S.E.Afr.-G.of Oman-Ind.Oc.-Sing. ca. 40–45–50–75mm. C. Also, dwarf form. Syn.: *S.mauritianus* Lam.

7. STROMBUS DENTATUS L. **Samar** or **Toothed Conch.** Moz., E.Afr.-Poly., Haw. 19–25–35–>50mm. C. Thin. Pattern variable.

8. STROMBUS DILATATUS Swainson. **Dilate Conch** or **Owl-wing Stromb.** And.Sea-New Cal. ca.28–40–50–60mm. C. Cp. *S. variabilis.*

9. STROMBUS EPIDROMIS L. **Swan Conch** or **Sail Stromb.** W.Pac. to New Cal. 50–65–75–90mm. C.

10. STROMBUS ERYTHRINUS Dillwyn. **Elegant Conch** or **Corrugated Stromb.** Red Sea-E.Afr.-Samoa, Haw. (R) <18–23–29–>40mm. C.

11. STROMBUS FASCIATUS Born. **Lineated Conch.** Red Sea-Per.G. <25–28–35–50mm. C. Aperture color variable.

12. STROMBUS FRAGILIS Röd. **Fragile Conch.** Indon.-S.W.Pac., Haw.(R) ca.30–35–42–49mm. S. Thin.

13. STROMBUS FUSIFORMIS Sow. **Fusiform Conch.** Red Sea, E.Afr.-W.Ind.Oc. ca. 22–25–30–?45mm. UC.

– – *STROMBUS GALEATUS* Swainson. – See pl. 35, no. 2.

– – *STROMBUS GALLUS* L. **Rooster-tail Conch.** S.E.Fla.(R)-W.I.-Brazil, Berm. <90–100–150–192mm. S. Aperture color variable. See pl. 3.

14. STROMBUS GIBBERULUS L. **Humped** or **Hunchback Conch.** S.E.Afr.-Red Sea-Ind. Oc.-Aust. 30–35–50–70mm. VC. Color variable. 14A is red-mouthed form *S.g.albus* Mörch from the Red Sea, G.of Aden.

– – *STROMBUS GIGAS* L. – See pl. 35, no. 4.

– – *STROMBUS GOLIATH* Schröter. – See pl. 35, no. 5.

15. STROMBUS GRACILIOR Sow. **Panama** or **E.Pac. Fighting Conch.** G.of Cal.-Peru. <55–60–75–90mm. C. Yellow-brown per. Claw-like operc.

16. STROMBUS GRANULATUS Swainson. **Granulated Conch.** No.G.of Cal.-Ecu. <50–55–70–93mm. C. Yellow-brown per.

17. STROMBUS HELLI Kiener. **Hell's Conch.** Haw. 14–16–22–27mm. VS.

18. STROMBUS KLINEORUM Abbott. **The Kline's Conch.** Sri Lanka. Avg.35–38mm. UC.

19. STROMBUS LABIATUS Röd. **Plicate Conch.** E.Afr.-Fiji. ca.18–25–32–47mm. C. Color variable. Syn.: *S.plicatus* Lam.

20. STROMBUS LABIOSUS Wood. **Labiate** or **Thick-lipped Conch.** E.Afr.-Fiji. 20–25–35–51mm. UC. Color variable.

– – *STROMBUS LATISSIMUS* L. – See pl. 35, no. 3.

21. STROMBUS LATUS Gm. **Bubonian Conch.** W.Sahara-Angola, C.V. ca.70–75–100–146mm. C. Brown per. Syn.: *S.bubonius* Lam. – See also pl. 35, no. 6.

22. STROMBUS LENTIGINOSUS L. **Silver Lip; Silver** or **Freckled Conch.** E.Afr.-W.Pac. <60–65–80–>100mm. VC. Variable color and pattern.

Plate 34 | Strombidae

1. *STROMBUS LISTERI* Gray. G.of Oman-N.W.Ind.Oc.-W.Thailand.   ca.100–110–130–152mm. VS (was VR). Also, dwarf form.

2. *STROMBUS LUHUANUS* L. **Bloodmouth, Red-mouth** or **Strawberry Conch.** S.W.Pac. to Fiji. ca.40–45–55–70mm. VC.

3. *STROMBUS MARGINATUS* L. **Marginate Conch.** Bay of Bengal-New Cal. 32–38–50–67mm. UC. 3 subsp.: 3 is *S.m.succinctus* L.; 3A is *S.m.robustus* Sow.; not illus.: *S.m.septimus* Duclos.

4. *STROMBUS MICROURCEUM* Kira. **Micro Conch.** S.W.Pac. to Samoa. <15–20–25–30mm. UC. Variable color.

5. *STROMBUS MINIMUS* L. **Minute** or **Small Conch.** Indon.-Samoa. 18–25–40mm. C.

6. *STROMBUS MUTABILIS* Swainson. **Mutable Conch.** S.E.Afr.-W.Pac. 20–25–35–40mm. VC. Form, color and pattern q.v.

– – *STROMBUS PERUVIANUS* Swainson. – See pl. 35, no. 7.

7. *STROMBUS PIPUS* Röd. **Butterfly** or **Elegant Conch.** E.Afr.-S.W.Pac. to Society Is. ca.45–50–60–70mm. UC. Color and pattern variable.

8. *STROMBUS PLICATUS* Röd. **Pigeon Conch.** Zan.-Red Sea-Fiji. 19–25–35–62mm. S. 3 subsp.

9. *STROMBUS PUGILIS* L. **W.Indian Fighting Conch.** S.E.Fla.(R)-W.I.-Brazil. 52–70–80–100mm. VC. Also, albino and dwarf forms. Cp. *S.alatus.*

10. *STROMBUS RANINUS* Gm. **Hawk-wing Conch.** S.E.Fla.-W.I.-Brazil, Berm. 40–70–80–100mm. C. Being overcollected in Fla. Also, dwarf form, from 35mm. Juveniles (10A) resemble cones.

11. *STROMBUS SINUATUS* Lightfoot. **Laciniated Conch.** W.Pac. to Fiji. 80–85–100–120mm. UC.

12. *STROMBUS TAURUS* Reeve. **Bull Conch.** Mariana Is., Marshall Is. ca.85–88–100–132mm. VS. Heavy.

13. *STROMBUS TEREBELLATUS* Sow. **Little Augur Conch.** W.Ind.Oc.-Fiji. ca.25–30–40–49mm. UC. Very thin.

– – *STROMBUS THERSITES* Swainson. – See pl. 35, no. 8.

– – *STROMBUS TRICORNIS* Lightfoot. – See pl. 35, no. 9.

14. *STROMBUS URCEUS* L. **Little Bear Conch** or **Pitcher Stromb.** W.Pac. to New Heb. 20–35–45–61mm. VC. Color and pattern q.v. Several subsp. and color forms incl. yellow, orange.

15. *STROMBUS VARIABILIS* Swainson. **Variable Conch** or **Maculate Stromb.** S.W.Pac. to Poly. <40–44–50–60mm. C. Form and color variable. Cp. *S.dilitatus.*

16. *STROMBUS VITTATUS* L. **Vittate Conch** or **Riband-marked Stromb.** And.Sea-Fiji. <50–55–65–91mm. C. Color variable. 16A is subsp. *S.v.turritus* Lam. from the And.Sea (UC).

17. *STROMBUS VOMER* Röd. S.W.Pac. to New Cal., Haw.(VR) 50–60–80–100mm. UC-VS. Three subsp. Also, albino form.

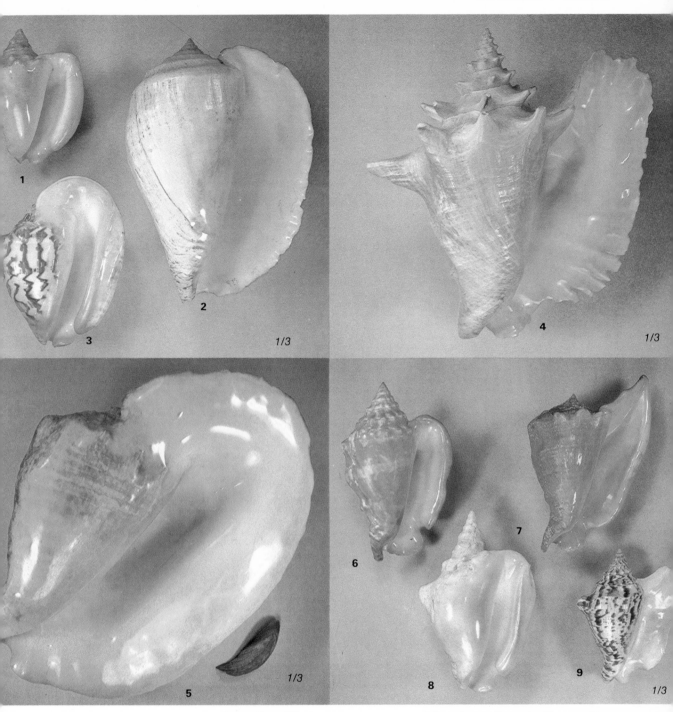

1/3

1/3

1/3

Larger Strombids

1. STROMBUS COSTATUS Gm. **Milk Conch.** S.Fla.(R)-W.I.-Brazil, Berm. ca.90–100–125–231mm. C. Heavy. Flaky per.

2. STROMBUS GALEATUS Swainson. **Galeate** or **Giant E.Pac. Conch.** No.G.of Cal.-Ecu. 150–160–190–223mm. UC. Very heavy. Aperture color variable. Largest Pan. gastropod. Edible.

3. STROMBUS LATISSIMUS L. **Widest Pacific** or **Heavy Frog Conch.** S.W.Pac. to Fiji. 130–140–155–222mm. UC. Heavy.

4. STROMBUS GIGAS L. **Queen** or **Pink Conch.** S.E.Fla.-W.I., Berm. 150–175–200–320mm. VC. Heavy; usually chipped. Thick flaky amber per. Brown claw-like operc. Also, albino, malformed and (?)sinistral forms. Edible.

5. STROMBUS GOLIATH Schröter. **Goliath Conch.** Brazil. ca.300–370mm. R. Very heavy.

6. STROMBUS LATUS Gm. **Bubonian Conch.** W.Sahara-Angola, C.V. ca.70–75–100–146mm. C. Brown per. Syn.: **S.bubonius** Lam. See also pl. 33, no. 21.

7. STROMBUS PERUVIANUS Swainson. **Peruvian Conch.** W.Mex.-N.Peru. 100–125–150–210mm. UC. Heavy. Thick brown per.

8. STROMBUS THERSITES Swainson. **Thersite Conch.** Ryukyus-Aust.-New Cal. ?100–130–150–160mm. R. Heavy.

9. STROMBUS TRICORNIS Lightfoot. Ind. Oc.-Poly., Haw. **Three-knobbed Conch.** Red Sea-G.of Aden. <70–80–110–154mm. UC. Coffee-brown per.

53

Plate 36 | Strombidae

1. **LAMBIS CHIRAGRA** L. **Chiragra** or **Gouty Spider Conch.** E.Ind.Oc.-E.Poly. 85–125–200–295mm. C. Color variable. **L.c. arthritica** Röd. is an UC subsp. from E.Afr.-C.Ind.Oc. Only the female (1B) differs from **L. chiragra**.

2. **LAMBIS CROCATA** Link. **Orange Spider Conch.** E.Afr.-Samoa. 70–80–110–204mm. UC (was C). White, brown or orange (S) forms.

2B. **LAMBIS CROCATA PILSBRYI** Abbott. **Pilsbry's Spider Conch.** Poly.-Marq. ca.160–240mm. R. ?Subsp.

3. **LAMBIS DIGITATA** Perry. **Elongate Spider Conch.** E.Afr.-Samoa. 110–115–130–171mm. VS.

4. **LAMBIS LAMBIS** L. **Common** or **Smooth Spider Conch.** E.Afr.-Tonga. <100–110–140–219mm. VC. Females are larger, with longer spines.

5. **LAMBIS MILLEPEDA** L. **Millipede** or **Thousand-footed Spider Conch.** Indon.-N.G. <100–105–120–219mm. C.

6. **LAMBIS SCORPIUS** L. **Scorpio** or **Scorpion Conch.** E.Afr.-Samoa. <100–110–140–170mm. C. Becoming UC.

7. **LAMBIS TRUNCATA** Lightfoot. **Giant Spider Conch** or **Wild-vine Root.** E.Afr.-Red Sea-Ind.Oc.-S.W.Pac. <230–240–300–385mm. UC. Heavy. Syn.: **L.bryonia** Gm.

8. **LAMBIS VIOLACEA** Swainson. **Violet Spider Conch.** Ind.Oc., esp. Maur. <100–110–120–130mm. R.

Plate 37

1. **EPITONIUM (Acrilla) ACUMINATA** Sow. S.Afr., W.Pac. 30–35–40–50mm. C. Pale yellow operc.

2. **EPITONIUM (Eglisia) BRUNNEA** Habe & Kosuge. W.Pac. 30–40–50–55mm. C.

3. **EPITONIUM (Clathrus) CLATHRUS** L. **Common Wentletrap.** North Sea-W.Eur.-Med. 20–22–26–30mm. C.

4. **EPITONIUM (Clathrus) COMMUNIS** Lam. Norway-Med. 13–25–35–40mm. C.?Syn. for **E.clathrus**.

5. **EPITONIUM (Gyroscala) CORONATUM** Lam. S.Afr. Avg.25–28mm. C.

6. **EPITONIUM (Dentiscala) GRANOSA** Q. & G. **Granulated Wentletrap.** W.Aust.-Vic.-Tas. 18–20–30–40mm. C.

7. **EPITONIUM IMPERIALIS** Sow. **Imperial Ladder Shell.** W.Pac., esp. Aust. 15–20–30–?40mm. UC.

8. **EPITONIUM (Gyroscala) LAMELLOSUM** Lam. **Banded** or **Lamellose Wentletrap.** S.Fla.-

Carib., Berm.; also W.Eur.-W.Afr. 19–25–32–38mm. C (W.Atl.: S).

9. EPITONIUM PALLASI Kiener. W.Pac. 14–20–30–38mm. UC.

10. EPITONIUM (Sthenorytis) PERNOBILIS Fischer & Bernardi. **Noble Wentletrap.** N.C.-S.E.Fla.-Barb.-Lesser Ant. 27–30–38–44mm. VR.

11. EPITONIUM (Gyroscala) PERPLEXUM Deshayes. W.Pac.-Haw. 13–20–30–?40mm. UC. Syn.: **E.perplexa** Pease.

12. EPITONIUM (Elegantiscala) RUGOSUM Kuroda & Ito. W.Pac., esp. Japan. Avg.50–60mm. VS.

13. EPITONIUM SCALARE L. **Precious Wentletrap.** N.W.Ind.Oc.-Fiji. 35–40–60–78mm. UC.

14. EPITONIUM (Cirsotrema) ZELEBORI Dunker. N.Z. 12–16–22–25mm. C.

15. AMAEA (Scalina) BRUNNEOPICTA Dall. Baja Cal.-G.of Cal.-C.R., Galáp. 20–28–35–43mm. UC.

16. AMAEA GAZEOIDES Kuroda & Habe. Japan-Tai. Avg.28–35mm. S.

17. AMAEA MAGNIFICUM Sow. **Magnificent Wentletrap.** W.Pac. 60–65–90–128mm. S. Thin. Ivory operc.

18. AMAEA SECUNDUM Kuroda & Ito. Japan-Tai. 40–45–55–60mm. S.

19. AMAEA THIELEI Boury. W.Pac. 14–18–22–28mm. C. Ivory operc.

20. OPALIA FUNICULATA Carpenter. **Sculptured** or **Scallop-edged Wentletrap.** S.Cal.-G.of Cal.-Pan. 10–12–15–19mm. VC. Syn.: **O.insculpta** Carpenter.

21. JANTHINA CAPREOLATA Montrouzier. W.Aust.-N.S.W. 10–15–20–30mm. C. 30mm. C.

22. JANTHINA EXIGUA Lam. **Dwarf** (or **Little**) **Purple** or **Violet Snail.** Tropical waters worldwide. 12–20mm. C. Very thin. Spire pointed.

23. JANTHINA GLOBOSA Swainson. **Round** or **Elongate Violet Snail.** Tropical waters worldwide. 10–15–25–40mm. C. Very thin. Bands at suture.

24. JANTHINA JANTHINA L. **Common** (or **Large**) **Purple** or **Violet Snail.** Tropical waters worldwide. 20–30–38–40mm. VC. Very thin. Pale top. Syn.: **J.violacea** Röd.

25. EULIMA MAJOR Sow. P.I. Avg.18–23mm. C.

26. BALCIS MARTINII Adams. S.E.Asia, esp. Tai. 25–43mm. UC.

Plate 38 | Hipponicidae – Calyptraeidae – Capulidae – Trichotropidae

1. HIPPONIX FOLIACEUS Q. & G. L. **White Hoof Shell.** Br.Col.-Peru; also, S.E.Fla.-W.I.-Brazil; also, Senegal; also, Ind.Oc.-Poly., Haw. 10–12–15–>18mm. C. Syn.: *H.antiquatus* L.

2. HIPPONIX CONICUS Schumacher. **Conical Horse Hoof** or **Bonnet Limpet.** E.Afr.-W.Pac., Haw. 9–25mm. C. Fibrous per. Often in clusters or on other shells. Also placed under genus Sabia.

3. CALYPTRAEA CHINENSIS L. **Chinese** or **Malay Hat; European Cup-and-Saucer.** England-Med.-Black Sea. W.Afr.-S.Afr. 10–12–18–29mm. C. Variable pale colors.

4. CALYPTRAEA FASTIGIATA Gould. **Pacific Chinese Hat.** Alaska-S.Cal. 8–12–20–25mm. C.

5. CALYPTRAEA MAMILLARIS Brod. Baja Cal.-G.of Cal.-Peru. 16–20–30–38mm. C. White to brown inside.

6. CALYPTRAEA TROCHIFORMIS Born. Ecu.-Chile; also, Angola, C.V. **Rayed (Peru-vian) Hat.** 28–30–40–50mm. C. Syn.: *"Patella trochiformis* Gm".

7. CALYPTRAEA (Sigapatella) NOVAE-ZELANDIAE Lesson. **Circular Slipper Shell.** N.Z. Avg.25–32mm. C.

– – **CREPIDULA ADUNCA** Sow. See pl. 86, no. 7.

8. CREPIDULA FORNICATA L. **Common American, Atlantic** or **Arched Slipper Limpet.** Wash.; Nova Scotia-Fla.-Texas; W.Eur.-Med. 20–25–40–52mm. VC.

9. CREPIDULA MACULOSA Conrad. **Spotted Slipper Shell** or **Limpet.** E. & W.Fla.-Veracruz, Bah. 20–25–35–50mm. C.

10. CREPIDULA ONYX Sow. **Onyx Slipper Limpet.** S.Cal.-Chile. 15–20–30–68mm. VC. Shaggy per. On other dead shells.

11. CREPIDULA PLANA Say. **Eastern White** or **Flat Slipper Limpet.** E.Canada-Fla.-Texas-Brazil, Berm. 12–15–25–30mm. C.

12. CREPIDULA (Maoricrypta) COSTATA

Sow. **Ribbed Slipper Shell.** N.Z. Avg.38–44mm. C. Form q.v.

13. CRUCIBULUM LIGNARIUM Brod. G.of Cal.-Ecu. 25–30–40–46mm. C.

14. CRUCIBULUM SCUTELLATUM Wood. **Imbricate Cup-and-Saucer.** Baja Cal.-G.of Cal.-Ecu.-?Peru. 25–35–50–77mm. C. White to brown.

15. CRUCIBULUM SPINOSUM Sow. **Spiny Cup-and-Saucer.** S.Cal.-Chile; I-P, Haw. 18–20–40–71mm. VC. Also, albino form.

16. CRUCIBULUM STRIATUM Say. **Striated Cup-and-Saucer.** Nova Scotia-E.& W.Fla. Avg.20–25mm. C.

17. SYPHOPATELLA WALSHI Reeve. Japan. Avg.22–26mm. UC. Thin yellow per. On other dead shells.

18. CHEILEA TORTILUS Reeve. Japan. 35–40–50–53mm. UC.

19. CAPULUS UNGARICUS L. **Hungarian** or **Fool's Cap.** Greenland-Fla., Berm.; also,

Arctic-Med. Avg.40–55mm. UC. Flaky, fibrous per.

20. TRICHOTROPIS CANCELLATA Hinds. **Cancellate Hairy-shell.** Bering Sea-Ore. Avg.20–25mm. C. Hairy brown per.

21. TRICHOTROPIS (Iphinoe) UNICARINATA Brod. & Sow. Japan. 15–17–22–27mm. UC. Coarse hairy brown per.

Plate 39

1. XENOPHORA CONCHYLIOPHORA Born. **Atlantic Carrier Shell.** N.C.-S.E.Fla.-W.I.-Brazil, Berm. 50–55–65–75mm. UC. Thin operc.

2. XENOPHORA CORRUGATA Reeve. S.E.-Afr.-W.Pac. 20–40–60–94mm. UC. White base with pale orange-brown streaks. Corals, stones, sand, some shells attached.

3. XENOPHORA CRISPA König. Med. 35–

40–55–63mm. UC. Usually shell fragments attached. Syn.: **X.mediterranea** Tiberi.

4. XENOPHORA DIGITATA Fischer. W. Afr. Avg.50–60mm. UC.

5. XENOPHORA JAPONICA Kuroda & Habe. Japan-Tai. 35–40–55–63mm. C.

6. XENOPHORA KONOI Habe. E.Ind.Oc.-W.Pac. 50–60–75–85mm. S.

7. XENOPHORA NEOZELANDICA Suter. N.Z. 50–60–75–90mm. C.

8. XENOPHORA PALLIDULA Reeve. **Pallid Carrier Shell.** S.Afr.-W.Pac. 22–50–80–100mm. UC. Often with gastropods at base, bivalves above, sponges on top.

9. XENOPHORA PERONIANA Iredale. Qld.-Vic., Haw. Avg.40–50mm. C. Usually bivalve fragments and pebbles attached.

10. XENOPHORA ROBUSTA Verrill. **Robust Carrier Shell.** W.Mex. 30–40–65–108mm. C. Horny brown operc.

11. XENOPHORA SENEGALENSIS Gray. Senegal-Angola, C.V. 30–35–45–50mm. C.

12. XENOPHORA SOLARIOIDES Reeve. Japan-Tai. 20–25–30–38mm. UC. Deeply concave white base. Shells, shell fragments or pebbles attached.

13. XENOPHORA TENUIS Fulton. Japan-Tai. 38–40–50–57mm. S. Deeply concave white base. Small shell fragments attached.

Plate 40 | Xenophoridae – Lamellariidae

1. **XENOPHORA TURRIDA** Kuroda. W.-C.Pac. Avg.40–50mm. Orange-brown base. Sand and pebbles attached.

2. **XENOPHORA (Onustus or Tugurium) CALCULIFERA** Reeve. **Pebble Carrier Shell.** W.Pac. 40–50–65–78mm. C. Cp. **X.exustus.** Usually small pebbles attached.

3. **XENOPHORA (Tugurium) CARIBAEUM** Petit. **Caribbean Carrier Shell.** Fla.Keys-W.I. 44–50–65–75mm. UC.

4. **XENOPHORA (Onustus or Tugurium) EXUTUS** Reeve. Ind.Oc.-W.Pac. 38–45–65–105mm. C. Thin. Cream to yellowish-brown. Only fine sand often attached. Cp. **X.calculifera.**

5. **XENOPHORA (Onustus) INDICUS** Gm. **Indian Carrier Shell.** ?Ind.Oc.-W.Pac. Avg. 60–70mm. UC.

6. **XENOPHORA (Tugurium) LONGLEYI** Bartsch. Dry Tortugas, Fla. 100–120–145–230mm. S.

7. **STELLARIA SOLARIS** L. **Sunburst Carrier Shell.** W.Pac. 60–70–90–110mm. UC. No attached objects.

8. **LAMELLARIA DIEGOENSIS** Dall. **San Diego Ear Shell** or **Lamellaria.** S.Cal.-G.of Cal. 15–20mm. UC. Very thin. Clear glossy per.

9. **LAMELLARIA STEARNSI** Dall. Alaska-S.Cal. 15–20mm. UC.

10. **VELUTINA LAEVIGATA** L. **Velvet Shell** or **Smooth Velutina.** Arctic-S.Cal.; Arctic-Mass.; also, N.W.Eur. 13–20mm. C. Very thin. Yellowish-brown per.

Plate 41

1. **TRIVIELLA APERTA** Swainson. S.Afr. 15–25mm. C.

2. **TRIVIA MERCES** Iredale. **Common Southern Bean Cowrie.** Aust.-N.Z. Avg.12–13mm. C. Usually beach spec. Syn.: **T.australis** Lam.

3. **TRIVIA MONACHA** DaCosta. **Common European** or **Spotted Cowrie.** W.Eur.-Med. Avg.8–12mm. C.

4. **TRIVIA EDGARI** Shaw. **Rice Grain Bean Cowrie.** S.Afr.-Ind.Oc.-Tonga, Haw. 6–13mm. C. Syn.: **T.oryza** Lam.

5. **TRIVIELLA OVULATA** Lam. S.Afr. 14–20mm. C. Usually beach spec.

6. **TRIVIA PEDICULUS** L. **Coffee Bean** or **Louse Trivia.** N.C.-Fla.-W.I.-Brazil, Berm. 10–15mm. C.

7. **TRIVIA RADIANS** Lam. **Radiating Trivia.** Baja Cal.-Ecu. 15–21mm. C.

8. **TRIVIA SANGUINEA** Sow. **Sanguine Trivia.** G.of Cal.-Ecu. 8–15mm. C.

9. *TRIVIA SOLANDRI* Sow. **Sea Button.**
S.Cal.-G.of Cal.-Peru. 13–20mm. C.

10. *ERATO VITELLINA* Hinds. **Apple
Seed.** No.Cal.-Baja Cal. 8–13mm. UC.

11. *PEDICULARIA CALIFORNICA*
Newcomb. **Californian Pedicularia.** C.-S.Cal.
7–15mm. UC. Now placed under Ovulidae,
rather than Triviidae.

12. *JENNERIA PUSTULATA* Lightfoot.
Pustulate Trivia. No.G.of Cal.-Ecu. 15–27mm.
C. Now placed under Ovulidae, rather than
Triviidae.

13. *CYPRAEA (Sc.) ACHATIDEA* Sow.
Agate Cowrie. W.Med.-S.W.Afr. 22–35–38–
42mm. VS.

14. *CYPRAEA (Er.) ALBUGINOSA* Gray.
White-spotted Cowrie. G.of Cal.-Ecu., Galáp.
12–25–29–33mm. UC. Fades to pale violet. Cp.
C.marginalis, C.poraria.

15. *CYPRAEA (Cy.) ANGELICAE* Clover.
Liberia. 19–25mm. R. Usually beach spec. ?Form
of *C.petitiana.*

16. *CYPRAEA (Not.) ANGUSTATA* Gm.
Brown-toothed Cowrie. N.S.W., S.Aust. 19–
36mm. C. Plump; convex base with dark spots.

17. *CYPRAEA (Zon.) ANNETTAE* Dall.
G.of Cal.-Peru. 22–30–38–52mm. C. Cp. *C.
nigropunctata.*

18. *CYPRAEA (Or.) ANNULUS* L. **Gold-
ringer** or **Ring Cowrie.** S.E.Afr.-Cook Is.,
?Haw. 10–22–28–34mm. VC. Variable. Used
by natives for money, ornament.

19. *CYPRAEA (Or.) ANNULUS OB-
VELATA* Lam. **Tahitian Gold-ringer.** Cook
Is., E.Poly.-Marq. 14–18–22–26mm. C. Thick
lateral callus; large broad teeth. ?Separate species.

20. *CYPRAEA (Mau.) ARABICA* L. **Arabian
Cowrie.** S.E.Afr.-Haw. 25–44–50–105mm.
VC. Arabica Group. Base flat or concave; no
spire blotch. See: *C.eglantina, C.grayana, C.
histrio, C.maculifera, C.scurra.*

Plate 42 | Cypraeidae

1. *CYPRAEA (Mau.) ARABICA NIGER*
Roberts. The color form illus. by 1, 1A, 1B is a rare color variant of **C.arabica** from New Cal.

2. *CYPRAEA (Mau.) ARABICULA* Lam.
Little Arabian Cowrie. G.of Cal.-Peru, Galáp. 16–22–26–35mm. C. Cp. **C.robertsi.**

3. *CYPRAEA (Ly.) ARGUS* L. **Eyed Cowrie.**
E.Afr.-Fiji. 47–65–80–107mm. UC. Pattern q.v. Base pale brown with 3 v.lge. dark brown spots and 1 faint one.

4. *CYPRAEA (Pal.) ASELLUS* L. **Little Ass Cowrie.** E.Afr.-C.Pac. 11–18–22–25mm. C. Brownish black bands often fade to dull brown.

5. *CYPRAEA (Ly.) AURANTIUM* Gm. **Golden** or **Orange Cowrie.** P.I.-Poly. 58–88–100–117mm. R. Fresh shells deep reddish orange; juvenile shells brighter orange (illus.). A famous and classic rarity.

– – *CYPRAEA (Pus.) BISTRINOTATA* S. & S. – See pl. 44, no. 3.

6. *CYPRAEA (Er.) BOIVINII* Kiener.
Indon.-Japan-P.I. 14–25–30–37mm. UC.

7. *CYPRAEA (Ly.) CAMELOPARDALIS*
Perry. **Giraffe Cowrie.** Red Sea-G.of Aden. 31–40–50–81mm. S. Black staining between teeth. Cp. **C.nivosa, C.vitellus.**

8. *CYPRAEA (Cyp.) CAPENSIS* Gray. **Cape Cowrie.** S.Afr. 24–27–32–38mm. UC. Pale mauve color fades rapidly. Fine ridges cover dorsum. Rarely collected live.

1/1

1. CYPRAEA (Ra.) CAPUTDRACONIS Melvill. **Dragon's Head Cowrie.** Easter Is. 17–26–32–45mm. UC. Cp. *C.caputserpentis.*

2. CYPRAEA (Ra.) CAPUTSERPENTIS L. **Snake's** or **Serpent's Head Cowrie.** S.E.Afr.-Haw. 15–25–32–43mm. VC. Cp. *C.caput-draconis, C.englerti.*

3. CYPRAEA (Ly.) CARNEOLA L. **Carnelian** or **Orange-banded Cowrie.** S.E.Afr.-Poly., Haw. 17–38–50–94mm. VC. Giant form, *C. carneola leviathon* S. & S., to 130mm., has nodules on margin. 3B is *C.carneola propinqua* Garrett from Aust.-Sol., now considered a separate species.

4. CYPRAEA (Err.) CAURICA L. **Thick-edged Cowrie.** S.E.Afr.-Samoa. 18–38–44–70mm. VC. Pattern and form q.v. 4C is form *C.caurica niger.* 4D is var. *C.caurica corrosa* Gronovius.

5. CYPRAEA (Ma.) CERVINETTA Kiener. **Little Deer** or **Panama Cowrie.** G.of Cal.-Peru, Galáp. 32–50–70–115mm. C. Also striped form and dwarfs (<40mm.). Cp. *C.cervus* (plumper; bolder teeth).

6. CYPRAEA (Ma.) CERVUS L. **Atlantic Deer Cowrie.** N.C.-Fla.-Cuba-Yucatan. ?Berm. 42–75–95–190mm. UC. Lge. posterior lip. Cp.

C.cervinetta (cylindrical, flatter). The largest cowrie. Being over-collected.

Plate 44 | Cypraeidae

1. *CYPRAEA (Ov.) CHINENSIS* Gm. **Chinese Cowrie.** S.E.Afr.-Poly., Haw.(R). ?7-30–38–52mm. C. Pale violet lateral spots; orange staining between teeth.

2. *CYPRAEA (Pus.) CICERCULA* L. **Chick Pea Cowrie.** Moz.-E.Afr.-Haw. 8–16–18–23mm. UC. Spire blotch. Cp. *C.globulus.*

3. *CYPRAEA (Pus.) CICERCULA SUB-LAEVIS* S. & S. S.E.Afr.-Poly. 10–15–18–23mm. UC. Dark brown dorsal splotches. Wide teeth. Adults granular. Cp. *C.globulus.* Syn.: *C.bistrinotata* S. & S. (preferred by some authorities).

4. *CYPRAEA (Lur.) CINEREA* Gm. **Atlantic Gray** or **Ashen Cowrie.** N.C.-Fla.-W.I., Berm., G.of Mex.-Brazil. 15–20–25–42mm. UC. Dark purplish-brown quickly fades to pale tan.

5. *CYPRAEA (Er.) CITRINA* Gray. **Citrine Cowrie.** S.Afr.-Moz. 13–20–25–30mm. UC. Usually faded beach spec.

6. *CYPRAEA (Pal.) CLANDESTINA* L. **Clandestine Cowrie.** S.E.Afr.-C.Pac. 8–15–19–25mm. C. Pattern q.v.

7. *CYPRAEA (Ov.) COLOBA* Melvill. N.Ind. Oc. 20–25–28–37mm. UC (was R). Possibly related to *C.chinensis.*

8. *CYPRAEA (Not.) COMPTONII* Gray. S.Aust.-N.Tas. 17–21–23–32mm. UC. Fine spots on base. 8B, 8C are color form *C.c. trenberthae* Trenberth.

9. *CYPRAEA (Pal.) CONTAMINATA* Sow. **Contaminated Cowrie.** E.Afr.-P.I.-N.E.Aust. 8–11–13–16mm. VS. No posterior terminal spots. Cp. *C.gracilis.*

10. *CYPRAEA (Bl.) COXENI* Cox. **Cox's Cowrie.** N.G.-Sol. 14–20–24–29mm. UC.

11. *CYPRAEA (Cr.) CRIBRARIA* L. **Sieve Cowrie.** S.E.Afr.-C.Pac. 10–25–32–42mm. C. 11A is form *C.c.niger.*

12. *CYPRAEA (Err.) CYLINDRICA* Born. **Cylindrical Cowrie.** P.I.-N.W.Aust.-Guam-New Cal. 18–25–30–47mm. C. Bluish. No lateral spotting. Cp. *C.hirundo, C.kieneri, C. teres.*

13. *CYPRAEA (Zo.) DECIPIENS* E.A.Smith. **Hump-backed Cowrie.** N.W.Aust. 46–52–70mm. UC.

14. *CYPRAEA (Not.) DECLIVIS* Sow. **Sloping Cowrie.** N.S.W.-Tas. 15–20–25–32mm. S. Color q.v. Tiny brown spots on adult dorsum.

15. *CYPRAEA (Mau.) DEPRESSA* Gray. **Depressed Cowrie.** E.Afr.-C.Pac. 23–35–42–56mm. C. Arabica Group. Heavy, callused; small spots; coarse well-marked teeth; most rounded.

1. *CYPRAEA (Pal.) DILUCULUM* Reeve. **Dawn** or **Daybreak Cowrie.** S.E.Afr.-Sey - Maur. 11–25–29–36mm. C. Brown spots on base. ?Subsp. of *C.ziczac.*

2. *CYPRAEA (Er.) EBURNEA* Barnes. **Ivory** or **Pure White Cowrie.** N.G.-Cook Is. 23–32–38–58mm. S.

3. *CYPRAEA (Lu.) EDENTULA* Gray. **Toothless Cowrie.** S.Afr. 17–21–25–34mm. UC. No teeth. Usually beach.

4. *CYPRAEA (Mau.) EGLANTINA* Duclos. **Eglantine Cowrie.** W.Pac.-Samoa. 35–44–52–80mm. C. Arabica Group. Small spire blotch; strong longitudinal lines may cross spots. Most elongated of group. 4D, 4E are color form *C.e.niger* Roberts from New Cal. See *C.arabica* for related sp.

5. *CYPRAEA (Er.) ENGLERTI* Summers & Burgess. **Father Englert's Cowrie.** Easter Is.

20–27mm. VS. Orange-brown base. Only 2 spec. known just 10 years ago. Cp. *C.caputdraconis, C.caputserpentis.*

6. *CYPRAEA (Er.) EROSA* L. **Eroded Cowrie.** S.E.Afr.-Poly., Haw. 16–32–38–71mm. VC. 6B is a rostrate form. Cp. *C.nebrites* (?subsp.).

7. *CYPRAEA (Err.) ERRONES* L. **Wandering Cowrie.** And.-Samoa. 13–20–28–43mm. VC. Greenish dorsum; white teeth. Cp. *C.ovum.*

8. *CYPRAEA (Cr.) ESONTROPIA* Duclos. Maur. 12–19–25–36mm. VS. Deltoid shape. Cp. *C.gaskoini* (sm. dorsal spots).

9. *CYPRAEA (Tal.) EXUSTA* Sow. Red Sea-G.of Aden. 52–65–70–91mm. R. Pyriform shape; brownish-black base; v.fine teeth. Cp. *C.talpa.*

10. *CYPRAEA (Err.) FELINA* Gm. **Cat** or **Kitten Cowrie.** S.E.Afr.-Samoa. 10–14–19–

27mm. C. Form and color q.v. Lge. black spots on lateral margins. 10B, 10C are a rounded form from the Red Sea-Arabian G., *C.f.fabula* Kiener. 10D is a slender bluish form from the Ind.Oc.-Fiji, *C.f.listeri* Gray.

11. *CYPRAEA (Pur.) FIMBRIATA* Gm. **Fringed Cowrie.** S.E.Afr.-C.Pac. excl. S.Aust., Haw. 7–10–13–21mm. VC. 11B is a form from S.Afr., *C.f.durbanensis* S. & S.

Plate 46 | Cypraeidae

1. CYPRAEA (Zo.) FRIENDI Gray. **Friend's** or **Scott's Cowrie.** W.-S.Aust. 42–65–80–107mm. S (some forms R). Form, color, pattern ext.v. 1B, 1C are rare form *C.f.jeaniana* Cate. Cp. *C.thersites.*

2. CYPRAEA (Bar.) FULTONI Sow. Off S.Afr. 50–66mm. Ext.R. A great rarity found in the stomachs of deep-water fish. Cp. *C.teulerei, C.mus.*

3. CYPRAEA (Lu.) FUSCODENTATA Gray. S.Afr. 24–28–32–43mm. UC. Orange basal ridges and teeth. Beach spec. only.

4. CYPRAEA (Zon.) GAMBIENSIS Shaw. Senegal-Sierra Leone, C.V. 24–29mm. VS (was VR). Lateral callus; some lateral spotting. ?Subsp. of *C.zonaria.*

5. CYPRAEA (Er.) GANGRANOSA Dillwyn. **Gangranous Cowrie.** E.Afr.-Aden-N.G. 9–16–20–27mm. UC (was VS). Magenta spots on tips of base. Cp. *C.quadrimaculata.* 5B is subsp. *C.g.reentsii* Dunker from And.Sea.

6. CYPRAEA (Cr.) GASKOINI Reeve. Fiji, Haw.(R). 10–19–23–27mm. VS. Cp. *C. esontropia* (lge.dorsal spots).

7. CYPRAEA (Pus.) GLOBULUS L. **Globular Cowrie.** E.Afr.-Haw. 9–16–19–24mm. UC. Smooth dorsum; orange base. Cp. *C.cicercula.*

8. CYPRAEA (Bl.) GOODALLI Sow. Guam-Poly. 8–10–13–20mm. S.

9. CYPRAEA (Pur.) GRACILIS Gaskoin. **Graceful Cowrie.** E.Afr.-Fiji. 9–16–19–30mm. VC. Brown spots on lateral margins, base and posterior terminals. Cp. *C.contaminata.* 9C is subsp. *C.g.macula* Angas from N.E.-E.Aust. 9D is subsp. *C.g.notata* Gill from Red Sea-G.of Oman.

10. CYPRAEA (Nu.) GRANULATA Pease. **Granulated Cowrie.** Haw. 15–22–28–43mm. S. Dull surface, except juveniles. Cp. *C.nucleus* (more elongated).

11. CYPRAEA (Mau.) GRAYANA Schilder. Red Sea-G.of Oman-Pak. 17–44–52–79mm. C. Arabica Group. Occasional faint spire blotch; longitudinal lines do not cross distinct spots; fine teeth. ?Subsp. of *C.arabica.* See *C.arabica* for related sp.

1. *CYPRAEA (Er.) GUTTATA* Gm. Great Spotted Cowrie. Japan-Tai.-New Heb., esp. P.I. 40–55–62–70mm. Ext.R. Less than 20 known 10 years ago; still a much desired rarity.

2. *CYPRAEA (Pur.) HAMMONDAE* Iredale. P.I., Aust. 9–13–15–18mm. C. 2 is the scarce form *C.h.dampierensis* Schilder & Cern. from W.Aust. 2A, 2B, 2C is the lighter, more pyriform P.I. form *C.h.raysummersi* Schilder.

3. *CYPRAEA (Er.) HELVOLA* L. Honey or Red Cowrie. S.E.Afr.-Poly.,-Haw. 8–15–23–36mm. VC. Several distinct forms. Syn.: *C. callista* Shaw.

4. *CYPRAEA (Um.) HESITATA* Iredale. Umbilicate or **Wonder Cowrie.** N.S.W.-Tasm. 54–75–100–121mm. UC. Not illus.: albino form *C.h.howelli* Iredale; dwarf form *C.h.beddomei* Schilder. ?Subsp. of *C.armeniaca* Verco.

5. *CYPRAEA (Nes.) HIRASEI* Roberts. Japan, P.I., Aust. 40–42–47–61mm. VR.

6. *CYPRAEA (Bi.) HIRUNDO* L. E.Afr.-Samoa. 8–16–19–24mm. UC. Bluish. Form illus.: *C.h.neglecta* Sow. (dark dorsal blotches). Cp. *C.kieneri, C.ursellus.*

7. *CYPRAEA (Mau.) HISTRIO* Gm. E.Afr.-N.W.Aust. 23–40–55–88mm. C. Arabica Group Strong spire blotch; network of distinct lge. spots; body color pale tan. See *C.arabica* for related sp.

8. *CYPRAEA (Pal.) HUMPHREYSII* Gray. E.Afr.-Samoa. 10–12–14–26mm. UC. Orange base with brown spots. ?Form of or syn. for *C.lutea.*

9. *CYPRAEA (Ad.) HUNGERFORDI* Sow. Japan. Qld. 22–32–38–41mm. S. Brown dots form dorsal band. *C.h.coucomi* Schilder is a form from Aust. (not illus.).

Plate 48 | Cypraeidae

1. CYPRAEA (Bl.) INTERRUPTA Gray. And.Sea-P.I. 14–19–24–28mm. UC (was R). Bands unequally spaced.

2. CYPRAEA (Na.) IRRORATA Gray. **Bedewed Cowrie.** C.Pac.-Poly. 8–10–13–17mm. C.

3. CYPRAEA (Lur.) ISABELLA L. Moz.-E.Afr.-Haw. 11–25–35–54mm. VC. Cp. **C. isabellamexicana.**

4. CYPRAEA (Lu.) ISABELLAMEXICANA Stearns. G.of Cal.-Pan., Galáp. 16–25–35–54mm. VS. Brown lateral calluses. Usually dead spec.

5. CYPRAEA (Bi.) KIENERI Hidalgo. E.Afr.-Samoa. 8–12–15–24mm. C. Variable bluish base pattern with brown blotches; brown spots on lateral margins; attenuated teeth. Cp. **C. hirundo, C.ursellus.**

6. CYPRAEA (Er.) LABROLINEATA Gaskoin. **Lined Lip Cowrie.** Indon.-Samoa; Haw. 8–15–18–31mm. C. Cp. **C.cernica, C. gangranosa.** Syn.: **C.flaveola** L. (Preferred by some writers.)

7. CYPRAEA (Er.) LAMARCKI Gray. S.E.Afr.-Sing., ?P.I. 18–37–41–51mm. C. Orange-brown spots on lateral margins. Cp. **C. miliaris, C.ocellata.**

8. CYPRAEA (Pal.) LENTIGINOSA Gray. **Freckled Cowrie.** Red Sea, Per.G.-Sri Lanka. 17–25–30–38mm. S (was VS). Brown spots on lateral margins and base.

– – CYPRAEA LEVIATHAN S. & S. – See pl. 43, no. 3B.

9. CYPRAEA (St.) LIMACINA Lam. E.Afr.-Samoa. 12–22–27–37mm. C. Black dorsum fades quickly to gray. Spots granular in adults; teeth do not cross base. Cp. **C.staphylaea.**

10. CYPRAEA (Lur.) LURIDA L. **Lurid Cowrie.** Med.-Angola; C.V. 14–40–48–66mm. C. Cp. **C.pulchra.**

11. CYPRAEA (Pal.) LUTEA Gm. Ind.Oc.-P.I.-W.Aust. 9–14–19–22mm. C. Cp. **C. humphreysii** (?form or syn.).

12. CYPRAEA (Ly.) LYNX L. **Lynx Cowrie.** S.E.Afr.-Red Sea-Haw.(VR). 18–38–50–85mm. VC. Color and pattern q.v. Orange staining between teeth.

13. CYPRAEA (Mau.) MACULIFERA Schilder. **Reticulated Cowrie.** P.I.-Poly., Haw. 31–44–54–89mm. C. Arabica Group. Base has dark columellar blotch. See **C.arabica** for related sp.

1. *CYPRAEA (Le.) MAPPA* L. **Map Cowrie.**
E.Afr.–Red Sea–Poly. 40–64–76–100mm. C.
Color and pattern q.v. 1B is P.I. pink base form,
C.m.panerythra Melvill. Not illus.: *C.m.alga*
Perry from E.Afr.–Red Sea has bright orange
teeth.

2. *CYPRAEA (Er.) MARGINALIS* Dillwyn.
Margin Cowrie. S.E.Afr.–G.of Oman. 15–19–
25–35mm. VS. Violet base fades. Cp. *C.ocellata.*

3. *CYPRAEA (Zo.) MARGINATA* Gaskoin.
Marginate Cowrie. S.W.Aust. 43–60–64–
70mm. VR. Color and pattern q.v.

4. *CYPRAEA (An.) MARIAE* S. & S. P.I.–
E.Poly., Haw. 9–12–15–20mm. VS. Often beach
spec. (illus.).

5. *CYPRAEA (No.) MARTINI* Schepman.
P.I.–New Heb.–New Cal. 12–16–18–20mm.
VR. Often beach spec. (illus.).

6. *CYPRAEA (Mau.) MAURITIANA* L.
Humpback, Mourning or **Chocolate Cowrie.**
S.E.Afr.–Haw. 43–65–80–130mm. VC.

7. *CYPRAEA (Pur.) MICRODON* Gray.
E.Afr.–Samoa. 6–15mm. UC. Transverse band.
Very tiny teeth.

8. *CYPRAEA (Er.) MILIARIS* Gm. **Millet
Cowrie.** Sing.–Japan–P.I.–Aust. 17–32–38–
56mm. VC. Cp. *C.lamarcki.*

9. *CYPRAEA (Mo.) MONETA* L. **Money
Cowrie.** Moz.–E.Afr.–Haw. 10–20–30–40mm.
VC. Form and color q.v. Still used for money in
Africa.

Plate 50 | Cypraeidae

1. *CYPRAEA (Mu.) MUS* L. **Mouse Cowrie.** Venez.-Columbia. 30–38–45–67mm. VS. Brown-stained base and teeth. Cp. *C.teulerei.*

2. *CYPRAEA (Er.) NEBRITES* Melvill. E.Afr.-Red Sea-Per.G. 15–22–24–42mm. UC. ?Subsp. of *C.erosa.*

3. *CYPRAEA (Ps.) NIGROPUNCTATA* Gray. **Black Spotted Cowrie.** Ecu.-N.Peru, Galáp. 17–27–29–41mm. VS (was S). Many black spots on sides to base. Cp. *C.annettae.*

4. *CYPRAEA (Ly.) NIVOSA* Broderip. C. Ind.Oc.-And.-N.Indon. 34–38–45–75mm. VS (was ext.R). Cp. *C.vitellus.*

5. *CYPRAEA (Nu.) NUCLEUS* L. Moz.-E.Afr.-Haw.(VR). 11–16–20–31mm. C. Glossy shell. Cp. *C.granulata* (less elongated).

6. *CYPRAEA (Er.) OCELLATA* L. **Ocellate Cowrie.** Moz.-G.of Oman-Sri Lanka. 14–

25–30–?56mm. UC. Brown staining on teeth. Cp. *C.lamarcki.*

7. *CYPRAEA (Ad.) ONYX* L. Moz.-E.Afr.-Sol. 24–32–38–57mm. C. Deep brown base, 7C, 7D is subsp. *C.o.adusta* Lam. from E.Afr.-Maur. (orange to reddish-orange teeth. UC). 7E is subsp. *C.o.melanesiae* S. & S. from Indon.-N.Aust.-Sol. (red teeth. S). 7F is subsp. *C.o. succincta* L. from Pak.-Indon. (white flakes under surface layer. VC). Also VR albino form *C.o. nymphae* Jay (not illus.).

8. *CYPRAEA (Err.) OVUM* Gm. Indon.-Japan-New Cal. 16–22–26–41mm. C. Yellow to orange teeth. Cp. *C.errones.* Syn.: *C.chrysostoma* Schilder.

9. *CYPRAEA (Ad.) PALLIDA* Gray. **Pallid Cowrie.** G.of Oman-N.Ind.Oc.-Indon. 17–23–26–32mm. UC (was VS). White base and teeth.

Cp. *C.xanthodon.* The VR *C.vredenburgi* Schilder is similar, but has fossula on columella.

10. *CYPRAEA (Bl.) PALLIDULA* Gaskoin. **Rhinoceros Cowrie.** Japan-P.I.-Aust.-Samoa. 11–18–21–29mm. C. Bands equally spaced. Cp. *C.interrupta.* Syn.: *C.rhinoceros* Souverbie. 10B, 10C is subsp. (or ?sep.sp.) *C.p.dayritiana* Cate from P.I. (lacks smudges and fine banding. UC.).

1. CYPRAEA (Cy.) PANTHERINA Lightfoot. **Panther Cowrie.** Red Sea-G.of Aden. 37–57–65–118mm. VC. Color and pattern q.v. Color forms: funebralis (1B, 1C), red and melanistic.

2. CYPRAEA (Zon.) PETITIANA Crosse. Senegal, C.V. 19–22–25–30mm. R. ?Dwarf form of **C.pyrum**.

3. CYPRAEA (Zon.) PICTA Gray. Senegal-Gambia, C.V. 19–24–28–36mm. R. Cp. **C. zonaria** (more oval; coarser teeth).

4. CYPRAEA (Not.) PIPERITA Gray. **Peppered Cowrie.** S.Aust.-N.Tas. 16–19–22–31mm. UC. Brown spots in broken bands. Syn.: **C.bicolor** Gaskoin.

5. CYPRAEA (Er.) PORARIA L. **Porous Cowrie.** E.Afr.-Poly., Haw. 10–16–19–28mm. VC. Cp. **C.albuginosa.**

6. CYPRAEA (Ad.) PULCHELLA Swainson. **Beautiful Little Cowrie.** Japan-Tai.-P.I.-N. Britain. 23–35–38–48mm. S. Teeth stained dark orange. 6C is subsp. **C.p.pericalles** Melvill & Standen from G.of Oman (UC, was VS). Cp. **C.pyriformis.**

7. CYPRAEA (Lur.) PULCHRA Gray. **Beautiful Cowrie.** G.of Suez-G.of Oman. 21–38–45–76mm. S. Brown teeth. Cp. **C.lurida** (darker).

8. CYPRAEA (Gu.) PULICARIA Reeve. **Flea-spotted Cowrie.** W.-S.W.Aust. 13–17–20–22mm. UC. Cylindrical. Brown spots in broken bands. Deeply concave fossula.

9. CYPRAEA (No.) PUNCTATA L. **Dotted Cowrie.** E.Afr.-Poly. 7–13–16–22mm. UC.

10. CYPRAEA (Ad.) PYRIFORMIS Gray. **Pear-shaped Cowrie.** Indon.-P.I.-N. to N.E. Aust. 16–20–25–34mm. UC. Teeth stained brown to black. Cp. **C.pulchella, C.subviridis.**

11. CYPRAEA (Zon.) PYRUM Gm. **Pear Cowrie.** Med.-S.W.Afr. 17–32–38–52mm. C. Fresh spec. have purple aperture. Cp. **C.petitiana** (?dwarf form).

12. CYPRAEA (Bl.) QUADRIMACULATA Gray. **Four-spotted Cowrie.** P.I.-N.Aust. 14–22–25–32mm. UC.

13. CYPRAEA (Bl.) RASHLEIGHANA Melvill. Haw. 11–18–22–45mm. R. Heavy callus. Illus. spec. is faded. Cp. **C.teres.**

14. CYPRAEA (Ly.) REEVEI Sow. **Reeve's Cowrie.** W.-S.W.Aust. 26–32–36–45mm. R. Thin. Rarely collected live.

15. CYPRAEA (Ps.) ROBERTSI Hidalgo. ?G.of Cal., Nicaragua-Peru, Galáp. 13–20–25–32mm. C. Dark brown spots on salmon-pink lateral margin. Convex base. Cp. **C.arabicula** (finer, sharper teeth).

Plate 52 | Cypraeidae

1. *CYPRAEA (Zo.) ROSSELLI* Cotton. W.Aust. 44–49–52–64mm. Ext.R. Dark brown base.

2. *CYPRAEA (Zon.) SANGUINOLENTA* Gm. **Blood Cowrie.** Senegal-Gambia, C.V. 14–21–25–28mm. VS. Purplish-brown spots on lateral margins and base.

3. *CYPRAEA (Pal.) SAULAE* Gaskoin. **Saul's Cowrie.** P.I.-N.E.Aust. 15–20–25–29mm. S. Brown spots on lateral margins. Pale orange staining between teeth.

4. *CYPRAEA (Ly.) SCHILDERORUM* Iredale. **Sandy Cowrie.** Guam-Poly., Haw. 22–28–33–43mm. UC. Fine white teeth. Cp. *C.sulcidentata.*

5. *CYPRAEA (Mau.) SCURRA* Gm. **Jester Cowrie.** E.Afr.-Haw. 23–38–43–57mm. UC. Arabica Group. Pale brown; fresh spec. purplish-brown; large lateral spots; cylindrical. See *C. arabica* for related sp.

6. *CYPRAEA (Eu.) SEMIPLOTA* Mighels. **Little Spotted Cowrie.** Haw. 7–14–17–37mm. R (was UC). Smooth base. Being overcollected. Illus. spec. is sub-fossil. Fresh spec. have dark brown dorsum with tiny white spots. Cp. juvenile *C.staphylaea.*

7. *CYPRAEA (Ne.) SPADICEA* Swainson. **Chestnut Cowrie.** S.Cal.-Baja Cal. 30–40–50–81mm. C.

8. *CYPRAEA (Er.) SPURCA SPURCA* L. **European Yellow Cowrie.** Med.-Angola; Red Sea. 12–23–28–39mm. VC. Brown lateral spots. Several forms.

8C. *CYPRAEA (Er.) SPURCA ACICU-LARIS* Gm. **Atlantic Yellow Cowrie.** N.C.-W.I.-Yucatan-Brazil, Berm. C. Often treated as sep.sp.

9. *CYPRAEA (St.) STAPHYLAEA* L. **Grape** or **Pustulose Cowrie.** S.E.Afr.-Samoa. 7–17–20–28mm. C. Globular; teeth cross base. Cp. *C.limacina.* 9B, 9C is form *C.s.descripta* Iredale.

10. *CYPRAEA (Tr.) STERCORARIA* L. **Rat Cowrie.** Senegal-Angola, C.V. 26–55–70–97mm. UC. Variable color. Melanistic (10A) and greenish forms.

Plate 53

1. *CYPRAEA (Bi.) STOLIDA* L. E.Afr.-Samoa. 15–22–30–46mm. S. Strong dark blotches; heavy teeth. 1C is a red-toothed form from Mal. 1D is subsp. *C.s.erythraeensis* Sow. (speckled blotches; S, was ext.R), possibly a sep.sp.

2. CYPRAEA (Ad.) SUBVIRIDIS Reeve. **Greenish Cowrie.** N.W.Aust.-Fiji. 18–28–32–?63mm. UC. White base and teeth. Cp. **C. pyriformis.**

3. CYPRAEA (Ly.) SULCIDENTATA Gray. **Groove-toothed Cowrie.** Haw. 20–27–35–77mm. UC. Fresh spec. fade rapidly. Tan to brown base; irregular large teeth. Cp. **C.ventriculus.**

4. CYPRAEA (Pr.) SURINAMENSIS Perry.

Surinam Cowrie. S.E.Fla.-Brazil. 23–25–30–48mm. R (was ext.R). Illus. spec. is faded. Usually found in the stomaches of fishes.

5. CYPRAEA (Tal.) TALPA L. **Mole** or **Chocolate-banded Cowrie.** S.E.Afr.-Poly., Haw. 23–50–70–104mm. VC. Deep brown base.

6. CYPRAEA (Bl.) TERES Gm. **Tapering Cowrie.** S.E.Afr.-Haw. ?7–25–32–45mm. C. Not illus.: subsp. **C.t.pellucens** Melvill from Panama, Galáp.

7. CYPRAEA (Pus.) TESSELLATA Swainson. Haw. 15–27–32–55mm. VS (was R). Pale broad bands across base.

8. CYPRAEA (Ch.) TESTUDINARIA L. **Tortoise Shell Cowrie.** E.Afr.-W.Poly. 74–90–110–114mm..UC. Heavy.

9. CYPRAEA (Pro.) TEULEREI Cazenavette. **White Mouth Cowrie.** S.Arabia. 33–40–48–67mm. UC (was VR). Toothless. Cp. **C.mus, C.fulton.**

Plate 54 | Cypraeidae

1. *CYPRAEA (Zo.) THERSITES* Gaskoin. **Black Cowrie.** S.Aust. 62–65–72–99mm. VS. Deep brown color partially covers base. ?Subsp. of *C.friendi*. *C.t.contraria* is a rare form.

2. *CYPRAEA (Cy.) TIGRIS* L. **Tiger Cowrie.** S.E.Afr.-Haw. 42–65–85–153mm. VC. Color, pattern and form q.v. Heavy. Giants from Haw. are called *C.t.schilderiana* Cate.

3. *CYPRAEA (Er.) TURDUS* Lam. **Thrush Cowrie.** E.Afr.-Red Sea-G.of Oman. 16–30–38–57mm. UC. Color and pattern variable.

4. *CYPRAEA (Bi.) URSELLUS* Gm. **Little Bear** or **Swallow Cowrie.** S.E.Afr.-Samoa. 6–12–15–19mm. S. Globular; broad teeth; strong patterns. Cp. *C.hirundo, C.kieneri.*

– – *CYPRAEA (Le.) VALENTIA* Perry. **Prince Cowrie.** P.I. 63–98mm. Ext.R. Illus. see pl. 4.

5. *CYPRAEA (Ly.) VENTRICULUS* Lam. **Ventral Cowrie.** Sol.-New Cal.-Poly. 32–45–50–76mm. S. Thick lateral callus; tan base; regular large white teeth. Cp. *C.sulcidentata.*

6. *CYPRAEA (Zo.) VENUSTA* Sow. S.W. Aust. 49–58–67–85mm. VS. Color and pattern q.v.

1, 1A, 2, 2A, 2B, 2C, 3, 3A, 4, 4A, 5, 5A, 5B, 5C, 5D, 6, 6A, 6B, 7, 8

1. CYPRAEA (Ly.) VITELLUS L. **Pacific Deer** or **Milk-spotted Cowrie.** S.E.Afr.-Haw. 20–35–45–100mm. VC. Cp. **C.camelopardalis, C.nivosa.**

2. CYPRAEA (Ad.) WALKERI Sow. Sey.-P.I.-Aust. 14–19–23–37mm. C. Violet base. 2B is form or subsp. **C.w.bregeriana** Crosse from Sol.-New Cal.-Fiji (?sep.sp.). 2C is form **C.w. surabajensis** Schilder from P.I. (large, elongated; pale violet base).

3. CYPRAEA (Ad.) XANTHODON Sow.

Yellow-toothed Cowrie (teeth and base are pale orange). Qld. 16–25–30–35mm. C. Large lateral brown spots. Cp. **C.pallida.**

4. CYPRAEA (Ma.) ZEBRA L. **Measled** or **Zebra Cowrie.** S.E.Fla.-W.I.-Brazil. 32–60–70–125mm. UC (was C). Ocelot-like spots on lateral margins.

5. CYPRAEA (Pal.) ZICZAC L. **Zigzag Cowrie.** Moz.-E.Afr.-Poly. 8–15–20–26mm. C.

6. CYPRAEA (Zon.) ZONARIA Gm. **Zoned**

Cowrie. Senegal-Angola, C.V. 15–20–25–43mm. S (was VS). Pale orange base with pale violet border with large brown lateral spots. Cp. **C.picta.**

7. OVULA COSTELLATUM Lam. E.Afr., Tai.-Japan, Aust. ca.35–45mm. S. Aperture pink to mauve.

8. OVULA OVUM L. **Egg Cowrie** or **Great Egg Shell.** Moz.-E.Afr.-W.Pac. 50–60–75–100mm. C (was VC). Aperture reddish-brown.

73

Plate 56 | Ovulidae

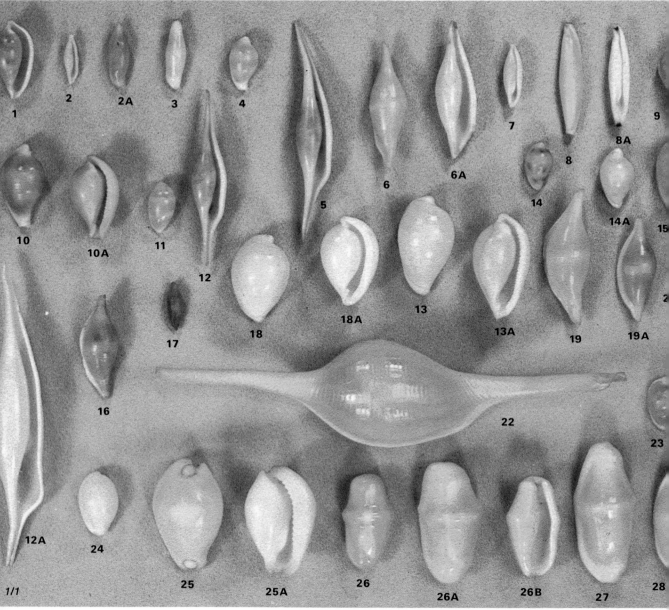

1. *PSEUDOSIMNIA ADRIATICA* Sow. Med., esp. Italy. 15–18–22–24mm. UC.

2. *SIMNIA AEQUALIS* Sow. C.Cal.-G.of Cal.-Pan., Galáp. 10–22mm. C. 2A is subsp. *S.a.vidleri* Sow. from Cal.

3. *PHENACOVOLVA ANGASI* Reeve. Qld.-N.S.W. 15–22mm. UC.

4. *DIMINOVULA BIMACULATA* Adams. W.Pac., esp. Aust. Avg.12–15mm. UC.

5. *PHENACOVOLVA LONGIROS-TRATA* Sow. – See no. 12.

6. *PHENACOVOLVA BIROSTRIS* L. S. Afr.-W.Pac., Cook Is., Haw. 20–63mm. C. Syn.: *P.brevirostris* Schumacher.

7. *CYMBULA DEFLEXA* Sow. Malaysia-Qld. 15–22mm. UC.

8. *HIATA DEPRESSA* Sow. S.Pac., esp. W. Aust. 12–28mm. UC.

9. *XANDAROVULA FORMOSANA* Azuma. Tai. 12–18mm. UC.

10. *PRIMOVULA FRUMENTUM* Sow. Tai. Avg.20mm.UC.

11. *PRIONOVULA FRUTICUM* Reeve. Tai. Avg. 12–15mm. UC.

12. *PHENACOVOLVA LONGIROS-TRATA* Sow. Tai.-Japan. Avg.35–45mm. UC. Dealers call form 12A *V.honkakujiana* Sow. – See also no. 5.

13. *PSEUDOSIMNIA MARGINATA* Sow. W.Pac., esp. Tai.-Japan. 19–25mm. C.

14. *PSEUDOSIMNIA PUNCTATA* Duclos. W.Pac. 9–15mm. C.

15. *PRIMOVULA PYRIFORMIS* Sow. Ind. Oc.-Qld. 18–22mm. UC.

16. *PHENACOVOLVA ROSEA* A.Adams. Tai.-Japan. Avg.25–30mm. C.

17. *PROSIMNIA SEMPERI* Weinkauff. W.Pac., esp. Aust. Avg.12–15mm. UC.

18. *PSEUDOSIMNIA SINENSIS* Sow. Tai.-Japan. Avg.18–22mm. C.

19. *VOLVA SOWERBYANA* Weinkauff. S.Afr.-W.Pac. 20–35mm. UC.

20. *CRENAVOLVA STRIATULA* Sow Ind.Oc.-Aust. 9–16mm. C.

21. *CRENAVOLVA STRIATULA TINCTURA* Garrard. Qld. 8–12mm. C. A subsp.

22. *VOLVA VOLVA* L. **Shuttlecock** or **Elongated Egg Cowrie.** S.E.Afr.-W.Pac. 55–60–85–186mm. C.

23. *PSEUDOSIMNIA WHITWORTHI* Cate. Japan. Avg.12–15mm. UC.

24. *CALPURNUS LACTEUS* Pease. W.Pac. 11–17mm. C.

25. *CALPURNUS VERRUCOSUS* L. **Little Egg Cowrie.** S.E.Afr.-W.Pac. 22–32mm. VC.

26. *CYPHOMA GIBBOSUM* L. **Common Flamingo Tongue.** N.C.-Fla.-Brazil, Berm. 19–25–35–44mm. C (was VC). Being over-collected.

27. *CYPHOMA SIGNATUM* Pilsbry & McGinty. **Fingerprint Flamingo Tongue.** Fla. Keys, Bah.-Brazil, Berm. (R). Avg.28–33mm. UC.

28. *CYPHOMA INTERMEDIUM* Sow. Fla.-W.I.-Brazil, Berm. 30–38mm. S.

1. *ATLANTA PERONI* Lesueur. **The Atlanta.** Atl. and Pac. 4–6mm. UC. A very thin, glassy pelagic heteropod.

2. *CARINARIA LAMARCKI* Peron & Lesueur. E.Pac.; Berm.-G.of Mex.; Med.; I-P. ca.25–50mm. VR. The very thin external shell of a heteropod. A classic rarity. Syn.: *C.mediterranea* Lam.

3. *NATICA ADANSONI* Blainville. Morocco-Angola; Madeira, C.V. 15–20–30–35mm. C.

4. *NATICA (Naticarius) ALAPAPILIONIS* Röd. **Butterfly Moon Shell.** Ind.Oc.-Fiji, Haw. 14–25–30–35mm. C. Thick per. Spirally-ribbed calcareous operc.

5. *NATICA (Naticarius) CANRENA* L. **Colorful Atlantic Moon Shell.** N.C.-Fla.-W.I.-Brazil, Berm. 22–30–40–56mm. C. Thick ribbed white operc.

6. *NATICA CHEMNITZI* Pfeiffer. Baja Cal.-G.of Cal.-N.Peru. 25–38mm. VC. Color and pattern variable. Related to *N.marochiensis* Gm.

7. *NATICA (Stigmaulax) ELENAE* Récluz. Baja Cal.-Ecu. 25–32mm. C.

8. *NATICA FANEL* Récluz. Mauritania-Angola, C.V. 20–25–30–35mm. C.

9. *NATICA FASCIATA* Röd. **Solid Moon Shell.** W.Pac. Avg.19–25mm. UC. Calcareous operc.

10. *NATICA FULMINEA* Gm. W.Sahara-Angola. 20–25–30–35mm. UC.

11. *POLINICES HELICOIDES* Gray. – See pl. 58, no. 5.

12. *NATICA (Naticarius) MACULATUS* von Salis. Med., esp. Italy. 30–35–50–60mm. UC. Syn.: *N.hebraeus* Martyn.

13. *NATICA (Notocochlis) LINEATA* Lam. **Lineated Sand Snail.** Ind.Oc.-W.Pac. 18–20–35–50mm. C. Grooved calcareous operc. Syn.: *N.lineata* Röd.

14. *NATICA (Naticarius) MILLEPUNCTATA* Lam. Med. 25–30–45–56mm. UC. Syn.: *N. stercusmuscarum* Gm.

15. *NATICA ONCA* Röd. W.-C.Pac. 17–20–25–30mm. C. Calcareous operc. Syn.: *N.chinensis* Lam.

16. *NATICA RUFILABRIS* Reeve. W.Pac. Avg.18–22mm. C. Shiny white operc.

17. *NATICA STELLATUS* Hedley. **Stellate Sand Snail.** Ind.Oc.-W.Pac. 24–28–38–?50mm. C. Calcareous operc.

18. *NATICA TURTONI* E.A.Sm Mauritania-Dahomey. 20–30mm. UC.

19. *NATICA VITELLUS* L. **Banded** or **Yolk Sand Snail.** Ind.Oc.-W.Pac. 28–32–⌣ 50mm. C. Calcareous operc. 19B is *N.v.spadicea* Gm., a form from Japan-Tai.

20. *NATICA ZEBRA* Lam. W.Med.-N.Afr. 25–35mm. UC.

21. *POLINICES (Neverita) ALBUMEN* L. **Albumen Moon Shell.** Ind.Oc.-W.Pac. ca.30–35–40–50mm. C.

22. *POLINICES AURANTIUM* Lam. **Orange Moon Shell.** W.Pac. 25–30–40–50mm. C. Pale yellow to deep orange. Orange-brown operc. Syn.: *P.aurantia* Röd.

23. *POLINICES BIFASCIATUS* Griffith & Pidgeon. **Two-striped Moon Shell.** G.of Cal.-Pan. <20–25–35–58mm. C. Syn.: *P.bifasciatus* Gray.

Plate 58 | Naticidae

1. *POLINICES (Conuber) CONICUS* Lam. **Conical Sand Snail.** N.W.Aust.-N.S.W., Tas. 20–25–40–45mm. VC.

2. *POLINICES (Neverita* or *Glossaulax) DIDYMA* Röd. **Hepatic Moon Shell.** S.E.Afr.-W.Pac. 30–40–60–90mm. C. Color variable. Horny operc. Syn.: *Uber bicolor* Philippi.

3. *POLINICES (Neverita) DUPLICATUS* Say. **Shark's Eye; Atlantic** or **Double Moon Shell.** Mass.-Fla.-Texas. 25–30–50–98mm. VC. Horny brown operc.

4. *POLINICES FLEMINGIANA* Récluz. **Fleming's Moon Shell.** W.Pac. ca.20–25–35–50mm. C. Thin horny operc., typical of genus.

5. *POLINICES HELICOIDES* Gray. **Helicoid Moon Shell.** Baja Cal.-G.of Cal.-Peru. Avg. 40–50mm. C. Syn.: *P.glauca* Lesson. See also pl. 57, no. 11.

6. *POLINICES HEPATICUS* Röd. **Brown Moon Snail.** S.E.Fla.-Texas, W.I.-Venez. 25–30–40–45mm. C. Syn.: *P.brunneus* Link.

7. *POLINICES (Mammilla) MELANO-STOMUS* Gm. **Black-mouthed Moon Shell.** E.Afr.-W.Pac., Haw. 18–30–40–46mm. UC. Horny reddish-brown operc.

8. *POLINICES OTIS* Brod. & Sow. G.of Cal.-Ecu., Galáp. 30–40mm. UC.

9. *POLINICES TUMIDUS* Swainson. **White** or **Pear-shaped Moon Shell.** S.E.Afr.-W.Pac., Haw. 25–30–45–?75mm. C. Horny yellowish-brown operc. Syn.: *Natica mammila* L., *P.pyriformis* Récluz.

10. *POLINICES (Neverita) RECLUZIANUS* Deshayes. **Recluz's Moon Shell.** S.Cal.-G.of Cal. 20–30–50–84mm. C. Reddish-brown operc.

11. *POLINICES (Conuber) SORDIDUS* Swainson. **Leaden** or **Sordid Moon Shell.** Aust. 20–30–40–50mm. C. Color variable. Orange-brown operc. Syn.: *P.plumbeus* Lam.

12. *POLINICES VESTITUS* Kuroda. Japan. Avg.30–38mm. C.

13. *AMAUROPSIS ISLANDICA* Gm. **Iceland Moon Shell.** Arctic Seas-Va. 18–22–30–38mm. UC. Flaky thin yellow-brown per. Horny operc.

14. *LUNATIA HEROS* Say. **Common Northern Moon Shell.** Canada-N.C. 50–60–90–112mm. VC. Thin pale yellowish-brown per. Pale brown operc.

15. *LUNATIA LEWISII* Gould. **Lewis'** or **Western Moon Shell.** Br.Col.-Baja Cal. 75–85–115–166mm. VC.

16. *SINUM DEBILE* Gould. **Frail Ear Shell.** S.Cal.-Baja Cal.-Pan. 15–18–22–28mm. UC. Syn.: *S.pazianum* Dall.

17. *SINUM GRAYI* Deshayes. G.of Cal.-Pan. Avg.35–44mm. UC. Syn.: *S.cortezi* J. & R.Burch.

18. *SINUM JAVANICUM* Griffith & Pidgeon. **Flat Baby Ear.** Japan-Tai. 25–30–45–61mm. C. Thin yellowish-brown operc.

19. *SINUM PERSPECTIVUM* Say. **Common Baby Ear.** Md.-Fla.-Texas-W.I.-Brazil, Berm. 13–25–40–50mm. C. Thin pale brown per.

20. *SINUM UNDULATUS* Lischke. Japan. 22–25–30–32mm. UC. Thin horny operc.

21. *EUNATICINA OLDROYDI* Dall. **Oldroyd's Fragile Moon Shell.** Ore.-S.Cal. 30–40–60–75mm. C.

1. *TONNA ALLIUM* Dillwyn. **Costate** or **Ribbed Tun.** E.Afr.-W.Pac. 50–60–80–90mm. C. Color variable. Cp. ***T.tesselata.***

2. *TONNA CANALICULATA* L. **Channelled Tun.** Moz.-E.Afr.-W.Pac. 50–60–90–300mm. C. Thin. Cp. ***T.galea.*** Syn.: ***T.cepa*** Rod., ***T.olearium*** Brug. (and L.).

3. *TONNA CEREVISINA* Hedley. **Reeve's Tun** or **Beer Barrel.** S.W.Pac. ca.150–175–200–ca.250mm. C. Thin.

4. *TONNA CUMINGII* Hanley. Indon.-W.Pac. 80–110mm. UC.

5. *TONNA DOLIUM* L. **Spotted Tun** or **Cask.** E.Afr.-Fiji, Haw. 45–50–70–85mm. C. Also, dwarf form, <50mm.

6. *TONNA GALEA* L. **Giant** or **Helmet Tun.** N.C.-Texas, W.I.-Brazil; Med.; Senegal-Angola; E.Afr.-Ind.Oc.-S.W.Pac. ca.100–120–150–>180mm. UC. Brown per. Cp. ***T.canaliculata.***

7. *TONNA LUTEOSTOMA* Küster. **Goldmouthed Tun.** Japan-N.Z. 50–100–150–178mm. C (was UC). Pattern variable. 7A is form ***T.l. procellara*** Euthyme from S.Afr.

Plate 60 | Tonnidae

1. *TONNA MACULOSA* Dillwyn. **Atlantic Partridge** or **Spotted Tun.** S.E.Fla.-W.I.-Brazil, Berm. 47–80–110–134mm. UC. Flaky per.

2. *TONNA PERDIX* L. **Pacific Partridge Tun.** S.E.Afr.-Poly., Haw. 70–75–125–227mm. C. Thin. Variable pattern.

3. *TONNA SULCOSA* Born. **Banded Tun.** Ind.Oc.-W.Pac. 50–60–100–125mm. C. Dark brown per. Cp. *T.tetracotula.* Syn.: *T.fasciatum* Brug.

4. *TONNA TESSELATA* Lam. **Tesselate Tun.** S.Afr., W.Pac. 50–60–100–150mm. C. Pale tan per. Cp. *T.allium, T.dolium.*

5. *TONNA TETRACOTULA* Hedley. **Hedley's** or **Deep-water Tun.** Indon., S.Qld.-N.S.W., N.Z. 60–100–150–200mm. S. ?Subsp. of *T.sulcosa.*

6. *TONNA VARIEGATA* Lam. **Variegated Tun.** S.E.Afr.-S.W.Pac. 80–100–120–150mm. C. Pale buff per.

7. *TONNA ZONATA* Green. **Oil Lamp Tun.** E.Afr.-Indon., Japan-Tai. 70–80–120–160mm. UC.

8. *MALEA POMUM* L. **Apple** or **Pacific Grinning Tun.** S.Afr., E.Afr.-W.Pac., Haw. 38–45–65–85mm. C.

9. *MALEA RINGENS* Swainson. **Great Grinning Tun.** W.Mex.-Peru. 90–100–150–234mm. UC. Also, dwarf form <80mm.

10. *EUDOLIUM INFLATUM* Kuroda & Habe. **Inflated False Tun.** Japan. Avg.40–50mm. S.

11. *EUDOLIUM PYRIFORME* Sow. **Pear-shaped False Tun.** Japan. Avg.50mm. UC.

2/3

1. *CASSIS CORNUTA* L. Horned or **Giant Helmet.** E.Afr.-Poly., Haw. 60–125–250–387mm. VC. Heavy. Female larger, with more but smaller knobs.

2. *CASSIS (Hypocassis) FIMBRIATA* Q. & G. Fimbriate Helmet. W.Aust. 60–65–85–113mm. UC.

3, 4. *CASSIS FLAMMEA* L. Flame or **Princess Helmet.** S.Fla.-W.I.-Brazil, Berm. 60–75–115–132mm. C (Fla.: R).

– – *CASSIS MADAGASCARIENSIS* Lam. Emperor or **Queen Helmet.** (Not illus.). Fla.-W.I., Berm. 100–125–175–>250mm. C (Fla.: VR). Pale cream color, with three rows of large nodules. Outer lip and parietal shield salmon-colored. Used for cameos.

5. *CASSIS (Hypocassis) NANA* Tenison-Woods. Dwarf Helmet. Qld.-N.S.W. 40–45–55–63mm. UC.

6. *CASSIS TESSELATA* Gm. West African Helmet. Senegal-Angola. ca.150–175–225–267mm. UC. Thin.

7. *CASSIS TUBEROSA* L. King Helmet. N.C.-Fla.-W.I.-Brazil, Berm.; C.V. 100–125–175–301mm. C (Fla.: R).

8. *CASMARIA ERINACEUS* L. Common or **Striped Bonnet.** E.Afr.-Red Sea-Poly., Haw. 20–25–50–79mm. C. Color and pattern variable. Cp. *C.ponderosa.* Syn.: *C.vibex* L. Also, subsp. *C.e.vibexmexicana* Stearns from Baja Cal.-Pan., Galáp. (not illus.).

9. *CASMARIA PONDEROSA* Gm. Ponderous Bonnet. S.E.Afr., Red Sea-Poly., Haw. 25–32–55–62mm. C. Color variable. Shoulder often nodulose. Cp. *C.erinaceus.* Several subsp. incl. *C.p.atlantica* Clench from Fla.Keys-Bah.-Carib. (not illus.).

10. *CYPRAECASSIS COARCTATA* Sow. Contracted Cowrie-helmet. No.G.of Cal.-Peru. 40–50–70–80mm. UC.

11. *CYPRAECASSIS RUFA* L. Bull Mouth or **Red Helmet.** S.E.Afr.-E.Poly. 100–125–175–195mm. VC. Heavy. Used for cameos.

Plate 62 | Cassididae

1. CYPRAECASSIS TENUIS Wood. **Galápagos Cowrie-helmet.** So.G.of Cal.-Ecu., Galáp. 100–110–130–157mm. S.

2. CYPRAECASSIS TESTICULUS L. **Reticulated Cowrie-helmet.** N.C.-Fla.-W.I.-Brazil, Berm; also, W.Afr. 25–30–60–76mm. C.

3. GALEODEA ECHINOPHORA L. **Mediterranean Spiny Bonnet.** Med. 60–70–80–ca.100mm. C. Syn. for genus: **Cassidaria**.

4. GALEODEA RUGOSA L. **Mediterranean Rugose Bonnet.** Med., W.Afr. 50–80–100–140mm. UC. Syn.: **G.tyrrhena** Gm.

5. GALEOOCORYS LEUCODOMA Dall. **Alabaster False Tun.** Japan-Tai. Avg.55–65mm. S. Thin yellowish-brown per. Syn.: **G.leucodon** Dall.

6. MORUM CANCELLATUM Sow. W.Pac. Avg.60–70mm. UC (was S). Also, yellow to orange form.

7. MORUM GRANDE A.Adams. W.Pac. Avg.50–60mm. UC (was S).

8. MORUM ONISCUS L. **Atlantic Woodlouse** or **Morum.** S.E.Fla.-Brazil, Berm. 19–27mm. C. Thin grayish per.

9. MORUM TUBERCULOSUM Reeve. Baja Cal.-G.of Cal.-Peru. 12–20–30–38mm. C.

10. PHALIUM AREOLA L. **Checkerboard Helmet.** S.E.Afr.-Samoa. 40–50–75–89mm. C.

11. PHALIUM BANDATUM Iredale. **Banded** or **Coronated Helmet.** Ind.Oc.-Indon.-W.Pac. 70–75–115–136mm. C. Cp. **P.glaucum**.

12. PHALIUM (Semicassis) BISULCATUM Schubert & Wagner. **Japanese Helmet.** S.E.Afr.-Fiji. 38–50–70–85mm. C. Color and pattern variable. 12A is form **P.b.booleyi** Sow. from Japan. 12C is form **P.b.diuturna** from Aust. 12B is form **P.b.pila** Reeve from Japan-Tai. Syn.: **P.persimilis** Kira, **P.pfeifferi** Hidalgo.

13. PHALIUM (Tylocassis) CICATRICOSUM Gm. **Smooth Scotch Bonnet.** S.E.Fla.(R)-W.I., Berm. 30–35–50–60mm. UC. Was considered subsp. of **P.granulatum**.

14. PHALIUM (Semicassis) CANALICULATA Brug. Bay of Bengal-Sri Lanka. Avg. 40–50mm. C.

15. PHALIUM DECUSSATUM L. **Decussated Bonnet.** Indon.-W.Pac. Avg.50–65mm. C.

16. PHALIUM (Semicassis) FAUROTIS Jousseaume. S.E.Afr.-W.Ind.Oc. 35–40–50–60mm. C.

17. PHALIUM (Semicassis) GLABRATUM Dunker. **Bald** or **Smooth Bonnet.** Indon.-Melanesia. 40–45–60–65mm. C. Spec. illus. is subsp. **P.g.angasi** Iredale from N.W.Aust.-Qld.-N.S.W. **P.g.bulla** Habe from Japan, S.E.China, Haw. (not illus.), may be sep.sp.

1. **PHALIUM (Tylocassis) GRANULATUM** Born. **Scotch Bonnet.** N.C.-Fla.-Texas-G.of Mex.-Brazil, Berm. 38–50–70–121mm. C. Being overcollected. Illus. spec. is form **P.g. inflatum** Shaw.

2. **PHALIUM (Tylocassis) GRANULATUM CENTRIQUADRATUM** Val. G.of Cal.-Peru, Galáp. 40–45–60–83mm. C. A subsp.

3. **PHALIUM (Tylocassis) GRANULATUM UNDULATUM** Gm. Med., Azores, Canary Is. 40–50–65–134mm. C. A subsp.

4. **PHALIUM GLAUCUM** L. **Glaucous** or **Gray Bonnet.** S.E.Afr.-Sol. 80–90–115–137mm. C. Cp. **P.bandatum.**

5. **PHALIUM (Xenophalium) INORNATUM** Pilsbry. **Unadorned Bonnet.** C.Japan-Tai. Avg. 25–38mm. C.

6. **PHALIUM (Xenophalium) LABIATUM** Perry. **Labiate, Lipped** or **Agate Helmet.** S.E. Afr.; S.Aust.-C.Pac.; S.Am. (UC). 40–45–65–75mm. C. Spec. illus. is subsp. **P.l.iredalei** Bayer from S.E.Afr.

7. **PHALIUM (Xenophalium) PYRUM** Lam. **Pear Helmet.** S.Afr.; W.Pac. 38–50–75–90mm. C. Variable thickness. Several forms.

8. **PHALIUM (Semicassis) SABURON** Brug. **Saburon Helmet.** W.Eur., Med.-Ghana, Azores. 45–50–60–70mm. UC.

9. **PHALIUM (Semicassis) SEMIGRANOSUM** Lam. **Half-grained Helmet.** W.Aust.-Vic.-Tas. 25–35–50–63mm. C.

10. **PHALIUM STRIGATUM** Gm. **Striped Bonnet.** Japan-Tai. 45–50–75–102mm. C. Syn.: **P.flammiferum** Röd.

11. **PHALIUM (Xenophalium) THOMSONI** Brazier. **Thomson's Helmet.** S.Qld.-Vic.-Tas., No. N.Z. 40–50–75–90mm. UC. Thin.

12. **FICUS COMMUNIS** Röd. **Atlantic, Common** or **Paper Fig Shell.** N.C.-Fla.-G.of Mex. 60–80–110–165mm. VC. Syn.: **F.papyratia** Say.

13. **FICUS FICUS** L. S.E.Afr.-W.Pac. 45–50–75–83mm. C.

14. **FICUS GRACILIS** Sow. **Elongated Fig Shell.** And.Sea, Japan-Tai. 90–100–140–181mm. C.

15. **FICUS SUBINTERMEDIUS** Orbigny. **Common Fig Shell.** W.Pac. 50–60–80–90mm. C.

16. **FICUS VENTRICOSA** Sow. Baja Cal.-G.of Cal.-Peru. 75–80–120–138mm. C.

Plate 64 | Cymatiidae

1. *ARGOBUCCINUM ARGUS* Gm. S.Afr. 60–70–90–115mm. C. Heavy. Velvety yellow-brown per.

2. *ARGOBUCCINUM AUSTRALASIAE* Perry. **Hairy Triton** or **Southern Rock Whelk.** W.Aust.-Qld., Tas., N.Z. 50–70–100–150mm. C. Bristly dark brown per. Horny brown operc.

3. *FUSITRITON LAUDANUM* Finlay. N.Z. Avg.100–110mm. UC. Thin dull gray per.

4. *FUSITRITON MURRAYI* Smith. S.Afr. Avg.90–120mm. UC.

5. *FUSITRITON OREGONENSIS* Redfield. **Hairy** or **Oregon Triton.** Japan; also Bering Sea-So.Cal. Avg.100–125mm. C. Thick, bristly yellowish-brown per. Thick horny brown operc. 5A is *F.o.galea* Kuroda, a deep sea form from Japan.

6. *RANELLA GIGANTEA* Lam. Med., Portugal-W.Afr.-S.Afr.-Aust. 100–150–180–217mm. UC. Yellow-brown per. Syn.: *R. olearium* L.

7. *APOLLON FACETUS* Iredale. Qld. Avg. 20–25mm. UC. ?Form of A. pusillum Brod. Syn. for genus: *Gyrineum.*

8. *APOLLON GYRINUM* L. **Tadpole Triton.** W.Pac. 19–25–35–50mm. C. White to yellow.

9. *APOLLON (Biplex) HIRASEI* Kuroda & Habe. Japan-Tai. Avg.30–38mm. UC. Yellowish per.

10. *APOLLON NATATOR* Röd. Ind.Oc.-Poly. Avg.30–35mm. UC.

11. *APOLLON (Biplex) PERCA* Perry. **Winged Frog Shell** or **Maple Leaf.** W.Pac., esp.Japan-Tai. <40–42–55–90mm. UC.

12. *APOLLON (Biplex) PULCHELLA* Forbes. **Tiny Winged Frog Shell** or **Cockaroo.** Qld. 13–23mm. UC. ?Form of *A.perca.*

13. *APOLLON ROSEUM* Reeve. **Rosy Frog Shell.** W.Pac. Avg.15–20mm. UC.

14. *CYMATIUM AFRICANUM* A.Adams.

S.Afr. 60–75–90–112mm. C. ?High-spired form of *C.dolarium.*

15. *CYMATIUM (Mayena) AUSTRALASIA* Iredale. **Australian Triton** or **Rock Whelk.** S.E.Afr.-S.Aust.-N.Z. 50–60–100–125mm. C. Thick brown velvety per. Brown horny operc.

16. *CYMATIUM BOSCHI* Abbott & Lewis. G.of Oman. ca.50–60–80–106mm. S (was R.)

17. *CYMATIUM (Ranularia) CAUDATUM* Gm. **Caniculated Triton.** W.Pac. 38–55–65–75mm. C.

18. *CYMATIUM (Linatella) CINGULATUM* Lam. **Poulsen's** or **Ventricose Triton.** N.C. to Texas (R), Brazil, Berm. Also, S.E.Afr.-W.Pac., Haw. 38–50–70–>75mm. UC.

19. *CYMATIUM CORRUGATUS* Lam. W.Eur.-W.Med., esp.Italy. ca.45–55–70–100mm. UC. Soft fibrous per. (illus.).

1. *CYMATIUM DOLIARUM* Lam. S.Afr.-Moz. <25-32-38->44mm. C. Cp. *C. africanum* (?high-spired form).

2. *CYMATIUM DUNKERI* Lischke. W.Pac. 60-65-75-96mm. UC.

3. *CYMATIUM FEMORALE* L. **Angular Triton.** S.E.Fla.(R)-W.I.-Brazil, Berm. 75-100-125-240mm. S. Thin deciduous per. Sm. claw-shaped operc.

4. *CYMATIUM (Turritriton) GIBBOSUM* Brod. G.of Cal.-Peru, Galáp. 20-25-45-71mm. C.

5. *CYMATIUM (Ranularia) GUTTURNIUM* Iredale. W.Pac., Haw.(R). ca.45-50-70->75mm. C. Form variable. Aperture yellow to orange.

6. *CYMATIUM (Septa) HEPATICUM* Röd. **Liver-colored Triton.** W.Pac. <25-30-40->50mm. C. Cp. *C.rubeculum.*

7. *CYMATIUM (Tritoniscus) LABIOSUM* Wood. **Lip Triton.** N.C.-E.& W.Fla.-W.I.-Brazil. Also, S.E.Afr.-Red Sea-Fiji, Haw.(R). 18-20-25-?38mm. S.

8. *CYMATIUM LOEBBECKEI* Lischke. W.Pac. Avg.35-50mm. C.

9. *CYMATIUM LOTORIUM* L. **Washing Bath Triton.** E.Afr.-W.Pac. <95-100-120-157mm. UC. Heavy. Fawn, yellow-orange to red.

10. *CYMATIUM MORITINCTUM* Reeve. **Dog-head Triton.** S.C.-Fla.-W.I.-Brazil, Berm.; Mad.-W.Pac. 38-55-70->75mm. UC.

11. *CYMATIUM (Gutturnium) MURICINUM* Röd. **Knobbed** or **White-mouthed Triton.** S.E.Fla.-W.I.-Brazil, Berm.; also, S.E.Afr.-Poly., Haw.; Galáp. 25-35-50-75mm. C.

12. *CYMATIUM (Cymatriton) NICO-BARICUM* Röd. **Golden-** or **Orange-mouthed Triton.** S.E.Fla.-W.I.-Brazil, Berm.; also, S.E. Afr.-Poly., Haw. ca.15-50-65-103mm. C. Syn.: *C.chlorostomun* Lam.

13. *CYMATIUM (Septa) PARTHENO-PEUM* von Salis. **Giant Hairy Triton.** N.C. to Texas(S)-Brazil, Berm.; G.of Cal.-Galáp.; also, Med.; S.E.Afr.-Haw. 60-75-100-150mm. C. Various geographic forms. Thick fibrous brown per. (13A). Syn.: *C.australasiae* Perry, *C.costatum* Born, *C.echo* Kuroda & Habe.

14. *CYMATIUM PERRYI* Emerson & Old. India-Sri Lanka. <80-95-115->125mm. UC (was S).

15. *CYMATIUM (Septa) PILEARE* L. **Common Hairy Triton.** S.C.-Texas-Brazil, Berm. (all UC); Baja Cal.-G.of Cal.-Pan.; also, S.E.Afr.-Red Sea-Poly., Haw. 38-60-90-138mm. VC. Aperture brown to red. Thick hairy brown per. 15A is *C.p.aquatile* Reeve from W.Pac.-Haw. 15B is *C.p.intermedius* Pease from W.Pac.-Haw. Avg.35-45mm. These are now considered sep. sp.

83

Plate 66 | Cymatiidae

1. **CYMATIUM PYRUM** Lam. **Pear Triton.** S.E.Afr.-Poly., Haw. 50-70-100-121mm. C. Thin, bristly per.

2. **CYMATIUM RANZANII** Bianconi. S.E. Afr.-Arabian G. 115-120-150-194mm. VS (was VR).

3. **CYMATIUM (Septa) RUBECULUM** L. **Red** or **Robin Redbreast Triton.** S.E.Afr.-W.Pac., Haw. Also, subsp. in S.E.Fla.-W.I., Brazil. 20-25-35->50mm. C. Color and pattern variable. Cp. **C.hepaticum.**

4. **CYMATIUM SARCOSTOMA** Reeve. **Flesh-colored Hairy Triton.** Red Sea, Indon.-W.Pac., Haw.(R). Avg.60-75mm. C.

5. **CYMATIUM (Cabestana) SPENGLERI** Perry. S.&E.Aust.-Tas.-N.Z. 65-70-100->150mm. C. Heavy. Horny operc.

6. **CYMATIUM (Gutturnium) TABULATA** Menke. **Ploughed Triton.** S.W.Aust.-N.S.W.-N.Z. <35-38-50-70mm. C. Variable form and color.

7. **CYMATIUM TENUILIRATUM** Lischke. Japan. Avg.40-50mm. C. Hairy brown per.

8. **CYMATIUM (Ranularia) TESTUDINARIA** Adams & Reeve. P.I. 50-60-70-75mm. UC.

9. **CYMATIUM TRIGONUM** Gm. Senegal-Angola, C.V. 30-32-38-50mm. S.

10. **CYMATIUM TRILINEATUM** Reeve. Red Sea-Arabian G. <38-50-70-83mm. C.

11. **CYMATIUM (Septa) VESTITUM** Hinds. **Panamanian Hairy Triton.** G.of Cal.-Ecu., Galáp. 38-45-60-80mm. C. Thick, bristly per.

12. **CYMATIUM (Cabestana) WATER-HOUSEI** A.Adams & Angas. W.Aust.-N.S.W.-Tas., N.Z. ca.25-30-40->63mm. C. Thick brown hairy per. Horny operc.

13. **CYMATIUM (Linatella) WIEGMANNI** Anton. Baja Cal.-G.of Cal.-Peru. 50-60-75-114mm. VS (but beach spec. C). Thin yellowish-brown per. (illus.).

14. *AUSTROSASSIA PARKINSONIANA* Perry. Vic.-N.S.W., Tas. Avg.38-45mm. C. Velvety, thin yellowish per.

15. *PHANOZESTA SEMITORTA* Kuroda & Habe. Japan. Avg.35-40mm. C.

1/3 1/3

1/2

1. *CHARONIA NODIFERA* Lam. **Knobbed Triton.** Med.-Canary Is., Maur.-Angola. 120–200–250–395mm. UC. ?Related to *C.rubicunda*. Syn.: *C.lampas* L.

2. *CHARONIA POWELLI* Cotton. W.Aust. 65–100–125–>150mm. UC. ?Related to *C. rubicunda*.

3. *CHARONIA RUBICUNDA* Perry. **Red Rock Whelk** or **Trumpet.** S.Aust.-N.S.W., Tas., N.Z. 100–110–140–150mm. C.

4. *CHARONIA SAULIAE* Reeve. **Japanese** or **Saul's Triton.** Japan-Tai. 125–150–200–250mm. C. Edible.

5. *CHARONIA TRITONIS* L. **Triton's Trumpet** or **Pacific Triton.** S.E.Afr.-Poly., Haw. 100–150–300–480mm. UC. Variable pattern. Being overcollected.

6. *CHARONIA VARIEGATA* Lam. **Atlantic Triton's Trumpet.** S.C. to Fla.(R)-W.I.-Brazil,

Berm. Also, Med., Canary Is., C.V. 100–150–250–350mm. C. ?Subsp. of *C.tritonis*.

7. *DISTORSIO ANUS* L. **Warp Shell** or **Old Woman.** S.E.Afr.-W.Pac., Haw. 38–50–70–84mm. C. Heavy.

8. *DISTORSIO CLATHRATA* Lam. **Atlantic Distortio** or **Distorted Triton.** N.C.-Fla.-Texas-Mex., Carib.-Brazil. 20–40–60–89mm. C. Thin brown per.

9. *DISTORSIO CONSTRICTA* Brod. **Constricted Distortio.** G.of Cal.-Ecu. 25–30–40->70mm. C.

10. *DISTORSIO DECUSSATA* Val. **Decussate Distortio.** G.of Cal.-Ecu. 30–40–60–82mm. C.

11. *DISTORSIO FRANCESAE* Iredale. **France's Warp Shell.** S.W.Pac. Avg.40–60mm. S. Hairy brown per., as illus. ?Form of *D. reticulata*.

12. *DISTORSIO KURZI* Petuch & Harasewych. W.Pac. Avg.40–60mm. S.

13. *DISTORSIO PERDISTORTA* Fulton. Japan-Tai. Avg.40–60mm. C. Form illus., *D.p. horrida* Kuroda & Habe, is coarsely reticulated.

14. *DISTORSIO RETICULATA* Röd. S.E. Afr.-Poly., ?Haw. 38–45–65–90mm. C. Light. *D.r.decipiens* Reeve is a color form.

Plate 68 | Bursidae – Colubrariidae

1. *BURSA ALBIVARICOSA* Reeve. W.Pac. Avg.60–70mm. C. ?Syn. for ***B.rana.***

– – *BURSA BUBO* L. – See no. 10.

2. *BURSA BUFO* Röd. E.Afr.-W.Pac. 50–70–100–140mm. UC. Smooth parietal shield. Variable color. Cp. ***B.lampas.***

3. *BURSA BUFONIA* Gm. S.E.Afr.-C.Pac., Haw. 40–50–70–80mm. UC.

4. *BURSA CAELATA* Brod. **Gaudy Frog Shell.** Baja Cal.-G.of Cal.-Peru; also, rarely, S.E.Fla.-Brazil, Berm. 25–35–50–55mm. C.

5. *BURSA CALIFORNICA* Hinds. **Californian Frog Shell.** S.Cal.-G.of Cal. 70–80–100–160mm. C.

6. *BURSA CRUMENA* Lam. S.E.Afr.-W.Pac. 38–40–60–100mm. C. Cp. ***B.rana.***

7. *BURSA CRUENTATA* Sow. S.Afr.-Poly., Haw. 20–25–35–45mm. UC. Spec. illus. has red coralline growths.

8. *BURSA FOLIATA* Brod. E.Afr.-Ind.Oc. 55–65–80–90mm. UC. ?Form or subsp. of *B. crumena.*

9. *BURSA GRANULARIS* Röd. S.E.Afr.-Poly., Haw.; also subsp. in S.E.Fla.-W.I.-Brazil. 25–35–50–83mm. C.

10. *(BURSA LAMPAS* L.) **Lamp Shell or Giant Frog Shell.** S.W.Afr.-S.E.Afr.-Poly., Haw. 100–140–200–320mm. C. Color and pattern variable. Heavy. Cp. ***B.bufo.*** Syn. for ***B. BUBO*** L., now accepted as the correct name.

11. *BURSA NANA* Brod. & Sow. G.of Cal.-Ecu. 38–42–50–58mm. C.

12. *BURSA NOBILIS* Reeve. **Noble Frog Shell.** W.Pac. 25–45–65–113mm. C. Syn.: ***B. margaritula*** Deshayes.

13. *BURSA PUSTULOSA* Reeve. Senegal-Angola, C.V. 30–35–45–65mm. UC.

14. *BURSA RANA* L. **Elegant Frog Shell.** Ind.Oc.-W.Pac. 38–45–65–100mm. C. Variable color. Cp. ***B.crumena.*** Syn.: ***B.elegans*** Sow.

15. *BURSA ROSA* Perry. E.Afr.-Poly., Haw. <25–35–50–55mm. UC. Variable color.

16. *BURSA RUBETA* L. S.E.Afr.-Poly. 65–80–100–110mm. C. Heavy. Large spec. called ***B.r.gigantea*** Smith appear to be ***B.bubo***.

17. *BURSA SPINOSA* Lam. **Spiny Frog Shell.** Ind.Oc. 40–50–70–76mm. C. Syn.: ***B. echinata*** Link.

18. *BURSA SUBGRANOSA* Beck. W.Pac. Avg.60–75mm. UC.

19. *BURSA THOMAE* Orbigny. **St. Thomas Frog Shell.** S.C.-Fla.-W.I.-Brazil. 13–20–30–41mm. UC.

20. *COLUBRARIA MACULOSA* Gm. **Spotted Colubraria.** Red Sea-Poly., Haw. 38–60–80–90mm. UC. Heavy.

21. *COLUBRARIA OBSCURA* Reeve. **Obscure Dwarf Triton.** S.E.Fla.(R)-Tortugas-W.I.-Brazil, Berm.; ?W.Pac. 25–30–40–50mm. UC.

1. MUREX (Mca.) KUSTERIANUS Tapperone-Canefri. G.of Oman. 60–80–100–120mm. C. Heavy. White to brown.

2. MUREX (Mu.) MACGILLIVRAYI Dohrn. **Macgillivray's Woodcock.** Aust. 50–55–65–75mm. C. ?Form of *M.brevispinus*.

3. MUREX (Ptp.) MACROPTERUS Deshayes. **Frill-wing Murex.** C.Cal.-Baja Cal. 35–50–60–75mm. C. Smooth and rough forms. Cream, tan to deep purplish-brown.

4. MUREX (Mar.) MARTINETANA Röd. Red Sea-P.I.-Ryukyu Is. Haw. <22–30–38–55mm. VS.

5. MUREX (Ch.) MAURUS Brod. N.Cal., Marq.; ?off S.Afr.-Moz. 60–65–75->95mm. S. White and dark brown bands; reddish-violet aperture margin. Cp. *M.microphyllus*. Syn.: *M. steeriae* Reeve.

6. MUREX (Mca.) MEGACERUS Sow. Mauritania-Angola, Canary Is. <65–70–80–110mm. UC. Also, albino form. Cp. *M.saharicus*.

7. MUREX (Ho.) MELANAMATHOS Gm. **Black-spined African Murex.** Senegal-Angola. 30–32–35–45mm. R.

8. MUREX (Ch.) MERGUS Vokes. Fla.-Surinam. ?25–40–45–50mm. VS. Light to dark brown.

9. MUREX (Ch.) MICROPHYLLUS Lam. **Scorched Murex.** E.Afr.-W.Pac., Haw. 35–75–90–124mm. Syn.: *M.torrefactus* Sow.

10. MUREX (Mu.) MINDANAOENSIS Sow. P.I. 60–70–90–114mm. C.

11. MUREX (Si.) MOTACILLA Gm. **Frog Murex.** W.I. (Dominica-Barbados). 50–57–62–65mm. VS.

12. EUPLEURA MURICIFORMIS Brod. **Murex-shaped Drill.** S.Baja Cal.-G.of Cal.-Ecu. 25–30–35–59mm. C.

– – MUREX NIGRITUS Philippi. – See pl. 74, no. 12.

13. MUREX (Mu.) NIGROSPINOSUS Reeve. **Black-spine Murex.** W.Pac., esp.P.I. ca.60–65–75–143mm. C. ?Form of *M.tribulus*.

14. EUPLEURA NITIDA Brod. W.Mex.-Pan. 13–19–22–25mm. C.

15. MUREX (Mco.) NODULIFERA Sow. W.Pac. 15–18–25–30mm. S.

16. MUREX (Ce.) NUTTALLI Conrad. **Nuttall's Hornmouth** or **Thorn Purpura.** C. Cal.-Baja Cal. ca.35–40–50–63mm. C. White to dark brown. *M.monoceros* Sow. is a form without wing-like varices.

17. MUREX (De. or As.) OBELISCUS A. Adams. W.Mex.-C.R. 15–20–26–33mm. C.

18. MUREX (Ho.) OXYCANTHA Brod. W. Mex.-S.Ecu. Avg.35–45mm. UC. Cp. *M. melanamathos*.

19. MUREX (Mco.) OXYTATUS M.Smith. **Hexagonal Murex.** S.Fla.-S.Carib. 20–22–26–38mm. C. Cream to flesh-pink. Syn.: *M. hexagonus* Lam.

20. MUREX (Ch.) PALMAROSAE Lam. **Rose-branch Murex.** Sri Lanka-P.I.-S.W.Japan. 65–70–85–133mm. UC. Cp. *M.saulii*. Syn.: *M.foliatus* Perry.

21. MUREX (Mco.) PAUXILLUS A.Adams. So.G.of Cal.-C.Am. 10–13–16–18mm. C.

22. MUREX (Pa.) PAZI Crosse. E.Fla.-Bah.-Cuba-Honduras. 25–28–35–?90mm. UC (was R). Syn.: *M.atlantis* Clench & Farfante, *M. nuttingi* Dall.

91

Plate 74 | Muricidae

1. *MUREX (Mu.) PECTEN* Lightfoot. **Venus Comb; Thorny** or **Spiny Woodcock.** ?E.Afr., S.E.Japan-P.I.-Qld.-Sol. 75–110–120–187mm. UC. Syn.: *M.tenuispina* Lam., *M.triremis* Perry.

2. *MUREX (Mar.) PELLUCIDUS* Reeve. E. Afr.-P.I.-S.E.Japan. 32–36–43–?77mm. UC. White to pale pink, brown.

3. *MUREX (Ptn.) PHYLLOPTERUS* Lam. W.I. (Guadeloupe-Martinique). 65–70–80–94mm. VR. Orangish-brown. Ext.R yellow and violet color forms.

4. *MUREX (Si.) PLICIFEROIDES* Kuroda. S.E.Japan-Tai.-P.I. <75–90–105–146mm. C. Syn.: *M.pliciferus* Sow., *M.propinquus* Kuroda & Azuma.

5. *MUREX (Ptp.) PLORATOR* Adams & Reeve. Indon.-S.E.Japan. 22–25–35–52mm. C.

6. *MUREX (Ph.) POMUM* Gm. **Apple Murex.** N.C.-Fla.-W.I.-Brazil, Berm. 44–50–'60–133mm. VC. Juveniles have hairy per.

7. *OCENEBRA POULSONI* Cpr. S.Cal.-Baja

Cal. 25–30–40–62mm. VC.

8. *MUREX (Mca.) PRINCEPS* Brod. **Prince Murex.** So.G.of Cal.-Peru, Galáp. ca.50–75–90–140mm. C. Usually quite encrusted.

9. *MUREX (Mca.) RADIX* Gm. **Radix** or **Root Murex.** C.R.-S.Ecu. ca.40–60–75–150mm. C.(S. form.) Syn.: *M.nitidus* Brod.

10. *MUREX (Mca.) CALLIDINUS* Berry. Guat.-C.R. Avg.80–95mm. UC. ?Geographic form of *M.radix*.

These 2 geographic forms of *M.radix* are also considered sep.sp.:

11. *MUREX (Mca.) AMBIGUUS* Reeve. **Ambiguous Murex.** S.Mex.-Pan. ca.65–90–110–179mm. C.

12. *MUREX (Mca.) NIGRITUS* Philippi. **Northern Radix Murex; Black Murex** or **Black-and-White Murex.** G.of Mex. ca.75–90–110–200mm. VC.

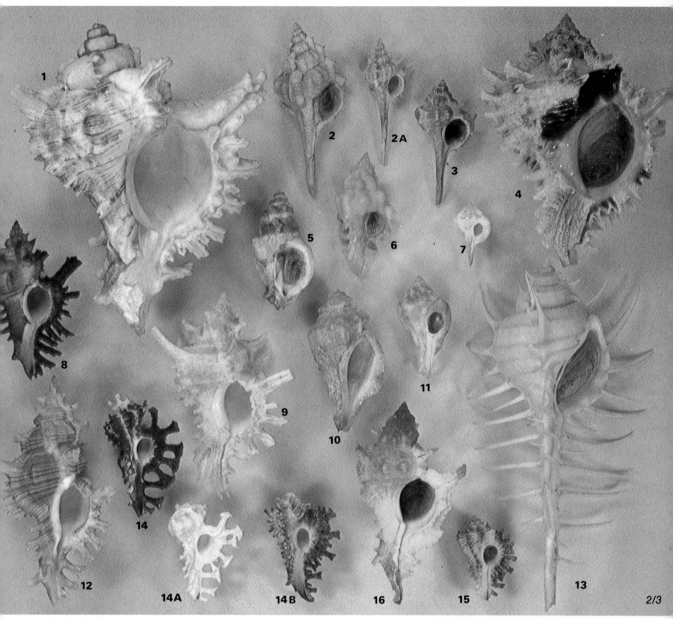

1. MUREX (Ch.) RAMOSUS L. **Branched, Giant** or **Ramose Murex.** S.E.Afr.-W.Pac. 75–100–125–327mm. C.

2. MUREX (Mu.) RECTIROSTRIS Sow. S.E.Japan-Tai. ca.35–50–60–80mm. C. 2A is **M.sobrinus** A.Adams, a smaller, spinier Japanese form (?sep.sp.).

3. MUREX (Mu.) RECURVIROSTRIS Brod. **Bent-beak Murex.** Baja Cal.-Ecu. <35–50–60–88mm. C. Cp. **M.tricornis.** Several subsp. or forms.

4. MUREX (Ph.) REGIUS Swainson. **Regal Murex.** So.G.of Cal.-Peru. ca.60–75–90–180mm. C.

5. MUREX (Ce.) RORIFLUUS Adams & Reeve. W.Japan-Korea-China. <32–35–45–50mm. C. Surface usually chalky.

6. MUREX (Ch.) ROSSITERI Crosse. S.E. Japan-Fiji-Loyalty Is. 32–45–50–55mm. VS. Cp. **M.artemis.** Syn.: **M.saltatrix** Kuroda.

7. MUREX (Mu.) RUBIDUS F.C.Baker. **Rose Murex.** N.C.-E.& W.Fla.-Bah. 16–24–28–55mm. C. Color q.v., with bright yellow and orange forms. ?Subsp. of **M.recurvirostris.**

8. MUREX (Ch.) RUBIGINOSUS Reeve. S.E.Japan-Aust. 55–70–85–130mm. UC. Pale flesh, orange, to deep brown.

9. MUREX (Mca.) SAHARICUS Locard. Mauritania-Senegal, Canary Is. ca.60–65–70–75mm. UC. Off-white to tan. Cp. **M. megacerus.**

10. VITULARIA SALEBROSA King & Brod. Baja Cal.-G.of Cal.-Col., Galáp. 25–60–70–107mm. C. Light to dark brown.

11. MUREX (?Max.) SANTAROSANA Dall. **Santa Rosa Murex.** S.Cal.-Baja Cal. 25–30–35–42mm. UC.

12. MUREX (Ch.) SAULII Sow. Japan-N.G. 60–75–90–110mm. VS. Cp. **M.palmarosae.**

13. MUREX (Mu.) SCOLOPAX Dillwyn. **Woodcock Murex.** Red Sea-N.Ind.Oc.-P.I.-N.W.Aust. ca.85–100–120–151mm. C. Also, "black" form.

14. MUREX (Ho.) SCORPIO L. **Scorpion Murex.** Red Sea, Indon.-P.I. 30–35–45–65mm. C. Brown to brownish-black. Also, albino form. 14B is form **M.digitatus** Sow. from the Red Sea. Cp. **M.secunda.** Syn.: **M.varicosus** Sow.

15. MUREX (Ho.) SECUNDUS Lam. India. Indon.-Aust.-New Cal. <24–28–32–40mm. UC. Tan to deep purplish-brown. Also white form with orange-brown bands. Usually quite encrusted.

16. MUREX (Si.) SENEGALENSIS Gm. **Brazilian Murex.** S.Carib.-S.Brazil. <38–50–65–77mm. UC. White to tan. Cp. **M.tenuivaricosus.**

93

Plate 76 | Muricidae

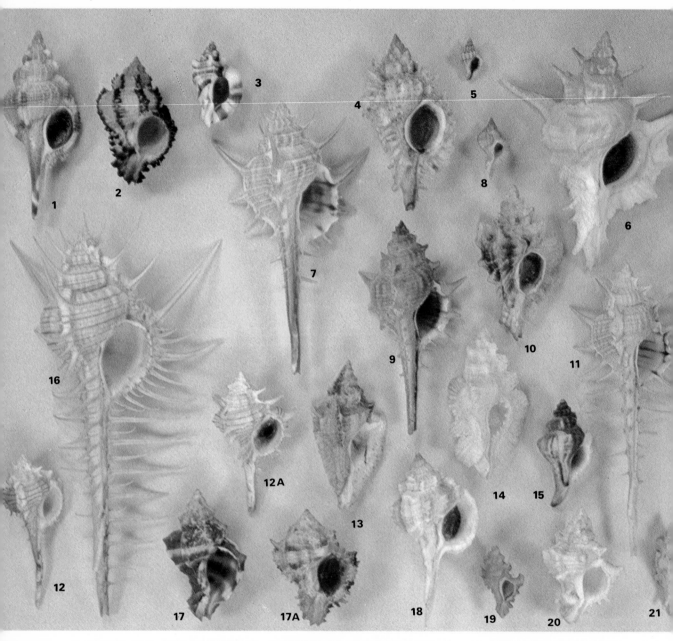

1. MUREX (Mu.) SERRATOSPINOSUS Dunker. N.Ind.Oc.-Indon. ca.60–70–90–100mm. VS (was R). Syn.: **M.malabaricus** E.A.Smith.

2. MUREX (He.) STAINFORTHI Reeve. N.W.Aust. ca.35–40–50–75mm. C. White with fine brown lines. Also orange and black forms.

3. MUREX (Ptn.) STIMPSONI A.Adams. Korea-Japan. Avg.30–35mm. Cp. **M.alatus** (longer spire). S.

4. MUREX (Ph.) SUPERBUS Sow. Japan-Tai., P.I. 40–50–60–76mm. UC. Cp. **M. laciniatus.**

5. UROSALPINX TAMPAENSIS Conrad. **Tampa Drill.** W.Fla. 12–15–20–25mm. C.

6. MUREX (Si.) TENUIVARICOSUS Dautz. C.-S.Brazil. 50–70–85–114mm. UC. Cp. **M. senegalensis** (shorter spines).

7. MUREX (Mu.) TERNISPINA Lam. **Triple-spined Murex.** S.India, P.I. <70–75–90–108mm. VC. Cp. **M.pecten.** ?Form of **M. tribulus.**

8. MUREX (Si.) THOMPSONI Bullis. Fr. Guiana-Surinam. 23–24–28–35mm. UC. ?Form of **M.woodringi** Clench & Farfante, a subsp. of **M.recurvirostris.**

9. MUREX (Mu.) TRAPA Röd. **Triple Spine Murex.** Malaysia-Tai.-P.I. 60–70–80–124mm. VC. Syn.: **M.rarispina** Lam.

10. MUREX (Ptp.) TRIALATUS G.B. Sowerby. **Western Three-winged Murex.** No. Cal.-Baja Cal. ca.50–60–70–93mm. Also, albino and dark brown forms. ?Form of **M.macroptera** Deshayes.

11. MUREX (Mu.) TRIBULUS L. **Bramble Murex.** E.Afr.-Fiji; ?Red Sea. <65–75–90–110mm. C. Form and color q.v. **M. aduncospinosus, M.nigrospinosus** and **M.terni-spina** are probably forms.

12. MUREX (Mu.) TRICORNIS Berry. Baja Cal.-So.G.of Cal. ca.45–50–60–>80mm. C. ?Form of **M.elenensis.**

13. MUREX (Ptc.) TRIFORMIS Reeve. **Triangle** or **Three-shaped Murex.** W.Aust.-N.S.W.-Tas. <38–40–50–63mm. C. Dark operc. Cp. **M.acanthopterus.**

14. MUREX (Mar.) TRIPTERUS Born. Red Sea, W.Pac., Haw. ca.40–45–50–58mm. UC. White to orange.

15. MUREX (Eu.) TRIQUETRA Reeve. S. Baja Cal.-Pan. <32–40–45–55mm.

16. MUREX (Mu.) TROSCHELI Lischke. S.E.Japan-P.I. <110–125–150–188mm. UC.

17. MUREX (Ph.) TRUNCULUS L. Portugal-W.Med.-Morocco, Canary Is. 35–45–55–>80mm. C. Form and pattern q.v. Edible. Canary Is. form: **M.turbinatus** Lam.

18. MUREX (Ptn.) TWEEDIANUS Macpherson. S.Qld. <50–55–65–75mm. C. Cream to brown.

19. MUREX (Por.) UNCINARIUS Lam. S.Afr. 12–18–25–30mm. S, but C as beach spec.

20. MUREX (Mca.) VARIUS Sow. Senegal-Angola. 35–40–45–65mm. VS. Syn.: **M.clausi** Dunker.

21. MUREX (Ptn.) VESPERTILIO Kira. S.E.Japan. 25–30–35–50mm. UC.

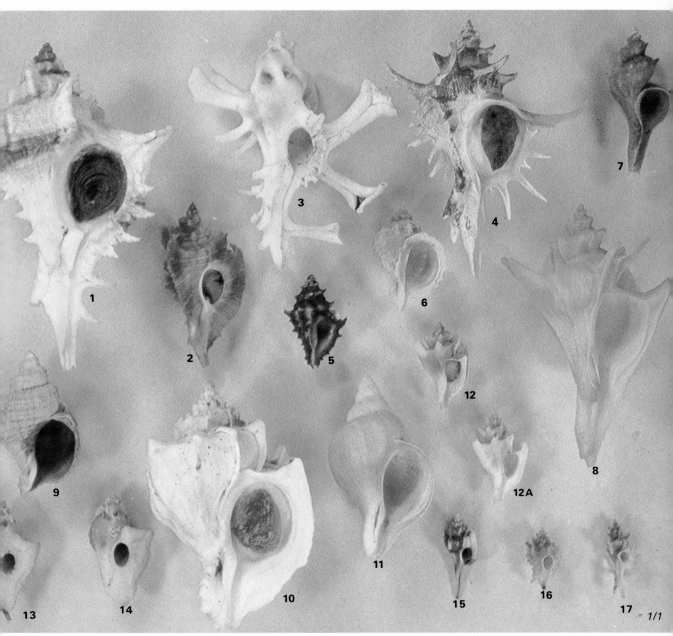

1/1

1. *MUREX (?Si.) VIRGINEUS* Röd. E.Afr., Red Sea-B.of Bengal. 65-75-95-160mm. White to brown. Heavy. Syn.: *M.anguliferus* Lam.

2. *MUREX (Oc.) VOKESAE* Emerson. **Wrinkled Wing Murex.** S.Cal.-Baja Cal. ca. 35-40-50-68mm. UC. Related to *M.erinaceoides.* Syn.: *M.rhyssus* Dall.

3. *MUREX (Ho.) ZAMBOI* Burch & Burch. P.I.-Sol. 38-45-50-58mm. C. Canal salmon-pink. Spines unequal in length. Also, pink form. Cp. *M.anatomicus.*

4. *MUREX (Poi.) ZELANDICUS* Q. & G. **Zealandic** or **Spiny Murex.** N.E.New Zealand. 40-50-55->62mm. UC.

5. *MUREX (Mco.) ZETEKI* Hert. & Strong. No.G.of Cal.-Ecu., Galáp. 18-19-22-28mm. C. Form and color q.v.

6. *EMOZAMIA LICINUS* Hedley & Petterd. **Southern Trophon** or **Broad Emozamia.** S. Aust., Tas. Avg.20-25mm. UC. Horny operc.

7. *TROPHON BEEBEI* Hertlein & Strong. So.G.of Cal. 25-30-40-52mm. UC. *Zacotrophon* (?Thaididae).

8. *TROPHON CERROSENSIS CATA-LINENSIS* Oldroyd. **Catalina Trophon** or **Forreria.** S.Cal. 50-60-75-85mm. R. (?Thaididae).

9. *TROPHON GEVERSIANUS* Pallas. Magellanic region, esp. Falkland Is. 38-42-50-60mm. UC.

10. *TROPHON LACINIATUS* Dillwyn. Straits of Magellan. 40-50-60-85mm. UC.

11. *TROPHON VARIANS* Orbigny. Magellanic region. Avg.40-50mm. S.

12. *BOREOTROPHON TRIANGULATUS* Cpr. **Triangular Trophon.** C.-S.Cal. Avg.19-23mm. S. Syn.: *B.peregrinus* Dall.

13. *TYPHIS CLARKI* Keen & Campbell. No. G.of Cal.-Pan.Bay. 18-20-25-30mm. S. White to purplish-brown.

14. *TYPHIS CORONATUS* Brod. Baja Cal.-Ecu. 25-28-35-40mm. UC. Syn.: *T.quadratus* Hinds.

15. *TYPHIS CUMINGII* Brod. W.Mex.-Ecu. 18-20-22-?32mm. S.

16. *TYPHIS RAMOSUS* Habe & Kosuge. S. China Sea. 15-20mm. VS.

17. *TYPHIS TOSAENSIS* Azuma, S.E.Japan-Tai. Avg.19-22mm. VS.

Plate 78 | Coralliophilidae

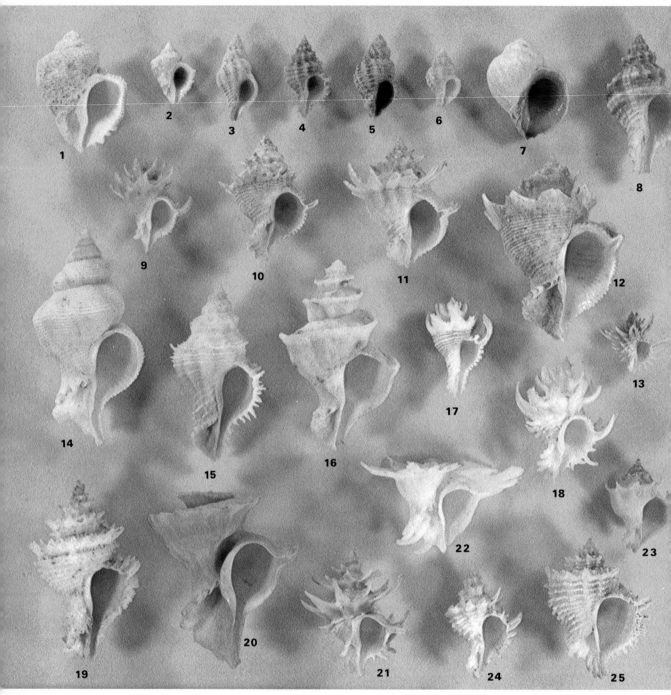

1. *CORALLIOPHILA ABBREVIATA* Lam. Abbreviated or **Short Coral Shell.** S.C.-S.E. Fla.-W.I.-Brazil. 19-25-35-38mm. C. Horny yellow-brown operc.

2. *CORALLIOPHILA CARIBAEA* Abbott. Caribbean Coral Shell. S.E.Fla.-W.I. 13-15-20-25mm. VC. Horny deep red operc.

3. *CORALLIOPHILA COSTULARIS* Lam. E.Afr.-W.Pac. 24-30-50-60mm. UC.

4. *CORALLIOPHILA LAMELLOSA* Philippi. Med. 20-25-35-40mm. UC.

5. *CORALLIOPHILA MEYENDORFFI* Calcara. Med.-W.Afr., E.Afr. 20-25-35-38mm. C.

6. *CORALLIOPHILA PARVA* E.A.Smith. G.of Cal.-Galáp. 10-12-16-24mm. C.

7. *CORALLIOPHILA VIOLACEA* Kiener. Purple Coral Snail. E.Afr.-Haw.; Galáp. 25-

28-35-47mm. C. Usually with coralline encrustations. Syn.: *C.neritoidea* Lam.

8. *LATAXIENA FIMBRIATA* Hinds. W.Pac., esp.Japan-Tai. 25-28-35-38mm. C.

9. *LATIAXIS ARMATUS* Sow. Armed Latiaxis. Japan-Tai. 23-27-35-39mm. S.

10. *LATIAXIS CARINIFEROIDES* Shikama. Japan. Avg.30-35mm. S.

11. *LATIAXIS DEBURGHIAE* Reeve. Japan-Tai. 18-22-30-35mm. UC.

12. *LATIAXIS DUNKERI* Kuroda & Habe. Japan-Tai. 38-50mm. UC.

13. *LATIAXIS ECHINATA* Azuma. Japan-Tai. 13-15-20-25mm. S.

14. *LATIAXIS EUGENIAE* Bernardi. Japan-Tai. 32-40-55-60mm. UC. Syn.: *L.idoleum* Jonas.

15. *LATIAXIS FEARNLEYI* Emerson & D'Attilio. India, W.Pac. 35-38-45-50mm. S.

16. *LATIAXIS GYRATUS* Wood. India, W. Pac., esp.Japan-Tai. 35-38-45-53mm. UC.

17. *LATIAXIS JAPONICUS* Dunker. Japan-Tai., P.I., Haw. 25-30-38-50mm. UC.

18. *LATIAXIS KINOSHITAI* Fulton. Japan-Tai., P.I. Avg.25-35mm. S.

19. *LATIAXIS LISCHKEANUS* Dunker. W.Pac., esp.Japan-Tai. 25-30-40-52mm. UC.

20. *LATIAXIS MAWAE* Griffith & Pidgeon. Japan-Tai. 35-40-55-64mm. UC.

21. *LATIAXIS PAGODUS.* A.Adams. Japan-Tai. <18-20-32-38mm. UC.

22. *LATIAXIS PILSBRYI* Hirase. W.Pac., esp.Japan. 18-22-32-44mm. S.

23. *LATIAXIS PURPURATUS* Chenu. Japan-

Tai. Avg.25–32mm. S. ?Form of *L.deburghiae*.

24. *LATIAXIS TOSANUS* Hirase. Japan-Tai., Haw. 24–26–32–35mm. UC.

25. *LATIAXIS WINCKWORTHI* Fulton. Japan-Tai. Avg.30–37mm. UC.

Plate 79

1. *MAGILUS ANTIQUUS* Montfort. **Common Tube-forming Coral Dweller.** Red Sea, E.Afr.-Ind.Oc.-W.Pac. Juveniles (1A) avg.20–25mm., adults to >150mm. UC. No. 1 is illus. in coral.

2. *QUOYULA MADREPORARUM* Sow. Red Sea, Ind.Oc.-W.Pac., Haw.; also Med.; also G.of Cal.-Pan. <10–20–30–35mm. C. Feeds on corals.

3. *RAPA RAPA* L. **Papery Rapa** or **Bubble Turnip.** W.Pac. 40–50–70–80mm. C. 3B is *Rapa incurva* Dunker, possibly a form of *R. rapa*.

4. *RAPANA BEZOAR* L. Thailand-W.Pac. 45–50–60–69mm. C.

5. *RAPANA RAPIFORMIS* Born. **Turnip Shell.** E.Afr.-W.Pac. 44–60–90–110mm. C.

6. *RAPANA THOMASIANA* Crosse. W.Pac., esp.Japan; also, Black Sea. 70–80–120–178mm. C. Form variable. Syn.: *R.venosa* Val.

7. *FORRERIA BELCHERI* Hinds. **Giant Forreria** or **Belcher's Chorus Shell.** C.Cal.-?Baja Cal. 75–100–125–187mm. UC.

8. *NEORAPANA GRANDIS* Sow. Galáp. 44–60–80–90mm. UC. Color variable. Syn.: *Acanthina grandis* Gray.

9. *NEORAPANA MURICATA* Brod. G.of Cal.-Ecu. 40–50–70–78mm. UC.

10. *NEORAPANA TUBERCULATA* Sow. G.of Cal. 35–50–60–114mm. C. ?Subsp. of *N.muricata*.

Plate 80 | Thaididae

1. THAIS ACULEATA Deshayes. W.Pac., esp.Fiji. 18–25–40–60mm. C. ?Form of **T. hippocastaneum**.

2. THAIS BISERIALIS Blainville. Baja Cal.-G.of Cal.-Chile, Galáp. 25–35–50–81mm. C. ?Subsp. of **T.haemastoma**.

3. THAIS BRONNI Dunker. Japan. 40–45–60–66mm. C.

4. THAIS (Mancinella) BUFO Lam. **Toad Purple.** S.E.Afr.-W.Pac. 25–30–50–65mm. C.

5. THAIS CALLIFERA Lam. Mauritania-Angola. 20–25–35–45mm. C.

6. THAIS CHOCOLATA Duclos. Ecu.-Peru-?Chile. 50–55–75–93mm. S.

7. THAIS CINGULATA L. S.Afr. 26–30–38–41mm. C.

8. THAIS DELTOIDEA Lam. **Deltoid Dog-winkle.** Fla.-W.I., Berm. 25–30–40–50mm. VC. Form q.v.

9. THAIS ECHINATA Blainville. **Prickly Purple.** W.Pac. 30–35–45–50mm. C.

10. THAIS (Mancinella) ECHINULATA Lam. E.Afr.-W.Pac. 34–38–45–50mm. C.

11. THAIS (or NUCELLA) EMARGINATA Deshayes. **Emarginate Dogwinkle.** Bering Sea-Baja Cal. Avg.25–28mm. VC. Variable form.

12. THAIS FORBESI Dunker. W.Afr. Avg. 30–35mm. C.

13. THAIS HAEMASTOMA L. **Florida Dogwinkle.** N.C.-Fla.-W.I.-Brazil; also, Med.-W.Afr.-S.W.Afr. 35–50–75–100mm. VC. Variable form.

14. THAIS HIPPOCASTANUM L. I-P. 25–30–45–55mm. C.

15. THAIS INTERMEDIA Kiener. **Intermediate Thais.** Ind.Oc.-W.Pac., Haw. 25–30–38–53mm. C.

16. THAIS (Mancinella) KIENERI Deshayes. W.Pac. 28–35–50–60mm. C.

17. THAIS KIOSQUIFORMIS Duclos. Baja Cal.-Peru. 16–30–45–65mm. VC.

18. THAIS (Mancinella) MANCINELLA L. **Pimpled Purple.** Ind.Oc.-W.Pac. 20–35–50–60mm. C.

19. THAIS MELONES Duclos. W.Mex.-Peru, Galáp. ca.30–35–45–54mm. C.

20. THAIS (Dicathais) ORBITA Gm. **Cartwheel Purple.** S.-E.Aust., N.Z. 35–50–70–80mm. C. Syn.: **T.succincta** Martyn.

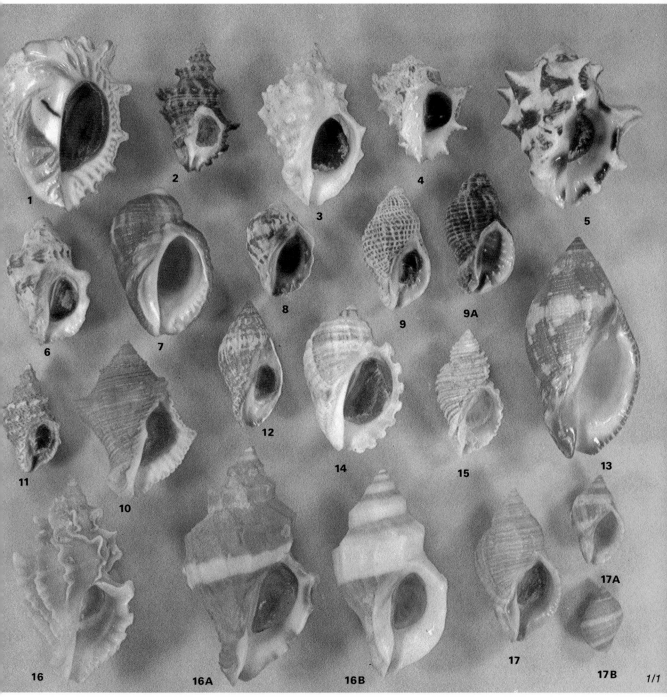

1. THAIS PLANOSPIRA Lam. G.of Cal.-Peru, Galáp. 35–40–55–62mm. UC.

2. THAIS RUGOSA Born. Ind.Oc.-W.Pac., esp.India. Avg.28–35mm. C.

3. THAIS (Mancinella) SIRO Kuroda. W.Pac. Avg.35–45mm. C.

4. THAIS (Mancinella) SPECIOSA Val. Baja Cal.-G.of Cal.-Peru. Avg.28–36mm. C.

5. THAIS (Mancinella) TUBEROSA Röd. E.Afr.-W.Pac. Avg.45–50mm. C. Variable color.

6. ACANTHINA ANGELICA Oldroyd. G.of Cal. 25–39mm. C.

7. ACANTHINA IMBRICATA Lam. Falkland Is. Avg.35–40mm. S.

8. ACANTHINA LUGUBRIS Sow. S.Cal.-Baja Cal., ?Galáp. 20–25–35–44mm. C.

9. ACANTHINA SPIRATA Blainville. **Spotted Thorn Drupe** or **Angular Unicorn.** Puget Sound-S.Cal. 25–28–35–42mm. C. Illus. is form **A.s.punctulata** Sow. (with rounded shoulders) from C.Cal.-Baja Cal.

10. CYMIA TECTA Wood. C.R.-Ecu. ca. 30–40–50–68mm. C. Cream to brown.

11. LEPSIELLA SCOBINA Q. & G. **Oyster Borer.** N.Z. Avg.25–30mm. C.

12. NASSA FRANCOLINA Brug. Ind.Oc.-W.Pac., Haw. 33–40–55–70mm. C. ?Syn. for **N.serta.**

13. NASSA SERTA Brug. **Garland Nassa.** E.Afr.-W.Pac., Haw. 38–42–52–58mm. VC.

14. NEOTHAIS SCALARIS Menke. **White Rock Shell.** N.Z. Avg.38–50mm. C.

15. NUCELLA CANALICULATA Duclos. **Channeled Dogwinkle.** Aleutian Is.-C.Cal. 25–

30–40–53mm. C. Members of this genus were formerly placed under **Thais**.

16. NUCELLA LAMELLOSA Gm. **Frilled Dogwinkle.** Alaska-C.Cal. 38–45–65–92mm. VC. Form and color q.v.

17. NUCELLA LAPILLUS L. **Atlantic** or **Northern Dogwinkle** or **Horsewinkle.** Labrador-N.Y.; also, Norway-Portugal. 18–30–50–>80mm. VC. Form and color q.v. Once used for purple dye.

Plate 82 | Thaididae – Columbariidae

1. PURPURA COLUMELLARIS Lam. So. G.of Cal.-Chile. <35–45–65–79mm. UC.

2. PURPURA PATULA L. **Wide-mouthed Purpura.** S.E.Fla.-W.I., Berm. 50–55–75–88mm. C. Once used by Indians for purple dye.

3. PURPURA PATULA PANSA Gould. Baja Cal.So.G.of Cal.-Col., Galáp. 25–40–65–98mm. C. ?Sep.sp.

4. PURPURA PERSICA L. **Princely Purple.** Ind.Oc.-W.Pac. to New Heb. ca.60–70–90–102mm. C. Heavy.

5. DRUPA ALBOLABRIS Lam. **White-lipped Castor Bean.** E.Afr.-W.Pac. 13–18–22–25mm. C. ?Syn. for **D.ricinus.**

6. MORULA FUSCA Kiener. Japan. 17–27mm. VC.

7. DRUPA (Drupina) GROSSULARIA Röd. **Finger Drupe.** E.Ind.Oc.-Haw. 25–28–35–45mm. VC.

8. DRUPA (Drupina) LOBATA Blainville. Red Sea, E.Afr.-W.Pac. Avg.25–30mm. UC. ?Form of **D.grossularia.**

9. DRUPA MORUM Röd. **Mulberry Drupe** or **Rough Castor Bean.** E.Afr.-W.Pac., Haw. 20–25–35–40mm. C.

10. DRUPA RICINA L. **Spotted Drupe** or **Spider-like Castor Bean.** S.E.Afr.-W.Pac., Haw. 19–22–28–32mm. C. Cp. **D.albolabris** (?Syn.).

11. DRUPA RUBUSIDAEUS Röd. **Porcupine Castor Bean.** Ind.Oc.-W.Pac., Haw. 20–25–40–60mm. UC.

12. MACULOTRITON BRACTEATUS Hinds. W.Pac., esp.Aust., Haw. 13–19mm. C.

13. MORULA FERRUGINOSA Reeve. Baja Cal.-G.of Cal. Avg.21–26mm. C.

14. MORULA (Cronia) FISCELLA Gm. Red Sea, Ind.Oc.-W.Pac., Haw. 20–25–35–40mm. UC.

Now placed under Muricidae: **Murex (Muricodrupa) funiculus** Wood.

15. MORULA FUNICULATUS Wood. Tonga. Avg.20mm. UC.

– – **MORULA FUSCA** Kiener. – See no. 6.

16. MORULA (Cronia) MARGARITICOLA Brod. **Shouldered Castor Bean.** S.E.Afr.-W.Pac. 13–22–30–40mm. C.

17. MORULA MARGINALBA Blainville. **Mulberry Whelk.** S.Qld.-N.S.W. 13–19–25–30mm. VC.

18. MORULA NODULOSA C.B.Adams. **Blackberry Drupe.** S.C.-Fla.-W.I.-Brazil. 13–15–20–25mm. C.

19. MORULA SPINOSA H.& A.Adams. Red Sea, W.Pac., Haw. ca.20–25–35–40mm. C. Color variable.

20. CRONIA AVELLANA Reeve. **Filbertnut Purple.** W.Aust. 19–22–28–35mm. C.

21. *CRONIA PSEUDAMYGDALA* Hedley. **Pseudo–almond Purple.** N.Qld.–N.S.W. 19–22–28–35mm. C.

22. *COLUMBARIUM EASTWOODAE* Kilburn. S.Afr.–off Moz. 40–50–65–73mm. S.

23. *COLUMBARIUM HEDLEYI* Iredale. S.Qld.–N.S.W. Avg.40–52mm. S.

24. *COLUMBARIUM PAGODA* Lesson. Japan–Tai. 50–55–75–88mm. C.

Plate 83

1. *AFROCOMINELLA ELONGATA* Dunker. S.Afr. 39–61mm. C. Pattern variable. Brown per.

2. *ANCISTROLEPIS UNICUS* Pilsbry. Japan. Avg.50–60mm. S. Brown per.

3. *BABYLONIA AMBULACRUM* Sow. And. Sea. 35–40–60–75mm. S. Thin yellowish per.

4. *BABYLONIA AREOLATA* Lam. **Spotted Babylon** or **Ivory Shell.** S.E.Asia. 40–45–65–98mm. VC. Thin yellowish per.

5. *BABYLONIA CANALICULATA* Schumacher. **Channeled Babylon.** S.E.Asia, esp. Thailand, Sri Lanka. 40–45–60–65mm. C.

6. *BABYLONIA FORMOSAE* Sow. **Formosan Babylon.** W.Pac. 35–40–55–60mm. C.

7. *BABYLONIA JAPONICA* Reeve. **Japanese Babylon.** Japan–Korea. 50–55–70–75mm. VC. Brown per.

8. *BABYLONIA KIRANA* Habe. Ryukyu Is. Avg.35–40mm. UC.

9. *BABYLONIA PALLIDA* Perry. **Grooved Babylon.** S.E.Asia. Avg.40–50mm. C. Illus. shows thin brown per.

10. *BABYLONIA PERFORATA* Sow. Tai. Avg.70–85mm. UC.

11. *BABYLONIA PINTADO* Kilburn. Off S.Afr. Avg.40–50mm. S.

12. *BABYLONIA SPIRATA* Lam. **Spiral Babylon.** Sri Lanka. Avg.50–65mm. C. Tip of spire purplish.

13. *BABYLONIA ZEYLANDICUS* Brug. S.E.Asia, esp.India, Sri Lanka. Avg.50–65mm. C.

14. *BERINGIUS EYERDAMI* A.G.Smith. Alaska–Wash. Avg.100–125mm. S. Syn. for genus: **Jumala.**

15. *BERINGIUS (Japelion) HIRASEI* Pilsbry. Japan. Avg.90–110mm. S.

16. *BUCCINANOPS GLOBOSUM* Kiener. Uruguay–Argentina. Avg.36–48mm. C.

17. *BUCCINANOPS SQUALIDUS* King. Argentina. Avg.70–80mm. C.

18. *BUCCINULUM (EUTHRIA) CORNEUM* L. S.W.Eur.–Med. 35–40–55–70mm. C.

19. *BUCCINULUM LINEUM* Martyn. N.Z. 20–25–35–40mm. C.

20. *BUCCINULUM MULTILINEUM* Powell. **Many–lined Whelk.** N.Z. Avg.26–34mm. C.

21. *BUCCINUM ISAOTAKII* Kira. Japan. Avg.80–95mm. S.

22. *BUCCINUM LEUCOSTOMA* Lischke. Japan. 55–75–90–120mm. UC.

Plate 84 | Buccinidae

1. *"BUCCINUM" PERRYI* Jay. Japan, Bering Sea. 35–38–50–60mm. C. Thin. Hairy yellowish-brown per. Now placed under genus *Volutharpa*.

2. *BUCCINUM UNDATUM* L. **Common Northern** or **Wavy Whelk.** Arctic-N.J.; also, W.Eur.-W.Med. 50–65–85–110mm. C. Horny oval operc. Gray per. Edible.

3. *BURNUPENA DELALANDII* Kiener. S.Afr. Avg.32–38mm. C.

4, 6. *CANTHARUS (Pollia) UNDOSA* L. **Waved Buccinum.** E.Afr.-W.Pac. 25–35–40–42mm. C. Thick dark brown per.

5. *CANTHARUS CANCELLARIUS* Conrad. **Cancellate Lesser Whelk.** N.C.-E.& W.Fla.-Texas-Yucatan. 15–30mm. C.

7. *CANTHARUS ELEGANS* Griffith & Pidgeon. Baja Cal.-G.of Cal.-Peru. 25–35–50–65mm. C.

8. *CANTHARUS ERYTHROSTOMUS* Reeve. **Red-mouthed Buccinum Whelk.** W. Pac. Avg.28–35mm. C. Silky per.

9. *CANTHARUS (Pollia) FUMOSUS* Dillwyn. Moz.-E.Afr.-Ind.Oc.-W.Pac. 22–35mm. C.

10. *CANTHARUS GEMMATUS* Reeve. W. Mex.-Peru. 25–35mm. C. Olive-green per.

11. *CANTHARUS MULTANGULUS* Philippi. **False Drill.** N.C.-Fla.-Yucutan, Bah., Cuba. 20–32mm. C.

12. *CANTHARUS PAGODUS* Reeve. W. Mex.-Pan.-?Peru. 40–56mm. UC. Velvety brown per.

13. *CANTHARUS RINGENS* Reeve. W. Mex.-Ecu. Avg.25–28mm. C. Smooth dull brown per.

14. *CANTHARUS SANGUINOLENTUS* Duclos. Baja Cal.-G.of Cal.-Ecu. Avg.20–25mm. C.

15. *CANTHARUS TINCTUS* Conrad. **Tinted** or **Painted Cantharus** or **Gaudy Lesser Whelk.** N.C.-Fla.-Texas, W.I. 15–20–25–32mm. C. Juveniles resemble *Thais*.

16. *CANTHARUS BERRYI* McLean. W.Mex. 17–20–30–33mm. UC.

17. *CANTHARUS VIBEX* Brod. Baja Cal.-Pan. 25–35mm. C. Rough brown per.

18. *CANTHARUS VIVERATUS* Kiener. Mauritania-Angola. Avg.35–40mm. C.

19. *COMINELLA ADSPERSA* Brug. **Speckled Whelk.** N.Z. 40–63mm. VC.

20. *COMINELLA QUOYANA* A.Adams. N.Z. 19–25mm. C.

21. *COMINELLA VIRGATA* H.& A.Adams. **Red-mouthed Whelk.** N.Z. 27–38mm. C.

22. *ENGINA INCARNATA* Deshayes. Red Sea-C.Pac. to Poly. 13–20mm. VC. Variable color.

23. *ENGINA MENDICARIA* L. **Little Dove Shell.** S.E.Afr.-W.Pac. 12–21mm. VC.

24. *ENGINA PULCHRA* Reeve. W.Mex.-Pan.-Ecu.; also, W.Pac. to Poly. 15–27mm. C. ?Syn. for Pac. form: *E.elegans* Dunker.

1. *HINDSIA KIRAI* Habe. Japan. Avg.40–48mm. C.

2. *HINDSIA MAGNIFICA* Lischke. Japan. 35–48mm. C. 2A is ***H.m.lischkei Makiyama***.

3. *HINDSIA SINENSIS* Sow. Tai. Avg.32–38mm. C.

4. *KANAMARUA ADONIS* Dall. Japan. Avg. 33–37mm. UC. Also placed under Colubrariidae.

5. *KELLETIA KELLETI* Forbes. **Kellet's Whelk.** So.Cal.-Baja Cal. 100–110–125–171mm. VC.

6. *MACRON AETHIOPS* Reeve. **Ethiopian** or **Ribbed Macron.** Baja Cal.-G.of Cal.(R). 35–40–60–87mm. UC. Rough (6) and smooth (6A) forms. Velvety grayish-green per.

7. *METULA AMOSI* Vanatta. G.of Cal.-Pan. 30–35–40–56mm. UC.

8. *NEPTUNEA DECEMCOSTATA* Say. **New England, Brown Corded** or **Ten-ridged Neptune.** Nova Scotia-N.C. 70–75–110–170mm. C. Heavy. ?Subsp. of ***N.lyrata***.

9. *NEPTUNEA HEROS* Gray. Bering Sea. Avg.90–115mm. UC.

10. *NEPTUNEA INTERSCULPTA* Sow. Japan. 110–155mm. C. Edible.

11. *NEPTUNEA KUROSIO* Oyama. Japan. Avg.70–85mm. C.

12. *NEPTUNEA LYRATA* Gm. **Ridged Whelk.** Alaska-N.Cal.; also, Japan. 90–100–125–140mm. UC.

13. *NEPTUNEA TABULATA* Baird. **Tabled Neptune** or **Whelk.** Br.Col.-S.Cal. 75–85–100–114mm. UC.

14. *NORTHIA NORTHIAE* Griffith & Pidgeon. W.Mex.-Pan.-?Ecu. 40–45–60–78mm. C.

15. *PENION ADUSTA* Philippi. **Northern Siphon Whelk.** N.Z. Avg.90–120mm. C. Syn. for genus: ***Verconella***.

16. *PENION MANDARINA* Duclos. **Southern Siphon Whelk.** N.Z. Avg. 100–125mm. UC.

17. *PENION MAXIMA* Tryon. **Giant Whelk** or **Spindle.** S.Aust.-N.S.W., Tas. Avg.150–200mm. C. Horny operc.

18. *PENION OLIGOSTIRA* Tate. S.Aust. Avg.80–100mm. UC.

Plate 86 | Buccinidae

1. *PHOS ARTICULATUS* Hinds. G.of Cal.-Peru. 30–46mm. C. Variable form.

2. *ENGONIOPHOS UNICINCTUS* Say. Senegal. 20–30mm. C. Violet aperture when fresh. Syn.: *Phos grateloupianus* Petit.

3. *PHOS SENTICOSUS* L. **Thorny Phos** or **Light Shell.** W.-C.Pac. 25–30–38–42mm. VC. Color and pattern q.v.

4. *PISANIA PUSIO* L. **Miniature Triton Trumpet.** S.E.Fla.-W.I.-Brazil, Berm. 25–30–38–45mm. C.

5. *PISANIA (CADUCIFER) CINIS* Reeve. W.Mex.-Galáp. Avg.25–30mm. UC. Some authors regard **Caducifer** as a separate genus.

6. *PRODOTIA IGNEA* Gm. Reeve. W.Pac., Haw. Avg.32–38mm. C. Pattern q.v. Syn.: *Pisania (Ecmanis) tritinoides* Reeve.

7. *SEARLESIA DIRA* Reeve. **Dire Whelk.** Alaska-C.Cal. 25–35–42–53mm. C. Often with *Crepidula adunca* Sow. attached, as illus.

8. *SIPHONALIA CASSIDARIAEFORMIS* Reeve. Japan. 40–45–55–62mm. C. Form, color and pattern q.v.

9. *SIPHONALIA FILOSA* A.Adams. Japan. Avg.60–75mm. C.

10. *SIPHONALIA FUNERA* Pilsbry. Japan. Avg.35–40mm. C. Color and pattern variable.

11. *SIPHONALIA FUSOIDES* Reeve. Japan. 45–50–60–63mm. C.

12. *SIPHONALIA MIKADO* Melvill. Japan. 35–45–55–60mm. C.

13. *SIPHONALIA SIGNUM* Reeve. Japan. 35–40–50–53mm. C. Color and pattern q.v.

14. *SIPHONALIA TROCHULUS* Reeve. Japan. Avg.35–42mm. C.

15. *SOLENOSTEIRA CAPITANEA* Berry. No.G.of Cal. Avg.50–55mm. C. Illus. shows gritty brown per.

16. *SOLENOSTEIRA GATESI* Berry. G.of Cal.-W.Mex. Avg.42–48mm. C. Pale brown per. with fine spines.

17. *SOLENOSTEIRA MACROSPIRA* Berry. No.G.of Cal. 30–35–45–66mm. C. Color variable. Fringed per.

18. *TRAJANA PERIDERIS* Dall. G.of Cal.-W.Mex. 20–30mm. C.

19. *TRIUMPHIS DISTORTA* Wood. El Salvador-Ecu. Avg.35–40mm. C. Color and pattern q.v. Formerly placed under genus **Cominella**.

– – VOLUTHARPA PERRYI Jay. – See pl. 84, no. 1.

20. *VOLUTOPSIUS LARGILLIERTI* Petit. North Sea. Avg.90–100mm. UC.

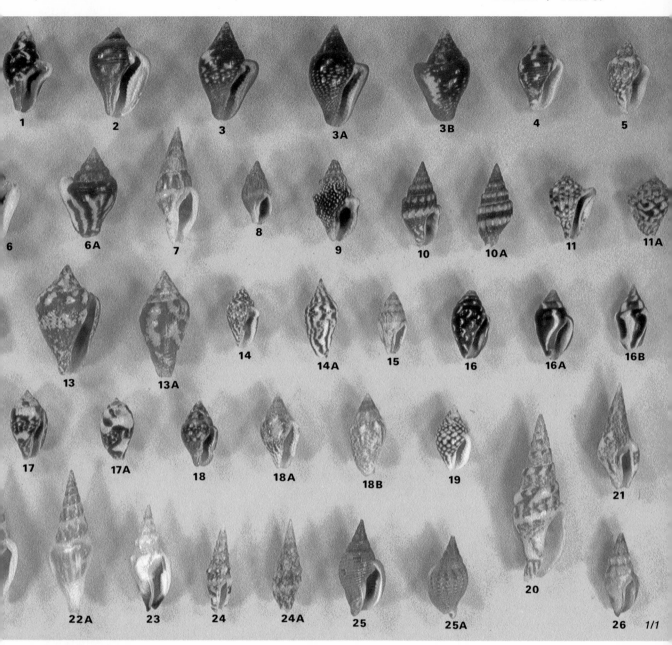

1   2   3   3A   3B   4   5

6   6A   7   8   9   10   10A   11   11A

13   13A   14   14A   15   16   16A   16B

17   17A   18   18A   18B   19   21

22A   23   24   24A   25   25A   20   26   1/1

1. COLUMBELLA HAEMASTOMA Sow. G.of Cal.-Ecu., Galáp. Avg.20–23mm. C. Pattern q.v. Also placed under *Pyrene*.

2. COLUMBELLA LABIOSA Sow. Nicaragua-Ecu. Avg.20–23mm. C. Olive per. Also placed under *Pyrene*.

3. COLUMBELLA MAJOR Sow. So.G.of Cal.-Peru. 19–22–28–33mm. C. Cp. *C.strombiformis*.

4. COLUMBELLA MERCATORIA L. **Common Dove Shell** or **Columbella**. S.E.Fla.-W.I.-Brazil, Berm. 13–19mm. VC. Variable color and pattern.

5. COLUMBELLA SCRIPTA Lam. **Varicolored Dove Shell**. W.Pac. 13–20mm. C. Color and pattern q.v. Syn.: *C.(Euplica) versicolor* Sow. Also placed under *Pyrene*.

6. COLUMBELLA STROMBIFORMIS Lam. No.G.of Cal.-Peru. Avg.20–25mm. C. Shaggy olive per. Cp. *C.major*. Also placed under *Pyrene*.

7. COLUMBELLA TURRITA Sow. Guat.-Ecu. Avg.25–30mm. C. Also placed under *Strombina*.

8. AMPHISSA VERSICOLOR Dall. **Joseph's Coat Amphissa**. Br.Col.-Baja Cal. 11–15mm. C. Variable color. Genus formerly placed under *Buccinidae*.

9. ANACHIS BOIVINI Kiener. Nicaragua-Col. Avg. 18–20mm. C.

10. ANACHIS SCALARINA Sow. G.of Cal.-W.Mex.-Pan. Avg.20–22mm. C.

11. MICROCITHARA HARPIFORMIS Sow. El Salvador-Pan. 15–20mm. C.

12. MITRELLA BICINCTA Gould. Japan, Hong Kong. 11–20mm. C. Color and pattern q.v.

13. PARAMETARIA DUPONTII Kiener. **False Cone** or **Dupont's Dove Shell**. G.of Cal.-W.Mex. 13–18–25–28mm. C. Variable color and form.

14. PYRENE EPAMELLA Duclos. W.Pac. Avg.15–20mm. C. Syn.: *P.philippinarum* Récluz.

15. PYRENE FLAVA Brug. E.Afr.-Poly. 15–17–20–25mm. C. Variable color and pattern.

16. PYRENE OCELLATA Link. W.Pac. 15–20mm. C. Syn.: *P.fulgurans* Lam.

17. PYRENE PUNCTATA Brug. W.Pac. 14–16–22–25mm. C. Color and pattern variable.

18. PYRENE RUSTICA L. Med., Morocco-Angola. 15–20mm. C. Color and pattern q.v. Also placed under *Columbella*.

19. PYRENE TESTUDINARIA Link. W. Pac. 15–20–30–41mm. C.

20. STROMBINA DEROYAE Emerson & D'Attilio. Ecu., Galáp. Avg.15–18mm. S.

21. STROMBINA DORSATA Sow. No.G.of Cal.-Ecu. Avg.23–26mm. C.

22. STROMBINA FUSINOIDEA Dall. Baja Cal.-Pan. 30–35–40–49mm. C.

23. STROMBINA LANCEOLATA Sow. Ecu., Galáp. Avg.25–32mm. UC. Thin brown per.

24. STROMBINA MACULOSA Sow. No. G.of Cal.-Pan. Avg.20–25mm. C.

25. STROMBINA PULCHERRIMA Sow. W.Mex.-C.R. Avg.20–23mm. UC.

26. STROMBINA RECURVA Sow. Baja Cal.-Peru. 20–30mm. UC.

Plate 88 | Melongenidae

1. *VOLEMA (Hemifusus) TERNATANUS*
Gm. W.Pac., esp.Japan. ca.90–150–200–225mm.
C. May lack shoulder spines. Edible.

2. *VOLEMA (Hemifusus) TUBA* Gm. Japan.
ca.90–185mm. C. Velvety per. Edible.

3. *MELONGENA CORONA* Gm: **American,
Florida** or **Common Crown Conch.** Fla.-
Gulf States-Yucatan. 50–60–80–>180mm. VC.
Light brown per. Thin claw-like operc. Several
var. May lack shoulder spines. 3A is *M.c.bicolor*
Say from Fla.-Dry Tortugas. Avg.30–38mm.
Melongena is a subgenus of *Volema*.

4. *MELONGENA GALEODES* Lam. W.Pac.
50–75mm. C. Illus. with per.

5. *MELONGENA MELONGENA* L. **W.I.
Crown Conch.** W.I. 70–80–120–170mm. C.
May lack shoulder spines.

6. *VOLEMA (?Melongena) MYRISTICA*
Röd. **Heavy Crown Conch.** Japan. 34–45–
65–80mm. UC.

7. *MELONGENA PARADISIACA* Röd. S.
E.Afr.-Sing. Avg.44–52mm. C. Syn. for *Volema
pyrum* Gm.

8. *MELONGENA PATULA* Brod. & Sow.
Pacific Crown Conch. No.G.of Cal.-Pan. 65–
75–125–212mm. C. May have spines. Thick
fibrous per.

9. *PUGILINA COCHLIDIUM* L. **Winding
Stair Shell.** Ind.Oc.-W.Pac. ca.65–75–100–
150mm. UC. Syn.: *Volegalea wardiana* Iredale.
?Syn.: *Melongena pugilina* Born. *Pugilina* is a
subgenus of *Volema*.

10. *PUGILINA COLOSSEUS* Lam. **Giant
Stair Shell.** Japan. ca.100–150–250–388mm.
UC. Hairy per.

11. *PUGILINA MORIO* L. **Giant Hairy
Melongena.** Martinique-Brazil; also, Mauritania-
Angola. 75–100–125–>160mm. C. May lack
shoulder spines. Thick per.

12. *BUSYCON CANALICULATUM* L.
Channeled Whelk. Mass.-Fla.; also, No.Cal.
ca.100–125–175–215mm. C. Thick velvety
golden-brown per. Rarely, sinistral form. Illus. is
of juvenile.

13. *BUSYCON CARICA* Gm. **Knobbed
Whelk.** Mass.-Fla. ca.100–125–175–241mm. C.
Rarely, sinistral form from N.J.

14. *BUSYCON COARCTATUM* Sow.
Turnip Whelk. Bay of Campeche, Mex. 100–
110–140–195mm. UC (was R).

15. *BUSYCON PERVERSUM* L. **Lightning,
Perverse** or **Left-handed Whelk.** N.J.-Fla.-
Gulf States-Yucatan. ca.60–75–150–370mm.
VC. Color variable. Also, albino from (R). Syn.:
B.contrarium Conrad.

16. *BUSYCON SPIRATUM* Lam. **True Pear
Whelk.** N.C.-Fla.-Texas-Yucatan. 50–75–125–
>200mm. C. Rarely, sinistral form. Syn.: *B.
pyrum* Dillwyn.

17. *SYRINX ARUANUS* L. **False Trumpet
Shell.** Arafura Sea-Qld. 250–300–500–>700mm.
UC. The largest living gastropod. Thick brown

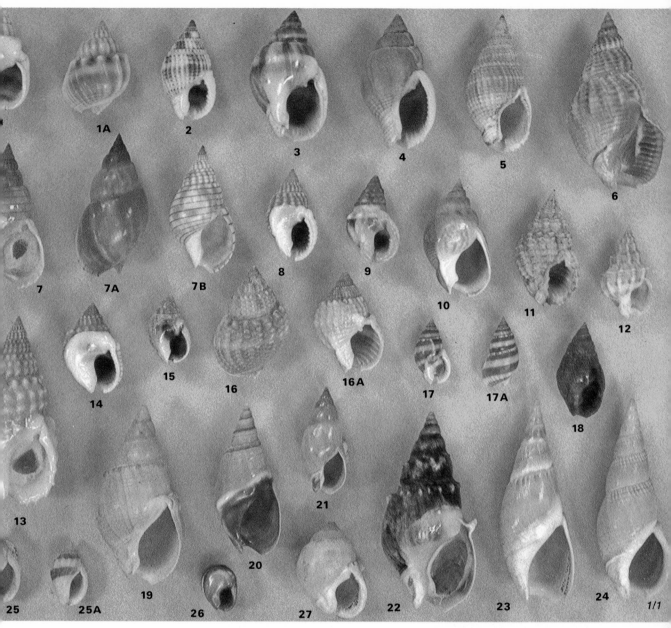

per. Horny operc. Juveniles have cylindrical apex. Edible.

Plate 89

1. NASSARIUS ARCULARIUS L. **Little Box Dog Whelk.** S.E.Afr.-Fiji. 18–22–27–30mm. C. Syn. for genus: **Nassa.**

2. NASSARIUS BICOLOR Dunker. Ind.Oc.-W.Pac., esp.Qld. 18–25mm. C. ?Syn. for **N. albescens** Dunker.

3. NASSARIUS CORONATUS Brug. **Coronated Dog Whelk.** S.E.Afr.-W.Pac. 25–32mm. C.

4. NASSARIUS DORSATUS Röd. W.Pac. 25–30–38–45mm. C.

5. NASSARIUS EUGLYPTUS Sow. W.Pac. 25–33mm. C. ?Syn. for **N.crematus** Hinds.

6. NASSARIUS FOSSATUS Gould. **Channeled** or **Giant Western Dog Whelk, Nassa** or **Basket Shell.** Br.Col.-Baja Cal. 35–38–45–50mm. C.

7. NASSARIUS GLANS L. **Acorn Dog Whelk.** S.E.Afr.-W.Pac. 30–32–40–50mm. C. Variable color.

8. NASSARIUS LIVESCENS Philippi. W.

Pac., esp.Japan. Avg.20–25mm. C.

9. NASSARIUS LUTEOSTOMA Brod. & Sow. G.of Cal.-Peru. 18–22mm. C.

10. NASSARIUS MUTABILIS L. Med. 17–20–25–28mm. VC.

11. NASSARIUS MYRISTICATUS Hinds. Nicaragua-Pan. Avg.28–32mm. C.

12. NASSARIUS PAGODUS Reeve. Baja Cal.-G.of Cal.-Ecu. 15–18–22–25mm. C.

13. NASSARIUS PAPILLOSUS L. **Papillose Dog Whelk.** E.Afr.-Poly., Haw. 25–35–45–50mm. UC.

14. NASSARIUS PULLUS L. **Olive Dog Whelk.** E.Afr.-W.Pac. Avg.18–22mm. C. ?Syn. for **N.arcularius plicatus** Röd.

15. NASSARIUS TEGULUS Reeve. **Western Mud Dog Whelk** or **Slate Nassa.** C.Cal.-Baja Cal. Avg.17–19mm. C.

16. NASSARIUS VARIEGATUS A.Adams. **Jewelled Dog Whelk.** S.E.Afr.-W.Pac. 22–25–28–30mm. C. Syn.: **N.gemmulata** Gray or Lam.

17. NASSARIUS ZONALIS A.Adams. Japan-Ryukyu Is. 16–20mm. UC.

18. ILYANASSA OBSOLETA Say. **Eastern Mud Whelk, Black Dog Whelk** or **Mud Basket Shell.** G.of St. Lawrence-N.E.Fla.; also, Br.Col.-C.Cal. 18–25mm. VC. Usually eroded. Formerly considered subgenus of **Nassarius.**

19. BULLIA ANNULATA Lam. S.Afr. 40–45–50–60mm. C. Syn. for genus: **Dorsanum.**

20. BULLIA CALLOSA Gray. Angola-S.Afr. Avg.35–40mm. C. Color variable. Dark brown when fresh.

21. BULLIA MIRAN Brug. Mauritania-Senegal. 20–30mm. C.

22. DORSANUM MONILIFERUM Val. Argentina. Avg.40–48mm. UC.

23. BULLIA NATALENSIS Krauss. S.Afr.-Moz. 38–42–48–55mm. UC.

24. BULLIA VITTATUM L. Ind.Oc. 35–38–45–50mm. C.

25. CYLLENE LYRATA Lam. W.Afr. Avg. 15–18mm. C.

26. CYCLOPE NERITEA L. S.W.Eur.-Med.-Black Sea. 8–10–12–17mm. C.

27. DEMOULIA RETUSA Lam. S.Afr. 20–27mm. C. Color and pattern variable.

Plate 90 | Fasciolariidae

1. *CYRTULUS SEROTINUS* Hinds. New Cal., Poly.-Marq. Avg.70–80mm. S. Syn. for genus: *Clavella*.

2. *FASCIOLARIA AURANTIACA* Lam. **Orange Band Shell.** N.coast of S.Am.-Brazil. 70–100–110–125mm. S.

3. *FASCIOLARIA HUNTERIA* Perry. **Banded Tulip.** N.C.-Fla.-Alabama. 60–65–90–120mm. C. ?Subsp. of **F.lilium** Fischer.

4. *FASCIOLARIA LILIUM TORTUGANA* Hollister. Fla. 50–60–85–100mm. UC.

5. *FASCIOLARIA TARENTINA* Lam. W Med. Avg.32–38mm. C.

6. *FASCIOLARIA TULIPA* L. **True Tulip.** N.C.-Fla.-Texas, W.I.-Brazil. 60–75–150–275mm. C. Pale orange to red, brown.

7. *PLEUROPLOCA FILAMENTOSA* Röd.

Threaded Band Shell. E.Afr.-W.Pac. 60–100–125–140mm. C. *Pleuroploca* also treated as subgenus of *Fasciolaria*.

8. *PLEUROPLOCA GIGANTEA* Kiener. **Florida Horse Conch.** N.C.-Fla.-Texas-Yucatan. 125–200–400–ca.600mm. C. Variable color. Juveniles bright reddish orange. Thick flaky brown per. Horny oval brown operc. Second largest gastropod in the world.

9. *PLEUROPLOCA GRANOSA* Brod. G.of Cal.-Peru. 80–100–150–175mm. C. Dark reddish brown per.

10. *PLEUROPLOCA PRINCEPS* Sow. **Panama Horse Conch.** G.of Cal.-Ecu. 150–175–250–400mm. C. Smooth brown per. Ridged operc.

11. *PLEUROPLOCA SALMO* Wood. **Granose Horse Conch.** G.of Cal.-Peru. 80–

100–125–152mm. C. Rough brown per.

12. *PLEUROPLOCA TRAPEZIUM* L. S.E. Afr.-W.Pac., esp.Japan. 90–100–125–248mm. C. Flaky brown per. Syn.: **P.audouini** Jonas.

1. LATIRUS ARMATUS A.Adams. Senegal; Madeira, Canary Is. 40–55mm. UC.

2. LATIRUS BELCHERI Reeve. W.Pac. to Fiji. 30–35–50–63mm. UC.

3. LATIRUS CARINIFERUS McGINTYI Pilsbry. S.E.Fla.-W.I. 45–50–70–80mm. UC. UC.

4. LATIRUS FILOSUS Schubert & Wagner. Gabon-Angola. 40–45–55–62mm. UC.

5. LATIRUS INFUNDIBULUM Gm. **Brown-lined Latirus** or **Spindle**. S.E.Fla.-W.I.-Brazil. 40–50–65–75mm. UC (Fla.: S).

6. LATIRUS KANDAI Kuroda. Japan. Avg. 36–40mm. UC.

7. LATIRUS MEDIAMERICANUS Hertlein & Strong. W.Mex.-Ecu. Avg.50–55mm. UC. Thick brown per.

8. LATIRUS NODATUS Gm. **Nodular, Knobbed Latirus** or **Spindle**. W.Pac., Haw. 70–75–85–102mm. UC. Syn.: **L.nodus** Martyn.

9. LATIRUS POLYGONUS Gm. S.E.Afr.-W.Pac. 40–55–70–105mm. C. Brown per.

10. LATIRUS RUDIS Reeve. W.Pan. Avg. 36–44mm. C. Olive-brown per.

11. LATIRUS TURRITUS Gm. W.Pac. 30–35–45–55mm. C.

12. LEUCOZONIA CERATA Wood. So.G. of Cal.-Pan., Galáp. 35–40–60–90mm. C. Deep brown per. Also placed under **Latirus**.

13. LEUCOZONIA NASSA Gm. **Chestnut Latirus** or **Common Lesser Tulip Shell**. Fla.-Texas, W.I.-Brazil. 35–50mm. C.

14. LEUCOZONIA OCELLATA Gm. **White-spotted Latirus**. S.E.Fla.-W.I.-Brazil. 19–27mm. C (Fla.: R).

15. LEUCOZONIA (Latirolagena) SMARAG-DULUS L. **Precious Stone Shell**. W.-C.Pac. 34–38–45–50mm. VC. Dark brown furry per.

16. OPEATOSTOMA PSEUDODON Burrow. **Banded Tooth** or **Thorn Latirus**. So. G.of Cal.-Peru. 35–45–55–64mm. C. Syn.: **Leucozonia cingulata** Lam.

17. PERISTERNIA AUSTRALIENSIS Reeve. W.Pac., esp.Aust. Avg.25–32mm. C.

18. PERISTERNIA FASTIGIUM Reeve. Ind.Oc.-Fiji. Avg.25–30mm. UC. Syn.: **P. rhodostoma** Dunker.

19. "PERISTERNIA INCARNATA" Kiener. **Flesh-colored Peristernia**. N.W.-N.Aust.-E.Qld. 23–30mm. C. Preoccupied name; not **P.incarnata** Deshayes.

20. PERISTERNIA NASSATULA Lam. S.E. Afr.-W.Pac. 30–40mm. C.

Plate 92 | Fasciolariidae

1. *FUSINUS AMBUSTUS* Gould. **Scorched Spindle.** G.of Cal.-W.Mex. 35–40–50–71mm. C. Syn. for genus: *Fusus*.

2. *FUSINUS AUSTRALIS* Q. & G. **Australian** or **Southern Spindle.** W.Aust.-Vic. Avg.75–110mm. C. Horny operc.

3. *FUSINUS COLPOICUS* Dall. G.of Cal. Avg.60–66mm. C.

4. *FUSINUS COLUS* L. **Distaff Spindle.** S. E.Afr.-C.Pac. 75–100–150–190mm. C. Light buff per.

5. *FUSINUS DUPETITTHOUARSI* Kiener. **DuPetit's** or **Ornamented Spindle.** Baja Cal.-G.of Cal.-Ecu. ca.100–125–200–250mm. C. Fibrous pale yellow-brown per. (illus.).

6. *FUSINUS FERRUGINEUS* Kuroda & Habe. Japan. Avg.85–100mm. UC.

7. *FUSINUS FORCEPS* Perry. Japan. 100–120–160–220mm. UC. A form from India lacks ridges on the whorls.

8. *FUSINUS FREDBAKERI* Lowe. G.of Cal.-W.Mex. Avg.38–48mm. C.

9. *FUSINUS IRREGULARIS* Grabau. **Irregular Spindle.** Baja Cal.-G.of Cal. 85–100–150–233mm. UC.

10. *FUSINUS KOBELTI* Dall. C.-S.Cal. 30–40–55–65mm. UC. Thick pale brown per.

11. *FUSINUS (Aptyxis) LUTEOPICTA* Dall. **Painted Spindle.** S.Cal.-Baja Cal. 19–27mm. C.

12. *FUSINUS NICOBARICUS* Röd. **Nicobar Spindle.** W.Pac.-Poly., Haw. 75–100–135–150mm. C.

13. *FUSINUS PANAMENSIS* Dall. W.Mex.-Ecu. 75–90–120–150mm. UC. Olive per.

14. *FUSINUS PERPLEXUS* A.Adams. **Perplexed Spindle.** W.Pac., esp.Japan. 75–100–130–>140mm. C. Thick pale yellowish per. Cp. *F.ferrugineus*.

15. *FUSINUS ROSTRATUS* Olivi. W.Med., Morocco. 25–30–50–70mm. UC.

16. *FUSINUS SYRACUSANUS* L. W.Med. 25–30–45–60mm. C.

17. *FUSINUS TORULOSUS* Lam. S.Afr.-Moz. Avg.75–90mm. UC.

18. *FUSINUS TUBERCULATUS* Lam. W. Pac. 100–120–160–175mm. C.

19. *GRANULIFUSUS HAYASHII* Habe. Japan-Tai. 44–50–60–63mm. UC.

20. *GRANULIFUSUS NIPPONICUS* Smith. Japan-Tai. 32–45–60–65mm. C.

2/3

1. CYMBIUM CYMBIUM L. **False Elephant's Snout.** Canary Is.-Senegal. 100–130–150–200mm. C. Tan to reddish-brown; dead shells may be ivory. Brown per. Heavy. Syn.: *C. porcina* Lam.

2. CYMBIUM MARMORATUM Link. **Marble Cymbium.** Senegal. 100–120–140–175mm. UC. Marbled white and brownish-red. Thin brown per. Syn.: *C.gracilis* Broderip.

3. CYMBIUM OLLA L. Portugal-Algeria-Morocco. 85–100–120–150mm. UC. Reddish-brown. Thin tan per.

4. CYMBIUM PEPO Lightfoot. **African Neptune Volute.** W.Sahara-Dahomey. 130–150–175–270mm. UC. Brownish-red, often with white mottling. Thick brown per. Syn.: *C. neptuni* Gm.; *C.patulum* Brod.; *?C.tritonis* Brod.

5. CYMBIUM CUCUMIS Röd. Senegal. 100–120–140–180mm. UC. Tan shell and per. Aperture chestnut brown. Cp. *C.cymbium.* Syn.: *C.rubiginosa* Swainson.

6. CYMBIUM GLANS Gm. **Elephant's Snout.** Senegal-G.of Guinea-?Angola. 100–200–250–362mm. C. Creamy brown, rim often dark brown; creamy-orange aperture. Dark brown per. Syn.: *C.proboscidalis* Lam.

7. CYMBIUM MAROCANUS Pallary. **Moroccan Cymbium.** Morocco-W.Sahara. 95–110–130–155mm. S. Pale brown, often with whitish blotches; flesh aperture.

8. CYMBIUM PACHYUS Pallary. Cameroon. 90–100–110–127mm. UC. Heavy. Reddish-brown.

Plate 94 | Volutidae

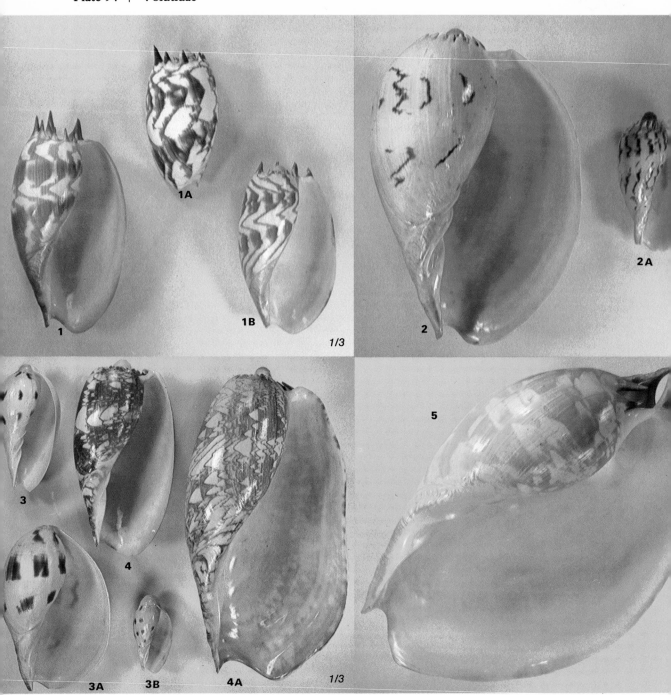

1A

1

1B

1/3

2

2A

3

4

5

3A

3B

4A

1/3

1. *MELO AMPHORA* Lightfoot. **Giant Baler** or **Melon Shell.** Ind.Oc.-W.Aust.-Qld.-N.G. 125–200–250–483mm. C. Heavy. Variable pattern. Thin brown per. Syn.: *M.diadema* Lam.

2. *MELO BRODERIPII* Gray. P.I. 90–200–250–355mm. VC. Often confused with *Melo aethiopicus* L., **Ethiopian Volute,** a scarce sp. from N.G. with fewer, less erect spines that are higher than the protoconch (not illus.).

3. *MELO MELO* Lightfoot. **Indian Volute.** India-Sing.-S.China Sea. 125–175–200–362mm. VC. Variable pattern. Thin brown per.

4. *MELO MILTONIS* Gray. **Southern Baler** or **Milton's Melon Shell.** S.W.Aust. <175–200–250–445mm. UC. Variable purplish-brown and cream pattern. Thin brown per. Cp. *M.amphora* (less cylindrical).

5. *MELO UMBILICATUS* Brod. in Sow. **Umbilicate Melon.** Torres Strait-S.Qld. 300– 350–375–424mm. UC. Variable color and pattern. Recurved spines cover protoconch.

1. *VOLUTA (Vol.) ABYSSICOLA* Adams & Reeve. **Abyssal Volute.** W.& E.S.Afr. 45–63–75–105mm. UC. Cp. ***V.lutosa.***

2. *VOLUTA (Fe.) AFRICANA* Reeve. **African Volute.** S.Afr. 42–50–60–75mm. UC.

3. *VOLUTA (Od.) AMERICANA* Reeve. **American Bat Volute.** Brazil. 35–45–55–65mm. UC. Form and color variable.

4. *VOLUTA (Ad.) ANCILLA* Lightfoot. S. Brazil–S.Argentina–Falkland Is. 135–190mm. UC. Deciduous per. Cp. ***V.paradoxa.***

5. *VOLUTA (Ly.) ANNA* Lesson. Maur., Moluccas. 50–63mm. R. Beach spec. only. Spec. illus. is faded.

6. *VOLUTA (Al.) ARABICA* Gm. **Arab** or **Arabic Volute.** N.Z. 75–125–175–195mm. C. Form and color q.v.

7. *VOLUTA (Hap.) ARAUSIACA* Lightfoot. **Vexillate Volute.** N.Sri Lanka. 70–85–105mm.

R. Pattern variable. Syn.: ***V.vexillum*** Gm.

8. *VOLUTA (Ly.) ARCHERI* Angas. W.I. (Montserrat-Martinique). 33–36–39–43mm. R. Illus. spec. dead collected.

9. *VOLUTA (Cym.) AULICA* Sow. **Courtier Volute.** P.I. 75–95–110–165mm. S. Form, col. and patt. q.v. 9A is form ***V.a.cathcartiae*** Reeve, which has little or no coronation.

10. *VOLUTA (Fus.) BARNARDI* Rehder. Off E.S.Afr. 74–85–100–117mm. R. Dull white, but dead shells orange-yellow. Bulbous protoconch. Cp. ***V.clarkei*** (fewer spiral threads). Note: illus. is of ***V.clarkei, V.barnardi*** is illus. on p. 96, no. 1.

11. *VOLUTA (Ly.) BARNESII* Gray. So.G.of Cal.-Peru. 25–26–30–35mm. UC.

– – *VOLUTA BECKII* Brod. – See pl. 101, no. 1.

12. *VOLUTA (Voc.) BEDNALLI* Brazier. N.Aust. 75–80–95–155mm. R (was VR).

13. *VOLUTA (Am.) BENTHALIS* McMichael. Qld. 28–38mm. R. Cp. ***V.undulata*** (larger).

14. *VOLUTA (Ad.) BRASILIANA* Lam. **Brazilian Volute.** S.Brazil-Argentina. 80–85–100–183mm. C.

15. *VOLUTA (Cal.) BULLATIANA* Weaver & duPont. S.Afr. 50–55–62–70mm. UC. Always dead collected. Syn.: ***V.bullata*** Swainson.

16. *VOLUTA (Am.) CANALICULATA* McCoy. **Channeled Volute.** Qld. 30–35–50–69mm. C (once ext.R). White and pink forms.

17. *VOLUTA (Ly.) CASSIDULA* Reeve. Japan. 24–33mm. UC. Dark brown per.

18. *VOLUTA (Fu.) CLARA* Sow.Japan. 55–75–90–120mm. C. Cp. ***V.formosana.*** Form ***V.c. noguchii*** Hayashi has higher spire and bolder spiral sculpture.

Plate 96 | Volutidae

1. *VOLUTA (Fus.) CLARKEI* Rehder. Moz. 50–55–70–98mm. UC (was VR). Thin brownish-pink per. Cp. *V.barnardi*. Note: illus. is of *V. barnardi, V.clarkei* is illus. on pl. 95, no. 10.

2. *VOLUTA (Cyl.) COMPLEXA* Iredale. **Spotted Volute.** Aust. 45–75–85–100mm. C. Also, dwarf form. Syn.: *V.punctata* Swainson.

3. *VOLUTA (Fu.) CONCINNA* Brod. **Notable Japanese Volute.** Japan. 95–125–150–186mm. UC.

4. *VOLUTA (Ly.) CUMINGII* Brod. Baja Cal.-G.of Cal.-Peru. 20–25–30–33mm. C.

5. *VOLUTA (Cym.) CYMBIOLA* Gm. Indon.-N.Aust. 55–60–65–85mm. R (was VR). Light and dark color forms.

6. *VOLUTA (Am.) DAMONII* Gray. W. Aust.-N.Qld. 74–80–95–138mm. UC. Form and pattern q.v. 6B is lightly patterned form *V.d. keatsiana* Ludbrook.

7. *VOLUTA RUPESTRIS* Gm. – See pl. 99, no. 13.

8. *VOLUTA (Ly.) DELESSERTIANA* Petit. **Delessert's Volute.** Mad.-Sey. 42–45–50–55mm. UC (was S). Cp. *V.mitraeformis.*

9. *VOLUTA (Fu.) DELICATA* Fulton. **Delicate Volute.** Japan. 26–30–40–55mm. C.

10. *VOLUTA (Ly.) DELICIOSA* Montrouzier. Qld.-N.S.W.-New Cal. 26–36mm. UC.

11. *VOLUTA (Cym.) DESHAYESI* Reeve. New Cal. 65–70–80–105mm. UC (was R.).

12. *VOLUTA (Sc.) GOULDIANA* Dall. N.C.-E.& W.Fla.-G.of Mex.-Texas. 30–60–80–125mm. S. Several color forms. Syn.: *V.dohrni* Sow.

13. *VOLUTA (Sc.) GOULDIANA FLORIDA* Clench & Aguayo. A form with slightly angled early whorls and faint short axial ribs.

14. *VOLUTA (Zi.) DUFRESNEI* Donovan. **Angular Volute.** Brazil-C.Argentina. 100–120–140–207mm. UC. Form q.v. Syn.: *V.angulata* Swainson.

15. *VOLUTA (Vo.) EBRAEA* L. **Hebrew Volute.** N.-N.E.Brazil. 90–100–120–222mm. UC. Color and pattern variable. Syn.: *V.hebraea* L.

16. *VOLUTA (Am.) ELLIOTI* Sow. **Elliot's Volute.** W.Aust. 50–65–75–110mm. UC. Cp. *V.jamrachi.*

17. *VOLUTA (Am.) EXOPTANDA* Reeve. **Much-desired Volute.** S.Aust. 85–90–100–105mm. R. Do not confuse with *V.(Fu.) exoptanda* Shikama.

1. *VOLUTA (Cym.) FLAVICANS* Gm. **Yellow Volute.** N.T., Aust.-Papua, N.G. 60–70–90–100mm. UC. Heavy. Often with shoulder tubercles. Color and pattern variable.

2. *VOLUTA (Fu.) FORMOSANA* Azuma. Japan-Tai. 50–70–85–133mm. C (was VS). Cp. *V.cancellata, V.clara.*

3. *VOLUTA (Er.) FULGETRA* Sow. **Lightning Volute.** S.Aust. 75–100–135–200mm. S (was UC). Variable color; also, albino form.

4. *VOLUTA (Al.) FUSUS* Quoy & Gaimard. **Spindle** or **Little Volute.** N.Z. 55–65–70–81mm. S. Variable form. Syn.: *V.gracilis* Swainson.

–– *VOLUTA GILCHRISTI* Sow. – See pl. 101, no. 2.

5. *VOLUTA (Am.) GRAYI* Ludbrook. **Shuttle** or **Gray's Volute.** N.T.–S.W.Aust. 45–65–

85–128mm. UC. Also, dwarf form. Syn.: *V. pallida* Griffith & Pidgeon.

6. *VOLUTA (Voc.) GROSSI* Iredale. Qld.-N.S.W. 60–90–120–174mm. R.

7. *VOLUTA (Fu.) HAMILLEI* Crosse. N. Tai.-Japan. 75–100–120–156mm. C. Cp. *V. rupestris.*

8. *VOLUTA (Voc.) HARGREAVESI* Angas. W.Aust. 65–70–85–128mm. R.

9. *VOLUTA (Fu.) HIRASEI* Sow. Japan. 90–120–140–184mm. C.

10. *VOLUTA (Cyt.) HUNTERI* Iredale. **Marbled** or **Marked Volute.** Qld.-N.S.W. 90–100–125–163mm. C. Color variable. Syn.: *V.marmorata* Swainson.

11. *VOLUTA (Cym.) IMPERIALIS* Lightfoot. **Imperial Volute.** P.I. 75–120–150–250mm.

C. Heavy. Pattern variable. Form *V.i.robinsona* Burch has triangular shape; lacks tent-like markings.

12. *VOLUTA (Am.) JAMRACHI* Gray. W. Aust. 45–50–60–70mm. UC. Form rectangularly ovate. Dark spots at suture. Cp. *V.ellioti, V. macandrewi.*

13. *VOLUTA (Tem.) JOHNSONI* Bartsch. Tai.-P.I. 100–130mm. VS (was ext.R). Silky grayish-brown per.

Plate 98 | Volutidae

1. *VOLUTA (Sc.) JUNONIA* Lam. (not Shaw). **Juno's Volute** or **Junonia.** N.C.-E.& W.Fla.-G.of Mex.-Yucatan. 70–75–90–154mm. UC (was S).

2. *VOLUTA (Fu.) KANEKO* Hirase. Tai.-Japan. 100–110–130–167mm. UC (was R). Form variable.

3. *VOLUTA (Ly.) KURODAI* Kawamura. Vietnam-S.China Sea. 57–60–70–95mm. VS. Becoming rarer.

4. *VOLUTA (Hap.) LAPPONICA* L. S.India-N.Sri Lanka. 57–60–75–100mm. C. 4B is a rare deep-water form *V.l.loroisi* Val., with axial stripes.

4B. *VOLUTA (Hap.) LOROISI* Val. S.India. 60–70–90–100mm. R. Was considered form of *V.lapponica.*

5. *VOLUTA (Vol.) LUTOSA* Koch. W.S.Afr. 44–60–75–90mm. UC. Cp. *V.abyssicola.*

6. *VOLUTA (Ly.) LYRAEFORMIS* Swainson. **Lyre-formed Volute.** Kenya. 80–95–110–133mm. VR.

7. *VOLUTA (Am.) MACANDREWI* Sow. W.Aust. <36–40–50–91mm. S (was R). Cp. *V.undulata,* white color form. Dwarf form illus.

8. *VOLUTA (Am.) MACULATA* Swainson. **Maculated Volute.** Qld. 48–55–65–75mm. 7A is golden form. Syn.: *V.caroli* Iredale.

9. *VOLUTA (Cym.) MAGNIFICA* Gebauer. **Magnificent Volute.** S.Qld.-N.S.W. 150–200–225–300mm. UC.

–– *VOLUTA (Li) MAMMILLA* Sow. **False Baler** or **Melon Shell.** S.Aust.-N.S.W. ca.100–200–250–295mm. UC. (Not illus.) Large mammilary protoconch; lacks strong axial ribs of *V. roadnightae.*

10. *VOLUTA (Fu.) MENTIENS* Fulton. Japan. 70–100–125–217mm. C. Cp. *V.daviesi.*

11. *VOLUTA (Ly.) MITRAEFORMIS* Lam. **Southern Lyre Shell** or **Mitre-shaped Volute.** W.Aust.-Vic. 29–38–45–55mm. VC. Also, golden form. Cp. *V.delessertiana.*

12. *VOLUTA (Am.) MOLLERI* Iredale. N.S.W. 63–70–85–105mm. UC (was VR).

13. *VOLUTA (Vo.) MUSICA* L. **Common Music Volute.** W.I. (Dominican Rep.-Greater Ant.)-Venez. 38–50–65–111mm. UC. Form and color q.v. Has operc.

1. *VOLUTA (Cym.) NIVOSA* Lam. **Snowy Volute.** W.Aust. 50–55–65–95mm. C. Color and pattern q.v. 1A–B is form *V.n.oblita* E.A. Smith, with shoulder nodules or spines.

2. *VOLUTA (Cym.) NOBILIS* Lightfoot. **Noble Volute.** Sing.-Tai. 65–80–100–193mm. C. Form, color and pattern q.v. 2A is a juvenile form.

3. *VOLUTA (Er.) PAPILLOSA* Swainson. **Marbled** or **Papillose Volute.** Aust. 65–110–130–150mm. UC. Cp. *V.sericata.*

– – *VOLUTA PARADOXA* Lahille. – See pl. 101, no. 3.

4. *VOLUTA (Na.) PARABOLA* Garrard. **Minute Volute.** Qld. 30–32–35–38mm. S.

5. *VOLUTA (Cyl.) PERISTICTA* Mc-Michael. **Dotted Volute.** Qld. <44–50–55–75mm. Related to *V.pulchra.*

6. *VOLUTA (Cyl.) PERPLICATA* Hedley. **Entangled Volute.** N.E.Aust. 58–75mm. Ext. R. Usually beach spec.

7. *VOLUTA (Fe.) PONSONBYI* E.A.Smith. Off S.Afr. 54–65–75–131mm. VR.

8. *VOLUTA (Am.) PRAETEXTA* Reeve. **Webby Volute.** W.Aust. 39–45–50–67mm. UC.

9. *VOLUTA (Amp.) PRIAMUS* Gm. **Spotted Volute.** Portugal-W.Afr., Canary Is. 45–50–60–80mm. VS.

10. *VOLUTA (Cyl.) PULCHRA* Sow. **Beautiful Volute.** Qld. 40–50–60–90mm. VC. Form, color and pattern q.v. 10C is form *V.p.perryi* Ostergaard & Summers. Another form (not illus.) is *V.nielseni* McMichael.

11. *VOLUTA (Ly.) QUEKETTI* Smith. S. Afr. 36–55mm. Ext.R. Found in fish stomachs or on Xenophora shells. Spec. illus. is faded juvenile.

– – *VOLUTA ROADNIGHTAE* McCoy. – See pl. 101, no. 4.

12. *VOLUTA (Cym.) ROSSINIANA* Bernardi. New Cal. 115–125–140–183mm. VR. Heavy. Wing-like projection on outer lip. Orange aperture. Cp. *V.imperialis* (longer spines).

13. *VOLUTA (Fu.) RUPESTRIS* Gm. **Asian Flame Volute.** W.Tai.-Japan. 78–110–125–146mm. C. Cp. *V.hamillei.*

Plate 100 | Volutidae – Volutomitridae

1. *VOLUTA (Cym.) RUTILA* Brod. **Blood-red Volute.** N.E.Aust. 65–70–85–125mm. C.

1A. *VOLUTA (Cym.) RUTILA NORRISII* Gray. N.G.-Sol. 50–70–85–90mm. C. Color and pattern q.v. This subsp. often has shoulder nodules. Syn.: *V.piperita* Sow.

2. *VOLUTA (Er.) SERICATA* Thornley. **Silk-like Volute.** Qld.-N.S.W. 75–90–100–125mm. UC. Cp. *V.papillosa.*

3. *VOLUTA (Cym.) SOPHIA* Gray. N.T.-N.Qld. 44–50–60–75mm. C. Hollow shoulder spines. Color and pattern variable.

– – VOLUTA SOWERBYI Kiener. – See pl. 101, no. 5.

4. *VOLUTA (Te.) STUDERI* Martens. Qld. 38–50mm. C.

5. *VOLUTA (Al.) SWAINSONI* Marwick.

Southern or **Swainson's Volute.** N.Z. 90–100–125–225mm. C. Form and pattern q.v.

6. *VOLUTA (Ly.) TAIWANICA* Lam. P.I.-Tai.-Japan. 52–70mm. R (was VR). New sp. (1975).

7. *VOLUTA (Cyl.) THATCHERI* McCoy. Coral Sea-New Cal. 50–65–85–125mm. VS (was R).

8. *VOLUTA (Am.) TURNERI* Griffith & Pidgeon. Aust. 40–65–75–81mm. UC. Color and pattern q.v.

9. *VOLUTA (Am.) UNDULATA* Lam. **Wavy Volute.** S.W.Aust.-N.S.W.-Tas. 60–75–85–122mm. C. Form, color and pattern q.v. Also, albino form. Syn.: *V.angasii* Sow.

10. *VOLUTA (No.) VERCONIS* Tate. **Verco's Volute.** W.-S.Aust. 23–25–28–32mm. S.

11. *VOLUTA (Cym.) VESPERTILIO* L. **Bat Volute.** P.I.-N.T., Aust. 45–55–75–142mm. VC. Often with shoulder tubercles. Color and pattern q.v. 11D is pink or rose form. Also, albino and sinistral (11E) forms.

12. *VOLUTA (Cyl.) WISEMANI* Brazier. Qld. 60–85mm. UC. Color and pattern variable. Syn.: *V.randalli* Stokes.

13. *VOLUTA (Am.) ZEBRA* Leach. **Zebra Volute.** N.T.-Qld.-N.S.W. 25–28–38–55mm. VC. Color and pattern q.v. Illus. are golden (13B) and black (13C) color forms. Syn.: *V. lineata* Leach, *V.lineatiana* Weaver & duPont.

14. *VOLUTOMITRA GROENLANDICA* Beck. **False Greenland Miter.** Arctic-Norway; Arctic-Mass. 10–15–25–30mm. UC. Now considered to be closely related to Mitridae, rather than Volutidae.

2/3

1. *VOLUTA (Ad.) BECKII* Brod. S.Brazil-S.Argentina-Falkland Is. 220–250–275–455mm. S.

2. *VOLUTA (Ne.) GILCHRISTI* Sow. E. S.Afr. 100–125–150–216mm. UC. Dull tan per. Horny operc. Do not confuse with *V. (Vol.) gilchristi* Sow.

3. *VOLUTA (Ad.) PARADOXA* Lahille. **Paradox Volute.** S.Argentina-Falkland Is. 100–150–175–200mm. VS. Heavy. Only beach spec. Cp. *V.ancilla* (lighter; narrow aperture).

4. *VOLUTA (Li.) ROADNIGHTAE* McCoy. W.Aust., Vic. 110–130–160–225mm. VS (was UC).

5. *VOLUTA (Er.) SOWERBYI* Kiener. **Spindle-shaped Volute.** Aust.-Tas. 95–125–150–224mm. UC.

Plate 102 | Harpidae

1. HARPA AMOURETTA Röd. **Minor** or **Lesser Harp.** Moz.-E.Afr.-Red Sea-Marq., Haw.(R). 40–45–55–65mm. C. Form variable. Syn.: **H.minor** Lam. **H.a.crassa** (not illus.) is a form. See also no. 7.

2. HARPA ARTICULARIS Lam. **Articulate Harp.** Thailand-Fiji. ca.50–60–80–96mm. C. Deep brown, salmon and flesh bands across ribs. Syn.: **H.nobilis** Lam. Note: There has been much confusion in the naming of the various common I-P Harps.

3. HARPA COSTATA L. **Imperial Harp.** Mad., Maur. ca.60–70–90–110mm. VR. Syn.: **H.imperialis** Lam.

4. HARPA CRENATA Swainson. **Crenated Harp.** Baja Cal.-So.G.of Cal.-Col. 50–55–70–97mm. C.

– – HARPA DAVIDUS Röd. (not illus.). S.E.Afr.-Ind.Oc. to Indon. 60–65–90–119mm. C. Single well-spaced reddish-brown lines cross ribs.

5. HARPA MAJOR Röd. – See no. 9.

6. HARPA DORIS Röd. **Rosy** or **Rose Harp.** Senegal-Angola, C.V. Ascension Is. ca.40–50–65–77mm. R. Syn.: **H.rosea** Lam.

7. HARPA AMOURETTA Röd. – See no. 1.

8. HARPA HARPA L. **Noble** or **Common Harp.** E.Afr.-Tonga, Haw.(VR). 60–65–90–108mm. C. Groups of thin dark brown lines cross ribs. Syn.: **H.nobilis** Röd.

9. HARPA MAJOR Röd. **Swollen Harp.** E.Afr.-Marquesas, Haw. 60–65–90–126mm. C. Broad pinkish-brown bands cross ribs. Syn.: **H.conoidalis** Lam.

10. HARPA VENTRICOSA Lam. Red Sea, E.Afr.-W.-C.Ind.Oc. ca.60–65–90–110mm. C. Ribs are crossed by broad salmon and tan bands alternating with thin cream bands. Formerly called "H.major".

1/2

1/2

1/2

1/2

1 to 10. *HARPA* reverses. See descriptions in previous plate.

11. *TURBINELLA ANGULATA* Lightfoot. **West Indian Chank** or **Lamp Shell.** Fla.Keys (R), Bahamas, Cuba, Yucatan–E.Pan. 170–200–275–365mm. C. Very heavy. Thick pale brown per. Very rarely sinistral. Genus name changed from *Xancus* in 1957.

12. *TURBINELLA LAEVIGATA* Anton. **Brazilian Chank.** N.E.Brazil. Avg.100–130mm. UC. Heavy.

13. *TURBINELLA PYRUM* L. **Indian Chank.** India–Sri Lanka. 100–115–140–217mm. VC. Very heavy. Thick fibrous brown per. Sinistral spec., deeply revered by Buddhists and Hindus, are ext.R.

14. *VASUM (Altivasum) FLINDERSI* Verco. **Flinder's Vase.** S.Aust. Avg.130–160mm. R. Illus. here, but proper order is on pl. 107, following no. 26.

Plate 104 | Olividae

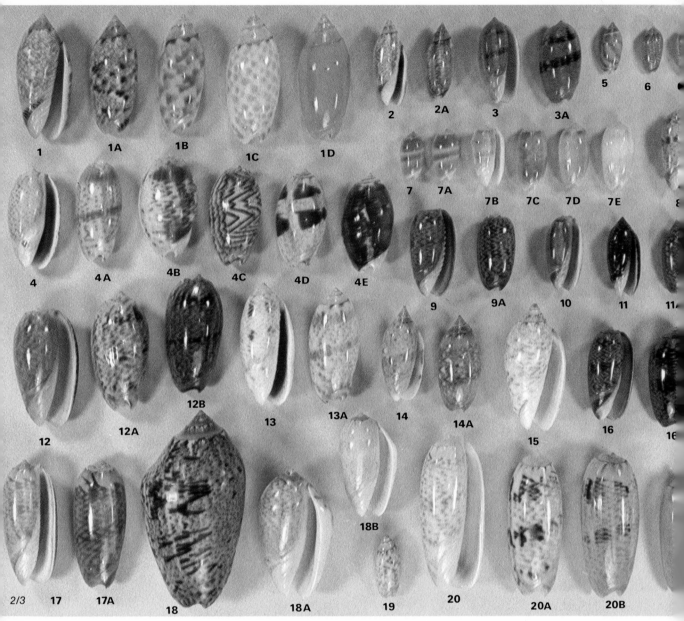

1. OLIVA ANNULATA Gm. E.Afr.-W.Pac., esp.P.I. 30–58mm. VC. Color and pattern q.v. Several color forms.

2. OLIVA AUSTRALIS Duclos. **Southern Olive.** W.Aust.-Vic., N.G. 20–22–30–32mm. C.

3. OLIVA BULBIFORMIS Duclos. **Bulb-shaped Olive.** P.I.-Moluccas-Sol. 21–25–32–35mm. C.

4. OLIVA BULBOSA Röd. S.E.Afr.-Red Sea-Ind.Oc.-Indon. 20–27–35–50mm. VC. Color and pattern q.v. Many color forms.

5. OLIVA BULOUI Sow. N.G.-New Britain-Sol. 16–18–25–30mm. UC.

6. OLIVA CALDANIA Duclos. Indon.-W.-N.Aust. 10–13–17–22mm. C. ?Form of **O. australis**.

7. OLIVA CARNEOLA Gm. **Carnelian Olive.** Indon.-Fiji. 13–15–19–24mm. VC. Several color forms incl. albino.

8. OLIVA CAROLINIANA Duclos. Moz.-Red Sea-S.W.Pac. 25–30mm. UC. Violet mouth. Cp. **O.mustelina.**

9. OLIVA CONCAVOSPIRA Sow. P.I.-Tai.-Japan. 25–30–35–44mm. UC.

10. OLIVA DACTYLIOLA Duclos. Indon.-Fiji. 30–35mm. UC.

11. OLIVA DUCLOSI Reeve. Tai.-Japan-Poly. 20–30mm. UC.

12. OLIVA ELEGANS Lam. Moz.-W.Pac. 30–35–40–50mm. VC. Color and pattern variable.

13. OLIVA EPISCOPALIS Lam. **Episcopal Olive.** E.Afr.-W.Pac., esp.P.I.-N.G.-Tas. ca. 30–40–50–58mm. VC. Violet inside mouth. Color and pattern q.v.

14. OLIVA FLAMMULATA Lam. N. Mauritania-Angola, C.V. 22–25–32–37mm. C. Also, yellowish and golden forms.

15. OLIVA FULGURATOR Röd. **Fusiform Olive.** W.I.-Lower Carib. 38–42–50–59mm. UC.

16. OLIVA FUNEBRALIS Lam. Sing.-W. Pac. 27–30–38–43mm. C.

17. OLIVA HIRASEI Kuroda & Habe. P.I.-Tai.-Japan. 35–45mm. UC.

18. OLIVA INCRASSATA Lightfoot. **Angled, Angulate** or **Giant Olive.** Baja Cal.-G.of Cal.-Peru. 32–40–50–95mm. VC. Heavy.

Also, golden (18B), albino and black (VR) forms.

19. OLIVA KALEONTINA Duclos. **Woven Olive.** So.G.of Cal.-Peru, Galáp. 17–19–23–33mm. VS.

20. OLIVA LIGNARIA Marrat. **Ornate Olive.** India-P.I.-N.Aust. 32–42–50–65mm. VC. Variable color. Also, albino, golden (20C) and brown forms. Syn.: **O.ornata** Marrat.

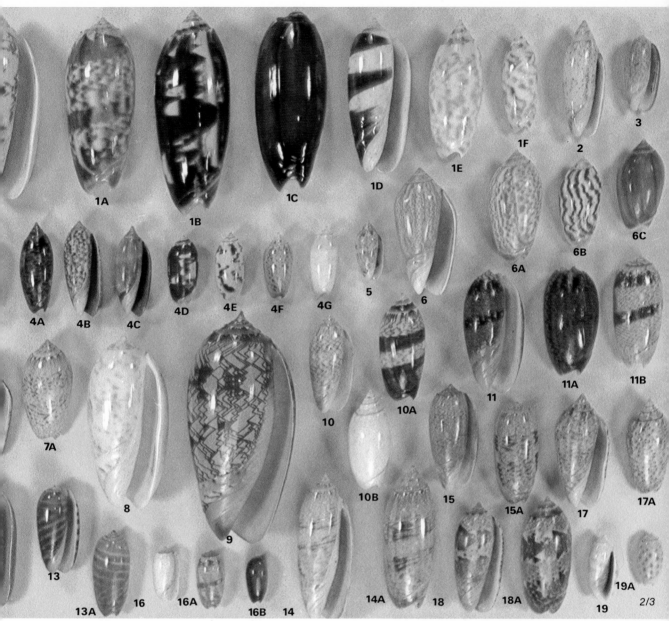

1. *OLIVA MINIACEA* Röd. **Red-mouthed** or **Pacific Olive.** P.I.-Tai.-Japan. 45–55–65–91mm. VC. Color and pattern ext.v. Several color forms. Cp. *O.tremulina.* Syn.: *O. erythrostoma* Lam., *O.porphyritica* Marrat.

2. *OLIVA MULTIPLICATA* Reeve. **Many-plaited Olive.** W.Pac., esp.Tai. 32–35–40–44mm. C.

3. *OLIVA MUSTELINA* Lam. India-P.I.-Japan. 29–32–38–49mm. C. Cp. *O.caroliniana.*

4. *OLIVA OLIVA* Röd. **Common Olive.** India-W.Pac. 18–22–30–40mm. VC. Color and pattern ext.v. Many forms, incl. albino and golden.

5. *OLIVA PAXILLUS* Reeve. E.Afr.-W.Pac. 12–27mm. C. Illus. is subsp. *O.p.sandwicensis* Pease, **Hawaiian Olive,** from Haw., avg.12–15mm.

6. *OLIVA PERUVIANA* Lam. **Peruvian Olive.** Peru-Chile. 32–35–40–50mm. C. Form, color and pattern q.v. Several forms.

7. *OLIVA POLPASTA* Duclos. **Polpast Olive.** Baja Cal.-G.of Cal.-Ecu. 19–32–38–42mm. C. Also, gold-banded form (7A).

8. *OLIVA PONDEROSA* Gm. **Ponderous** Olive. Ind.Oc. 45–50–70–85mm. C. ?Form of *O.miniacea.*

9. *OLIVA PORPHYRIA* L. **Tent** or **Camp Olive.** G.of Cal.-Pan., Galáp. 60–75–95–121mm. UC.

10. *OLIVA RETICULARIS* Lam. **Netted Olive.** S.E.Fla.-W.I.-Brazil, Berm. 25–30–38–58mm. C. Several forms, incl. albino (10B). Cp. *O.sayana.*

11. *OLIVA RETICULATA* Röd. **Blood Olive.** Ind.Oc.-New Cal. 32–38–45–50mm. C. Several color forms. Syn.: *O.sanguinolenta.*

12. *OLIVA RUBROLABIATA* H.Fischer. New Heb.-New Cal. 38–44–46–47mm. VR. Light and dark forms. The rarest olive.

13. *OLIVA RUFULA* Duclos. **Reddish Olive.** Moluccas-P.I. 25–28–35–38mm. C.

14. *OLIVA SAYANA* Ravenal. **Lettered Olive.** N.C.(R)-Fla.(R)-Gulf States, Cuba, Brazil. ca.30–40–50–83mm. VC. Pattern q.v. Also, albino and golden yellow forms. Cp. *O. reticularis.* Syn.: *O.litterata* Lam.

15. *OLIVA SCRIPTA* Lam. **Inscribed Olive.** W.I. 25–30–38–50mm. C. Syn.: *O.caribaeensis* Dall & Simpson.

16. *OLIVA SIDELIA* Duclos. Ind.Oc.-Sol. 17–23mm. C. 3 color forms.

17. *OLIVA SPICATA* Röd. **Veined Olive.** G.of Cal.-Pan. 25–30–38–85mm. VC. Color and pattern q.v. Many color forms, incl. albino.

18. *OLIVA SPLENDIDULA* Sow. **Splendid Olive.** W.Mex.-Pan. 35–38–45–50mm. UC.

19. *OLIVA TESSELLATA* Lam. **Tesselated Olive.** Ind.Oc.-New Cal. 18–19–25–36mm. C.

Plate 106 | Olividae

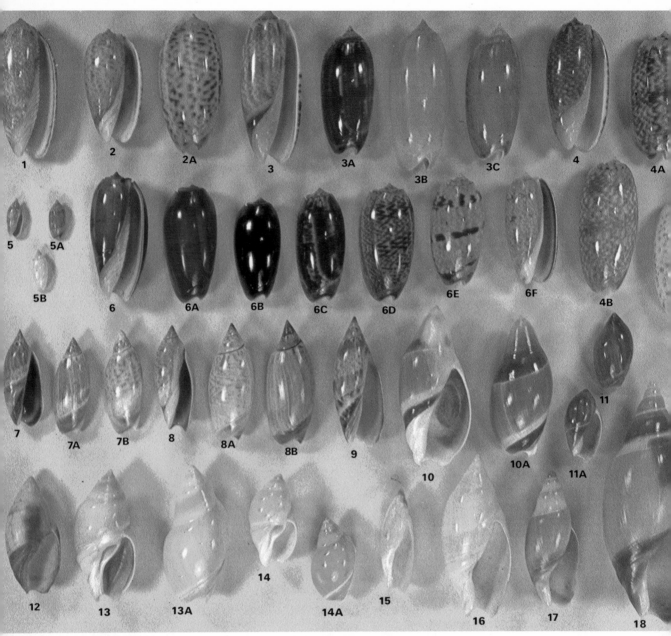

1. OLIVA TEXTILINA Lam. **Orange-mouthed Olive.** E.Afr.-W.Pac. 50–60–75–105mm. UC. Syn.: **O.sericea** Röd.

2. OLIVA TIGRINA Lam. **Tiger Olive.** E. Afr.-Red Sea-New Cal. 25–35–40–60mm. C.

3. OLIVA TREMULINA Lam. E.Afr.-W.Pac. 30–45–50–102mm. UC. Several color forms. Fleshy white aperture. Cp. **O.miniacea.**

4. OLIVA TRICOLOR Lam. **Three-colored Olive.** Ind.Oc.-W.Pac. 38–40–45–58mm. C.

5. OLIVA UNDATELLA Lam. Baja Cal.-G.of Cal.-Ecu. 12–18mm. C. 5B is an albino form. Resembles an **Olivella.**

6. OLIVA VIDUA Röd. **Moor Olive.** Ind. Oc.-W.Pac. ca.28–40–50–60mm. C. Color and pattern q.v. Many color forms. Syn.: **O.oliva** of various authors (not L.).

7. AGARONIA HIATULA Gm. N. Mauritania-Dahomey. 35–50mm. C.

8. AGARONIA TESTACEA Lam. **Panama False Olive.** No.G.of Cal.-Peru. ca.25–35–50–66mm. C.

9. AGARONIA TRAVASSOSI Morretes. Brazil. 48–60mm. S.

10. ANCILLA ALBICALLOSA Lischke. Japan. ca.46–70mm. C.

11. ANCILLA CINNAMOMEA Lam. Red Sea, E.Afr.-Ind.Oc. 19–32mm.

12. ANCILLA CONTUSA Reeve. S.Afr. 40–52mm. UC.

13. ANCILLA GLABRATA L. Lower Carib.-Brazil. 30–75mm. UC. Cream to orange.

14. ANCILLA LIENARDI Bernardi. Venez.-N.Brazil. ca.25–38mm. UC.

15. ANCILLA MUSCAE Pilsbry. **Elongate Ancilla.** N.W.-N.Aust. ca.30–63mm. C. Very thin. Syn.: **A.elongata** Gray.

16. ANCILLA TANKERVILLEI Swainson. Venez.-Brazil. 50–75mm. UC.

17. ANCILLISTA CINGULATA Sow. **Australian Olive.** N.-E.Aust. 38–91mm. UC.

18. ANCILLISTA VELESIANA Iredale. **Girdled Ancilla.** Qld.-N.S.W. 50–55–75–95mm. UC.

1. *BARYSPIRA AUSTRALIS* Sow. Indon., N.Z. 32–38mm. C.

2. *BARYSPIRA MAMMILLA* Sow. Tai.-Japan. 32–38mm. C. Syn.: *A.suavis* Yokoyama.

3. *BARYSPIRA MUCRONATA* Sow. **Brown Olive.** N.Z. 35–45mm. C.

4. *BARYSPIRA URASIMA* Taki. Japan. 32–37mm. C.

5. *OLIVANCILLARIA ACUMINATA* Lam. W.Sahara-Congo. 30–40–60–70mm. C.

6. *OLIVANCILLARIA AURICULARIA* Lam. Brazil-Argentina. Avg.30–35mm. UC. ?Subsp. of *O.vesica.*

7. *OLIVANCILLARIA DESHAYESIANA* Duclos. Argentina. 25–35mm. C.

8. *OLIVANCILLARIA GIBBOSA* Born. E. Afr.-Ind.Oc. 40–50–65–75mm. C. Color q.v. Also, albino form.

9. *OLIVANCILLARIA NEBULOSA* Lam. Ind.Oc.-Indon. 40–50–70–78mm. C.

10. *OLIVANCILLARIA STEERIAE* Reeve. E.-S.Brazil. Avg.40mm. C.

11. *OLIVANCILLARIA URCEUS* Röd.

Brazil-Argentina. 40–60mm. C. Syn.: *O.brasiliana* Lam.

12. *OLIVANCILLARIA VESICA* Gm. Brazil-Argentina. Avg.45–55mm. C.

13. *OLIVELLA ANAZORA* Duclos. G.of Cal.-N.Peru. 10–18mm. C.

14. *OLIVELLA BIPLICATA* Sow. **Purple or Two-plaited Dwarf Olive.** Br.Col.-Baja Cal. 20–32mm. VC. Color q.v.

15. *OLIVELLA DAMA* Wood. **Dama Dwarf Olive.** G.of Cal.-W.Mex. 10–22mm. VC.

16. *OLIVELLA GRACILIS* Brod. & Sow. W.Mex.-Pan. 10–20mm. UC.

17. *OLIVELLA PULCHELLA* Duclos. Mauritania-Zaire, C.V. 12–18mm. C.

18. *OLIVELLA VOLUTELLA* Lam. C.Am.-Ecu.-?Peru. 15–28mm. VC. 2 color forms.

19. *OLIVELLA ZANOETA* Duclos. No. G.of Cal.-Ecu. 15–17mm. C. 2 color forms.

20. *MELAPIUM LINEATUM* Lam. S.Afr. Avg.30mm. UC.

21. *VASUM CAPITELLUM* L. Puerto

Rico-Trinidad, N.coast of S.Am. 50–60–70–75mm. UC.

22. *VASUM CERAMICUM* L. **Ceram Vase** or **Heavy Whelk.** E.Afr.-E.Poly. 80–90–115–161mm. C. Heavy.

23. *VASUM MURICATUM* Born. **Caribbean Vase.** S.Fla.-W.I.-C.Am. 65–90–115–142mm. C. Heavy. Thick dark brown per. Thick dark brown claw-shaped operc.

24. *VASUM RHINOCEROS* Gm. **Rhinoceros Vase.** E.Afr.-Red Sea. Avg.75–85mm. VC.

25. *VASUM TUBIFERUM* Anton. **Imperial Vase.** S.W.Pac. 55–60–70–111mm. C.

26. *VASUM TURBINELLUS* L. **Common Pacific Vase** or **Horned Heavy Whelk.** E.Afr.-W.Poly. ca.40–50–70–85mm. VC.

– – *VASUM (Altivasum) FLINDERSI* Verco. **Flinder's Vase.** S.Aust. Avg. 130–160mm. R. Illus. on pl. 103, no. 14.

125

Plate 108 | Vasidae – Marginellidae

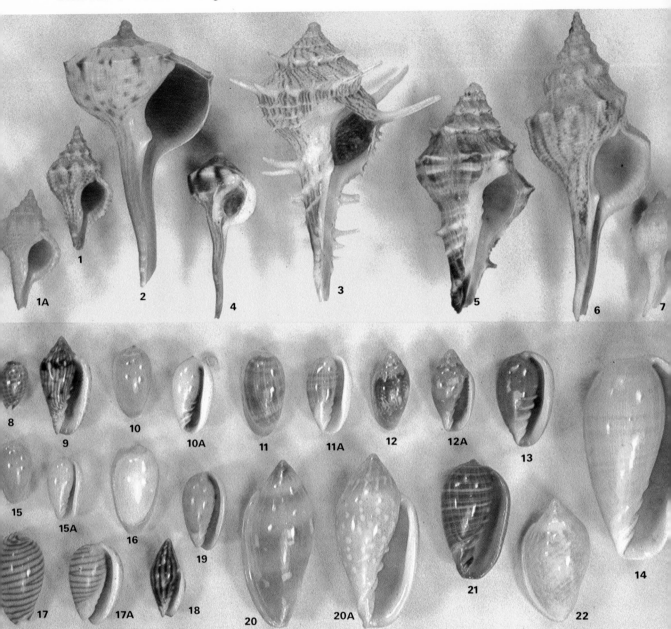

1. TUDICULA AFRA Gm. Mauritania-Guinea. Avg.30–35mm. C.

2. TUDICULA SPIRILLUS L. **Spiral Tudicula** or **Whelk.** India-Sri Lanka. 50–55–70–82mm. S.

3. TUDICULA ARMIGERA A.Adams. **Armored Tudicula** or **Spined Whelk.** N.T.-Qld. 50–60–70–75mm. UC. White to pinkish.

4. TUDICULA INERMIS Angas. **Unspotted Tudicula.** W.Aust.-N.T. Avg.38–50mm. UC.

5. TUDICULA RASILISTOMUM Abbott. **Spineless Whelk.** S.Qld.-N.S.W. 50–55–75–90mm. UC.

6. AFER CUMINGII Reeve. **Cuming's Spindle Whelk.** Tai-S.China Sea. 55–65–70–76mm. C.

7. AFER PORPHYROSTOMA Adams & Reeve. Mauritania, Canary Is. Avg.30–35mm. UC.

(For abbreviations of Marginellidae genera or subgenera see p. 192.)

8. MARGINELLA (Pe.) ACCOLA Roth & Coan. W.Pan. 10–13mm. S.

9. MARGINELLA (Gl.) ADANSONI Kiener. Senegal. 20–25mm. UC.

10. MARGINELLA (Pru.) AMYGDALA Kiener. W.Sahara-Guinea. 8–15–18–22mm. C.

11. MARGINELLA (Bu.) ANGUSTATA Sow. India-Sri Lanka. 13–19–22–25mm. C.

12. MARGINELLA (Gl.) AURANTIA Lam. Senegal. 17–22mm. UC.

13. MARGINELLA (Cry.) BERNARDII Largilliert. Tai. 13–19–22–25mm. C (was S). ?Syn.: **M.tricincta** Hinds.

14. MARGINELLA (Bu.) BULLATA Born. **Bubble Margin Shell.** Brazil. 42–50–60–90mm. UC (was R).

15. MARGINELLA (Pru.) CARNEA Storer. **Orange Margin Shell** or **Ruddy Rim Shell.** Fla.-Carib.-Yucatan. 11–20mm. C.

16. MARGINELLA (Pru.) CINCTA Kiener. Senegal; also, W.I. 18–25mm. UC. See also pl. 109, no. 10.

17. MARGINELLA (Pe.) CINGULATA Dillwyn. **Belted Margin Shell.** W.Sahara-Senegal, Canary Is., C.V. 17–23mm. C. Syn.: **M.lineata** Lam.

18. MARGINELLA (Ma.) CLERYI Petit. Mauritania-Gambia. 18–22mm. UC.

19. MARGINELLA (Pe.) CORNEA Lam. Mauritania-Dahomey, C.V. 16–21–25–29mm. C. Syn.: **M.persicula** Röd.

20. MARGINELLA (Ma.) DESJARDINI Marchad. W.Sahara-Ivory Coast. 30–40–50–56mm. UC. 20A is probably **M.SEBASTIANI** Marche-Marchaud & Rossi. There is much confusion between these two species, **M.glabella** and **M.goodalli.** Cp. **M.glabella, M.goodalli.**

21. MARGINELLA (Cry.) ELEGANS Gm. Burma-S.W.Thailand. 25–32mm. C. Dark red lip.

22. MARGINELLA (Ma.) GLABELLA L. Morocco-Senegal, Canary Is., C.V. Avg.25–32mm. C. Cp. **M.desjardini.**

1. *MARGINELLA (Ma.) GOODALLI* Sow. Senegal-Guinea. 24–30–40–50mm. S (was VS). Cp. *M.desjardini.*

2. *MARGINELLA (Pru.) GUTTATA* Dillwyn. **White-spotted Margin Shell.** S.E. Fla.-W.I. 13–22mm. C.

3. *MARGINELLA (Ma.) HARPAEFORMIS* Sow. Senegal-Equatorial Guinea. 15–20mm. S.

4. *MARGINELLA (Ma.) HELMATINA* Rang. Senegal-Angola. 15–20–30–37mm. UC.

5. *MARGINELLA (Pe.) INTERRUPTO-LINEATA* Mühlfeld. S.Carib.; also, Mauritania-Guinea. 9–13mm. C.

6. *MARGINELLA (Ma.) IRRORATA* Menke. W.Sahara-Senegal. 20–30mm. UC.

7. *MARGINELLA (Pru.) LABIATA* Kiener. **Royal Margin Shell.** W.I.-Yucatan-C.Am. 24–32mm. C (was S). See also no. 12.

8. *MARGINELLA (Cl.) LARGILLIERI* Kiener. E.Brazil. 17–20–25–35mm. S.

9. *MARGINELLA (Gl.) LIMBATA* Lam. Mauritania-Gambia. 22–30mm. UC. Pattern variable. Cp. *M.petitii.*

10. *MARGINELLA (Pru.) CINCTA* Kiener.– See pl. 108, no. 16.

11. *MARGINELLA (Ma.) MOSAICA* Sow. S.Afr. <20–30mm. S. Usually beach spec.

12. *MARGINELLA (Pru.) LABIATA* Kiener. Spec. with immature lip. See no. 7.

13. *MARGINELLA (Ma.) ORNATA* Redfield. S.Afr. 21–32mm. UC. Color variable. Usually beach spec.

14. *MARGINELLA (Pe.) PERSICULA* L. Mauritania-Guinea, C.V. 14–18–22–25mm. C (was S). Pattern variable. *M.p.avellana* Lam. (14C) is a form with smaller dots.

15. *MARGINELLA (Ma.) PETITII* Duval. Mauritania-Sierra Leone. 19–34mm. S. ?Form of *M.(Gl.)limbata.*

16. *MARGINELLA (Ma.) PIPERATA* Hinds. S.Afr. 15–>25mm. C. Banded and yellowish color forms.

17. *MARGINELLA (Af.) PRINGLEI* Tomlin. S.Afr. 70–100–115–126mm. S (was R). Once considered a volute, this is the largest *Marginella.*

18. *MARGINELLA (Pru.) PRUINOSA* Hinds. **Glowing Margin Shell.** W.I.-G.of Mex.-E.Pan. <13–17mm. C.

19. *MARGINELLA (Pru.) PRUNUM* Gm. ?Fla.-S.Carib.-Brazil. 20–27mm. C. Color variable.

20. *MARGINELLA (Ma.) PSEUDOFABA* Sow. Mauritania-Guinea. 26–30–35–44mm. VS.

21. *MARGINELLA (Pru.) ROOSEVELTI* Bartsch & Rehder. Bah.-Carib. Avg.22–25mm. VS. ?Color form of *M.carnea.*

22. *MARGINELLA (Ma.) ROSEA* Lam. **Rose Margin Shell.** S.Afr. 17–28mm. C. Usually beach spec.

23. *MARGINELLA (Pru.) SAPOTILLA* Hinds. W.Pan.-Ecu. 16–20–24–27mm. C.

– – *MARGINELLA SEBASTIANI* – See pl. 108, no. 22.

24. *MARGINELLA (Ma.) STRIGATA* Dillwyn. And.Sea-Sing. 28–32–38–42mm. C (was S). Also, dwarf form.

25. *MARGINELLA (Cry.) VENTRICOSA* G.Fischer. Thailand-Sing. 20–27mm. C.

127

Plate 110 | Mitridae

(For abbreviations of Mitridae genera and subgenera see p. 192.)

1. MITRA (St.) ACUMINATA Swainson. E.Afr.-Poly., Haw. 18–20–25–35mm. C.

2. MITRA (Co.) ACUPICTUM Reeve. W.Pac. 13–23–27–38mm. S.

3. MITRA (Mi.) AMBIGUA Swainson. E. Afr.-Poly., Haw. 39–45–55–70mm. C.

4. MITRA (Su.) ANNULATA Reeve. Maur. 19–23–27–33mm. C.

5. MITRA (St.) AURICULOIDES Reeve. W.Pac. to Haw. Avg.19–23mm. UC.

6. MITRA (Ne.) AURORA Dohrn. **Dawn Miter.** E.Afr.-Red Sea-E.Poly., Haw. 19–21–25–?45mm. S.

7. MITRA (Zi.) BACILLUM Lam. W.Pac. to Poly. 19–25mm. C.

8. MITRA (Mi.) BALDWINI Melvill. Haw. 20–25mm. S.

9. MITRA (Ne.) BELCHERI Hinds. Baja Cal.-Pan. <75–100–120–148mm. UC. Deep brown per.

10. MITRA (Mi.) BOISSACI Montrouzier. W.Pac. 15–19–22–25mm. S.

11. MITRA (Co.) CADAVEROSUM Reeve. E.Afr.-Poly. 13–16–20–25mm. C.

12. MITRA (Ve.) CAFFRUM L. **Negro Miter.** Moz.-W.Pac. 38–40–45–52mm. C.

13. MITRA (Mi.) CALODINOTA Berry. G.of Cal.-C.R. 20–30mm. UC.

14. MITRA (Mi.) CARDINALIS Gm. **Cardinal Miter.** E.Afr.-Poly. 38–45–60–70mm. C.

15. MITRA (Sw.) CASTA Gm. E.Afr.-W. Pac. 20–30–45–52mm. C. Brown band is an epidermis layer.

16. MITRA (Neo.) CLATHRUS Gm. G.of Aden.-Poly., Haw. 13–25–35–50mm. C.

17. MITRA (Ve.) COCCINEUM Reeve. W.Pac. 50–65–75–80mm. C. Color and pattern variable. Syn.: **M.ornatum coccineum** Reeve.

18. MITRA (Mi.) COFFEA Schubert & Wagner. Mad.-Poly., Haw. 32–50mm. S.

19. MITRA (Ne.) CONTRACTA Swainson. E.Afr.-Poly., Haw. <25–30–35–50mm. UC. Form, color and pattern q.v. Dark brown per.

20. MITRA (Im.) CONULARIS Lam. **Cone-shaped Miter.** Red Sea-Fiji. 15–16–20–25mm. C.

21. MITRA (Pt.) CONUS Gm. W.Pac. 17–25–30–36mm. UC. Syn.: **M.conulus** Lam.

22. MITRA (Ne.) CORONATA Lam. **Crowned Miter.** S.E.Afr.-Poly., Haw. 11–13–20–35mm. UC. Form and color q.v. ?Syn. for **M.lugubris** Swainson.

23. MITRA (Ve.) COSTELLARIS Lam. W. Pac. 32–35–45–50mm. UC.

1. MITRA (Pt.) CRENULATA Gm. **Crenulated Miter.** E.Afr.-Poly., Haw. 18–21–28–38mm. UC.

2. MITRA (Co.) CRUENTATUM Gm. Red Sea-Samoa. 13–15–19–22mm. C. Color and pattern variable.

3. MITRA (Ne.) CUCUMERINA Lam. **Ridged** or **Cucumber Miter.** Red Sea-S.E.Afr.-Poly., Haw. 9–13–19–34mm. C. Brown per.

4. MITRA (Ve.) CURVILIRATUM Sow. India-P.I. <30–43–50–>55mm. C.

5. MITRA (Pt.) DACTYLUS Lam. W.Pac. 25–30–35–52mm. C.

6. MITRA DENNISONI Reeve. W.Pac. Avg. 50–60mm. S. Sold by dealers as **M.taylorianum** Sow.

7. MITRA (Co.) DESHAYESI Reeve. Maur.-Tonga. 10–12–18–29mm. UC.

8. MITRA (Di.) EDENTULA Swainson. E. Afr.-Poly., Haw. Avg.35–40mm. S.

9. MITRA (Mi.) EREMITARUM Röd. **Adusta Miter.** Indon.-Fiji. 38–40–55–80mm. C. Dark brown per. Cp. **M.incompta.** Syn.: **M.adusta** Lam.

10. MITRA (Su.) ERYTHROGRAMMA Tomlin. Nicaragua-Col. 15–25mm. C.

11. MITRA (Co.) EXASPERATUM Gm. S. E.Afr.-Poly., Haw. 13–19–23–26mm. C. ?Syn. for **M.pacificum** Reeve.

12. MITRA (Pt.) FENESTRATA Lam. And.-Poly., Haw. 19–32mm. UC.

13. MITRA (Ne.) FERRUGINEA Lam. **Rusty Miter.** S.E.Afr.-Poly., Haw. 26–30–40–58mm. C.

14. MITRA (Do.) FILARIS L. W.Pac. 19–25–35–55mm. C.

15. MITRA (Sw.) FISSURATA Lam. Red Sea-E.Afr.-Ind.Oc. Avg.28–38mm. UC.

16. MITRA (Ca.) FLAMMEA Q. & G. Maur.-Fiji, Haw. 19–27mm. UC.

17. MITRA (Ve.) FORMOSENSE Sow. **Formosan Miter.** Indon.-Fiji. 31–40–50–55mm. C.

18. MITRA (Su.) GIGANTEA Reeve. Pan.-Ecu. 40–50–60–70mm. S. Greenish-brown per.

19. MITRA (Do.) GLORIOLA Cernohorsky. P.I. Avg.40–50mm. UC.

20. MITRA (Do.) GRANATINA Lam. Red Sea-Poly., Haw. 23–35–45–64mm. C.

21. MITRA (Co.) GRANOSUM Gm. Maur.-Fiji. 19–30–40–52mm. C.

22. MITRA (Ve.) GRUNERI Reeve. P.I.-Samoa. 18–20–25–32mm. UC.

23. MITRA (Su.) HINDSII Reeve. Baja Cal.-G.of Cal.-Ecu. 25–30–35–38mm. C. Olive-brown per.

24. MITRA (Su.) IDAE Melvill. **Ida's Miter.** C.Cal.-Baja Cal. 32–40–50–77mm. UC. Variable form. Blackish per. Syn.: **M.catalinae** Dall, **M.diegensis** Dall.

25. MITRA (Mi.) IMPERIALIS Röd. **Imperial Miter.** S.E.Afr.-Red Sea-Poly. 38–42–50–60mm. UC. Syn.: **M.pertusa** L.

26. MITRA (Mi.) INCOMPTA Lightfoot. E. Afr.-Poly., Haw. 44–50–70–160mm. UC. Brown per. Cp. **M.eremitarum.** Syn.: **M.terebralis** Lam., **M.tesselata** Martyn.

Plate 112 | Mitridae

1. MITRA (Mi.) INQUINATA Reeve. Japan-Tai. 45–50–60–75mm. S. Syn.: **M.hanleyana** Dunker.

2. MITRA (Ve.) INTERMEDIA Kiener. **Intermediate Miter.** E.Afr.-N.Aust. 38–40–50–63mm. C. Now considered form of **M.rugosum** Gm. See also pl. 113, no. 3B–C.

3. MITRA (Ca.) ISABELLA Swainson. W. Pac. 50–65–85–100mm. UC.

4. MITRA (Mi.) LATRUNCULARIA Reeve. S.Afr. 18–20–25–34mm. C. Usually beach spec.

5. MITRA (St.) LENS Wood. G.of Cal.-Peru. Avg.36–40mm. C. Dark brown per.

6. MITRA (Ne.) LIENARDI Sow. New Cal., Haw. Avg.25–27mm. UC.

7. MITRA (St.) LITTERATA Lam. **Lettered Miter.** S.E.Afr.-Poly., Haw. 11–20–25–31mm. C. Form, color and pattern q.v.

8. MITRA (Ve.) LYRATUM Lam. **Lyre-Like Miter.** W.Pac. to Sol. 32–40–45–51mm. S. Syn.: **M.subdivisum** Gm.

9. MITRA (Su.) MALLETI Petit. G.of Cal. Avg.20–24mm. UC. Olive per.

10. MITRA (Ve.) MELONGENA Lam. And. Sea-Fiji. 38–44–48–52mm. S.

11. MITRA (Mi.) MITRA L. **Episcopal, Orange-spotted** or **Giant Miter.** S.E.Afr.-Poly., Haw. ca.40–75–110–170mm. VC. Heavy. Thin yellowish per. Syn.: **Mitra episcopalis** L.

12. MITRA (Pt.) NUCEA Gm. E.Afr.-Poly. 28–32–40–57mm. C.

13. MITRA (Sc.) OCELLATA Swainson. S. E.Afr.-W.Pac. 13–19–25–?38mm. C.

14. MITRA (Im.) OLIVAEFORMIS Swainson. **Olive-shaped Miter.** Maur.-Poly., Haw. 8–12–15–25mm. C.

15. MITRA (Mi.) PAPALIS L. **Papal Miter.** E.Afr.-Poly., Haw. 50–85–110–162mm. UC (was C). Secretes purple dye when disturbed.

16. MITRA (Neo.) PAPILIO Link. Maur.-G.of Aden-Poly., Haw. 19–25–40–64mm. C.

17. MITRA (St.) PAUPERCULA L. **Poor Miter.** S.E.Afr.-Red Sea-Poly., Haw. 13–20–30–39mm. C. Thin brown per. Form and pattern q.v.

18. MITRA (Ca.) PIA Dohrn. W.Pac. 19–30–45–50mm. UC.

19. MITRA (Ve.) PLICARIUM L. **Plicate** or **Plaited Miter.** And.Sea-Samoa. 30–35–45–50mm. VC.

20. MITRA (Pu.) PULCHELLUM Reeve. Fla.-W.I. 11–15mm. VS.

21. MITRA (Im.) PUNCTATA Swainson. E.Afr.-Poly., Haw. 11–15mm. C.

22. MITRA (Mi.) PUNCTICULATA Lam. Mad., Indon.-Fiji. 25–35–45–52mm. UC.

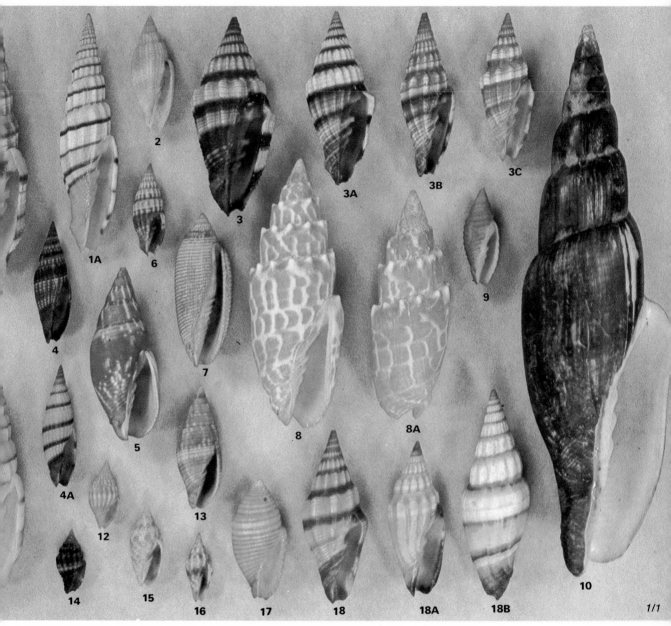

1. *MITRA (Ve.) REGINA* Sow. Ind.Oc.-P.I. 44–50–60–70mm. S. 1A is form *M.r. filiareginae* Cate.

2. *MITRA (Mi.) ROSACEA* Reeve. Thailand-W.Pac. 10–20–30–37mm. S.

3. *MITRA (Ve.) RUGOSUM* Gm. **Rugose Miter.** E.Afr.-W.Pac. 32–35–45–50mm. VC. 3B–C is form *M.rugosum intermedia* Kiener. See also pl. 112, no. 2.

4. *MITRA (Co.) SANGUISUGA* L. **Blood Sucker Miter.** W.Pac. to N.G. 20–25–35–50mm. UC.

5. *MITRA (St.) SCUTULATA* Gm. G.of Aden-India-Poly. 22–25–35–47mm. C. Color and pattern variable.

6. *MITRA (Co.) SEMIFASCIATUM* Lam. Red Sea-Ind.Oc.-Samoa. 13–18–24–32mm. C.

7. *MITRA (Pt.) SINENSIS* Reeve. Japan-Tai. Avg.38–45mm. UC.

8. *MITRA (Mi.) STICTICA* Link. **Pontifical Miter.** E.Afr.-Poly., Haw. 30–50–65–87mm. C. Syn.: *M.cardinalis* Röd. (not Gm.), *M. pontificalis* Lam.

9. *MITRA (Su.) SULCATA* Sow. So.G.of Cal.-Ecu. 19–20–30–53mm. UC.

10. *MITRA (Mi.) SWAINSONII* Brod. Baja Cal.-G.of Cal.-Ecu. 70–80–95–135mm. UC. Olive-black per. Syn.: *M.mexicana* Dall, *M. zaca* Strong, Hanna & Hertlein.

11. *MITRA (Ve.) TAENIATUM* Lam. **Filleted Miter.** W.Pac. 38–50–60–76mm. VS (was UC).

12. *MITRA (Pu.) UNIFASCIALIS* Lam. Red Sea-Poly., Haw. 13–17mm. UC.

13. *MITRA (Mi.) VARIABILIS* Reeve. W. Pac. 25–30–37–44mm. C.

14. *MITRA (Pu.) VARIATA* Reeve. Fla.-Carib. 13–21mm. S.

15. *MITRA (Sc.) VARIEGATA* Gm. **Variegated Miter.** S.E.Afr.-W.Pac. 16–25–32–38mm. UC. Color and pattern q.v.

16. *MITRA (Su.) VERRUCOSA* Reeve. P.I.-Samoa. 13–16–22–32mm. UC.

17. *MITRA (St.) VEXILLUM* Reeve. Ind. Oc.-Sol. Avg.25–30mm. C.

18. *MITRA (Ve.) VULPECULA* L. **Little Fox Miter.** W.Pac. 32–40–50–62mm. C. Color and pattern q.v.

Plate 114 | Cancellariidae

1. *CANCELLARIA ASPERELLA* Lam. Ind. Oc.-W.Pac. Avg.25–30mm. UC.

2. *CANCELLARIA BICOLOR* Hinds. **Two-colored Nutmeg.** Japan-Tai. Avg.15–18mm. C.

3. *CANCELLARIA CANCELLATA* L. Med., C.V., Morocco-Angola. 26–30–40–50mm. UC.

4. *CANCELLARIA CASSIDIFORMIS* Sow. No.G.of Cal.-Peru. 30–35–55–66mm. C.

5. *CANCELLARIA FOVEOLATA* Sow. S.Afr. Avg.19–24mm. UC. Color variable. Usually beach spec.

6. *CANCELLARIA FUNICULATA* Hinds. Japan-Tai. Avg.29–35mm. S.

7. *CANCELLARIA INDENTATA* Sow. G.of Cal.-Ecu. Avg.27–32mm. UC.

8. *CANCELLARIA LAMELLOSA* Hinds. S.E.Afr.-W.Pac. 13–22mm. UC.

9. *CANCELLARIA LATICOSTA* Löbbecke. Japan-Tai. 30–42mm. C.

10. *CANCELLARIA NODULIFERA* Sow. Japan. 45–60mm. UC.

11. *CANCELLARIA OBESA* Lam. Baja Cal.-G.of Cal.-Ecu. 30–32–40–57mm. UC.

12. *CANCELLARIA OBLIQUATA* Lam. Ind.Oc.-W.Pac. Avg.15–18mm. C.

13. *CANCELLARIA PISCATORIA* Gm. Morocco-Benin. Avg.25–30mm. UC.

14. *CANCELLARIA REEVEANA* Crosse. Japan-Tai. 28–32–38–43mm. C.

15. *CANCELLARIA RETICULATA* L. **Common Nutmeg.** N.C.-E.& W.Fla.-Texas, W.I.-Brazil. 25–30–45–55mm. VC. Also, albino form.

16. *CANCELLARIA RIGIDA* Sow. Mauritania-Senegal. Avg.20–25mm. UC.

17. *CANCELLARIA TEXTILIS* Kiener. **Textile Nutmeg.** W.Pac.15–18–25–30mm. UC. ?Form of *Trigonostoma scalata* Sow.

18. *CANCELLARIA URCEOLATA* Hinds. Baja Cal.-G.of Cal.-Ecu. Avg.23–28mm. C.

19. *SYDAPHERA SPENGLERIANA* Deshayes. Indon.-W.Pac. Avg.50–60mm. C. ?Subgenus of *Aphera*.

20. *TRIGONOSTOMA BULLATUM* Sow. W.Mex.-Pan. 25–40mm. S.

21. *TRIGONOSTOMA GONIOSTOMA* Sow. No.G.of Cal.-Pan. Avg.20–25mm. UC.

22. *TRIGONOSTOMA SEMIPELLUCIDA* Adams & Reeve. Japan. Avg.20–24mm. UC.

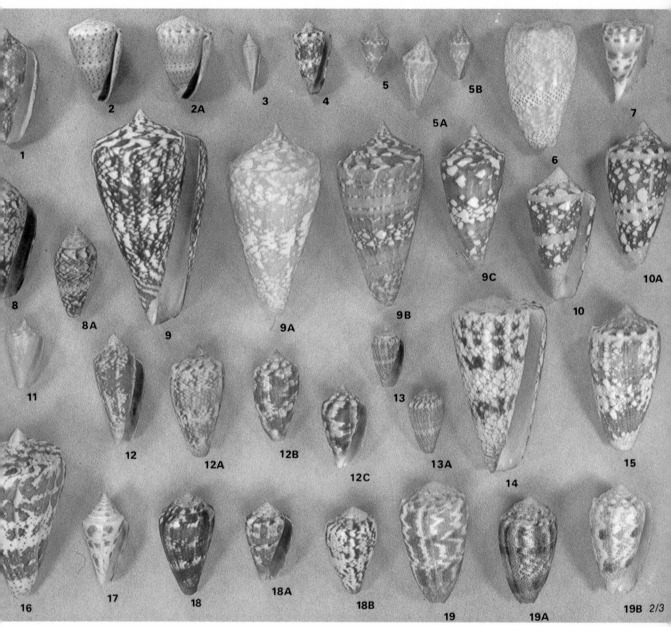

1. CONUS ABBAS Hwass. **Abbas Cone.** S. India-Sri Lanka. 30–32–40–77mm. UC. Cp *C.canonicus, C.dalli, C.textile.*

2. CONUS ABBREVIATUS Reeve. **Abbreviated Cone.** Haw. 17–22–30–58mm. C. Cp. *C.encaustus, C.miliaris* (?subsp.).

3. CONUS ACULEIFORMIS Reeve. **Spindle Cone.** Ind.Oc.-Sol. 24–26–30–54mm. UC. Cp. *C.insculptus, C.vimineus* (?form).

4. CONUS ACUMINATUS Hwass. Red Sea-G.of Aden-N.W.Ind.Oc. 22–25–35–50mm. UC.

5. CONUS ACUTANGULUS Lam. **Sharp-angled Cone.** E.Afr.-Poly., Haw. 15–18–25–32mm. UC. Cp. *C.eugrammatus.*

6. CONUS ADAMSONI Broderip. **Rhodo-dendron Cone.** W.Pac. 40–42–45–56mm. Ext. R. A classic rarity. Syn.: *C.rhododendron* Jay.

7. CONUS ADVERTEX Garrard. Qld.-N.S.W. 25–28–32–40mm. UC.

8. CONUS AEMULUS Reeve. Senegal-Angola. <25–28–32–35mm. C. Cp. *C.bulbus, C.echinophilus* (?dwarf form), **C.ermineus.** Syn.: *C.obtusus.*

9. CONUS AMADIS Gm. India-Indon. 50–55–75–100mm. UC. Cp. *C. thalassiarchus.* Syn.: *C.castaneofasciatus* Sow. (?subsp.).

10. CONUS AMMIRALIS L. **Admiral Cone.** Ind.Oc.-W.Pac. 37–40–60–82mm. UC. Cp. *C. archithalassus.*

11. CONUS AMPHIURGUS Dall. N.C.-Fla.-Texas-W.I.-Yucatan. 17–25–35–60mm. R. Color q.v. Cp. *C.vittatus.* Syn.: *C.juliae* Clench.

12. CONUS ANEMONE Lam. **Anemone** or **Southern Cone.** Aust. 29–35–50–92mm. C. Form, color and pattern q.v. Cp. *C.compres-sus* (?form), **C.peronianus** (?form), some *C. papilliferus* patterns. Syn.: *C.novaehollandiae* A.Adams, *C.remo* Brazier.

13. CONUS APLUSTRE Reeve. N.S.W. 20–22–26–30mm. C.

14. CONUS ARANEOSUS Lightfoot. **Cob-web Cone.** Ind.Oc. 40–60–75–101mm. C. Yellow deep inside mouth. Cp. *C.nicobaricus* (?subsp.).

15. CONUS ARCHITHALASSUS ?Hwass. Ind.Oc. 29–40–50–65mm. R. ?Coronate form of *C.ammiralis.*

16. CONUS ARCHON Brod. **Magistrate Cone.** G.of Cal.-Pan. 35–45–60–97mm. UC. Cp. *C.aurantius, C.cedonulli.*

17. CONUS ARCUATUS Brod. & Sow. **Arched Cone.** G.of Cal.-Col. 30–32–38–52mm. C. Cp. *C.cancellatus.* Syn.: *C.lizardensis* Crosse.

18. CONUS ARDISIACEUS Kiener. G.of Oman. Avg.30–38mm. S.

19. CONUS ARENATUS Hwass. **Sand-dusted Cone.** S.E.Afr.-W.Pac. 28–30–40–84mm. VC. Cp. *C.pulicarius.* Syn.: *C.arenosus* Röd.

133

Plate 116 | Conidae

1. *CONUS ARGILLACEUS* Perry. Yemen-N.W.Ind.Oc. 45–52–60–65mm. S. Syn.: *C. splendidulus* Sow.

2. *CONUS ARMADILLO* Shikama. Japan-Tai., Sol. 49–60–70–80mm. VR. ?Form of *C. duplicatus* Sow. (not illus.).

3. *CONUS AUGUR* Lightfoot. **Auger Cone.** S.E.Afr.-Ind.Oc. 40–45–55–73mm. UC.

4. *CONUS AULICUS* L. **Court Cone.** E. Afr.-Poly. 70–75–100–162mm. UC. Often with pinkish tone. Cream to pale orange inside mouth. Venomous. Cp. *C.magnificus, C.pennaceus.*

5. *CONUS AURANTIUS* Hwass. **Golden Cone.** W.I. (V.I.-Neth.Ant.). 30–36–45–71mm. S. Cp. *C.archon, C.cedonulli, C.regius.*

6. *CONUS AUREUS* Hwass. Ind.Oc.-Poly. 30–50–55–65mm. S. Cp. *C.paulucciae* (?form), *C.telatus.*

7. *CONUS AURICOMUS* Hwass. **Clavus Cone.** Ind.Oc.-Poly., Haw. 20–30–40–60mm. S. Thin. Cp. juvenile *C.aulicus* (thick, heavier).

8. *CONUS AURISIACUS* L. **Orange Admiral Cone.** Indon.-Malaysia. 40–50–65–95mm. VR. Cp. pale form of *C.circumcisus.*

9. *CONUS AUSTINI* Rehder & Abbott.

Austin's Cone. S.E.Fla.-W.I.-Yucatan. 32–45–55–70mm. C (Fla.: R). ?Subsp. of *C.atractus* Tomlin.

10. *CONUS AUSTRALIS* Holten. **Austral Cone.** Japan-S.China Sea. 40–50–65–105mm. C. Fresh spec. have violet mouth. Cp. *C. laterculatus* (?subsp.).

11. *CONUS AXELRODI* Walls. Indon.-P.I.-Tai. 13–16–20–22mm. UC. Cp. *C.miliaris, C. musicus, C.sponsalis.*

12. *CONUS BAIRSTOWI* Reeve. S.Afr. 25–30–40–50mm. UC. ?Form of *C.infrenatus.* Usually beach spec.

13. *CONUS BARTHELEMYI* Bernardi. W.-S.Ind.Oc. 40–55–70–80mm. VS (was R). Color and pattern q.v. Cp. *C.gubernator.*

14. *CONUS BARTSCHI* Hanna & Strong. Baja Cal.-G.of Cal.-C.R. 30–35–40–50mm. S. ?Form of *C.brunneus.* Also, Cp. *C.regius.*

15. *CONUS BENGALENSIS* Okutani. Bay of Bengal. 60–90–110–120mm. VR. Cp. *C. gloriamaris.*

16. *CONUS BETULINUS* L. S.E.Afr.-Poly. 50–65–90–177mm. C. Very heavy. Cp. *C. suratensis* (?subsp.).

– – *CONUS BILIOSUS* Röd. – See *C.piperatus* (Syn.).

17. *CONUS BOCKI* Sow. Bay of Bengal-Sol. ca.50–60–70–85mm. S. ?Form of *C.sulcatus.*

18. *CONUS BOETICUS* Reeve. Red Sea-Fiji. 19–25–32–38mm. C. Pattern q.v. Cp. *C. pauperculus* (?form).

19. *CONUS BOSCHI* Clover. G.of Oman, India. 18–20–25–30mm. UC. Fresh spec. have deep violet mouth. Cp. juvenile *C.lucidus.*

20. *CONUS BRODERIPII* Reeve. Indon., P.I. 30–35–40–50mm. C. ?Form of *C.spectrum* or *C.collisus.*

1. *CONUS BRUNNEUS* Wood. Wood's Brown Cone. Baja Cal.-G.of Cal.-Ecu. 30–35–45–71mm. C. Juveniles are white with brown axial stripes. Cp. *C.bartschi* (?Syn.).

2. *CONUS BULBUS* Reeve. W.Afr., esp. Angola. 15–20–25–45mm. UC. Cp. *C.naranjus* (?form), *C.zebroides* (?form).

3. *CONUS BULLATUS* L. Bubble Cone. Ind.Oc.-Poly., Haw. 40–45–50–71mm. R. Color fades.

4. *CONUS CABRITII* Bernardi. New Cal. 15–18–24–30mm. UC.

5. *CONUS CALIFORNICUS* Hinds. California(n) Cone. C.Cal.-Baja Cal. 19–20–30–49mm. C. Thick brown per., as on 5A.

6. *CONUS CANCELLATUS* Hwass. Cancellate Cone. Japan-Tai.-P.I. 30–35–40–50mm. C.

7. *CONUS CANONICUS* Hwass. E.Afr.-Marq. 26–30–35–70mm. C. Pinkish mouth. Cp. *C.abbas, C.tigrinus* (?Syn.).

8. *CONUS CAPITANELLUS* Fulton. S. Japan-Tai. 20–22–26–41mm. S.

9. *CONUS CAPITANEUS* L. Captain Cone. S.E.Afr.-Fiji, Haw. 30–50–60–90mm. VC. Violet mouth. Usually flawed. Cp. *C.vexillum.*

10. *CONUS CARACTERISTICUS* Fischer. Characteristic Cone. Ind.Oc.-W.Pac. 40–45–50–89mm. C. Form, color and pattern q.v. Syn.: *C.characteristicus* Dillwyn.

11. *CONUS CARDINALIS* Hwass. Cardinal Cone. Fla.-Bah.-Carib. 20–25–30–45mm. S. Color of mouth variable, often pinkish. Usually beach spec. Cp. *C.regius.*

12. *CONUS CATUS* Hwass. Cat Cone. S.E.Afr.-Poly., Haw. 25–28–35–44mm. VC. Color and pattern q.v. Cp. *C.monachus, C. nigropunctatus.*

13. *CONUS CEDONULLI* L. Bah.-Venez. 40–45–50–78mm. R. Form and pattern q.v. Usually dead, flawed spec. Live spec. may be dark brown. Cp. *C.aurantius, C.regius.*

14. *CONUS CENTURIO* Born. Centurion Cone. Ga.-W.I.-?Brazil. , 30–40–50–104mm. R. Usually dead, flawed spec. Cp. *C.delessertii.*

15. *CONUS CHALDEUS* Röd. Worm or Vermiculate Cone. S.E.Afr.-Pac. to Poly.-Galáp., Haw. 20–25–30–41mm. VC. Often has pink tone. ?Subsp. of *C.ebraeus.* Syn.: *C. vermiculatus* Lam.

16. *CONUS CINEREUS* L. Malaysia-W.Pac. 32–38–45–58mm. C. Color and pattern variable. Cp. *C.lienardi, C.spectrum.*

17. *CONUS CIRCUMACTUS* Iredale. W. Pac.-Fiji, Haw. 30–40–50–58mm. S. Pink tones. Variable pattern. Cp. *C.planorbis, C.striatellus, C.vitulinus.* Called *C.connectens* Adams by J. Walls.

18. *CONUS CIRCUMCISUS* Born. W.Pac.-New Heb., ?Haw. 40–60–65–80mm. VS (was R). Pattern q.v. Cp. *C.aurisiacus.*

19. *CONUS CLARUS* E.A.Smith. W.Aust.-Vic. 20–30–35–45mm. UC. Pink to pale orange mouth. Cp. *C.segravei.*

135

Plate 118 | Conidae

1. *CONUS CLASSIARIUS* Hwass. **Naval Cone.** Red Sea. Avg.28–32mm. UC. ?Syn. for *C.capitaneus.*

2. *CONUS CLENCHI* Martins. Brazil. Avg. 40–50mm. VS. ?Higher-spired form of *C.clerii.*

3. *CONUS CLERII* Reeve. N.E.Brazil-N. Argentina. 30–40–50–66mm. UC (was VS). Cp. *C.clenchi* (?form).

4. *CONUS CLOVERI* Walls. Senegal. 21–25–30–38mm. S. ?Form of *C.mercator.* Also called *C.soaresi* Iravao.

5. *CONUS COCCEUS* Reeve. W.Aust. 19–25–32–50mm. UC. Cp. pale *C.anemone.*

6. *CONUS COCCINEUS* Gm. Bay of Bengal-W.Pac. 30–38–45–56mm. UC. Cp. *C.cumingii.*

7. *CONUS COELINAE* Crosse. W.Pac., esp. New Cal.; Haw. 50–55–75–>120mm. S. White to pale tan base. ?Form of *C.virgo* (shoulder more roundly angled). *C.c.spiceri* Bartsch & Rehder (not illus.) is a rare Hawaiian subsp.

8. *CONUS COLLISUS* Reeve. S.India-Sol. 20–32–38–46mm. UC. 8A is form *C.c. andamenensis* E.A.Smith from And. Cp. *C. iodostoma, C.janus, C.stramineus, C.tegulatus.* Called *C.subulatus* Kiener by J.Walls.

9. *CONUS COMPRESSUS* Sow. S.Aust. Avg.40–50mm. C. ?High-spired form of *C. anemone.*

10. *CONUS CONCOLOR* Sow. W.Pac. 30–32–38–50mm. UC.

11. *CONUS CONSORS* Sow. E.Afr.-Sol. 50–65–75–113mm. UC. Cp. *C.magus, C.pöhlianus.*

12. *CONUS CORONATUS* Gm. **Coronate** or **Crowned Cone.** S.E.Afr.-Poly., Haw. 15–22–27–44mm. VC. Cp. *C.miliaris.* Syn.: *C. aristophanes* Sow.

13. *CONUS CROCATUS* Lam. **Saffron Cone.** Rewa Is., Thailand, New Cal., Sol., Samoa. 45–70mm. Ext.R. Wide-shouldered form illus. is *C.thailandus* da Motta.

14. *CONUS CUMINGII* Reeve. ?Bay of Bengal-Sol., ?Haw. 20–32–35–40mm. S. Usually flawed. Cp. *C.coccineus.*

15. *CONUS CUNEOLUS* Reeve. C.V. 17–22–28–34mm. S. Pattern q.v. Called *C.balteus* Wood by J.Walls.

16. *CONUS CYANOSTOMA* A.Adams. Qld.-N.S.W. 15–16–20–25mm. C. Most spec. have very little color or pattern. Spec. illus. does not have typical bluish tinge.

17. *CONUS CYLINDRACEUS* Brod. & Sow. E.Afr.-Poly., Haw. 17–22–28–45mm. S.

18. *CONUS DALLI* Stearns. **Dall's Cone.** G.of Cal.-Pan., Galáp. 38–40–50–85mm. UC. Violet mouth. Cp. *C.abbas, C.canonicus.*

19. *CONUS DAUCUS* Hwass. **Carrot Cone.** E.& W.Fla., W.I.-Brazil. 22–30–40–61mm. UC. Also, yellow and albino forms.

20. *CONUS DELESSERTII* Récluz. **Sozon's Cone.** S.C.-Fla.-G.of Mex., Berm. 35–40–55–102mm. C. Usually flawed. Cp. *C.centurio.* Syn.: *C.sozoni* Bartsch; *C.largillierti* Kiener.

21. *CONUS DIADEMA* Sow. **Diadem Cone.** Baja Cal.-G.of Cal.-Ecu., Galáp. 25–30–40–67mm. C. Cp. *C.lividus.*

22. *CONUS DISTANS* Hwass. **Distant** or **Knobby-top Cone.** E.Afr.-Poly., Haw. 50–60–75–134mm. VC. Syn.: *C.kenyonae* Brazier.

1. *CONUS DORREENSIS* Peron & Lesueur. **Pontifical Cone.** W.Aust. 20–30–38–40mm. C. Per., often tinged greenish, bordered by 2 bands. Illus. 1A: without per. Syn.: *C.pontificalis* Lam.

2. *CONUS EBRAEUS* L. **Hebrew Cone.** S.E.Afr.-Poly., Haw.; also, C.R. 19–20–30–62mm. VC. Variable pattern. Cp. *C.chaldeus* (?subsp.). Often misspelled *C.hebraeus*.

3. *CONUS EBURNEUS* Hwass. **Ivory Cone.** S.E.Afr.-Poly. 22–35–50–78mm. VC. 3C, 3D, 3E are form *C.e.polyglotta* Weinkauff, esp. from P.I.

4. *CONUS ECHINOPHILUS* Petuch. Senegal. 8–12mm. VS. ?Dwarf form of *C.aemulus*.

5. *CONUS EMACIATUS* Reeve. E.Afr.-Poly. 30–40–50–56mm. VC. Cp. *C.flavidus, C.terebra, C.virgo.*

6. *CONUS ENCAUSTUS* Kiener. Poly., Marq. 20–25–28–40mm. C. Cp. *C.fulgetrum, C.miliaris.*

7. *CONUS EPISCOPUS* Hwass. **Episcopal Cone.** E.Afr.-Poly. 48–50–65–114mm. VC. White aperture. ?Form of *C.pennaceus.*

8. *CONUS ERMINEUS* Born. **Turtle Cone.** S.C.-G.of Mex., Carib.-Brazil; also, W.Sahara-Angola, C.V. 30–50–65–103mm. C. Color and pattern q.v. *C.grayi* Reeve (not illus.) is a form from W.Afr. *C.purpurascens* (?subsp.). Syn.: *C.guinaicus* Hwass, C. "*ranunculus* Hwass", C. *testudinarius* Hwass.

9. *CONUS ERYTHRAEENSIS* Reeve. **Red Sea Cone.** Red Sea. ?12–19–25–35mm. C.

10. *CONUS EUGRAMMATUS* Bartsch & Rehder. Japan-Tai.-P.I.; Haw.(R). 20–25–32–40mm. UC. Cp. *C.acutangulus, C.wakayamaensis* (?form).

11. *CONUS EXIMIUS* Reeve. Bay of Bengal-W.Pac. 30–32–38–55mm. UC. Pattern q.v.

12. *CONUS FERGUSONI* Sow. **Ferguson's Cone.** Baja Cal.-G.of Cal.-Ecu., Galáp. 65–70–85–163mm. C.

13. *CONUS FIGULINUS* L. **Fig** or **Clay Cone.** S.E.Afr.-Poly. 32–50–75–121mm. VC. Very heavy. 13B is form *C.f.loroisii* Kiener from India-P.I.

14. *CONUS FLAVESCENS* Sow. **Bahama Cone.** S.E.Fla.-Carib. 15–22–26–40mm. UC. Color and pattern q.v. Cp. *C.jaspideus.* Called *C.magellanicus* Hwass by J.Walls.

15. *CONUS FLAVIDUS* Lam. **Flavid** or **Yellow-tinged Cone.** S.E.Afr.-Poly., Haw. 25–28–35–64mm. VC. Cp. *C.emaciatus, C.lividus.* Syn.: *C.peasei* Brazier.

16. *CONUS FLOCCATUS* Sow. **Snow-flaked Cone.** P.I.-Fiji, Marshall Is. <30–32–42–65mm. VS (was R). Color and pattern q.v. Usually dead spec.

17. *CONUS FLORIDANUS* Gabb. **Florida Cone.** N.C.-E.& W.Fla. 30–35–45–52mm. C. J.Walls calls it *C.philippii* Kiener. Syn.: *C. floridensis* Sow.

18. *CONUS FLORIDULUS* A.Adams & Reeve. W.Pac., esp.P.I. Avg.25–30mm. VS. ?High-spired form of *C.muriculatus.*

137

Plate 120 | Conidae

1. CONUS FULGETRUM Sow. **Lightning Cone.** Red Sea-E.Afr.-Sol. 15–19–25–38mm. Cp. *C.encaustus, C.miliaris.*

2. CONUS FULMEN Reeve. **Thunderbolt Cone.** S.Japan-N.China Sea. 30–38–50–70mm. C. Cp. *C.kinoshitai.*

3. CONUS FURVUS Reeve. **Carpenter Cone.** N.Ind.Oc.-W.Pac. 25–40–50–60mm. C. Variable form, color and pattern. Syn.: *C. granifer* Reeve, *C.lignarius* Reeve.

4. CONUS FUSCOLINEATUS Sow. Guinea-Angola. 15–20–26–40mm. UC. Heavy. Variable pattern. Usually eroded. Called *C. variegatus* Kiener by J.Walls. Syn.: *C.africanus* Kiener.

5. CONUS GENERALIS L. **General Cone.** E.Afr.-Fiji. 40–50–65–89mm. VC. Dark violet to blackish base. Cp. *C.maldivus* (?subsp.).

6. CONUS GENUANUS L. Senegal-Angola. 30–38–50–82mm. UC.

7. CONUS GEOGRAPHUS L. **Geography Cone.** S.E.Afr.-Poly. 50–75–100–153mm. VC. Coronate shoulder. Venomous. Cp. *C.obscurus, C.tulipa.*

8. CONUS GLADIATOR Brod. **Gladiator Cone.** G.of Cal.-Ecu.-?Peru. 20–25–35–44mm. VC. Thick, rough brown per. Cp. *C.mus.*

9. CONUS GLANS Hwass. **Acorn Cone.** E. Afr.-Poly. 20–25–32–59mm. C.

10. CONUS GLAUCUS L. **Gray Cone.** Indon.-P.I. 27–32–38–60mm. C. Heavy glossy shell.

11. CONUS GLORIAMARIS Chemnitz. **Glory-of-the-Seas Cone.** W.Pac., esp.P.I., Sol. 75–80–100–150mm. VR. A famous and classic rarity. Cp. *C.bengalensis.*

12. CONUS GRADATUS Wood. Baja Cal.-G.of Cal.-Peru. 30–35–45–60mm. C. White mouth. Cp. *C.regularis* (?form), *C.scalaris* (?form). *C.recurvus* may also be a form.

13. CONUS GRANGERI Sow. Tai.-P.I. 40–45–50–76mm. UC. ?Subsp. of *C.sulcatus.* ?Syn.: *C.pseudosulcatus* Nomura (fossil).

14. CONUS GRANULATUS L. **Glory-of-the-Atlantic Cone.** S.E.Fla.-W.I. 26–30–40–61mm. R (Fla.: VR). Rarely collected live.

15. CONUS GUBERNATOR Hwass. **Governor's Cone.** S.E.Afr.-Ind.Oc. 40–50–65–106mm. UC. Color and pattern q.v. Cp. *C. barthelemyi.* 15B is **CONUS LEEHMANI** deMotta & Rockel (miscalled *C.gubernator* and *C.barthelemyi "pramparti"* Richard). S.

16. CONUS HIEROGLYPHUS Duclos. W.I. (?Jamaica, ?V.I.-Neth.Ant.). 13–15–18–22mm. UC. Syn.: *C.armillatus* C.B.Adams.

17. CONUS HIRASEI Kira. S.Japan-Tai. 40–45–55–84mm. R. Spec. illus. is faded.

18. CONUS HYAENA Hwass. Ind.Oc. to Bay of Bengal. 35–38–45–65mm. UC (was R). Cp. *C.piperatus.* ?Syn.: *C.mutabilis* Reeve.

Plate 121

1. CONUS ICHINOSEANA Kuroda. S. Japan-Tai., P.I. 40–44–50–69mm. VS. Cp. *C. orbignyi.*

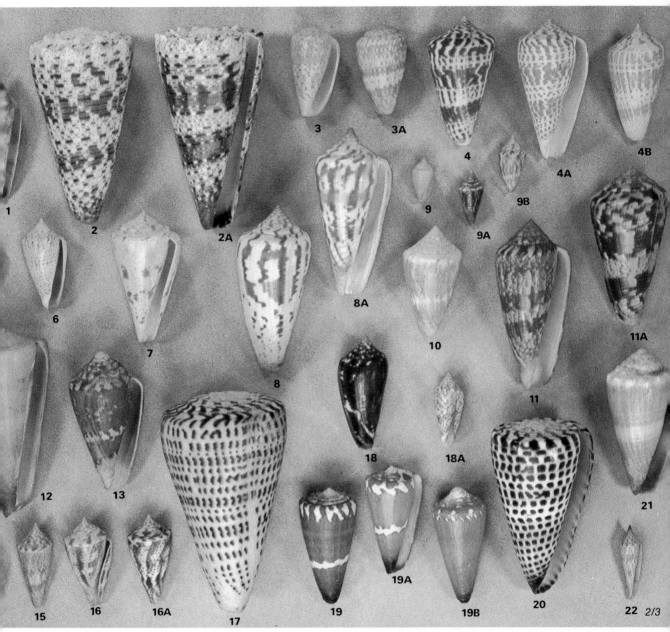

2. CONUS IMPERIALIS L. **Imperial Cone.** S.E.Afr.-Poly., Haw. 40–75–90–105mm. VC. Form and pattern q.v.

3. CONUS INFRENATUS Reeve. S.Afr. 20–25–38–50mm. C. Usually damaged beach spec. Cp. **C.natalis.**

4. CONUS INSCRIPTUS Reeve. **Inscribed Cone.** N.E.Afr.-Red Sea-N.Ind.Oc. 30–40–50–67mm. C. Cp. **C.collisus, C.stramineus.** ?Syn.: **C.keati** Sow. **C.adenensis** E.A.Smith is a form (not illus.).

5. CONUS INSCULPTUS Kiener. **Engraved Cone.** Bay of Bengal-Fiji. 19–22–26–38mm. C.

6. CONUS IODOSTOMA Reeve. E.Afr.-W. Ind.Oc. 25–30–40–45mm. UC. Usually imperfect. Cp. **C.collisus.**

7. CONUS IONE Fulton. **Iona Cone.** Japan-?Tai. 45–50–60–70mm. UC. Pale violet. Cp. **C.sieboldii.**

8. CONUS JANUS Hwass. E.Afr.-C.Ind.Oc. ?35–50–60–76mm. UC (was R). Mouth tinged yellow.

9. CONUS JASPIDEUS Gm. **Jasper Cone.** Fla.-W.I.-Brazil. 12–17–23–27mm. VC. Rounded sides. Color and pattern q.v. Cp. **C. flavescens.** 9A, 9B is form **C.j.stearnsi** Conrad from N.C.-Yucatan, with straight sides (13–19mm.). Syn.: **C.verrucosus** Hwass.

10. CONUS KERMADECENSIS Iredale. Ind.Oc.-W.Pac. 30–40–50–60mm. UC. Syn.: **C."kenyonae** Brazier".

11. CONUS KINOSHITAI Kuroda. W.Pac. to ?Sol. 40–50–65–73mm. R. Pattern q.v. Cp. **C.fulmen.**

12. CONUS KINTOKI Azuma & Toki. P.I. Avg.70–75mm. R. New sp.

13. CONUS KLEMAE Cotton. W.-S.Aust. 20–40–55–75mm. Color and pattern q.v. S. Cp. **C.anemone.**

14. CONUS LEGATUS Lam. **Ambassador Cone.** W.Pac. to Poly. 20–25–35–40mm. UC. Cp. **C.canonicus.**

–– CONUS LEEHMANI deMotta & Rockel – See pl. 120, no. 15B.

15. CONUS LEMNISCATUS Reeve. ?E.Afr.-G.of Oman-India. 20–30–35–50mm. R. Spire

usually imperfect. Syn.: **C.traversianus** E.A. Smith.

16. CONUS LENTIGINOSUS Reeve. S.India-Sri Lanka. 20–25–30–40mm. C.

17. CONUS LEOPARDUS Röd. **Leopard Cone.** E.Afr.-Poly., Haw. 40–75–100–221mm. VC. Very heavy. Cp. **C.litteratus.**

18. CONUS LIENARDI Bernardi & Crosse. New Cal. 25–27–32–45mm. S. Cp. **C.cinereus.** 18A is a rare melanistic form.

19. CONUS LITOGLYPHUS Hwass. **Lithograph** or **Pebble-carved Cone.** E.Afr.-Poly., Haw. 25–32–38–62mm. VC.

20. CONUS LITTERATUS L. **Lettered Cone.** E.Afr.-Poly. 50–70–85–170mm. VC. Very heavy. Pale orange bands; deep purple base. Dark per. Cp. **C.leopardus.**

21. CONUS LIVIDUS Hwass. **Livid Cone.** S.E.Afr.-Poly., Haw. 23–30–40–81mm. VC. Brownish. Coronated spire. Cp. **C.flavidus, C. sanguinolentus** (?subsp.).

22. CONUS LONGURIONIS Kiener. Ind. Oc. Avg.25–30mm. UC. ?Round-shouldered form of **C.aculeiformis.**

139

Plate 122 | Conidae

1. **CONUS LUCIDUS** Wood. **Spiderweb Cone.** Baja Cal.-G.of Cal.-Ecu., Galáp. 23–35–50–59mm. C. Thick silky horn-colored per.

2. **CONUS LYNCEUS** Sow. Ind.Oc.-P.I.-Aust. 40–50–60–84mm. UC.

– – **CONUS MAGELLANICUS** Hwass. – See **Conus flavescens**.

3. **CONUS MAGNIFICUS** Reeve. **Magnificent Cone.** E.Afr.-Poly. 38–50–65–92mm. UC. Reddish-brown. Spec. illus. is paler than usual. Cp. **C.aulicus, C.pennaceus.**

4. **CONUS MAGUS** L. **Magus Cone.** Ind.Oc.-Fiji. 38–40–50–94mm. VC. Color and pattern ext.v. Cp. **C.consors, C.pöhlianus.** Syn.: **C.raphanus** Hwass.

5. **CONUS MALACANUS** Hwass. **Malacca Cone.** N.Ind.Oc. 35–50–60–77mm. UC (was VS). Heavy. Pattern q.v.

6. **CONUS MALDIVUS** Hwass. **Maldive Cone.** E.Afr.-Bay of Bengal. 40–45–60–79mm. C. ?Subsp. of **C.generalis**.

7. **CONUS MARCHIONATUS** Hinds. Poly., Marq. 20–25–32–>40mm. UC. ?Subsp. of **C. nobilis**.

8. **CONUS MARMOREUS** L. **Marble Cone.** S.E.Afr.-Poly., Haw. 38–65–80–150mm. VC. Heavy. Thin horn-colored per. Very rare orange form, 8B, can be artificially created by heat.

The following are usually considered forms of **C.marmoreus** and not sep.sp. or subsp.:

9. **CONUS M. BANDANUS** Hwass. E.Afr.-W.Pac. C.

10. **CONUS M. CROSSEANUS** Bernardi. New Cal.-Samoa. VS.

11. **CONUS M. DEBURGHIAE** Sow. Indon. Ext.R.

12. **CONUS M. NIGRESCENS** Sow. New Cal.-Samoa. S.

13. **CONUS M. NOCTURNUS** Lightfoot. Indon. R.

14. **CONUS M. PSEUDOMARMOREUS** Crosse. W.Pac., esp. New Cal. S.

15. **CONUS M. SUFFUSUS** Sow. New Cal. UC. Albino (15) and intermediate (15A) forms.

16. **CONUS M. VIDUA** Reeve. I-P, esp.W.Pac. UC.

1. CONUS MERCATOR L. **Trader** or **Merchant Cone.** Senegal-Sierra Leone, C.V. 14–20–35–56mm. C. Color and pattern ext.v.

2. CONUS MILES L. **Soldier Cone.** S.E.Afr.-Poly., Haw. 40–50–75–117mm. VC. Heavy.

3. CONUS MILIARIS Hwass. S.E.Afr.-Poly., Easter Is. 19–25–30–36mm. VC. Cp. **C. coronatus, C.encaustus, C.fulgetrum.** ?Subsp.: **C.abbreviatus, C.tiaratus.**

4. CONUS MILNEEDWARDSI Jousseaume. **Glory-of-India Cone.** S.E.Afr.-Ind.Oc., China Seas. 50–80–100–163mm. Ext.R. A classic rarity. Often beach and juvenile.

5. CONUS MITRATUS Hwass. **Miter-like Cone.** E.Afr.-Poly. 15–20–25–40mm. UC.

6. CONUS MOLUCCENSIS Kuster. **Moluccan Cone.** Indon.-Ryukyus-New Cal. 35–38–48–60mm. R. Granulose and smooth forms. Pattern variable.

7. CONUS MONACHUS L. **Monk Cone.** E. Afr.-Fiji. 30–35–45–76mm. C. Color and pattern ext.v. Cp. **C.nigropunctatus.** Syn.: **C. achatinus** Hwass.

8. CONUS MONILE Hwass. **Necklace Cone.** N.Ind.Oc. 38–40–50–93mm. C.

9. CONUS MOZAMBICUS Hwass. **Mozambique Cone.** Senegal-S.Afr.-Moz. 20–40–45–70mm. UC. ?Same sp. as **C.algoensis** (not illus.) and **C.tinianus.** Syn.: **C.guineensis** Gm.

10. CONUS MUCRONATUS Reeve. **Alabaster Cone.** India, S.Japan-Tai.-P.I. 25–35–40–50mm. C. Often sold as **C.pseudosulcatus** Nomura. Syn.: **C.alabaster** Reeve.

11. CONUS MURICULATUS Sow. E.Ind. Oc.-W.Pac. 20–25–30–50mm. C. Also, granulose form. Cp. **C.floridulus** (?form), **C.flavidus, C.lividus.** Syn.: **C.sugillatus** Reeve.

12. CONUS MUS Hwass. **Mouse Cone.** S.E. Fla.-W.I., Berm.; also, W.Pan. 19–25–30–56mm. VC. Color variable. Cp. **C.gladiator.**

13. CONUS MUSICUS Hwass. **Music Cone.** S.E.Afr.-Fiji. 10–14–18–28mm. C. Color and pattern variable. ?Form or subsp. of **C.sponsalis.**

14. CONUS MUSTELINUS Hwass. **Weasel Cone.** E.Africa-Fiji. 38–50–70–89mm. C. Cp. **C.capitaneus.**

15. CONUS NAMOCANUS Hwass. Moz.-E.Afr.-Ind.Oc.-?W.Pac. 40–50–70–100mm. C. Thin. Pattern variable. Cp. **C.capitaneus, C. vexillum.**

16. CONUS NARANJUS Trovao. Angola. Avg.15–20mm. UC. ?Form of **C.bulbus.**

17. CONUS NATALIS Sow. **Natal Cone.** S. Afr. 25–32–38–52mm. C. Usually beach spec. Cp. **C.infrenatus, C.n.gilchristi** Sow. (not illus.) is a form.

Plate 124 | Conidae

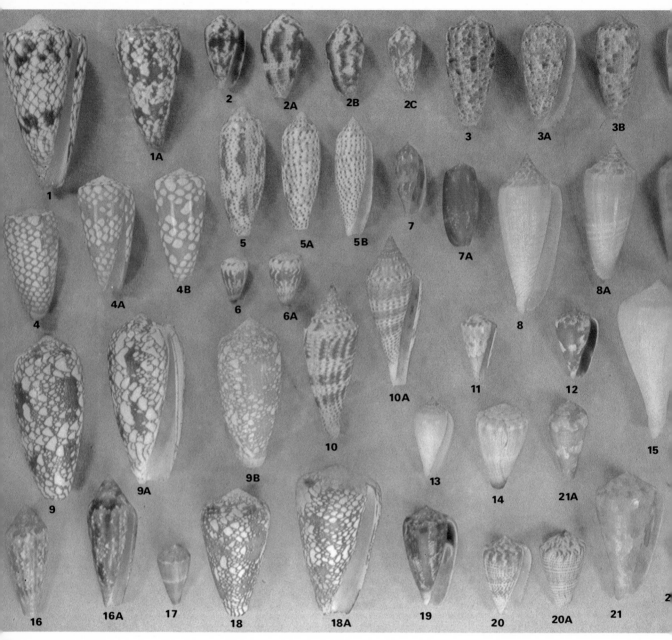

1. *CONUS NICOBARICUS* Hwass. **Nicobar Cone.** Ind.Oc.-P.I. 40–50–60–90mm. C. ?Subsp. of *C.araneosus.*

2. *CONUS NIGROPUNCTATUS* Sow. Red Sea-W.Pac. 20–28–32–41mm. VC. Color and pattern variable. Cp. variants of *C.magus, C. monachus.* Syn.: *C.decurtata.*

3. *CONUS NIMBOSUS* Hwass. **Stormy Cone.** Ind.Oc.-Marq. 30–35–45–65mm. UC (was S). Color variable.

4. *CONUS NOBILIS* L. **Noble Cone.** E. Ind.Oc.-Marq. 25–30–38–59mm. UC (was R). Being overcollected. Cp. *C.marchionatus* (?subsp.). See *C.victor* (?subsp.).

5. *CONUS NUSSATELLA* L. E.Afr.-Poly., Haw. 30–35–50–95mm. C. Color and pattern variable.

6. *CONUS NUX* Brod. **Nut Cone.** Baja Cal.-G.of Cal.-Ecu. 12–18–22–25mm. C. ?Subsp. of *C.sponsalis.*

7. *CONUS OBSCURUS* Sow. **Obscure Cone.** E.Afr.-Poly., Haw. 18–20–30–41mm. C. Very thin. Smooth shoulder. Cp. *C.geographus, C. tulipa.*

8. *CONUS OCHROLEUCUS* Gm. P.I.-N.G. 40–45–55–65mm. C. Cp. *C.pilkeyi, C.radiatus.*

9. *CONUS OMARIA* Hwass. E.Afr.-W.Pac. 28–45–60–70mm. VC. Pale orange deep inside mouth. ?Form of *C.pennaceus.*

10. *CONUS ORBIGNYI* Audouin. S.E.Afr.-W.Pac. 38–40–55–86mm. C. Cp. *C.ichinoseana.*

11. *CONUS OTOHIMEAE* Kuroda & Ito. S.Japan-Tai. 18–25–30–32mm. VS.

12. *CONUS PAPILLIFERUS* Sow. N.S.W.-?Vic. 20–22–30–45mm. UC. Color and pattern q.v. Cp. *C.anemone.*

13. *CONUS PARIUS* Reeve. P.I.-New Heb. 25–30–32–35mm. C. Cp. *C.radiatus* (darker).

14. *CONUS PARVULUS* Link. W.Pac. 20–25–35–43mm. C. Syn. or subsp.: *C.imperator* Woolacott.

15. *CONUS PATRICIUS* Hinds. **Patrician** or **Pear-shaped Cone.** G.of Cal.-Ecu. 45–65–85–140mm. C. Very heavy. Velvety brown per. Syn.: *C.pyriformis* Reeve.

16. *CONUS PAULUCCIAE* Sow. Mad.-Ind.

Oc. Avg.55–65mm. VR. ?Large form of *C. aureus.*

17. *CONUS PAUPERCULUS* Sow. Sol. Avg.25–30mm. UC. ?Form of *C.boeticus.*

18. *CONUS PENNACEUS* Born. E.Afr.-Poly., Haw. 35–50–65–85mm. VC. Thin yellowish per. There is much confusion over the relationship of this sp. to these possible forms: *C.episcopus, C.magnificus, C.omaria, C. stellatus.*

19. *CONUS PERONIANUS* Iredale. N.S.W.-Tas. 38–50–60–70mm. UC. Illus. spec. is quite dark. ?Form of *C.anemone.*

20. *CONUS PERPLEXUS* Sow. **Puzzled Cone.** Baja Cal.-G.of Cal.-Ecu. 15–18–22–33mm. VC. J.Walls considers it a Panamic subsp. of *C.puncticulatus.*

21. *CONUS PERTUSUS* Brug. **Pertusa Cone.** Moz.-E.Afr.-Poly., Haw. 20–22–28–64mm. UC. Color fades.

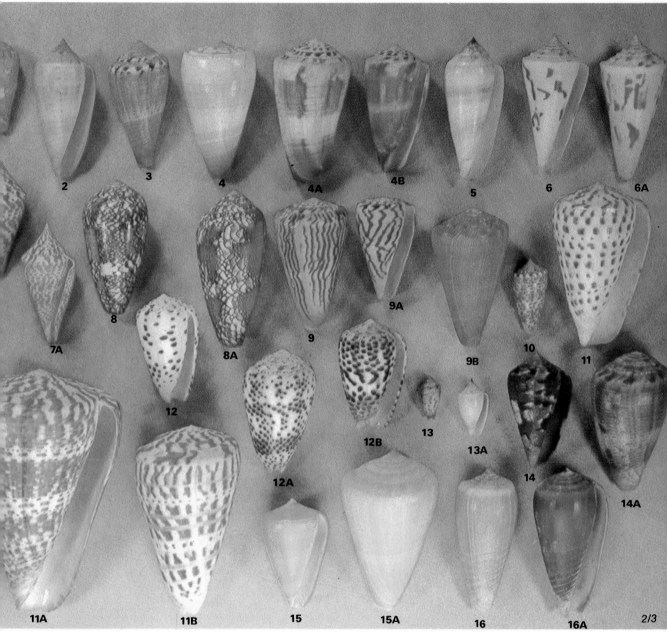

1. CONUS PICTUS Reeve. S.Afr. 20–28–35–50mm. S. Usually beach spec.

2. CONUS PILKEYI Petuch. P.I.-Fiji. 40–45–55–74mm. UC. Orange aperture. Illus. is of light color form. Cp. **C.ochroleucus.**

3. (CONUS PIPERATUS Dillwyn.) S.E.Afr., India-Sri Lanka. 35–38–45–60mm. C. Cp. **C. hyaena.** Syn. for **C.BILIOSUS** Röd.

4. CONUS PLANORBIS Born. E.Afr.-Poly. 30–40–50–65mm. C. Heavy. Cp. **C.circumactus, C.striatellus, C.vitulinus.**

5. CONUS PÖHLIANUS Sow. New Britain. 45–50–60–70mm. S (beach spec. C). Cp. **C. consors, C.magus.**

6. CONUS POORMANI Berry. W.Mex.-Col. 30–40–50–58mm. UC. Thick pale brown per. Cp. **C.villepinii.** ?Form of **C.recurvus.**

7. CONUS PRAECELLENS A.Adams. W. Pac. to Sol. 25–32–42–55mm. C. Syn.: **C. sowerbyi** Reeve.

8. CONUS PRAELATUS Hwass. E.Afr.-W. Ind.Oc. Avg.40–50mm. UC. ?Form of **C.pennaceus.**

9. CONUS PRINCEPS L. Prince Cone. G.of Cal.-Ecu. 35–45–60–130mm. UC. Thick bristly brown per. Being overcollected. 9B is form **C. p.lineolatus.** Val. Form **C.p.apogrammatus** Dall (not illus.) lacks markings.

10. CONUS PROXIMUS Sow. W.-S.Pac. 20–30–35–45mm. VS.

11. CONUS PULCHER Lightfoot. Small: **Butterfly Cone;** lge.: **Prometheus Cone.** W. Sahara-Angola. 50–60–75–250mm. C. Syn.: **C. papillionaceus** Hwass, **C.prometheus** Hwass.

12. CONUS PULICARIUS Hwass. **Flea-bitten Cone.** E.Afr.-Poly., Haw. 30–38–45–75mm. VC. Cp. **C.arenatus, C.vautieri** (?subsp.).

13. CONUS PUNCTICULATUS Hwass. S. Carib.-N.Brazil. 15–19–25–40mm. VC. Color and pattern q.v. Syn.: **C.papillosus** Kiener. Illus.: 13 is form **C.p.pygmaeus** Reeve (?sep.sp.); 13A is form **C.p.columba** Hwass.

14. CONUS PURPURASCENS Sow. **Purple Cone.** Baja Cal.-G.of Cal.-Ecu. 30–40–50–84mm. C. Color and pattern variable. Rough bristly brown per. ?Subsp. of **C.ermineus.**

15. CONUS QUERCINUS Lightfoot. **Oak Cone.** S.E.Afr.-Poly., Haw. 48–50–65–144mm. VC. Heavy.

16. CONUS RADIATUS Gm. **Radiant Cone.** P.I.-Fiji. 40–60–65–109mm. C. Cp. **C. ochroleucus, C.pilkeyi.**

143

Plate 126 | Conidae

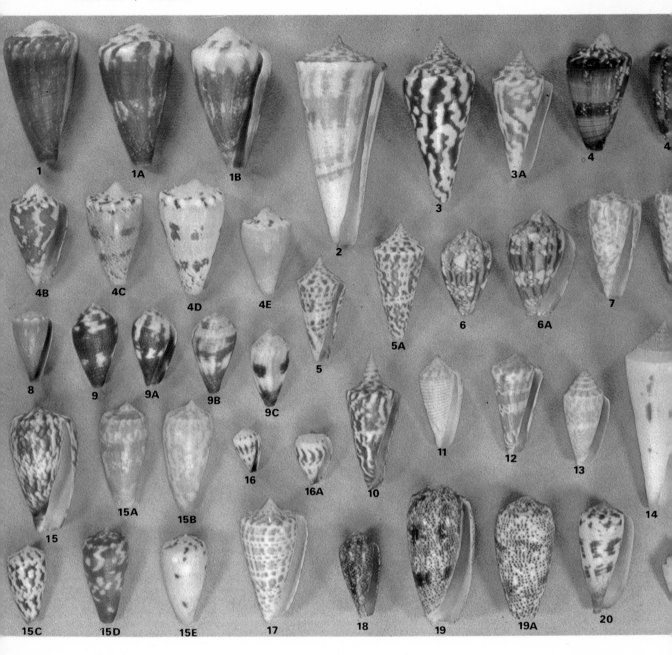

1. *CONUS RATTUS* Hwass. S.E.Afr.-Poly., Haw. 20-30-40-64mm. VC. Purple margin inside mouth.

2. *CONUS RECLUZIANUS* Bernardi. S. Japan-Tai.-P.I. 40-42-55-112mm. UC. Juveniles often violet or yellow. Cp. **C.tribblei, C. urashimanus, C.voluminalis.**

3. *CONUS RECURVUS* Brod. **Curved Cone.** Baja Cal.-G.of Cal.-Col. 38-50-65-100mm. UC. Cp. **C.scalaris, C.poormani** (?form).

4. *CONUS REGIUS* Gm. **Crown** or **Royal Cone.** S.Fla.-W.I.-Brazil. 30-35-50-84mm. C. Color and pattern q.v. Whitish mouth. Form **C.r.citrinus** Gm. is yellow or orange.

5. *CONUS REGULARIS* Sow. **Regular Cone.** Baja Cal.-G.of Cal.-Pan.-?Peru. 30-40-50-75mm. C. Mouth usually stained. ?Form of **C.gradatus.**

6. *CONUS RETIFER* Menke. **Netted Cone.** Ind.Oc.-Poly., Haw. 22-30-45-69mm. UC.

7. *CONUS RUFIMACULOSUS* Macpherson. Qld.-N.S.W. 30-35-40-50mm. C. Pink inside mouth.

8. *CONUS SANGUINOLENTUS* Q. & G. E.Afr.-Poly. 24-26-32-45mm. C. ?Subsp. of **C.lividus.**

9. *CONUS SCABRIUSCULUS* Dillwyn. W. Pac. to Poly. 20-25-32-51mm. C. Pattern variable.

10. *CONUS SCALARIS* Val. **Ladder Cone.** Baja Cal.-G.of Cal.-W.Mex. 30-40-50-84mm. C. Cp. **C.recurvus.** ?Form of **C.gradatus.**

11. *CONUS SCALPTUS* Reeve. P.I.-Sol. 24-32-38-50mm. S (beach spec.: UC). Name used by J.Walls. Often misnamed **C.mucronatus.**

12. *CONUS SCULLETTI* Marsh. N.Qld.-N.S.W. 30-37-45-60mm. UC.

13. *CONUS SEGRAVEI* Gatliff. S.Aust.-Vic. ca.25-32-38-54mm. S. ?Syn. for **C.clarus.**

14. *CONUS SIEBOLDII* Reeve. Japan-Tai.-?P.I. 55-60-75-115mm. C. Dull white. Thin greenish-gray per. Cp. **C.ione.**

15. *CONUS SPECTRUM* L. **Spectre Cone.** P.I., W.Aust.-Qld. 30-35-40-58mm. C. Color and pattern q.v. Cp. **C.broderipii** (?form), **C.**

cinereus, C.stigmaticus (?form). Syn.: **C.pica** Adams & Reeve.

16. *CONUS SPONSALIS* Hwass. E.Afr.-Poly., Haw. 15-17-20-32mm. VC. Pattern q.v. See **C.nux** (?subsp.).

17. *CONUS SPURIUS* Gm. **Alphabet Cone.** N.C.(R)-Fla.-G.of Mex.-Venez. 40-50-65-104mm. C. Heavy. Thin per.

18. *CONUS STELLATUS* Kiener. W.Ind.Oc. Avg.30-35mm. R. ?Form of **C.pennaceus.**

19. *CONUS STERCUSMUSCARUM* L. **Fly-specked Cone.** W.Pac. 37-40-50-60mm. C. Peach deep inside mouth. Cp. **C.arenatus** (coronated).

20. *CONUS STIGMATICUS* A.Adams. And.-Indon. 30-35-45-50mm. UC. ?Form of **C.spectrum** or **C.tegulatus.**

21. *CONUS STIMPSONI* Dall. S.E.Fla.-G.of Mex. 25-28-35-51mm. S.

2/3

1. *CONUS STRAMINEUS* Lam. E.Afr.-Sol. 30–32–40–60mm. C. Form variable. Reddish to purplish inside mouth. Cp. *C.collisus, C.inscriptus.*

2. *CONUS STRIATELLUS* Link. E.Afr.-Fiji. 30–38–45–70mm. C. Cp. *C.circumactus, C. planorbis, C.vitulinus.* Syn.: *C.pulchrelineatus* Hopwood.

3. *CONUS STRIATUS* L. **Striate Cone.** Moz.-E.Afr.-Poly., Haw. 60–65–80–129mm. VC. Pattern q.v.

4. *CONUS STUPELLA* Kuroda. S.Japan-Tai. 55–60–65–98mm. R.

5. *CONUS SULCATUS* Hwass. **Furrowed** or **Sulcate Cone.** Bay of Bengal-Sol. 40–45–55–87mm. C. Cp. *C.bocki* (?subsp.), *C. mucronatus.*

6. *CONUS SUMATRENSIS* Hwass. **Sumatran Cone.** Red Sea-E.Afr.-Ind.Oc. 39–50–60–73mm. UC. ?Form of *C.vexillum.*

7. *CONUS SURATENSIS* Hwass. **Surat Cone.** E.Afr.-Sol. 59–75–100–130mm. C. Very heavy. ?Subsp. of *C.betulinus.*

8. *CONUS SUTURATUS* Reeve. **Sutured Cone.** ?Ind.Oc.-W.Pac. to Haw. 25–28–32–46mm. C.

9. *CONUS TAENIATUS* Hwass. Red Sea-Per.G. <15–19–25–43mm. C.

10. *CONUS TEGULATUS* Sow. **Tiled Cone.** Ind.Oc.-Sol. 20–25–32–50mm. S. Form and pattern variable. Cp. *C.collisus andamanensis, C.stigmaticus* (?form).

11. *CONUS TELATUS* Reeve. **Webbed Cone.** So.P.I. 35–40–50–81mm. UC. Smooth and granulose forms. Cp. *C.aureus.*

12. *CONUS TERAMACHII* Kuroda. S.E.Afr., S.Japan-Tai. 50–80–95–103mm. R. Flesh color.

13. *CONUS TEREBRA* Born. E.Afr.-Poly. 37–40–50–93mm. C. Cp. *C.emaciatus.*

14. *CONUS TESSULATUS* Born. **Tesselate Cone.** S.E.Afr.-Poly., Haw.; also W.Mex.-C.R. 26–35–50–83mm. C.

15. *CONUS TEXTILE* L. **Textile** or **Cloth-of-gold Cone.** S.E.Afr.-Poly., Haw. 38–50–70–129mm. VC. Pattern q.v. Not venomous as sometimes stated. 15C is scarce form *C.t. panniculus* Lam. from Marq.

Plate 128 | Conidae

1. *CONUS THALASSIARCHUS* Sow. So. P.I. 40–60–75–106mm. C (once S). Color and pattern q.v.

2. *CONUS TIARATUS* Sow. **Turban** or **Roosevelt's Cone.** W.Mex.-Ecu. 15–25–35–49mm. UC (was C). Cp. **C.miliaris** (?subsp.). Syn.: **C.roosevelti** Bartsch & Rehder.

3. *CONUS TIGRINUS* Sow. S.W.Pac. ca. 35–40–50–60mm. C. Cp. **C.abbas.** ?Syn. for **C.canonicus** or **C.textile.**

4. *CONUS TIMORENSIS* Hwass. **Timor Cone.** Maur.-Indon.-N.G. 25–27–35–45mm. S. Usually faded dead spec.

5. *CONUS TINIANUS* Hwass. S.Afr.-Moz. 30–35–42–50mm. C. Color and pattern q.v. Usually beach spec. Cp. **C.mozambicus** (?same sp.). Syn.: **C.aurora** Lam., **C.rosaceus** Dillwyn.

6. *CONUS TORNATUS* Sow. **Grooved Cone.** Baja Cal.-G.of Cal.-Ecu. 15–22–26–45mm. C. Cp. **C.ximines.**

7. *CONUS TRIBBLEI* Walls. Tai.-P.I. 48–60–75–120mm. UC. Cp. **C.recluzianus, C. urashimanus.**

8. *CONUS TRIGONUS* Reeve. W.Aust.-N.T. 35–45–55–92mm. S. Form and color variable. Usually dead spec. (UC).

9. *CONUS TULIPA* L. **Tulip Cone.** E.Afr.-Poly. 30–45–60–95mm. C. Bluish. Venomous; possibly fatal to man. Cp. **C.geographus, C. obscurus.**

10. *CONUS TYPHON* Kilburn. S.Afr.-Moz. 30–32–40–49mm. VS. Often covered with fine brown spiral lines. Also, albino form.

11. *CONUS URASHIMANUS* Kuroda & Ito. S.Japan-Tai.-P.I. 40–50–60–75mm. UC. Fresh spec. violet-toned. Cp. **C.recluzianus, C. tribblei.**

12. *CONUS VARIUS* L. **Spotted Cone.** E. Afr.-Fiji. 25–30–40–61mm. C. pattern q.v.

13. *CONUS VAUTIERI* Kiener. Poly.-Marq. Avg.26–32mm. UC. ?Subsp. of **C.pulicarius.**

14. *CONUS VENTRICOSUS* Gm. **Mediterranean Cone.** Adriatic, Med.-Angola, C.V. 15–22–32–73mm. VC. Sinistral spec. VR. Cp. **C.aemulus.** Syn.: **C.mediterraneus** Hwass.

15. *CONUS VENULATUS* Hwass. C.V. 20–28–35–50mm. S. No.15 is the pale or albino higher-spired form. **C.v.trochulus** Reeve. The more typical form is illus. on pl. 129, no. 1.

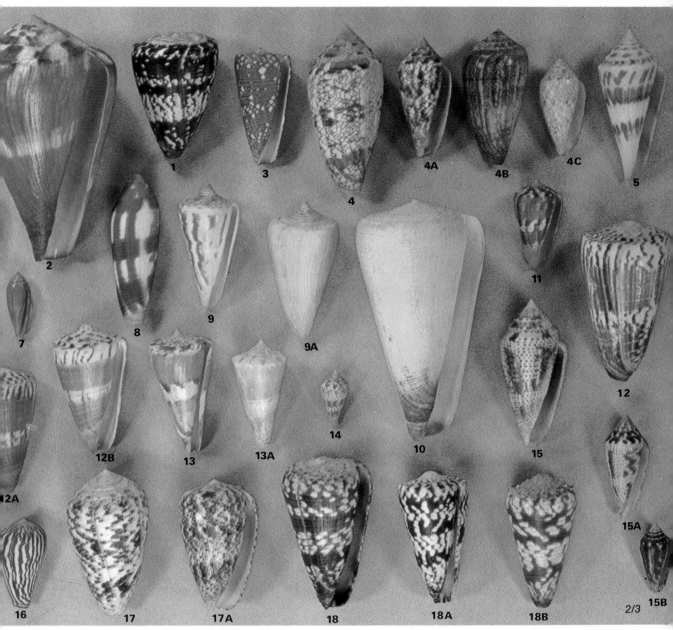

1. *CONUS VENULATUS* Hwass. – See pl. 128, no. 15.

2. *CONUS VEXILLUM* Gm. **Flag** or **Vexillum Cone.** S.E.Afr.-Poly., Haw. 50–60–75–163mm. C. Heavy. White mouth. Brown per. Juveniles yellow to green. Cp. *C.capitaneus, C.namocanus*. See *C.sumatrensis* (?form).

3. *CONUS VICTOR* Brod. Indon. Avg.40–45mm. Ext.R. ?Subsp. of *C.nobilis*.

4. *CONUS VICTORIAE* Reeve. **Queen Victoria's Cone.** W.Aust.-N.T. 30–40–50–70mm. C. Pattern q.v. 4B is form *C.v. cholmondeleyi* Marsh. 4C is subsp. *C.v.nodulosus* Sow. (pink inside mouth). Syn. of form: *C. complanatus* Sow.

5. *CONUS VILLEPINII* Fischer & Bernardi. S.E.Fla.-Yucatan. 30–50–65–72mm. UC (live: R). Usually dredged dead. Cp. *C.poormani, C. recurvus*.

6. *CONUS VIMINEUS* Reeve. **Wicker Cone.** ?Bay of Bengal, P.I. 25–32–38–50mm. UC. ?Form of *C.aculeiformis*.

7. *CONUS VIOLA* Cern. Okinawa, P.I.-N.

Aust. 22–25–35–50mm. R. Called *C.artoptus* by J.Walls.

8. *CONUS VIOLACEUS* Gm. **Violet Cone.** S.Ind.Oc. 40–42–50–80mm. UC. Syn.: *C. tendineus* Hwass.

9. *CONUS VIRGATUS* Reeve. **Virgate Cone.** Baja Cal.-G.of Cal.-Ecu. 33–42–50–75mm. C.

10. *CONUS VIRGO* L. **Virgin Cone.** S.E. Afr.-Poly. 50–60–80–151mm. VC. Deep purple base. Cp. *C.coelinae* (?form), *C.emaciatus*.

11. *CONUS VITTATUS* Hwass. **Ribboned Cone.** G.of Cal.-Ecu. 20–28–35–45mm. UC. Pattern variable. Thick, rough per. Cp. *C. amphiurgus, C.cardinalis*.

12. *CONUS VITULINUS* Hwass. **Calf** or **Veal Cone.** E.Afr.-Poly., Haw. 25–32–45–77mm. C. Cp. *C.circumactus, C.planorbis, C. striatellus*.

13. *CONUS VOLUMINALIS* Reeve. Bay of Bengal-Tai.-P.I. 30–35–40–54mm. UC.

14. *CONUS WAKAYAMAENSIS* Kuroda. Japan. Avg.22–28mm. S. ?Form of *C.eugrammatus*.

15. *CONUS XIMENES* Gray. **Interrupted Cone.** G.of Cal.-Peru. 24–30–40–61mm. VC. Cp. *C.tornatus*. 15A–B is *C.mahogani* Reeve (avg.25–35mm.) (?form or syn.).

16. *CONUS ZEBROIDES* Kiener. Angola. 15–20–25->40mm. C. ?Form of *C.bulbus*.

17. *CONUS ZEYLANICUS* Gm. S.E.Afr.-Ind.Oc.-?Malaysia. 35–38–48–76mm. C. Heavy.

18. *CONUS ZONATUS* Hwass. **Zoned Cone.** Seychelles-Ind.Oc.-Indon. 42–45–60–84mm. UC. Variable pattern.

Plate 130 | Terebridae

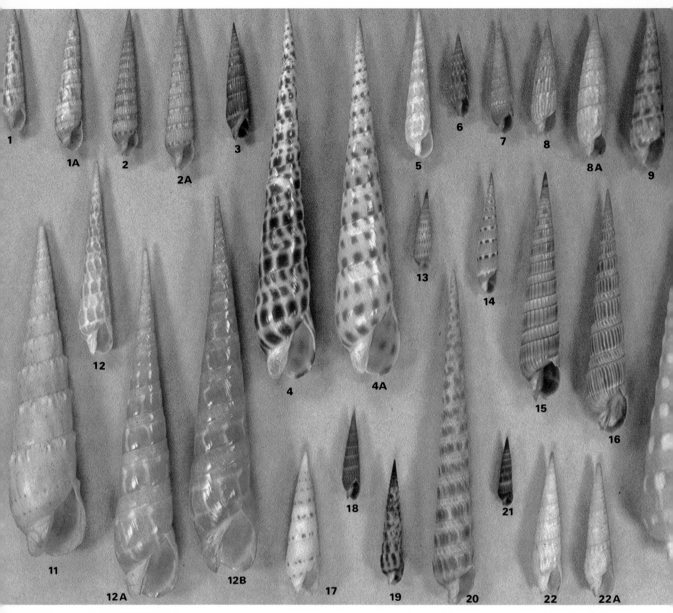

1. *TEREBRA AFFINIS* Gray. Moz.-Poly., Haw.; also G.of Cal. 20–25–45–67mm. VC.

2. *TEREBRA ALVEOLATA* Hinds. Tai. Avg.45–60mm. UC.

3. *TEREBRA (Duplicaria) ANOMALA* Gray. Tai., Aust. Avg.43–48mm. C.

4. *TEREBRA AREOLATA* Link. E.Afr.-W. Pac., Haw. 65–85–115–176mm. C. Note two natural repairs on no. 4. Syn.: *T.muscaria* L.

5. *TEREBRA ARGUS* Lam. E.Afr.-W.Pac., Haw. <50–55–70–80mm. C.

6. *TEREBRA ARMILLATA* Hinds. Baja Cal.-G.of Cal.-Peru. 15–25–30–64mm. C.

7. *TEREBRA BABYLONIA* Lam. E.Afr.-Per.G.-Poly., Haw. ca.30–35–50–75mm. C.

8. *TEREBRA CERITHINA* Lam. E.Afr.-Samoa, Haw. 20–35–50–76mm. C. Syn.: *T. spaldingi* Pilsbry.

9. *TEREBRA CHLORATA* Lam. E.Afr.-W. Pac., Haw. 50–55–65–90mm. C.

10. *TEREBRA (Hastula) CINEREA* Born. **Gray (Atlantic) Augur.** E.Fla.-W.I.-Brazil. Also, W.Mex.-Ecu. 25–35–40–50mm. C. *Hastula* is now considered a separate genus.

11. *TEREBRA CRENULATA* L. **Crenulated**

Augur. E.Afr.-W.Pac., Haw.; off W.Mex. 30–75–110–150mm. C.

12. *TEREBRA DIMIDIATA* L. **Dimidiate** or **Divided Augur.** Moz.-E.Afr.-W.Pac., Haw. <70–75–115–164mm. C.

13. *TEREBRA DISLOCATA* Say. **Atlantic** or **Common American Augur.** Md.-Fla.-Texas-W.I.-Brazil. Also, S.Cal.-Pan. 20–22–35–56mm. VC. Color variable.

14. *TEREBRA (Hastula) DIVERSA* E.A. Smith. S.E.Afr.-W.Pac. 19–25–35–49mm. C. Orange to brown. Cp. *T.strigilata.*

15. *TEREBRA (Duplicaria) DUPLICATA* L. **Duplicate Augur.** E.Afr.-W.Pac. ca.45–50–70–85mm. C. Color variable.

16. *TEREBRA DUSSUMIERI* Kiener. Tai.-Japan. <60–65–80–93mm. C.

17. *TEREBRA FELINA* Dillwyn. **Tiger Augur.** E.Afr.-W.Pac., Haw. 38–40–50–71mm. C.

18. *TEREBRA FLAVESCENS* Deshayes. Aust.-Fiji. 32–35–42–50mm. UC.

19. *TEREBRA FORMOSA* Deshayes. W. Mex.-Pan. Avg.70–75mm. UC.

20. *TEREBRA FUJITAI* Kuroda & Habe. Tai.-Japan. ca.90–110–115–130mm. VS.

21. *TEREBRA GLAUCA* Hinds. Baja Cal.-Ecu. 20–22–25–?45mm. C. Form and color variable.

22. *TEREBRA GOULDI* Deshayes. **Gould's Augur.** Haw. 30–35–45–65mm. UC.

23. *TEREBRA GUTTATA* Röd. **Eyed Augur.** E.Afr.-W.Pac., Haw. 57–90–120–210mm. UC. Syn.: *T.oculata* Lam.

1. TEREBRA (Hastula) HASTATA Gm. **Shiny Atlantic Augur.** S.E.Fla.(VS)-W.I.-Brazil, Berm. 18–20–30–40mm. C.

2. TEREBRA (Hastula) HECTICA L. **Bluish Augur.** E.Afr.-Poly., Haw. <28–30–45–75mm. C. Color and pattern variable.

3. TEREBRA (Hastula) INCONSTANS Hinds. Japan, Haw. <30–35–40–50mm. C.

4. TEREBRA (Hastula) LANCEATA Gm. **Lanced Augur.** E.Afr.-W.Pac., Haw. <25–35–55–63mm. C.

5. TEREBRA (Hastula) LUCTUOSA Hinds. W.Mex.-Ecu. 25–30–35–41mm. C. Grayish brown to black.

6. TEREBRA MACULATA L. **Big** or **Spotted Augur; Marlinspike.** E.Afr.-W.Pac., Haw.; also, off W.Mex., C.R. 70–100–150–274mm. VC. Edible. 16B is a juvenile.

7. TEREBRA (Hastula) MERA Hinds. W. Pac., esp.Sol. Avg.20–25mm. UC.

8. TEREBRA MICANS Hinds. Mauritania-Angola. Avg.25–35mm. C.

9. TEREBRA MONILIS Q. & G. **Necklace Augur.** E.Afr.-Poly. 25–32–40–50mm. C.

10. TEREBRA NEBULOSA Sow. Red Sea-Moz.-E.Afr.-W.Pac., Haw. 30–45–60–80mm. C.

11. TEREBRA ORNATA Gray. G.of Cal.-Ecu., Galáp. 30–45–65–92mm. C.

12. TEREBRA PERTUSA Born. **Perforated Augur.** And.-Haw. 32–50–65–75mm. UC. Yellow to orange.

13. TEREBRA PRETIOSA Reeve. **Precious Augur.** W.Pac. ca.60–75–100–125mm. UC.

14. TEREBRA (Duplicaria) RAPHANULA Lam. **Little Radish Augur.** S.Afr.-Fiji. 35–45–60–65mm. C.

15. TEREBRA ROBUSTA Hinds. **Robust Augur.** Baja Cal.-Galáp. 30–70–90–137mm. C. Syn.: **T.lingualis** Hinds.

16. TEREBRA SENEGALENSIS Lam. N. Mauritania-Angola. <70–80–100–110mm. C.

17. TEREBRA SEROTINA A.Adams. Japan-China Seas. 35–40–55–65mm. C.

18. TEREBRA SPECTABILIS Hinds. **Graceful Augur.** S.Afr., Japan-Tai. Avg.30–40mm. C.

19. TEREBRA STRIGATA Sow. G.of Cal.-Pan., Galáp. 80–85–100–144mm. UC (was C).

20. TEREBRA (Hastula) STRIGILATA L. **Strigate, Combed** or **Painted Augur.** W.Pac. to Melanesia, Haw. 19–25–45–?60mm. C. Cp. **T.diversa.** Syn.: **T.verreauxi** Deshayes.

21. TEREBRA STYLATA Hinds. Maur., W. Pac. Avg.30–38mm. C.

22. TEREBRA SUBULATA L. **Subulate** or **Chocolate Spotted Augur.** E.Afr.-W.Pac., Haw. <70–90–125–168mm. C.

23. TEREBRA TAURINUS Lightfoot. **Flame Augur.** S.E.Fla.-Texas-W.I.-Brazil. ca.75–90–120–178mm. S (was R).

24. TEREBRA TRISERIATA Gray. **Triseriate Augur.** W.Pac., Haw.(R). ca.60–65–85–95mm. UC.

25. TEREBRA VARIEGATA Gray. **Variegated Augur.** Baja Cal.-G.of Cal.-Ecu.-?Peru. 25–30–50–101mm. C.

Plate 132 | Turridae

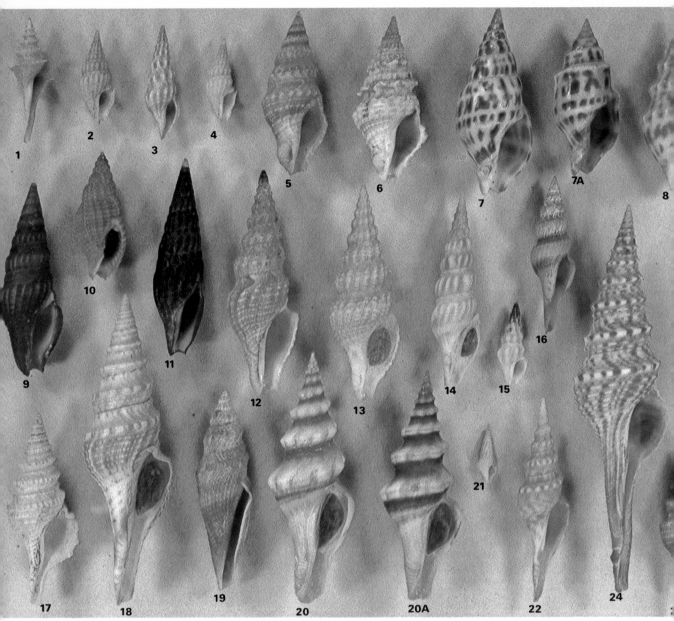

1. ANCISTROSYRINX PULCHERRISIMA Kuroda. Japan-Tai. 19–22–28–35mm. UC. Syn. for genus: *Cochlespira*.

2. CALLICLAVA ALBOLAQUEATA Cpr. Nicaragua-Pan.Bay. Avg.20–24mm. C.

3. CLATHRODRILLIA FLAVIDULA Lam. Japan. 28–40–60–75mm. C.

4. CLATHRODRILLIA SALVADORICA Hertlein & Strong. G.of Cal.-El Salvador. 20–30mm. UC.

5. CLAVATULA BIMARGINATA Lam. Mauritania-S.Afr. 30–40–50–65mm. C. Syn. for genus: *Pusionella, Perrona*.

6. CLAVATULA MURICATA Lam. Senegal-Gabon. 25–40mm. UC.

7. CLAVATULA NIFAT Brug. ?Algeria; Senegal-Angola. 30–40–55–70mm. C.

8. CLAVUS ECHINATUS Lam. Indon.-W. Pac. Avg.35–42mm. S.

9. CRASSISPIRA INCRASSATA Sow. G.of Cal.-Ecu. Avg.40–50mm. UC.

10. CRASSISPIRA MARTINENSIS Dall. G.of Cal. Avg.25–30mm. UC. ?Syn. for *Pseudomelatoma grippi* Dall.

11. CRASSISPIRA (Burchia) SEMINFLATA Grant & Gale. S.Cal.-Baja Cal. Avg.45–52mm. UC. Glossy black per. Syn.: *Pseudomelatoma redondoensis* T.Burch.

12. DRILLIA JEFFREYSII Smith. Japan. Avg.45–55mm. C.

13. DRILLIA PERCULATHRATA Kuroda. Japan. Avg.50–55mm. C.

14. DRILLIA RECURVIROSTATA Kuroda. Japan. Avg.45–50mm. C.

15. DRILLIA ROSEOLA Hertlein & Strong. No.G.of Cal.-Ecu. 15–18–22–31mm. UC.

16. FUSITURRIS UNDATIRUGA Bivona. Med., Canary Is., Mauritania-Angola. 35–40–55–70mm. UC.

17. GEMMULA COSMOI Sykes. Japan. 45–60mm. C.

18. GEMMULA UNEDO Kiener. W.Pac., esp. Japan. 60–70–90–105mm. C.

19. GENOTA MITRAEFORMIS Wood. Mauritania-Ivory Coast. 30–40–50–55mm. C.

20. KNEFASTIA TUBERCULIFERA Brod. No.G.of Mex.-W.Mex.-?Nicaragua. 40–45–65–88mm. C.

21. KYLIX PAZIANA Dall. G.of Cal. 12–17mm. S.

22. LEUCOSYRINX QUEENSLANDICA Powell. S.Qld., N.G. Avg.50mm. S.

23. LOPHIOTOMA ACUTA Perry. Red Sea-Samoa. 40–45–60–70mm. C. Syn.: *Turris tigrina* Lam.

24. LOPHIOTOMA INDICA Röd. **Indian Turris.** S.E.Afr.-Fiji. 50–60–80–93mm. C.

1. NIHONIA AUSTRALIS Roissy. W.Pac. Avg.80–95mm. UC.

2. POLYSTIRA ALBIDA Perry. **White Giant Turrid.** S.Fla.-Texas-G.of Mex., W.I. 70–80–100–122mm. C.

3. POLYSTIRA NOBILIS Hinds. **Noble Turrid.** No.G.of Cal.-Pan. 50–70–100–110mm. C. Syn. for genus: *Pleuroliria*.

4. POLYSTIRA OXYTROPIS Sow. Baja Cal.-Ecu. 20–30–40–53mm. C.

5. POLYSTIRA PICTA Reeve. No.G.of Cal.-Col. 32–40–50–55mm. C.

6. THATCHERIA MIRABILIS Angas. **Miraculous Thatcheria** or **Japanese Wonder Shell.** Japan-Tai. 60–65–75–109mm. UC.

7. TURRICULA COREANICA Adams & Reeve. Japan. Avg.32–35mm. C.

8. TURRICULA KADERLEYI Lischke. Japan. Avg.70–85mm. C.

9. TURRICULA KAMAKURANA Pilsbry. Japan. Avg.42–55mm. C.

10. TURRICULA NELLIAE GRANO-BALTEUS Hedley. Japan-Tai. Avg.30–38mm. UC.

11. TURRICULA SUBDECLIVIS Yokoyama. Japan-Tai. Avg.42–50mm. UC.

12. TURRICULA TORNATA Dillwyn. Ind. Oc.-W.Pac. Avg.60–75mm. C.

13. TURRIS BABYLONIA L. **Tower Turrid.** W.Pac. Avg.70–85mm. C. Old syn. for genus: *Pleurotoma.*

14. TURRIS CRISPA Lam. **Great Turrid.** Ind.Oc.-Fiji, Haw. 60–70–100–150mm. UC.

15. TURRIS LEUCOTROPIS A.Adams & Reeve. Japan. Avg.50–70mm. C.

16. TURRIS LÜHDORFI Lischke. Japan-Tai. 40–50–65–72mm. C.

17. TURRIS SOLOMONENSIS E.A.Smith. N.G.-Sol.-Fiji. 20–27mm. S.

18. TURRIS UNIZONALIS Lam. W.Pac. to Fiji. 18–25mm. C.

19. XENUROTURRIS CINGULIFERA Lam. Red Sea, S.E.Afr.-Fiji. ca.40–45–60–76mm. UC. Horny reddish-brown operc.

Plate 134 | Pyramidellidae – Acteonidae – Aplustridae – Bullidae

1. *PYRAMIDELLA ACUS* Gm. E.Afr.-W. Pac. 32–50–60mm. C. Color and pattern variable.

2. *PYRAMIDELLA DOLABRATA* Lam. **Giant Atlantic Pyram.** Fla.Keys-W.I.; also, W.Afr.-S.E.Afr. 20–25–35–39mm. C. See *P. terebellum*, no. 5.

3. *PYRAMIDELLA MACULOSA* Lam. E. Afr.-W.Pac. 25–40–45mm. C. ?Syn. for *P.acus*.

4. *PYRAMIDELLA SULCATA* A.Adams. **Sulcate Pyramidella.** E.Afr.-W.Pac., Haw. 25–28–35–50mm. C.

5. *PYRAMIDELLA TEREBELLUM* Müller. **Ringed Pyramidella.** E.Afr.-C.Pac., Haw. 20–25–32–35mm. C. ?Syn. for *P.dolabrata*.

6. *ACTEON ELOISEAE* Abbott. Muscat, Oman. Avg.29–32mm. R.

7. *ACTEON PUNCTOCAELATUS* Cpr. **Carpenter's Baby Bubble** or **Barrel Shell.** Br.Col.-Baja Cal. 10–12–16–20mm. C.

8. *ACTEON TORNATILIS* L. Norway-Med.-Zaire. 15–25mm. C.

9. *SOLIDULA SOLIDULA* L. **Solid Pupa.** S.E.Afr.-W.Pac. Avg.19–25mm. C. Variable pattern. Syn. for genus: *Pupa*.

10. *SOLIDULA SULCATA* Gm. **Sulcate Pupa.** S.E.Afr.-W.Pac. 17–26mm. C. Col. and patt. q.v.

11. *APLUSTRUM AMPLUSTRE* L. **Pink Bubble** or **Ship's Flag Shell.** Moz.-E.Afr.-W.Pac. to Marq., Haw. 14–25mm. UC. Fragile. Now placed by some writers under *Hydatina*.

12. *HYDATINA ALBOCINCTA* Hoeven. **Clown** or **White-banded Bubble.** ?E.Afr.; W. Pac., Haw. 25–30–45–60mm. C. Thin tan per. All *Hydatina* shells are very thin and fragile.

13. *HYDATINA PHYSIS* L. **Striped Bubble.** Red Sea, E.Afr.-Haw.; also, Mauritania-Zaire; S. Afr. 25–28–40–>50mm. C. Thin pale yellow per. *H.vesicaria* Lightfoot (not illus.) is a similar, rarer sp. or subsp.

14. *HYDATINA VELUM* Gm. S.E.Afr.-Ind. Oc. Avg.36–45mm. UC. ?Syn. for *H.zonata* Lightfoot.

15. *BULLINA NOBILIS* Habe. Japan-Tai. 16–21mm. S.

16. *BULLA ADAMSI* Menke. Qld., Haw. Avg.22–25mm. C.

17. *BULLA AMPULLA* L. **Large True Bubble.** S.E.Afr.-W.Pac. 32–35–50–60mm. VC. Color and pattern variable.

18. *BULLA BOTANICA* Hedley. **Common True Bubble.** W.-S.Aust.-N.S.W., Tas. 32–38–45–55mm. VC.

19. *BULLA GOULDIANA* Pilsbry. **California, Cloudy** or **Gould's Bubble.** S.Cal.-Ecu. 35–55–73mm. VC. Thin dark brown per.

20. *BULLA OCCIDENTALIS* A.Adams. **Common True, Florida** or **W.I. Bubble.** N.C.-S.E.Fla.-W.I. 13–25mm. VC. Syn.: *B. umbilicata* Röd. ?Syn. for *B.striata*, heavier.

21. *BULLA PUNCTULATA* A.Adams. Baja Cal.-G.of Cal.-Peru; also, W.Pac. 15–20–25–30mm. C. Syn.: *B.orientalis* Habe.

1/1

1. BULLA QUOYI Gray. **Brown Bubble Shell.** N.Z. 30–50mm. C.

2. BULLA STRIATA Brug. **Striate Bubble.** W.Fla.-Texas, W.I.-Brazil; also, Med. 20–22–30–40mm. C. ?Syn.: *B.adansoni* Philippi (2A), from W.Sahara-Angola, C.V.

3. BULLA VERNICOSA Gould. Thailand, W.Pac., Haw. Avg.42–50mm. C. Up to four faint dark bands.

4. ATYS CYLINDRICUS Helbing. **Cylindrical True Bubble Shell.** Moz.-E.Afr.-W.Pac. 12–15–22–30mm. C. Thin gray per.

5. ATYS NAUCUM L. **White** or **Nut Sheath Bubble.** E.Afr.-W.Pac. 17–25–32–45mm. C. Thin orange-brown striped per.

6. HAMINOEA ELEGANS Gray. **Elegant Paper Bubble.** S.E.Fla.-Texas, W.I.-Brazil; also, Mauritania. 13–20mm. C.

7. HAMINOEA HYDATIS L. W.Eur.-W. Med.-Morocco, Canary Is. 8–12–18–23mm. C.

8. HAMINOEA VESICULA Gould. **Gould's** or **Blister Paper Bubble.** S.E.Alaska-So.G.of Cal. 15–22mm. C.

9. PHILINE KURODAI Habe. Japan. 14–19mm. UC. Internal shell. Very thin, fragile.

10. SCAPHANDER LIGNARIUS L. **Woodgrained** or **Woody Canoe Shell.** Iceland-W. Eur.-Med. 32–40–60–80mm. C.

11. CAVOLINIA TRIDENTATA Forskål. Worldwide, pelagic. 5–7–15–20mm. C. Nos. 11–15 are Pteropods or "Sea Butterflies". All are glassy and very thin.

12. CAVOLINIA UNCINATI Rang. Worldwide, pelagic. 5–>10mm. C.

13. CLIO LANCEOLATA Lesueur. Worldwide, pelagic. <10–20mm. C. Syn. for genus: *Cleodora.*

14. CUVIERINA COLUMNELLA Rang. Worldwide, pelagic. 5–14mm. C. Syn. for genus: *Cuvieria.*

15. DIACRIA MUCRONATA Quay. Worldwide, pelagic. 5–>10mm. C.

16. APLYSIA PARVULA Mörch. **Small Sea Hare.** I-P, esp.Aust.; Haw.; also, W.I.; G.of Cal.; England-W.Atl. ca.10–20mm. C. Very thin horny internal shell.

17. AKERA SOLUTA Gm. **Papery Bubble Shell.** S.E.Afr.-W.Pac. 20–25–35–48mm. C. Very thin, fragile. Thin glassy per.

18. DOLABELLA SCAPULA Lam. **Hatchet Sea Hare.** E.Afr.-Maur.-Ind.Oc.-W.Pac. 30–140mm. C. Internal shell.

19. TYLODINA FUNGINA Gabb. **Yellow Umbrella Shell.** S.Cal.-C.R., Galáp. 14–16–22–30mm. C. Rubbery.

20. UMBRACULUM MEDITERRANEUM Lam. **Mediterranean Umbrella.** Med. 40–50–70–100mm. C.

21. UMBRACULUM SINICUM Gm. **Umbrella Shell.** S.E.Afr.-W.Pac., Haw. 50–65–85–100mm. C. Syn.: *U.indica* Lam.

153

Plate 136 | Amphibolidae – Melampidae – Siphonariidae – Trimusculidae

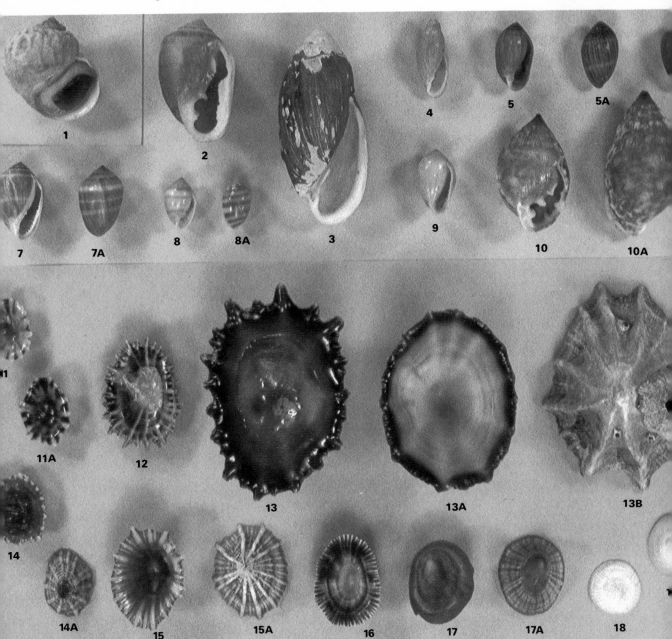

1. AMPHIBOLA CRENATA Martyn. N.Z. Avg.25–32mm. VC.

2. CASSIDULA ANGULIFERA Petit. **Angular Ear Shell.** N.Aust.-Qld. 25–35mm. C. Nos.2–10 are air-breathing salt-marsh snails.

3. ELLOBIUM AURISJUDAE L. **Judas Ear Shell.** W.Pac. 45–60mm. C. Illus. shows brown per.

4. ELLOBIUM STAGNALIS Orbigny. El Salvador-Ecu., Galáp. 18–25mm. C. Thin horny per.

5. MELAMPUS CAROLIANUS Lesson. C.R.-Ecu., Galáp. Avg.15–18mm. C.

6. MELAMPUS CASTANEUS Mühlfeldt. W.-C.Pac., Haw. 12–15mm. C.

7. MELAMPUS COFFEUS L. **Coffee-bean Marsh Snail.** S.Fla.-W.I.-Brazil, Berm. 12–15–18–20mm. VC.

8. MELAMPUS FASCIATUS Deshayes. **Brown-and-white Coffee Shell.** W.Pac. 11–15–20–25mm. C. ?Form of *M.flavus* Gm.

9. MELAMPUS LUTEUS Q. & G. **Necklace Coffee Shell.** E.Afr.-W.Pac. 12–15–20–25mm. C. ?Form of *M.flavus* Gm.

10. PYTHIA SCARABAEUS L. W.Pac. 25–30–40–50mm. C. Syn.: *P.pantherina* A.Adams.

11. SIPHONARIA ACMAEOIDES Pilsbry. Japan. 14–21mm. UC.

12. SIPHONARIA ASPERA Kuroda & Habe. S.Afr. Avg.25–30mm. UC.

13. SIPHONARIA GIGAS Sow. **Giant False Limpet** W.Mex.-Peru. 32–40–55–84mm. C. Largest of genus. Barnacles usually attached, as in 13B.

14. SIPHONARIA JAPONICA Donovan. Japan. 16–20mm. VC. Yellowish per.

15. SIPHONARIA LACINIOSA L. W.Pac., esp.Japan. 19–27mm. VC.

16. SIPHONARIA PECTINATA L. **Striped False Limpet.** E.Fla.-Texas-Mexico, W.I. Avg. 20–25mm. C.

17. PACHYSIPHONARIA LESSONI Blainville. Argentina. Avg.18–20mm. UC.

18. TRIMUSCULUS RETICULATUS Sow. **Reticulate Button Shell.** C.Cal.-G.of Cal.-W. Mex. 12–14–18–25mm. C.

1. SOLEMYA PANAMENSIS Dall. **Panama Veiled Clam.** S.Cal.-G.of Cal.-Pan. Avg.36–39mm. UC. Glossy fringed per.

2. ACILLA SCHENCKI Kira. Japan. 27–35mm, C.

3. NUCULA NUCLEUS L. **Common Nut Clam.** W.Eur.-Med.-W.Afr.-S.Afr. 10–15mm. C. Greenish per.

4. YOLDIA LIMATULA Say. **File Yoldia.** Maine-N.J.; also, Alaska-S.Cal. 18–30–50–75mm. C. Glossy, greenish per. illus. is subsp. *Y.l.gardneri* Oldroyd.

5. SACCELLA CONFUSA Hanley. Japan. 19–23mm. UC.

6. ARCA (Barbatia) BARBATA L. **Bearded Ark Shell.** Med. 30–35–50–65mm. C. Hairy blackish per.

7. ARCA NOAE L. **Noah's Ark.** W.Eur.-Med.-Senegal. 50–60–70–75mm. C. Hairy brown per. Edible.

8. ARCA SUBNAVICULARIS Iredale. N.W.Aust.-Qld. 55–60–80–100mm. C.

9. ARCA (Trisodos) TORTUOSA L. **Twisted Ark.** Aust. 60–70–80–100mm. C. White, tan to yellow. Silky brown per. ?Syn.: *Arca yongei* Iredale.

10. ARCA ZEBRA Swainson. **Turkey Wing.** N.C.-W.Fla.-Texas, Berm., Lesser Ant. 50–55–75–90mm. VC. Matted brown per. Syn.: *A. orientalis* Philippi.

11. ANADARA BRASILIANA Lam. **Incongruous** or **Brazil Ark.** N.C.-W.Fla.-Texas, W.I.-Brazil. 25–35–50–65mm. C. Thin pale brown per. Syn.: *A.incongrua* Say.

12. ANADARA TRANSVERSA Say. **Transverse Ark.** Mass.-Fla.-Texas, W.I. 13–20–32–38mm. C. Grayish-brown per.

13. NOETIA PONDEROSA Say. **Ponderous Ark.** Va.-S.E.Fla.-Texas-G.of Mex. 45–50–60–65mm. C. Thick velvety black per.

14. SENILIA SENILIS L. W.Afr. Avg.45–65mm. C. Heavy. Hairy dark brown per.

15. GLYCYMERIS DECUSSATA L. **Decussate Bittersweet.** S.E.Fla.-W.I.-Brazil. Avg.45–50mm. C. (Fla.: R).

16. GLYCYMERIS GIGANTEA Reeve. **Giant Bittersweet.** G.of Cal.-W.Mex. 65–70–85–100mm. C.

17. GLYCYMERIS LATICOSTATA Q. & G. **Large Dog Cockle.** N.Z. 40–50–65–75mm. C. Heavy.

18. GLYCYMERIS LONGIOR Sow. Uruguay. Avg.19–25mm. C.

19. GLYCYMERIS VIOLASCENS Lam. Med. 40–45–60–70mm. UC. Velvety dark brown per.

20. TUCETONA AMBOINENSIS Gm. **Amboina Dog Cockle.** E.Afr.-S.W.Pac. 12–20–40–50mm. C.

Plate 138 | Mytilidae

1. MYTILUS EDULIS L. **Blue** or **Edible Mussel.** Nearly worldwide. 40-50-75-105mm. VC. Glossy per. Edible.

2. PERNA CANALICULATA Gm. W.Pac. Avg.25-35mm. VC.

3. BRACHIDONTES MODIOLUS L. **Yellow** or **Lemon Mussel.** S.Fla.-W.I. 25-30-38-46mm. C. Syn.: **B.citrinus** Röd.

4. MYTELLA GUYANENSIS Lam. W.Mex.-N.Peru; also, Venez.-Brazil. Avg.35-55mm. C. Green to black.

5. ISCHADIUM RECURVUM Rafinesque. **Hooked Mussel.** Mass.-Fla.-Texas, W.I. 25-35-50-65mm. C.

6. PERNA VIRIDIS L. **Green Mussel.** Ind. Oc.-W.Pac. 35-40-60-65mm. C. Bright green per.

7. SEPTIFER BILOCULARIS L. **Deck Mussel.** S.E.Afr.-W.Pac. 25-30-45-50mm. C. Variable color.

8. MUSCULUS NIGER Gray. **Black Mussel.** Arctic-N.C.; also, Alaska-Wash. 30-50-70-75mm. C.

9. MUSCULUS WATSONI Smith. Japan. Avg.44-50mm. UC.

10. LITHOPHAGA LITHOPHAGA L. Med. 40-45-65-70mm. C. Brown per. Edible.

11. LITHOPHAGA TERES Philippi. **Chocolate Date Mussel.** E.Afr.-W.Pac. 50-60-80-120mm. C.

12. MODIOLUS ALBICOSTUS Lam. **White Ribbed** or **Narrow Horse Mussel.** W.Aust.-N.S.W., Tas. 60-70-90-100mm. C.

13. MODIOLUS AMERICANUS Leach. **Tulip Mussel** or **Common Horse Mussel.** N.C.-Fla.-Texas, W.I.-Brazil, Berm. 25-35-60-100mm. VC. Thick, hairy pale brown per. Silky yellow byssus. Syn.: **M.tulipa** Lam. The E.Pac. counterpart is **M.pseudotulipus** Olsson, Baja Cal.-Peru.

14. MODIOLUS BARBATUS L. **Bearded Horse Mussel.** W.Eur.-Med.-Morocco. 30-40-60-70mm. VC. Thick, shaggy, fringed per.

15. MODIOLUS CAPAX Conrad. **Capax** or **Fat Horse Mussel.** S.Cal.-Peru. 50-70-100-176mm. C. Hairy per.

16. GEUKENSIA DEMISSA Dillwyn. **Ribbed Mussel.** G.of St. Lawrence-N.C.-Fla.-Texas-Yucatan; also, No.Cal. 60-65-85-100mm. VC. Thin glossy per. Syn.: **Modiolus plicatula** Lam.

17. AMYGDALUM PALLIDULUM Dall. No.Cal.-Col. Avg.17-22mm. C.

18. BOTULA (Adula) FALCATA Gould. **Falcate Date Mussel** or **Pea-pod Shell.** Ore.-Baja Cal. 48-55-75-100mm. C. Thin, rubbery. Wrinkled brownish per.

19. LIOBERUS SALVADORICUS Hertlein & Strong. Baja Cal.-C.R. 15-25mm. UC.

Plate 139

1. PINNA CARNEA Gm. **Amber Pen Shell.** S.E.Fla.(S)-W.I. 100-150-200-275mm. C. Thin, fragile.

2. PINNA MURICATA L. E.Afr.-W.Pac., esp.Japan; Haw. ca.100-135mm. C. Thin, fragile.

3. ATRINA KINOSHITAI Habe. Japan. 60-70-90-110mm. UC. Thin, fragile. ?Syn. for **A. pectinata** L.

4. PTERIA BREVIALATA Dunker. Japan. 44–50–65–70mm. C. Brown per.

5. PTERIA LOVENI Dunker. Japan. 50–55–70–75mm. C. Brown per.

6. PTERIA STERNA Gould. **Western Wing Oyster.** So.Cal.-Baja Cal.-G.of Cal.-Peru. 40–60–90–100mm. C. Wrinkled per. A pearl oyster.

7. PINCTADA MARGARITIFERA L. **Black-Lip Pearl Oyster.** E.Afr.-W.Pac., Haw. 65–100–200–250mm. C. Thick, brittle, fringed per.

8. PINCTADA MAZATLANICA Hanley. **Panamanian Pearl Oyster.** Baja Cal.-G.of Cal.-Peru. 60–100–125–156mm. C. Thick, brittle, fringed per.

9. ISOGNOMON ALATUS Gm. **Flat** or **Winged Tree Oyster.** S.Fla.-Texas, W.I. 50–60–80–91mm. C.

10. ISOGNOMON JANUS Cpr. Baja Cal.-G.of Cal.-W.Mex. 35–45–65–80mm. C.

11. ISOGNOMON RECOGNITUS Mobile. **Western Tree Oyster** or **Purse Shell.** ?S.Cal., N.Baja Cal.-Peru. 20–30–45–50mm. C. Syn.: **Perna chemnitziana** Orbigny.

12. MALLEUS ALBUS Lam. **White Hammer Oyster.** ?Ind.Oc.-W.Pac. 75–100–150–220mm. C.

13. MALLEUS MALLEUS L. **Black** or **Common Hammer Oyster.** Ind.Oc.-W.Pac. 75–100–150–210mm. VC.

14. OSTREA ANGELICA Rochebrune. G.of Cal.-Ecu. 25–40–70–100mm. C.

15. OSTREA LURIDA Cpr. **Native Pacific, California** or **Olympic Oyster.** Alaska-Baja Cal. 50–80mm. VC.

16. CRASSOSTREA VIRGINICA Gm. **Eastern Oyster.** G.of St. Lawrence-G.of Mex., W.I.; introduced to W.coast of U.S., Haw. 50–75–125–150mm. VC. Dark brown per. Edible; includes form "Blue Point".

17. OSTREA (LOPHA) CUCULLATA Born. E.Afr.-W.Pac. 43–50–55–60mm. C. Cerith usually attached, as illus.

18. OSTREA (LOPHA) CRISTAGALLI L. **Cock's-comb Oyster.** Ind.Oc.-W.Pac., esp. P.I. 50–60–80–90mm. C.

19. OSTREA (LOPHA) HYOTIS L. **Hyotoid Oyster.** E.Afr.-W.Pac. 85–100–150–200mm. VC. Edible.

20. OSTREA (LOPHA) IMBRICATA Menke. W.Pac. 55–65–85–100mm. C.

21. OSTREA (LOPHA) MEGODON Hanley. G.of Cal.-Peru. 50–70–90–100mm. C.

157

Plate 140 | Plicatulidae – Pectinidae

1. *PLICATULA SIMPLEX* Gould. Japan. 10–16mm. C.

2. *PLICATULA SPONDYLOPSIS* Rochebrune. G.of Cal.-Ecu. 25–40mm. C.

3. *BATHYAMUSSIUM JEFFREYSI* Smith. Japan. 15–18mm. S. V.thin.

4. *LUTEAMUSSIUM SIBOGAI* Dautzenberg & Bavay. Japan. 25–36mm. UC. V.thin. Parasitic *Capulus tosaensis* Otuka US. leaves white scar.

5. *PARVAMUSSIUM CADUCUM* Smith. Japan. 18–26mm. UC. V.thin.

6. *AMUSIUM JAPONICUM* Gm. **Japanese Sun and Moon Shell.** W.Pac., esp.Japan. ca. 80–90–110–120mm. VC. Right valve yellowish white. Edible.

7. *AMUSIUM JAPONICUM BALLOTTI* Bernardi. **Ballot Saucer Scallop.** S.W.Pac., esp.E.Aust.-New Cal. 60–75–100–ca.150mm.

C. Subsp. Often with *Capulus dilatatus* A.Adams attached. Edible.

8. *AMUSIUM LAURENTI* Gm. **Laurent's Scallop.** G.of Mex.-W.I.-Honduras. 40–50–70–90mm. UC.

9. *AMUSIUM PAPYRACEUS* Gabb. **Paper Scallop.** Texas-G.of Mex.-W.I.-Brazil. 45–50–75–102mm. UC.

10. *AMUSIUM PLEURONECTES* L. **Sun and Moon Shell** or **Delicate Saucer Scallop.** Ind.Oc.-W.Pac. 60–65–85–103mm. C. Right valve white. Edible.

11. *PECTEN (Notovola) ALBICANS* Schröter. **Japanese Scallop.** Japan. 40–45–55–65mm. C. Color and pattern q.v. May have *Capulus dilitatus* A.Adams attached.

12. *PECTEN (Serratovola) ASPERA* Sow. **Rough Scallop.** W.Pac. 25–28–35–42mm. C. Syn.: *P.tricarinata* Anton.

13. *CHLAMYS (Mimachlamys) ASPERRIMUS* Lam. **Prickly Scallop, Fan Shell** or **Doughboy.** S.W.Aust.-N.S.W., Tas. 30–35–45–50mm. C. Color q.v.

14. *PECTEN (Lyropecten) AURANTIACUS* Adams & Reeve. W.Pac., esp.Okinawa. 20–28–35–38mm. S.

15. *CHLAMYS (Mimachlamys) AUSTRALIS* Sow. S.W.Aust. 60–75–90->100mm. C. Color ext.v.; yellow scarce.

16. *CHLAMYS (Equichlamys) BIFRONS* Lam. **Queen** or **Two-faced Scallop.** S.Aust.-N.S.W., Tas. 45–50–75–123mm. C. Purple inside. Edible.

17. *PECTEN (Mesopeplum) CAROLI* Iredale. **Carol's Scallop.** Vic.-N.S.W. 25–45mm. C.

– – *PECTEN CAURINUS* – See pl. 144, no. 9.

1. *ARGOPECTEN CIRCULARIS* Sow. **Pacific Calico Scallop.** S.Cal.-Peru. 28–40–65–106mm. C. Col. and patt. var. Cp. *A.gibbus.*

2. *ARGOPECTEN CIRCULARIS AEQUIS-ULCATUS* Cpr. **Speckled Scallop.** Cal.-Baja Cal.-G.of Cal. 45–100mm. UC. Subsp.

3. *CHLAMYS IRREGULARIS COOKEI* Dall, Bartsch & Rehder. **Cooke's Scallop.** Haw. 15–18–25–>30mm. S. See no. 16. *C.cookei* is now considered a syn. for *C.irregularis.*

4. *CHLAMYS DIEFFENBACHI* Gray. **Southern Fan Scallop.** N.Z. 15–50mm. C. Var. bright col.; yellow VS. Syn.: *C.celator* Finley.

5. *PECTEN DIEGENSIS* Dall. **San Diego Scallop.** S.Cal.-Baja Cal. 50–60–80–>100mm. S. *Capulus* sp. often attached.

6. *PECTEN FLABELLUM* Gm. Mauritania-Angola. 25–35–45–53mm. C. Col. and patt. q.v.

7. *ARGOPECTEN GIBBUS* L. **Calico Scallop.** Md.-Fla.-Texas-?Brazil, Berm. 25–30–50–78mm. VC. Var., bright colors. Edible. See also *A.nucleus.*

8. *PECTEN GLABER* L. Med. 25–30–50–66mm. C. Often bright red or orange. Yellow form (8C): *P.g.mytilene.*

9. *CHLAMYS (Mimachlamys) GLORIOSUS* Reeve. **Glory Scallop.** Ind.Oc.-W.Pac. 20–30–50–?75mm. C. Variable colors.

10. *AEQUIPECTEN GLYPTUS* Verrill. **Tryon's Scallop.** Mass.-Fla.-Texas. 22–63mm. UC.

11. *CHLAMYS HASTATA* Sow. **Spear Scallop.** C.-S.Cal. Avg.50–63mm. VS. Bright yellow, orange, red, purple.

12. *CHLAMYS HASTATA HERICIA* Gould. **Pacific Pink Scallop.** Alaska-S.Cal. 50–55–75–93mm. C. Variable colors. ?Sep. sp.

13. *CHLAMYS IMBRICATA* Gm. **Little Knobby Scallop.** S.E.Fla.-W.I., Berm. 20–25–40–53mm. S. Yellow inside.

14. *PECTEN INFLEXUS* Poli. Med. 18–25–30–35mm. UC.

15. *ARGOPECTEN IRRADIANS* Lam. **Atlantic Bay** or **Bearning Scallop.** Nova

16. *CHLAMYS IRREGULARIS* Sow. Red Sea; Japan; Haw. 25–30–38–42mm. UC. Usually yellow to red. See no. 3. Syn.: *C.albolineatus* G.B.Sow.

17. *CHLAMYS ISLANDICA* Müller. **Iceland** or **Northern Scallop.** Arctic Seas-Mass.; Alaska-Wash.; Japan. 60–80–100mm. VC. Cols. ext.v.

**– – *PECTEN JACOBEUS* L. – See pl. 144, no. 10.

18. *CHLAMYS JOUSSEAUMEI* Bavay. Japan. 12–15–18–20mm. UC.

19. *CHLAMYS "LAETUS"* Gould. Japan. 50–55–65–70mm. UC. Reddish shades. Syn. for *C.nipponensis.*

20. *LEPTOPECTEN LATIAURATUS* Conrad. **Kelp Scallop.** No.Cal.-?G.of Cal. 13–20–30–?53mm. C.

21. *CHLAMYS LEMNISCATA* Reeve. Japan. 16–18–22–25mm. UC. Tiny spines. Color q.v.

22. *CHLAMYS (Mimachlamys) LENTI-GINOSA* Reeve. W.Pac. 25–30–45–50mm. C.

Plate 142 | Pectinidae

1. *CHLAMYS (Annachlamys) LEOPARDUS* Reeve. **Leopard Scallop.** W.Pac. 40–50–65–75mm. C.

2. *AEQUIPECTEN LINEOLARIS* Lam. **Wavy-lined Scallop.** S.E.Fla.-Carib. 25–30–45–50mm. S.

3. *PECTEN LISCHKEI* Dunker. Uruguay-Argentina. Avg.60–75mm. UC. Color variable. Syn.: *P.patriae* Doello-Jurado.

4. *CHLAMYS (Scaeochlamys) LIVIDUS* Lam. **Scaly Scallop** or **Fan-Shell.** S.W.Pac., esp. Aust. 38–45–60–75mm. C.

5. *PECTEN LUCULENTUM* Reeve. W.Pac., esp.W.Aust. 35–38–45–55mm. UC.

6. *PLACOPECTEN MAGELLANICUS* Gm. **Atlantic Deep-sea Scallop.** Labrador-N.C. 70–100–150–230mm. C. Edible.

160 --*PECTEN MAXIMUS* L.-See pl. 144, no. 11.

-- *CHLAMYS MELICA* Iredale. – See pl. 144, no. 12.

7. *PECTEN (Notovola) MERIDIONALIS* Tate. **Commercial** or **King Scallop.** S.Qld.-N.S.W., Tas., N.Z. ca.70–80–110–>150mm. VC. Color variable. Edible. Illus. is form *P.m. fumata* Reeve.

8. *CHLAMYS MIRIFICA* Reeve. Red Sea; W.Pac., Haw. 18–20–25–44mm. R.

9. *HINNITES MULTIRUGOSUS* Gale. **Giant Rock Scallop.** Aleutians-Baja Cal. ca. 60–75–125–233mm. C. Free-swimming young resemble *Chlamys*.

10. *AEQUIPECTEN MUSCOSUS* Wood. **Mossy** or **Rough Scallop.** N.C.-Fla.-Texas, W.I.-?Brazil, Berm. 20–25–35–51mm. C. Variable bright colors.

11. *CHLAMYS NIPPONENSIS* Kuroda.

Japan-Korea. 35–40–60–85mm. C. ?Subsp. of *C.farreri*. See also pl. 141, no. 19.

12. *CHLAMYS (Mimachlamys) NOBILIS* Reeve. **Noble Scallop.** Ind.Oc.-W.Pac., esp. Japan. 45–55–85–>100mm. C. Variable colors, incl. purple, orange, yellow. ?Same sp. as *C. senatorius*.

13. *LYROPECTEN NODUSUS* L. **Lion's Paw** or **Knobbed Scallop.** N.C.-Fla.-Texas, Berm., W.I.-Brazil; Ascension Is. 35–50–75–165mm. UC. Variable colors, usually orange to red. Knobs often restored to enhance value.

14. *PECTEN NOVAEZELANDIAE* Reeve. **N.Z. Queen Scallop.** N.Z. 60–75–100–140mm. C. Color q.v. Edible.

15. *ARGOPECTEN NUCLEUS* Born. **Nucleus Scallop.** S.E.Fla.-W.I. 20–25–35–38mm. C. ?Subsp. of *A.gibbus*.

1. *AEQUIPECTEN OPERCULARIS* L. **Quin** or **Queen Scallop.** W.Eur.-Med. 35–40–60–80mm. C. Colors q.v. Edible.

2. *CHLAMYS ORNATA* Lam. **Ornate Scallop.** S.E.Fla.-W.I.-Brazil, Berm. 18–38mm. UC.

3. *PECTEN (Cryptopecten) PALLIUM* L. **Painted Scallop.** Red Sea, E.Afr.-W.Pac., esp. P.I. 40–45–60–92mm. VC. Var. cols. and patt.

4. *LEPTOPECTEN PALMERI* Dall. G.of Cal. 20–35–45–50mm. UC.

5. *PECTEN PROTEUS* Lightfoot. Sicily-Ionian Sea. Avg.45–55mm. UC. Variable color.

6. *PECTEN (Comptopallium) RADULA* L. **Flat-ribbed** or **Grater Scallop.** W.Pac., esp. P.I.-Guam. 40–45–65–80mm. C. Syn.: *P. pauciplicatum* Iredale.

7. *PECTEN RASTELLUM* Lam. Red Sea; P.I. 22–25–35–38mm. R.

8. *PECTEN RAVENELI* Dall. **Ravenel's Scallop.** N.C.-Fla.-Texas, W.I. 30–35–45–75mm. UC. Cp. *P.ziczac.*

9. *CHLAMYS (Annachlamys) REEVEI* Adams & Reeve. **Reeve's Scallop.** W.Pac., esp.P.I. 35–40–50–56mm. C. Syn.: *C.macasserensis* Chenu.

10. *CHLAMYS RUBIDA* Hinds. **Hind's Scallop.** Alaska-S.Cal. 35–45–60–65mm. C. Colors variable. Syn.: *C.hindsi* Cpr.

11. *PECTEN SCABRICOSTATUS* Lam. Aust. Avg.40–50mm. C.

12. *CHLAMYS SENATORIUS* Gm. E.Afr.-W.Pac., esp.P.I. 25–30–50–>75mm.C. Colors, often very bright, q.v. ?Same sp. as *P.nobilis*.

13. *CHLAMYS SENTIS* Reeve. N.C.-Fla.-W.I.-?Brazil. 20–25–35–55mm. C. Variable, often bright, colors.

14. *PECTEN (Notovola) SINENSIS* Sow. **Chinese Scallop.** Japan-Tai. 30–40–60–70mm. UC. Color and pattern q.v.

15. *PECTEN (Gloripallium) SPECIOSA* Reeve. **Scaled Scallop.** Okinawa. 30–35–45–50mm. VS.

16. *CHLAMYS (Excellichlamys) SPECTABILIS* Reeve. Red Sea; W.Pac. 18–42mm. S.

17. *CHLAMYS SQUAMATA* Gm. W.Pac. to Tonga. 32–35–45–62mm. C. Color and pattern q.v. Often misnamed *C.squamosa* Gm. ?Syn.: *C.larvata* Reeve.

18. *CHLAMYS SQUAMOSA* Gm. W.Pac. to Tonga. 25–30–45–60mm. C. Color and pattern q.v. Often misnamed *C.squamata* Gm.

19. *DECATOPECTEN STRIATUS* Schumacher. Japan. 25–30–40–48mm. C. 5 or 6 ribs. Often confused with *D.plica* L. (not illus.), which has 9 or more ribs.

20. *PECTEN SUPERBUS* Sow. Okinawa. 35–40–55–60mm. R.

161

Plate 144 | Pectinidae

1. CHLAMYS TEHUELCHUS Orbigny. Brazil-Argentina. 30–40–55–60mm. UC.

2. CHLAMYS TIGERINA Müller. **Tiger Scallop.** North Sea-W.Eur.-Med. 15–18–25–30mm. C. Color and pattern q.v.

3. CHLAMYS (Comptichlamys) TIGRIS Lam. ?E.Afr., W.Pac. 38–40–55–60mm. C.

4. PECTEN (Leptopecten) TUMBEZENSIS Orbigny. G.of Cal.-Peru. 20–30–35–40mm. UC: Variable pattern.

5. CHLAMYS VARIA L. **Variegated Scallop.** Norway-Med.-Senegal. 20–25–45–60mm. C. Color and pattern q.v. Edible.

6. PECTEN (Cryptopecten) VESICULOSUS Dunker. Japan. 22–25–30–38mm. UC.

7. CHLAMYS (Bractechlamys) VEXILLUM Reeve. **Frag Scallop.** W.Pac. 30–35–45–50mm. C. Variable color and pattern.

8. PECTEN ZICZAC L. **Zigzag Scallop.** N.C.-Fla.-Yucatan, W.I.-?Brazil, Berm. 30–50–85–127mm. C. Color and pattern q.v.; also orange or red. Cp. **P.raveneli.** See no. 20.

9. PECTEN (Patinopecten) CAURINUS Gould. **Giant Pacific** or **Weathervane Scallop.** Aleutian Is.-No.Cal. ca.100–150–200–288mm. C. Edible.

10. PECTEN JACOBEUS L. **Pilgrim** or **Jacob's Scallop.** Med. 50–75–100–130mm. C. Edible. Cp. **P.maximus.**

11. PECTEN MAXIMUS L. **Great Scallop.** W.Eur.-W.Med. 70–80–110–>130mm. C. Variable color and pattern. Edible. Cp. **P.jacobeus.**

12. CHLAMYS (Annachlamys) MELICA Iredale. **Carmine Banded Scallop.** N.W.Aust., Tas. 50–60–70–85mm. C. ?Form of **C.leopardus.** Cp. **C.flabellatus** Lam.

13. ARGOPECTEN PURPURATUS Lam.

Peru-Chile. 60–101mm. C. Rarely yellow.

14. PECTEN SERICEUS Hinds. **Silken Scallop.** G.of Cal.-Peru. 40–70–85–95mm. UC.

15. LYROPECTEN SUBNODUSUS Sow. **Pacific Lion's Paw** or **Blunt-knobbed Scallop.** Baja Cal.-G.of Cal.-Peru. 65–100–150–200mm. C. Reddish-purple inside.

16. CHLAMYS (Swiftopecten) SWIFTI Bernardi. **Swift's Scallop.** Aleutian Is.-Japan. ca.50–75–100–?120mm. C. Variable color.

17. CHLAMYS TOWNSENDI Sow. Persian G.-Pak. ca.100–125–160–175mm. UC. Var. patt.

18. PECTEN VOGDESI Arnold. Baja Cal.-G.of Cal.-Pan. Avg.60–95mm. UC.

19. PECTEN (Patinopecten) YESSOENSIS Jay. **Giant Ezo Scallop.** Japan. ca.100–125–150–>180mm. C. Edible.

20. PECTEN ZICZAC L. – See no. 8.

1. *SPONDYLUS AMERICANUS* Hermann. **Atlantic Thorny Oyster** or **Chrysanthemum Shell.** N.C.-Fla.-Texas, W.I.-Brazil. 63–75–125–193mm. C. Color q.v.: orange, red, purple, etc. Young resemble *Chama*.

2. *SPONDYLUS AURANTIUS* Lam. W.Pac., esp.P.I. 50–60–80–100mm. UC. Syn.: *S. versicolor* Schreibers.

3. *SPONDYLUS BUTLERI* Reeve. W.Pac. ca.75–85–115–135mm. C.

4. *SPONDYLUS CALCIFER* Cpr. **Lime-Carrier.** G.of Cal.-Ecu. 100–150–267mm. C.

5. *SPONDYLUS CRUENTIS* Lischke. Japan. 32–35–50–55mm. UC.

6. *SPONDYLUS DUCALIS* Röd. Red Sea-W.Pac. 50–60–80–100mm. C.

7. *SPONDYLUS MARISRUBRI* Röd. – See no. 11.

8. *SPONDYLUS LINGUAEFELIS* Sow. Haw. Avg.70–100mm. Ext.R. Color q.v. Syn.: *S.gloriosus* Dall, Bartsch & Rehder.

9. *SPONDYLUS IMPERIALIS* Chenu. **Imperial Thorny Oyster.** Ind.Oc.-W.Pac. 50–60–80–100mm. UC.

10. *SPONDYLUS LIMA* Chenu. Japan, P.I. 40–45–55–60mm. S.

11. *SPONDYLUS MARISRUBRI* Röd. **Red Sea Thorny Oyster.** Red Sea. 50–75–100–115mm. UC. See also no. 7. Sold as *S.gloriandus*. Often confused with *S.gaederopus* L., a similar Med.-W.Atl. sp.

12. *SPONDYLUS NICOBARICUS* Sow. W.Pac. 60–65–85–100mm. C.

13. *SPONDYLUS PESASINUS* Röd. W.Pac., esp.P.I. 60–70–90–110mm. C. Sold as *S.aculeatus* Chemnitz. Misnamed *S.sinensis* in Jap. books.

14. *SPONDYLUS PRINCEPS* Brod. **Pacific** or **Painted Thorny Oyster.** G.of Cal.-Pan. 55–75–125–185mm. C. White, orange, red. Spines usually bent. Syn.: *S.crassisquamatus* Lam., *S.pictorum* "Chemnitz".

15. *SPONDYLUS REGIUS* L. **Regal Thorny Oyster.** W.Pac. 75–125–175–225mm. UC. Illus. are of juveniles. Orange to red.

16. *SPONDYLUS SANGUINEUS* Dunker. W.Pac. Avg.30–40mm. UC.

17. *SPONDYLUS SINENSIS* Sow. **Chinese** or **Bearded Thorny Oyster.** W.Pac. 50–60–85–110mm. UC. Deep orange color form is illus. Syn.: *S.barbatus* Reeve.

18. *SPONDYLUS TENELLUS* Reeve. **Scarlet Thorny Oyster.** W.Aust.-N.S.W. ca. 50–60–75–95mm. C. Pink to scarlet red.

19. *SPONDYLUS WRIGHTIANUS* Crosse. **Long-spined Thorny Oyster.** W.Aust.-Qld. 50–75–100–135mm. C.

Plate 146 | Limidae – Anomiidae – Crassatellidae – et al.

1. LIMA LIMA L. **Spiny Lima** or **File Shell.** S.E.Fla.-Texas, W.I.-Brazil, Berm.; also, Ind. Oc.-W.Pac. 35–45–75–100mm. VC. I-P form: **L.l.vulgaris** Link; syn.: **L.sowerbyi** Deshayes.

2. LIMA SCABRA Born. **Rough Lima** or **File Shell.** S.C.-Fla.-Texas, W.I.-Brazil. 35–45–60–106mm. C. Brown per.

3. ANOMIA EPHIPPIUM L. **Saddle Oyster.** W.Eur.-Med.-W.Afr.; also, S.Atl. 40–50–60–70mm. VC.

4. ANOMIA PERUVIANA Orbigny. **Peruvian Jingle Shell.** C.Cal.-Peru. 25–30–50–63mm. C. Color variable. Illus. is of lower valve.

5. ANOMIA SIMPLEX Orbigny. **Common, Smooth** or **Atlantic Jingle Shell.** Nova Scotia-Fla.-G.of Mex., W.I.-Brazil. 25–30–40–50mm. VC. Color variable. Often stained black.

6. PLACUNANOMIA CUMINGII Brod. G.of Cal.-Ecu. 50–55–75–85mm. UC.

7. PODODESMUS (Monia) CEPIO Gray. **Pearly Monia.** Br.Col.-G.of Cal. 35–50–75–128mm. VC. ?So. form of **P.macroschisma.** Often attached to **Haliotis.**

8. PODODESMUS (Monia) MACRO-SCHISMA Deshayes. **False Pacific Jingle.** Alaska-Baja Cal.; also, Japan. 35–50–75–100mm. VC. Illus. is of lower valve.

9. CRASSATELLITES JAPONICUS Dunker. Japan. Avg.30–35mm. C.

10. EUCRASSATELLA GIBBOSA Sow. G.of Cal.-Peru. Avg.50–60mm. UC.

11. EUCRASSATELLA KINGICOLA Lam. **King Island Crassatella.** N.S.W.-Vic., Tas. 50–65–86–100mm. C. Thick dark brown per.

12. EUCRASSATELLA PULCHRA Reeve. **Beautiful Crassatella.** N.W.-N.Aust. Avg.65–75mm. UC. Chestnut brown per.

13. ASTARTE CASTANEA Say. **Chestnut** or **Smooth Astarte.** Nova Scotia-N.J.-?N.C. Avg.22–25mm. C. Pale brown per.

14. ASTARTE UNDATA Gould. **Wavy Astarte.** Labrador-N.J. 20–28mm. C. Dark brown per.

15. NEOTRIGONIA LAMARCKI Gray. N.S.W. Avg.25–30mm. C. Inside iridescent purple.

16. NEOTRIGONIA MARGARITACEA Lam. **Southern Brooch Shell.** N.S.W.-Vic., Tas. 30–38mm. C. Inside iridescent red to purple.

17. CARDITA AFFINIS Sow. G.of Cal.-W. Mex. 40–55–65–70mm. C. Syn.: **C.californica** Deshayes.

18. CARDITA BICOLOR Lam. Ind.Oc.-W. Pac., esp.P.I. Avg.38–45mm. C.

19. CARDITA CRASSICOSTA Lam. **Thick-ribbed Cardita.** W.Pac. 25–40–60–75mm. UC. Color and form q.v.

20. CARDITA FLORIDANA Conrad. **Florida** or **Broad-ribbed Cardita.** W.-S.Fla.-Texas-Mex. 25–28–35–38mm. VC. Gray per.

21. CARDITA (Fulvia) RACKETTI Dono-van. **Common Southern Cockle.** S.W.Aust.-N.S.W. Avg.38–45mm. C. Yellowish per.

22. CARDITA (Cardites) LATICOSTATA Sow. G.of Cal.-Peru. Avg.30–42mm. C. Color q.v. Syn.: **C.tricolor** Sow.

23. CARDITA SENEGALENSIS Reeve. Senegal. 27–42mm. C. Color variable.

24. GLANS HIRASEI Dall. Japan. 25–32mm. UC.

1. GLOSSUS HUMANUS L. **Heart Cockle.** W.Eur.-Med. 60–65–85–>100mm. C. Thick brownish per. Edible. Syn.: *Isocardium cor* L.

2. MEIOCARDIA VULGARIS Reeve. W. Pac., esp.P.I. 28–35–45–50mm. UC. ?Syn.: *Isocardia moltkianus* Spengler. See no. 3.

3. MEIOCARDIA TETRAGONA Adams & Reeve. W.Pac., esp.Japan. Avg.25–28mm. C. ?Syn. with *M.vulgaris*.

4. CODAKIA ORBICULARIS L. **Tiger Lucine** or **Lucina.** Fla.-Texas, W.I.-Brazil, Berm. 50–60–80–90mm. C.

5. CODAKIA PAYTENORUM Iredale. W. Pac. 30–35–40–50mm. C.

6. CODAKIA TIGERINA L. **(Pacific) Common Codakia.** E.Afr.-W.Pac. 50–55–70–100mm. C.

7. FIMBRIA FIMBRIATA L. **Basket Lucina.** W.Pac., Haw. 60–65–85–100mm. C. Heavy. Syn. for genus: *Corbis*.

8. LINGA PENNSYLVANICA L. **Pennsylvania Lucina.** N.C.-S.Fla.-W.I. 25–32–40–54mm. VC. Yellowish wrinkled per. Formerly placed under *Lucina*.

9. LUCINA PECTINATA Gm. **Thick or Comb Lucina.** N.C.-Fla.-Texas, W.I.-Brazil. 25–35–50–65mm. C. Syn.: *L.jamaicensis* Lam. Syn. for genus: *Phacoides*.

10. DIPLODONTA ORBELLA Gould. **Orb Diplodon.** Alaska-Pan. 19–27mm. C.

11. CHAMA (Arcinella) BRASILIANA Nicol. Brazil. Avg.40–45mm. UC.

12. CHAMA BRASSICA Reeve. **Cabbage Jewel Box.** E.Afr.-W.Pac., esp.P.I. Avg.55–70mm. C.

13. CHAMA CRENULATA Lam. Mauritania-Gabon, C.V. 35–50mm. UC.

14. CHAMA ECHINATA Brod. **Spiny Jewel Box.** G.of Cal.-Pan.-?Peru. Avg.45–60mm. C. Usually eroded.

15. CHAMA LAZARUS L. **Lazarus** or **(Pacific) Leafy Jewel Box.** W.Pac., esp.P.I. 50–60–90–>110mm. C. White and/or pale colors; rarely pure yellow or orange. Syn.: *C.pulchella*.

16. CHAMA MACEROPHYLLA Gm. **(Atlantic) Leafy Jewel Box.** N.C.-Fla.-G.of Mex., W.I.-Brazil, Berm. 25–40–65–75mm. C. Color q.v., often very bright.

17. CHAMA PELLUCIDA Brod. **Clear** or **Agate Jewel Box.** Ore.-Chile. 38–45–60–72mm. C.

18. CHAMA (Pseudochama) RETROVERSA Lischke. Japan. Avg.30–35mm. C.

19. CHAMA "RUBEA". P.I. Avg.60–70mm. UC.

20. ARCINELLA CORNUTA Conrad. **(Florida) Spiny Jewel Box.** N.C.-E.& W.Fla.-Texas. 25–30–40–55mm. C. Syn.: *Echinochama cornuta* L.

21. PSEUDOCHAMA PANAMENSIS Reeve. G.of Cal.-Pan. Avg.35–40mm. UC.

165

Plate 148 | Cardiidae

1. *ACANTHOCARDIA ACULEATA* L. **Spiny Cockle** or **Red Nose.** W.England-Morocco, Med. ca.50–80–>100mm. VC. Edible.

2. *ACANTHOCARDIA ECHINATA* L. **Prickly Cockle.** W.Eur.-Med. 40–75mm. C.

3. *ACANTHOCARDIA TUBERCULATA* L. **Rough Cockle.** S.England-Morocco, Med. Avg.50–65mm. VC. Col. and patt. vary. Edible.

4. *AMERICARDIA BIANGULATA* Brod. & Sow. **Western Strawberry Cockle.** S.Cal.-Ecu. 25–30–35–38mm. C. Formerly under *Trigoniocardia.*

5. *AMERICARDIA MEDIA* L. **Atlantic Strawberry Cockle** or **American Cockle.** N.C.-S.E.Fla.-W.I.-Brazil, Berm. 25–30–35-ca.45mm. C. Formerly under *Trigoniocardia.*

6. *CARDIUM COSTATUM* L. **Ribbed Cockle.** Mauritania-Angola, C.V. 75–80–100–110mm. UC.

7. *CARDIUM HEMICARDIUM* L. **Half Cockle.** W.Pac. 25–30–40–50mm. C.

8. *CARDIUM NEBULOSUM* Reeve. P.I. Avg.35–40mm. UC.

9. *CARDIUM PSEUDOLIMA* Lam. E.Afr., Per.G. Avg.70–100mm. UC.

10. *CARDIUM RINGENS* Brug. W.Afr.; also, E.Afr.-W.Pac. Avg.30–40mm. UC.

11. *CARDIUM VICTOR* Angas. Japan, P.I. Avg.30–35mm. R.

12. *CERASTODERMA EDULE* L. **Common** or **European Edible Cockle.** W.Eur.-Med.-W.Afr. 25–30–40–50mm. VC. Brown per. Edible. Formerly under *Cardium.*

13. *CLINOCARDIUM NUTTALLII* Conrad. **Basket** or **Nuttall's Cockle.** N.W.Pac.-Japan; Bering Sea-S.Cal. 50–75–100–?150mm. C. Thin brownish per. Edible. Syn.: *Cardium corbis* Martyn.

14. *CORCULUM CARDISSA* L. **True Heart Cockle.** W.Pac., esp.P.I. 38–45–60–75mm. C. White and/or pale colors.

15. *DISCORS AURANTIACA* A.Adams & Reeve. W.Pac. Avg.25–30mm. UC. Thin.

16. *FRAGUM FRAGUM* L. **White Strawberry Cockle.** E.Afr.-W.Pac. 25–35–40mm. C.

17. *FRAGUM UNEDO* L. **Strawberry Cockle.** W.Pac. 38–45–60–65mm. VC.

18. *LAEVICARDIUM ATTENUATUM* Sow. **Attenuated Cockle.** E.Afr.-W.Pac. Avg. 40–55mm. UC.

19. *LAEVICARDIUM ELATUM* Sow. **Giant** or **Great (Pacific) Egg Cockle.** S.Cal.-Pan. 60–125–190mm. C. Largest of Cardiidae.

20. *LAEVICARDIUM LAEVICARDIUM* L. **Common Egg Cockle.** N.C.-E.& W.Fla.-Texas, W.I.-Brazil, Berm. 25–35–50–80mm. C.

1. NEMOCARDIUM BECHEI Reeve. W. Pac., esp.Japan. 45–75mm. UC. Yellowish brown per. Syn.: *Pratulum probatum* Iredale.

2. NEMOCARDIUM LYRATUM Sow. **Lyrate Cockle.** E.Afr.-W.Pac. 35–40–50–63mm. UC. Formerly placed under *Discors*.

3. PAPYRIDEA CROCKERI Hertlein & Strong. Baja Cal.-G.of Cal. Avg.45–50mm. UC.

4. PAPYRIDEA SOLENIFORMIS Brug. **Spiny Paper Cockle.** N.C.-Fla.-W.I.-Brazil, Berm. 25–30–40–45mm. C.

5. TRACHYCARDIUM BELCHERI Brod. & Sow. W.Mex.-Pan. 35–40–50–55mm. UC.

6. TRACHYCARDIUM CONSORS Sow. **Scaly Cockle.** G.of Cal.-Ecu., Galáp. Avg. 60–70mm. C.

7. TRACHYCARDIUM ISOCARDIA L. **Prickly Cockle.** W.I.-N.coast of S.Am., Berm. 45–50–65–75mm. VC.

8. TRACHYCARDIUM MAGNUM L. **Magnum Cockle.** Fla.Keys-W.I.-Brazil, Berm. 50–55–75–90mm. UC.

9. TRACHYCARDIUM (Mexicardia) PROCERUM Sow. G.of Cal.-Chile. Avg.40–50mm. C.

10. VASTICARDIUM BURCHARDI Dunker. Japan. 60–65–85–90mm. C. Syn. for genus: *Acrosterigma*.

11. VASTICARDIUM FLAVUM L. E.Afr.-W.Pac. Avg.50–60mm. C. Yellowish-brown per.

12. VEPRICARDIUM MULTISPINOSUM Sow. **Many-spined Cockle.** W.Pac. Avg.38–50mm. C.

13. VEPRICARDIUM PULCHRICOSTATUM Iredale. Qld.-N.S.W. 45–50–65–75mm. C. ?Syn. for *V.multispinosum*.

14. AMIANTIS PURPURATA Lam. Brazil-Uruguay. Avg.50–60mm. C.

15. ANOMALOCARDIA AUBERIANA Orbigny. **Pointed Venus.** Fla.-Texas, Mex.-?Pan. 13–20mm. C.

16. ANOMALODISCUS SQUAMOSUS L. W.Pac., esp.Japan. Avg.28–35mm. VC.

17. ANTIGONA CHEMNITZII Hanley. E. Afr., W.-N.Aust. 50–60–85–100mm. C. Formerly placed under *Periglypta* or *Trigonoma*.

18. ANTIGONA LAMELLARIS Schumacher. **Frilled Venus.** Ind.Oc.-W.Pac. 40–45–55–63mm. C.

19. BASSINA DISJECTA Perry. **Wedding Cake Venus.** Ind.Oc., W.Aust.-N.S.W., Tas. Avg.50–65mm. UC. Syn. for genus: *Callanaites*.

20. BASSINA YATEI Gray. N.Z. Avg.50–60mm. C.

21. CALLISTA ERYCINA L. Ind.Oc. Avg. 70–90mm. UC.

Plate 150 | Veneridae

1. CHAMELEA GALLINA L. W.Eur.-Med. 25–30–38–45mm. C.

2. CHIONE AMATHUSIA Philippi. G.of Cal.-Peru. Avg.38–50mm. C.

3. CHIONE CANCELLATA L. **Cross-barred Venus.** S.C.-Fla.-Texas, W.I. 25–30–38–45mm. VC.

4. CHIONE GNIDIA Brod. & Sow. Baja Cal.-G.of Cal.-Peru. 40–60–80–110mm. C.

5. CHIONE LATILIRATA Conrad. **Imperial Venus.** N.C.-Fla.-Texas, W.I. 25–35mm. UC.

6. CHIONE PAPHIA L. **King Venus.** Fla. Keys(R)-W.I.-Brazil. Avg.30–38mm. UC.

7. CHIONE PULICARIA Brod. G.of Cal.-Col. Avg.40–48mm. C.

8. CHIONE SUBIMBRICATA Sow. G.of Cal.-Peru. 20–30–35–40mm. C. Formerly placed under **Anomalocardia**.

9. CHIONE SUBRUGOSA Wood. Baja Cal.-G.of Mex.-Peru. 25–35–45–50mm. VC. Edible. Formerly placed under **Anomalocardia**.

10. CHIONE TUMENS Verrill. Baja Cal.-G.of Cal. Avg.30–35mm. C. ?Subsp. of **C. subimbricata**.

11. CHIONE UNDATELLA Sow. **Frilled California Venus.** S.Cal.-W.Mex.-Peru. 25–35–50–65mm. VC. ?Subsp. of **C.californiensis** Brod.

12. CIRCE RIVULARIS Born. **Circular Tapestry Shell.** Qld. Avg.40–45mm. C. Variable pattern. Thin greenish-brown per.

13. CIRCE SCRIPTA L. E.Afr.-W.Pac. 25–30–45–50mm. VC. Variable pattern.

14. CIRCOMPHALUS PLICATA Gm. Mauritania-Congo. 50–70mm. UC. Syn.: **Venus foliaceo-lamellosa** of various authors.

15. CLAUSINELLA CALOPHYLLA Hanley. W.Pac. Avg.30–35mm. C.

16. COSTACALLISTA IMPAR Lam. **Purple-rayed Sulcate Venus.** N.W.Aust. 40–45–60–65mm. C.

17. COSTACALLISTA LILACINA Pallas. **Giant Sulcate Venus.** W.Aust. 40–50–70–>80mm. C.

18. COSTACALLISTA "SEMPERI". Aust. Avg.45–50mm. UC.

19. CRYPTOGRAMMA SQUAMOSA Moerch. **Scaled Venus.** W.Pac., esp.W.Aust. Avg.30–35mm. C.

20. DOSINIA GRATA Deshayes. **Delicate Dosinia.** Vic., Tas. Avg.32–38mm. C.

21. GAFRARIUM DIVARICATUM Gm. E.Afr.-W.Pac., esp.Japan. 30–50mm. VC. Variable pattern.

22. GAFRARIUM TUMIDUM Röd. Ind.Oc.-Fiji, esp.Japan. 28–40mm. C.

23. GOMPHINA UNDULOSA Lam. **Waved Venus.** W.Aust.-Vic., Tas. 20–30mm. C.

24. KATELYSIA PERONI Lam. W.Aust.-Vic., Tas. Avg.32–38mm. C.

25. LIOCONCHA CASTRENSIS L. **Chocolate Flamed Venus.** Ind.Oc.-W.Pac., esp.P.I. 32–40–50–60mm. C. Variable. pattern.

Plate 151

1. LIOCONCHA FASTIGIATA Sow. Ind. Oc.-W.Pac., esp.W.Aust.-Qld. 25–30–35–40mm. C.

2/3

2. LIOCONCHA LORENZIANA Dillwyn. Japan. Avg.30–35mm. UC.

3. LIOCONCHA TIGRINA Lam. W.Pac., esp.N.Aust.-Qld.; Haw. 35–50mm. C. ?Syn.: *L.hieroglyphica* Conrad.

4. MACROCALLISTA MACULATA L. **Calico Clam; Checkerboard** or **Spotted Venus.** N.C.-S.Fla.-W.I. 38–42–50–63mm. C. Glossy per.

5. MACROCALLISTA NIMBOSA Light-foot. **Sunray** or **Giant Venus.** N.C.-Fla.-Texas. 50–75–115–>175mm. Glossy per. Edible.

6. MEGAPITARIA AURANTIACA Sow. G.of Cal.-Ecu. <60–75–100–115mm. C. Orange to brown per. (illus.) over pinkish shell.

7. MEGAPITARIA SQUALIDA Sow. Baja Cal.-Peru. <60–75–100–115mm. C.

8. MERETRIX LUSORIA Röd. **Common Oriental Clam.** Ind.Oc., W.Pac., esp.Japan. 25–30–50–60mm. VC. Glossy per. Edible. ?Subsp. of *M.meretrix* L.

9. PAPHIA EUGLYPTA Philippi. W.Pac., esp.Japan. Avg.70–80mm. C.

10. PAPHIA EXARATA Philippi. W.Pac. 30–35–45–50mm. C.

11. PAPHIA JAPONICA Deshayes. W.Pac., esp.Japan; Haw. 25–30–40–45mm. VC. Also placed under *Tapes* or *Venerupis.* See pl. 152, no. 22.

12. PAPHIA SCHNELLIANA Dunker. Japan. 70–105mm. C.

13. PAPHIA SULCOSA Philippi. **Grooved Tapes.** W.Aust. Avg.55–65mm. C.

14. PAPHIA UNDULATA Born. W.Pac., esp.Japan. 38–45–60–68mm. C.

15. PERIGLYPTA EDMONDSONI Dall, Bartsch & Rehder. **Reticulate Venus.** Haw. Avg.50–65mm. C. Syn. for *Periglypta reticulata* L. *Periglypta* also considered a subgenus of *Antigona.*

16. PERIGLYPTA LISTERI Gray. **Princess** or **Lister's Venus.** S.E.Fla.-Texas, W.I. 45–60–75–?100mm. C.

17. PERIGLYPTA MULTICOSTATA Sow. **Many-ridged Venus.** G.of Cal.-Peru. 60–75–115–138mm. C.

18. PERIGLYPTA PUERPERA L. **Purple Venus.** E.Afr.-W.Pac. to Fiji, esp.Japan. 45–50–60–70mm. C.

19. PERIGLYPTA RETICULATA L. **Reti-culated Venus.** Ind.Oc.-W.Pac. 60–65–80–95mm. C. See no. 15.

Plate 152 | Veneridae

1. PITAR DIONE L. **Royal Comb Venus.** Texas-W.I.-E.Pan. 25–30–40–45mm. UC.

2. PITAR JAPONICUM Kuroda & Habe. Japan. 30–40mm. UC.

3. PITAR LUPANARIA Lesson. **Panamic Comb Venus.** Baja Cal.-Peru. <40–50–70–82mm. UC.

4. PITAR ROSEA Brod. & Sow. G. of Cal.-Peru. Avg.40–50mm. C.

5. PITARINA CITRINA Lam. W.-N.Aust.-N.S.W. Avg.35–45mm. C.

6. PLACAMEN ISABELLINA Philippi. W. Pac., esp.Tai. Avg.22–26mm. C.

7. PLACAMEN TIARA Dillwyn. W.Pac., esp.Japan. Avg.16–19mm. C.

8. PROTOTHACA GRATA Say. Baja Cal.-G. of Cal.-Chile. 20–25–35–40mm. VC. Color and pattern q.v.

9. PROTOTHACA MCGINTYI Olsson. C.R.-Pan. Avg.25–32mm. UC.

10. PROTOTHACA METODON Pilsbry & Lowe. G. of Cal.-Pan. 20–25–35–45mm. C. Formerly placed under **Chione**.

11. SUNEMEROE PEREXCAVATA Fulton. W.Aust. Avg.32–45mm. UC.

12. SUNETTA MENSTRUALIS Menke. W. Pac., esp.Japan. 30–40–55–65mm. C.

13. TAPES LITTERATA L. **Lettered Venus.** E.Afr.-W.Pac. 60–65–80–90mm. C. Variable pattern.

14. TAPES TURGIDA Lam. **Tapestry Shell** or **Turgid Tapes.** W.Pac., esp.S.W.Aust.-N.S. W.-Qld. Avg.60–75mm. C. Variable pattern. Edible.

15. TAWERA LAGOPUS Lam. **Banded Venus.** S.W.Aust.-N.S.W., Tas. 25–40mm. C.

16. TIVELA BYRONENSIS Gray. Baja Cal.-G. of Cal.-Ecu. 35–40–55–60mm. VC. ?Subsp. of **T.mactroides**.

17. TIVELA MACTROIDES Born. **Trigonal Tivela.** W.I.-Brazil. 25–38mm. C. See **T. byronensis**.

18. TIVELA PLANULATA Brod. & Sow. G. of Cal.-Ecu. 30–40–55–60mm. C.

19. TIVELA VENTRICOSA Gray. Brazil-Uruguay. Avg.50–55mm. UC.

20. VENERUPIS AUREA Gm. **Golden Carpet Shell.** W.Eur.-Med. Avg.25–35mm. C. Variable color and pattern.

21. VENERUPIS DECUSSATA L. **Crosscut Carpet Shell.** W.Eur.-Med.-W.Afr. Avg. 45–60mm. VC. Variable pattern. Edible.

22. VENERUPIS JAPONICUS Deshayes. Same as pl. 151, no. 11.

23. VENUS (Ventricola) FOVEOLATA Sow. Japan-Korea-China. Avg.40–45mm. VC.

24. VENUS VERRUCOSA L. **Warty Venus.** W.Eur.-Med.-W.Afr.-S.Afr. 32–40–55–60mm. VC. Dark brown per. Edible.

Plate 153

1. PETRICOLA PARALLELA Pilsbry & Lowe. Baja Cal.-G. of Cal.-Nicaragua. 25–35–45–60mm. C.

2. PETRICOLA PHOLADIFORMIS Lam. **False Angel Wing** or **American Piddock.** G.of St.Lawrence-Fla.-Texas, Brazil-Uruguay; also, W.Eur.-Med.-W.Afr. 25–30–50–70mm. C.

3. HIPPOPUS HIPPOPUS L. **Bear's Paw, Horse's Hoof, Horse Shoe, Spotted** or **Strawberry Clam.** W.Pac. to Tongo, esp.P.I. 50–75–125–423mm. C. Syn.: **H.maculatus** Lam.

4. TRIDACNA CROCEA Lam. **Crocus** or **Boring Clam.** Malaysia-Samoa. 60–70–100–150mm. UC.

5. TRIDACNA MAXIMA Röd. **Elongate Clam.** E.Afr.-Poly. ca.100–150–250–350mm. C. Syn.: **T.elongata** Lam. The largest shell in the world is **TRIDACNA GIGAS** Lam., **Giant Clam** (not illus.), E.Afr.-W.Pac. The largest recorded is 137cm. (54in.), weighing 230.5kg. (507lb.).

6. TRIDACNA SQUAMOSA Lam. **Fluted, Scaly** or **Frilled Clam.** S.E.Afr.-Samoa. 50–100–150–400mm. VC. White to yellow, often with orange.

7. AUSTROMACTRA CALOUNDRA Iredale. N.S.W. Avg.20–25mm. C.

8. MACTRA CORALLINA L. **Trough Shell.** N.Sea-W.Eur.-Med.-W.Afr. 40–45–55–60mm. VC. Pale brown per. Edible.

9. RAETA PLICATELLA Lam. **Channeled Duck** or **Surf Clam.** N.C.-Fla.-Texas, W.I.-Argentina. 50–55–65–75mm. C. Syn. for genus: **Labiosa.**

10. ATACTODEA STRIATA Gm. **Striated Little Trough** or **Triangle Shell.** W.Aust.-N.T.-Qld., N.G. 16–32mm. C.

11. PSAMMOTRETA OBESA Desh. **Pacific Grooved Macoma.** S.Cal.-Baja Cal. 50–60–75–90mm. C. Syn.: **Apolymetis biangulata** Cpr.

12. ARCOPAGIA MARGARITINA Lam. W.Pac., esp.Japan. 22–35mm. C.

13. GASTRANA FRAGILIS L. W.Eur.-Med.-Morocco. 28–30–40–45mm. UC.

14. MACOMA BALTHICA L. **Baltic Tellin** or **Little Macoma.** Arctic Seas-Baltic Sea-W. Eur.-N.Afr.; Arctic Seas-Georgia; also, Bering Sea-C.Cal. 13–20–30–38mm. VC. Thin grayish or yellowish flaky per.

15. MACOMA BREVIFRONS Say. **Short Macoma.** N.J.-Fla.-Texas, W.I.-Uruguay. 25–38mm. UC. Pale brown per.

16. QUIDNIPAGUS PALATAM Iredale. E. Afr.-W.Pac., esp.N.W.Aust.-Qld. 44–50–60–70mm. C. Syn.: **Tellina rugosa** Born.

17. SCUTARCOPAGIA LINGUAFELIS L.

Cat's Tongue. Ind.Oc.-Poly.; Haw. 40–50–60–65mm. C. Also placed under **Tellina.**

18. SCUTARCOPAGIA SCOBINATA L. **Rasp Tellin.** E.Afr.-W.Pac. 50–55–70–75mm. C. Also placed under **Tellina.**

19. STRIGILLA CARNARIA L. **Large Strigilla.** N.C.-Fla.-Carib. 15–18–22–25mm. VC.

20. STRIGILLA CHROMA Salisbury. Baja Cal.-Ecu. <15–18–22–25mm. VC. A similar Atl. sp. is **S.pseudocarnaria** Boss.

21. TELLIDORA BURNETI Brod. & Sow. Baja Cal.-G.of Cal.-Ecu. <20–30–40–50mm. C.

22. TELLIDORA CRISTATA Recluz. **White-crested Tellin.** N.C.-E.& W.Fla.-Texas. 25–28–35–38mm. C (once R).

23. TELLINA ALBINELLA Lam. **Southern White** or **Pink Tellin.** S.Aust.-Vic., Tas. Avg. 45–55mm. C. 23A is the deep pink form, **T.a. roseola** Iredale, from N.S.W.

24. TELLINA ALTERNATA Say. **Alternate Tellin.** N.C.-Fla.-Texas, W.I. 50–55–70–75mm. C. Variable color. Yellowish brown per.

25. TELLINA (Phylloda) FOLIACEA L. **Leaf** or **Leafy Tellin.** N.W.Aust.-Qld. 60–65–80–>90mm. UC.

Plate 154 | Tellinidae – Donacidae – Psammobiidae

2/3

1. TELLINA LISTERI Röd. **Speckled Tellin.** N.C.-Fla.-Brazil, Berm., W.I. 60–65–80–90mm. VC.

2. TELLINA PERRIERI Bertin. W.Pac., esp. Japan. Avg.45–52mm. C. Syn.: **T.consanguinea** Sow.

3. TELLINA PHARAONIS Hanley. E.Afr.-Red Sea. 32–40–55–63mm. C. Yellow to rose-red.

4. TELLINA PULCHELLA Lam. **Pretty Tellina.** Med.-W.Sahara. Avg.25–30mm. UC.

5. TELLINA PULCHERRIMA Sow. **Beautiful Tellina.** W.Pac. Avg.38–45mm. C.

6. TELLINA QUOYI Sow. **Pink-rayed Tellin.** N.W.Aust.-Qld. Avg.55–65mm. UC.

7. TELLINA RADIATA L. **Sunrise Tellin.** S.C.-Fla., Berm., W.I.-Guianas. 50–55–75–86mm. VC.

8. TELLINA STAURELLA Lam. E.Afr.-W.Pac., esp.Japan. 32–38–50–57mm. C.

9. TELLINA VIRGATA L. **Striped Tellin.** E.Afr.-W.Pac. 50–55–65–70mm. C.

10. DONAX CARINATUS Hanley. So.G.of Cal.-Col. <27–39mm. C.

11. DONAX DELTOIDES Lam. **Pipi.** S. Aust.-N.S.W., Tas. 40–45–60–63mm. VC. Thin brown per. Edible.

12. DONAX DENTICULATUS L. **Common Caribbean Donax.** S.W.Carib.-Venez. 20–25mm. VC. Color and pattern q.v. Edible.

13. DONAX SCORTUM L. **Hide Wedge Shell** or **Keeled Donax.** Ind.Oc. 50–60–80–90mm. C.

14. DONAX SERRA Röd. S.W.Afr.-S.Afr. Avg.60–70mm. C. Color variable.

15. DONAX TRUNCULUS L. **Abrupt Wedge Shell.** W.Eur.-Med.-N.Afr., Black Sea. 25–28–35–40mm. VC. Pale tan per. Edible.

16. DONAX VARIABILIS Say. **Florida Coquina** or **Coquina Clam.** N.Y.-Fla.-Texas. 13–20mm. VC. Color variable, incl. inside. **D.v.fossor** Say is the smaller, less colorful No. form.

17. ASAPHIS DEFLORATA L. **Gaudy Sand Clam** or **Asaphis.** S.E.Fla.-W.I.-Brazil, Berm.; also I-P. 40–45–60–85mm. C (Fla.: S). Color q.v.

18. ASAPHIS VIOLACEUS Forskäl. **Box Sunset Shell.** Sing.-Fiji. 40–45–60–70mm. UC.

19. GARI LINEOLATA Gray. **Pink Sunset Shell.** N.Z. 38–45–60–65mm. C.

20. GARI STANGERI Gray. **Purple Sunset Shell.** N.Z. Avg.40–55mm. C. Juveniles often yellow or orange.

21. HETERODONAX PACIFICUS Conrad. **False Pacific Donax.** S.Cal.-Pan. <13–15–22–27mm. C. Variable color.

22. SANGUINOLARIA BERTINI Pilsbry & Lowe. Baja Cal.-G.of Cal.-Peru. 50–55–75–92mm. C.

23. SANGUINOLARIA NUTTALLII Conrad. **Purple Clam.** S.Cal.-Baja Cal. 60–65–80–90mm. C. Glossy reddish-brown per.

24. SANGUINOLARIA CRUENTA Lightfoot. **Atlantic Sanguin.** S.Fla.-Texas, W.I.-Brazil. 38–50mm. UC. Inside flushed pink. **S. sanguinolenta** Gm. is a similar sp., not a syn.

25. SANGUINOLARIA TELLINOIDES A. Adams. G.of Cal.-Ecu. 50–60–80–90mm. C.

26. SOLETELLINA NITIDA Gray. **Shining** or **Golden Sunset Shell.** N.Z. 25–30–38–45mm. C.

27. TAGELUS DIVISUS Spengler. **Purplish Tagelus** or **Divided Sand Clam.** Mass.-Fla.-Texas, Berm., W.I.-Brazil. 25–38mm. C. Glossy per.

1. *SOLECURTUS STRIGILLATUS* L. S. W.Eur.-Med., Black Sea. Avg.70–85mm. C. Edible.

2. *SCROBICULARIA PLANA* da Costa. **Peppery Furrow Shell.** W.Baltic Sea-W.Eur.-Med.-W.Afr. 40–45–60–65mm. C. Edible.

3. *CUMINGIA CALIFORNIA* Conrad. **Californian Cuming Shell.** No.Cal.-Baja Cal. 18–20–26–32mm. VC.

4. *SEMELE BELLASTRIATA* Conrad. **Cancellate Semele.** N.C.-Fla.-Texas, W.I.-Brazil. 13–16–20–23mm. C.

5. *SEMELE PROFICUA* Pulteney. **White Atlantic Semele.** N.C.-Fla.-Texas, Berm., W.I.-Brazil. 15–20–30–38mm. C. Illus. is color form *S.p.radiata* Say, **Rayed Semele.**

6. *SEMELE RUPICOLA* Dall. **Rock-dwelling Semele.** C.Cal.-G.of Cal. 25–30–40–59mm. UC.

7. *SOLEN LUZONICUS* Dunker. Japan. Avg.38–48mm. UC.

8. *SOLEN VAGINOIDES* Lam. **Razor Shell.** W.Aust.-N.S.W., Tas. 50–75mm. VC.

9. *SOLEN VIRIDIS* Say. **Green Jackknife Clam.** R.I.-N.Fla., N.W.Fla.-Gulf States. Avg. 45–60mm. C.

10. *ENSIS DIRECTUS* Conrad. **Atlantic** or **Common Jackknife Clam.** Labrador-S.C. ca.

100–125–150–>200mm. C. Glossy greenish per. Edible.

11. *ENSIS ENSIS* L. **Sword Razor-shell.** W.Eur.-Med. 80–90–115–130mm. C.

12. *ENSIS SILIQUA* L. **Pod Razor-shell.** N.Sea, W.Eur.-Med. 80–100–160–200mm. C. Greenish per.

13. *SILIQUA COSTATA* Say. **Fragile** or **Atlantic Razor Clam.** G.of St. Lawrence-N.J. 35–40–60–65mm. VC.

14. *SILIQUA RADIATA* L. Ind.Oc.-W.Pac. 40–50–70–80mm. C. Brown to purple.

15. *MYA ARENARIA* L. **Soft-shell** or **Steamer Clam, Sand** or **Common Gaper.** Baltic Sea-W.Eur., Black Sea; Labrador-S.C.; introduced to Alaska-C.Cal.; also, Japan. 50–75–125–150mm. VC. Thin, flaky grayish to brownish per. Highly edible.

16. *MYA TRUNCATA* L. **Blunt** or **Truncated Gaper.** Arctic Seas-Mass.; Arctic Seas-Puget Sound; also, Japan. Avg.50–75mm. C. Thick brown per. Edible.

17. *CORBULA NASUTA* Sow. **Snub-nose Corbula.** Baja Cal.-G.of Cal.-Peru. 8–14mm. UC.

18. *HIATELLA ARCTICA* L. **Arctic Rock Borer.** W.Eur.-Med.; also, Arctic Seas-W.I.; Arctic Seas-Pan.; Haw. 18–20–30–70mm. C. Flaky gray or yellowish per.

19. *PANOPEA ZELANDICA* Q. & G. N.Z. 50–60–80–100mm. UC.

20. *ANCHOMASA SIMILIS* Gray. **N.Z. Rock Borer.** N.Z. Avg.85–100mm. C.

21. *BARNEA CANDIDA* L. **White Piddock.** W.Eur.-Med.-W.Afr. 25–35–60–70mm. C.

22. *BARNEA MANILENSIS* Philippi. **(Oriental) Angel Wing.** E.Afr.-W.Pac., esp. P.I. 70–90–115–125mm. VC.

23. *BARNEA SUBTRUNCATA* Sow. **Pacific Mud Piddock.** S.Ore.-Chile. Avg.50–65mm. C. Syn.: *B.pacifica* Stearns.

24. *BARNEA TRUNCATA* Say. **Fallen** or **False Angel Wing.** Maine-Fla.-Texas, W.I.-Brazil; also, Senegal-Ghana. 25–30–50–70mm. VC.

25. *CYRTOPLEURA COSTATA* L. **True Angel Wing.** Mass.-Fla.-Texas, W.I. 100–125–150–184mm. C.

26. *NETTASTOMELLA ROSTRATA* Val. **Beaked Piddock.** Puget Sound-S.Cal. 12–19mm. UC.

27. *PARAPHOLAS CALIFORNICA* Conrad. **California Piddock.** Ore.-S.Cal. 60–75–100–150mm. C.

28. *PENITELLA PENITA* Conrad. **Common Piddock.** Bering Sea-S.Cal. 28–45–60–75mm. C.

Plate 156 | Pholadidae – Pandoridae – Lyonsiidae – et al.

1. *ZIRFAEA CRISPATA* L. Great, Oval or **Rough Piddock.** Labrador-N.J.; also, W.Eur. 22–40–60–93mm. C. Brown per.

2. *ZIRFAEA PILSBRYI* Lowe. Pilsbry's or **(Pacific) Rough Piddock.** Bering Sea-Baja Cal. 50–60–85–100mm. C. Yellowish per.

3. *PANDORA ARCUATA* Sow. Baja Cal.-N.Peru. Avg.30–38mm. UC.

4. *PANDORA GOULDIANA* Dall. Gould's Pandora. G.of St. Lawrence-N.J. 20–30–40–48mm. C. Pearly inner layer.

5. *LYONSIA CALIFORNICA* Conrad. Californian Lyonsia. Puget Sound-Baja Cal. Avg.22–28mm. C. Thin olive per. over pearly shell.

6. *LYONSIA PATAGONICA* Orbigny. Uruguay. Avg.15–18mm. C.

7. *MYADORA STRIATA* Q. & G. Battle-axe or **Large Myadora.** N.Z. 25–30–38–44mm. C.

8. *THRACIA RUSHII* Pilsbry. Uruguay. Avg. 20–22mm. UC.

9. *PENICILLUS STRANGULATUM* Chenu. True Watering Pot. W.Aust.-Qld. ca.100–125–200–230mm. UC. Syn. for genus: *Aspergillum.*

10. *PENICILLUS GIGANTEUS* Sow. E. Afr., Japan-Tai. ca.200–305mm. S.

11. *PENICILLUS PENIS* L. Tai. Avg.100–135mm. UC.

12. *CUSPIDARIA APODEMA* Dall. Smooth Dipper Shell. Alaska-W.Mex. Avg. 12–16mm. UC.

13. *CUSPIDARIA CUSPIDATA* Olivi. Med. Avg.25–30mm. UC.

14. *CUSPIDARIA SUGANUMAI* Nomura. Japan. Avg.25–30mm. C.

15. *EUCIROA TERAMACHII* Kuroda. Japan. 35–40–50–60mm. S.

1. ACANTHOCHITONA DEFILIPPI
Tapparone-Canefri. Japan. Avg.38–50mm. C.

2. ACANTHOCHITONA EXQUISITA
Pilsbry. No.G.of Cal. Avg.25–30mm. UC.
Girdle has large bronzy tufts of spines.

3. CYANOPLAX HARTWEGII Cpr.
Hartweg's Baby Chiton. Wash.-Baja Cal. Avg.
30–40mm. C.

4. ISCHNOCHITON BONINENSIS Bergen-
hayn. Japan. Avg.25–30mm. C. Color q.v.

5. ISCHNORADSIA AUSTRALIS Sow. S.
Qld.-N.S.W.-Vic. ca.35–45–65–75mm. VC.

6. RADSIELLA TRIDENTATA Pilsbry.
G.of Cal. 12–15–20–29mm. C. Form and color
q.v.

7. LEPIDOZONA CLATHRATA Reeve.
Baja Cal., No.G.of Cal. 30–32–38–50mm. UC.

8. LEPIDOZONA COREANICA Reeve.
Korea-Japan-Tai. 20–25–30–35mm. C. Color
q.v.

9. DINOPLAX GIGAS Gm. S.Afr. Avg.50–
60mm. C.

10. STENOPLAX CONSPICUA Dall.
Conspicuous Chiton. S.Cal.-G.of Cal. 30–50–
75–114mm. C. Velvety girdle.

11. STENOPLAX HEATHIANA Berry.
Heath's Chiton. No.Cal.-Baja Cal. 45–55–70–
75mm. UC.

12. STENOPLAX MAGDALENENSIS
Hinds. **Magdalena** or **Gray Chiton.** Baja Cal.-
G.of Cal. 25–50–70–100mm. UC.

13. TONICELLA LINEATA Wood. **Lined
Red Chiton.** Japan; Aleutian Is.-S.Cal. 25–30–
40–50mm. C.

**14. CALLISTOCHITON CRASSICO-
STATUS** Pilsbry. S.Cal.-Baja Cal. 20–30mm.
C.

15. NUTTALLINA CALIFORNICA Reeve.
Br.Col.-S.Cal. Avg.25–38mm. C. Moss-like
girdle.

16. NUTTALLINA FLUXA Cpr. **Rough
Nuttall Chiton.** S.Cal.-Baja Cal. Avg.25–
35mm. C.

17. CHAETOPLEURA EURYPLAX Berry.
G.of Cal. 15–25–35–43mm. UC.

18. CHAETOPLEURA LURIDA Sow. So.
G.of Cal.-Peru. 15–20–30–35mm. C.

19. KATHARINA TUNICATA Wood.
Black Katy Chiton. Aleutian Is.-S.Cal. 50–
60–70–93mm. VC.

20. MOPALIA MUSCOSA Gould. **Mossy
Mopalia.** Alaska-Baja Cal. 25–30–45–64mm.
C. Form illus. is *M.m.lignosa* Wood, **Woody
Mopalia** (?sep. sp.).

21. LIOLOPHURA JAPONICA Lischke.
Japan. Avg.30–45mm. VC.

22. ACANTHOPLEURA ECHINATA
Barnes. Chile. Avg.70–90mm. UC.

Plate 158 | Chitonidae – Dentaliidae – Nautiloidae – Spirulidae – Argonautidae

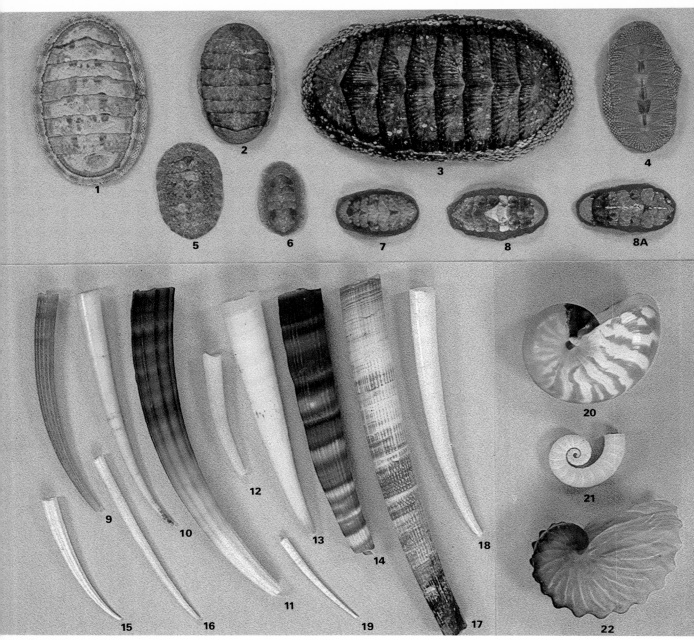

1. *CHITON ARTICULATUS* Sow. **Smooth Panama Chiton.** So.G.of Cal.-Pan. 30–45–65–100mm. C.
2. *CHITON MARMORATUS* Gm. **Marbled Chiton.** S.E.Fla.-W.I. 35–50–70–75mm. VC. Col. and patt. vary. Underside bluish-green.
3. *CHITON SULCATUS* Wood. Galáp. 50–60–80–100mm. C.
4. *CHITON TUBERCULATUS* Linne. **Common W.I. Chiton.** S.E.Fla.-W.I., Berm. 40–50–70–75mm. VC. Underside bluish-green.
5. *RHYSSOPLAX KURODAI* Taki & Taki. Japan. Avg.30–35mm. C.
6. *TONICIA ARNHEIMI* Dall. Galáp. Avg. 15–22mm. C.
7. *TONICIA FORBESII* Cpr. G.of Cal.-Pan. Avg.25–30mm. UC.
8. *ONITHOCHITON HIRASEI* Pilsbry. Japan-Tai.-S.China Sea. ca.20–45mm. C.
9. *DENTALIUM APRINUM* L. **Green Tusk Shell.** W.Pac. Avg.60–85mm. C.
10. *DENTALIUM CROCINUM* Pilsbry. Japan. 55–65–80–90mm. UC.

11. *DENTALIUM ELEPHANTINUM* L. **Elephant's Tusk Shell.** P.I.-Aust. 60–100mm. C.
12. *DENTALIUM ENTALIS* L. England-France. Avg.30–38mm. C.
13. *DENTALIUM FLORIDENSE* Henderson. **Florida Tusk Shell.** S.E.Fla.-W.I. 50–60–70–75mm. UC.
14. *DENTALIUM FORMOSUM* Adams & Reeve. **Beautiful Tusk Shell.** Japan-Tai. 65–90mm. UC.
15. *DENTALIUM OCTANGULATUM* Donovan. Japan-Tai. 25–30–40–>50mm. C.
16. *DENTALIUM RHABDOTUM* Pilsbry. Japan. Avg.45–55mm. C.
17. *DENTALIUM VERNEDEI* Sow. Japan-Tai. 95–105–130–140mm. C.
18. *DENTALIUM WEINKAUFFI* Dunker. Japan-Tai. 50–55–75–95mm. C. White to pale yellow, pink.
19. *FUSTIARIA (Laevidentalium) SPLENDIDA* Sow. W.Mex. 25–28–35–45mm. UC.
– – NAUTILUS MACROMPHALUS Sow. W.Pac., esp.New Cal. ca.125–150–175–200mm.

VS. Deep, concave umbilicus. Illus. on pl. 12.
20. *NAUTILUS POMPILIUS* L. **Chambered** or **Pearly Nautilus.** Ind.Oc.-C.Pac., esp.P.I. ca.125–224mm. VC. Illus. is juv. Pl. 12 illus. mature spec. and spec. pearled with acid. Edible.
– – NAUTILUS SCROBICULATUS Lightfoot. **Umbilicate Nautilus.** N.G.-Sol. ca.125–150–175–200mm. R. Deep, steep-walled umbilicus. Syn.: *N.umbilicata* Lam. Illus. on pl. 12.
21. *SPIRULA SPIRULA* L. **Common Spirula** or **Ram's Horn.** S.E.Afr.-W.Pac.; also, Mass.-Fla.-W.I.; W.Eur. 13–20–25–35mm. VC. Thin, fragile.
– – ARGONAUTA ARGO L. **Common Paper Nautilus.** S.E.Afr.-W.Pac., Haw.; Fla., Berm.; Med. 60–100–200–275mm. UC. This external shell is the egg case of the female *Argonauta*. Very thin, fragile. Illus. on pl. 12.
22. *ARGONAUTA HIANS* Lightfoot. **Brown Paper Nautilus.** S.E.Afr.-W.Pac.; Berm. 38–45–65–93mm. C.
– – ARGONAUTA NODUSA Lightfoot. **Paper Nautilus.** S.E.Afr.-C.Pac.; Brazil. 100–150–200–350mm. UC. Illus. on pl. 12.

Identification of Families

The following section describes the common characteristics of each of the principal families of seashells to assist in their identification. The illustrations show the most important characteristics of each of the principal classes. For their definitions and those of the other scientific words employed in the text, see the glossary on pages 208–213.

The principal features in identifying gastropods are the shape of the spire and body whorl, the type of surface sculpture, aperture, outer lip, columella, siphonal canal, umbilicus and operculum.

For bivalves, the principal features are the shape of the valves, the type of ligament, beaks, hinge, hinge teeth, pallial sinus, pallial line and adductor muscle scars.

The genera are listed in proper systematic order within the family if agreed upon by most authorities. If the arrangement is in some dispute or not yet established in an accepted form, they are listed in alphabetical order.

The simplified line drawings of examples of the principal genera in each family have been employed to help in the rapid identification of specimens. When the family is located, turn to the appropriate color plates for identification of the species.

Class: GASTROPODA
SUBCLASS: PROSOBRANCHIA
FAMILY
PLEUROTOMARIIDAE   *Pl. 13*
Slit Shells
Principal genera: ***Entemnotrochus***
Mikadotrochus
Perotrochus

(Also considered subgenera under single genus ***Pleurotomaria*** [*ill.*])

Large, conical shells with slit and slit band on outer edge of body whorl. Very fine beaded spiral threads on surface. Yellowish-orange to red color patterns. Some have umbilicus. Small, thin, round, horny, multispiral operculum. The most primitive form of gastropod, first occurring in the Cambrian Period, 500 million years ago. About fifteen species in one or three genera. In deep water, nearly all in Japonic and Caribbean provinces.

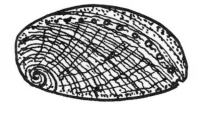

FAMILY
HALIOTIDAE   *Pls. 13–14*
Abalones, Ear Shells, Ormers
Sole genus: ***Haliotis*** [*ill.*]

Small to large, round to oval, spiral, depressed, ear-shaped, with small flattened spire. Large, saucer-shaped body whorl. Surface often with rough axial or spiral lines, ribs or folds. Row of round or oval holes along left margin; some earlier ones may be closed. Interior nacreous, sometimes iridescent; often with large muscle scar. Columellar margin thickened and flattened. No operculum. Herbivorous. Attached to rocks by large muscular, highly edible foot. Also used for jewelry, buttons and inlays. About 100 species in one genus. On or beneath rocks, mostly intertidal, shallow water. Temperate to tropical waters, mainly Australian, Californian, South African.

FAMILY
FISSURELLIDAE   *Pl. 15*
Keyhole Limpets
Principal genera: ***Diodora***
Fissurella [*ill.*]
Macroschisma

Mostly small, conical, oval, cap- or saucer-shaped. Most have spire with perforated subcentral apex, usually a slit or channel. Finely sculptured surface. Interior porcellaneous, with horseshoe-shaped muscle scar. No operculum. Herbivorous, feeding on seaweed. Attached to rocks and coral, mainly intertidal, shallow water. About 500 species in 20 to 30 genera. Worldwide, especially Panamic, Caribbean.

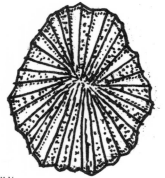

FAMILY

PATELLIDAE *Pls. 15–17*
True Limpets
Principal genera: ***Patella*** [*ill.*]
Cellana

Small to medium shells, conical, oval, cap- or saucer-shaped, with subcentral apex. Smooth or radially ribbed, with fine concentric growth lines; often eroded. ***Cellana*** have nacreous, often iridescent, interior; ***Patella*** have porcellaneous interior. No operculum. Herbivorous, feeding on seaweed, algae. Attached to rocks in intertidal zone. Many species in four genera. Temperate to tropical, ***Patella*** mainly in S. Africa, ***Cellana*** in Pacific.

FAMILY

ACMAEIDAE *Pl. 17*
Cap Limpets
Principal genus: ***Acmaea***
[*Ill.: Colisella*]

Mostly small, conical, oval, cap-shaped. Solid, subcentral apex. Surface smooth or with radial ribs or cords. Interior porcellaneous, sometimes colored, often with marginal pattern. Horseshoe- or pear-shaped central muscle scar. No operculum. Herbivorous, feeding on seaweed, algae. Attached to rocks in intertidal zone, especially at high tide mark. About 400 species in five or six genera. Worldwide, especially western N. America.

FAMILY

LEPETIDAE *Pl. 17*
Eyeless Limpets
Principal genus: ***Lepeta*** [*ill.*]

Small, thin, conical, oval. Smooth or finely ribbed surface. Colorless to white. Very few species in four genera. Deep water in Polar to temperate seas.

FAMILY

TROCHIDAE *Pls. 18–22*
Top Shells
Principal genera:

Lischkeia	***Trochus***
Monodonta	***Clanculus***
Tegula	***Tectus*** [*ill.*]
Calliostoma	***Umbonium***

Small to large shells, some very thick and heavy. Conical or turbinate, mainly with flat, round base. Surface smooth or variously sculptured, usually with spiral cords or threads. Some very colorful. Aperture rounded, nacreous, sometimes iridescent. Umbilicus usually open. Thin circular, brown, horny operculum with central nucleus. Herbivorous, feeding on protozoans, detritus. Trochus, Tectus used for jewelry, buttons. Intertidal, shallow water. Several hundred species in over 50 genera. Mainly temperate to tropical waters worldwide.

FAMILY

ANGARIIDAE *Pl. 23*
Dolphin Shells
Sole genus: ***Angaria***

Medium-sized thick, turbinate shells, with depressed spire. Spiral ornamentation, with tubercles or nodules, often spiny. Circular aperture with nacreous interior. Deep umbilicus. Horny, brown, round, concave, multispiral operculum. Sometimes placed under Trochidae. Shallow water, in coral reefs. A few species in one genus. Indo-Pacific tropical waters.

FAMILY

STOMATELLIDAE *Pl. 23*
False Ear or Wide Mouth Shells
Principal genera: ***Stomatella*** [*ill.*]
Pseudostomatella

Small, oval, flattened shells, trochiform to ear-shaped. Depressed spire with few whorls. Surface with very fine spiral cords. Aperture large, quite oblique, with nacreous interior. No umbilicus. Some with operculum. Herbivorous. Shallow water, in coral reefs. About 50 species in six genera. Tropical Pacific.

FAMILY
LIOTIIDAE   *Pl. 23*

Principal genera: *Liotia* [ill.]
                     Arene

Small top- to disk-shaped shells, deeply umbilicate. Short spire with rounded or keeled whorls. Ornamented with axial and spiral cords, some nodulose or spinose, in cancellate pattern, often with a pitted appearance, continuing into umbilicus. Round aperture with nacreous interior. Thick, continuous, flaring lip, some with varix. Round, concave, multispiral operculum with horny inner surface and bristly margins or with small calcareous granules. Also placed under Turbinidae or Cyclostrematidae, another small family. Mostly deep water; *Arene* usually intertidal. A few species in five or six genera. Worldwide, mainly Pacific and Panamic.

FAMILY
TURBINIDAE   *Pls. 23–26*
Turbans

Principal genera: *Astraea*
                     Guilfordia
                     Turbo [ill.]

Mostly medium to large, thick, heavy, turbinate or conical shells. Smooth surface, often colorful, or with spiral cords, often spiny or nodulose. Aperture round to elliptical. Nacreous interior. Smooth columella. Some with umbilicus. Thick, round to oval, calcareous operculum, often sculptured or colored; top spiral and convex, bottom flat. Herbivorous, feeding on marine algae. Intertidal, shallow waters, under coral rocks, on reefs, or in seaweed. Many species in about fifteen genera. Mainly subtropical to tropical.

Turbo subgenera:

Batillus	Ba.	*Ocana*	Oc.
Callopoma	Ca.	*Sarmaticus*	Sa.
Lunatica	Lt.	*Subninella*	Su.
Lunella	Lu.	*Taeniaturbo*	Ta.
Marmarostoma	Ma.	*Turbo*	Tu.
Ninella	Ni.		

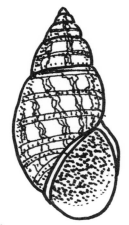

FAMILY
PHASIANELLIDAE   *Pl. 26*
Pheasant Shells

Principal genus: *Phasianella* [ill.]

Very small to medium-sized, elongate, conical shells, with few whorls. Smooth, glossy surface, some with very fine spiral lines. Many quite colorful with elaborate patterns. Almond-shaped aperture with porcellaneous interior. Simple, thin outer lip. Small umbilicus in some small species. Thick, calcareous, almond-shaped, usually convex, white operculum, with eccentric nucleus. Grassy bottoms in shallow water. About 40 species in three genera. Subtropical to tropical waters, especially Australia.

FAMILY
NERITOPSIDAE   *Pl. 27*

Sole genus: *Neritopsis*

Small, semi-globose shells, with depressed spire and flattened base. Large body whorl. Surface has granulose spiral cords. No umbilicus. Thick calcareous operculum set into apophysis. Closely related to Neritidae. Two species in one genus. Indo-Pacific.

FAMILY
NERITIDAE   *Pls. 27–28*
Nerites

Principal genera: *Nerita* [ill.]
                     Neritina
                     Smaragdia

Small, thick (except freshwater species), semi-globose shells, with depressed spire and flattened base. Large body whorl. Usually smooth; some pustulose or with spiral ribs on growth lines. Often very colorful. Semi-lunate aperture with teeth on both outer and inner lips. Prominent calloused pad on columella. Lacks umbilicus. Thick, smooth or granulate, calcareous operculum set into apophysis. Herbivorous, feeding on algae. On seaweed, seagrass, on or under rocks and corals, in rock crevices, in intertidal, shallow waters; often in brackish or fresh water, mangrove swamps; some even live on land. Several hundred species in about ten genera. Mainly subtropical to tropical waters.

FAMILY
LITTORINIDAE   *Pl. 28*
Periwinkles
Principal genera: ***Littorina*** [*ill.*]
Tectarius

Small, thick, conical, turbinate or globose shells. Generally smooth or with spiral lines or cords; some granulose or spiny. Ovate aperture with porcellaneous interior. Thin outer lip. Smooth, flattened or concave columella. Rarely with umbilicus. Spiral, horny, dark brown operculum. Edible, especially in Europe. Herbivorous, feeding mainly on algae, seaweeds. On rocks and seaweeds primarily in upper intertidal zone and above high-tide line; some in mangrove swamps and fresh water. Over 100 species in about 20 to 25 genera. Worldwide, primarily temperate to subtropical.

FAMILY
ARCHITECTONICIDAE   *Pl. 29*
Sundials
Principal genera: ***Architectonica*** [*ill.*]
Heliacus
Philippia

Small to medium-sized, usually thick, shells. Round, discoidal, with depressed spire and flat or somewhat convex base. Widely coiled body whorl. Surface generally with beaded, spiral ribs. Small, circular or oval aperture. Very large, deep umbilicus, with corrugated whorls, bordered by beaded keel. Female keeps egg-capsules in umbilicus. Very small, horny, conical concave operculum. ***Heliacus*** has spiral operculum. In seaweeds on sand, in intertidal, shallow waters. About 40 species in five or six genera. Subtropical to tropical waters, especially Pacific.

FAMILY
ORECTOSPIRIDAE   *Pl. 29*
Sole genus: ***Orectospira***

Medium-sized, thin conical shells, with high spire. Slightly overlapping whorls, sometimes crenulated. Aperture somewhat rectangular, with short anterior canal. Perforated umbilicus. Thin, horny, concave, pale yellow, multispiral operculum. On muddy bottoms in deep water. A few species in one genus, primarily Japonic.

FAMILY
TURRITELLIDAE   *Pls. 29–30*
Turret or Screw Shells
Principal genera: ***Turritella*** [*ill.*]
Vermicularia
Siliquaria

Mostly medium-sized to large, thick, elongated, turreted shells, with long pointed spires. Multi-whorled, with strongly sculptured spiral ridges. Rounded aperture with thin outer lip. No umbilicus. Thin, horny, round operculum; bristly in ***Siliquaria***. ***Vermicularia*** and ***Siliquaria*** placed by some authors under Vermetidae; ***Siliquaria*** also treated as separate family, Siliquariidae. Herbivorous. In sand or mud in shallow water, mainly below low-tide line. ***Vermicularia*** and ***Siliquaria*** sometimes fixed to substrate. About 50 species. The ***Turritella*** are treated as either one or several genera. Temperate to tropical, especially Indo-Pacific.

FAMILY
MODULIDAE   *Pl. 30*
Sole genus: ***Modulus***

Small, thick, top-shaped shells, with conical spire, usually depressed. Surface with grooved, spiral cords, some with axial ribs. Large, circular, lirate aperture, at oblique angle. Sharp tooth on base of columella. Small, narrow umbilicus. Thin, horny, multispiral operculum. In sand and seaweeds, in shallow water. A few species in one genus. Subtropical to tropical waters.

FAMILY
VERMETIDAE   *Pl. 30*
Worm Shells
Principal genera: ***Vermetus***
Petaloconchus
Serpulorbis
[*Ill.: Vermicularia*]

Long, thick, tubular, irregularly coiled shells. Early whorls spirally coiled at apex. Longitudinal ridges; some with spiral cords or growth lines. Thin, horny, round, multispiral operculum. Feed on diatoms, plankton and detritus, often by spinning a mucous net. Attached to substrate in shallow waters, sometimes forming entire reefs. Several species in a few genera. Temperate to tropical waters.

FAMILY
CERITHIIDAE   *Pl. 31*
Horn Shells or Ceriths
Principal genus: ***Cerithium*** [*ill.*]

Small to medium-sized, elongated, multi-whorled shells, with high spire. Often strongly sculptured with spiral ribs or cords, some nodulose. Small, oblique aperture, sometimes lirate. Columella smooth or with one central fold. Short, recurved siphonal canal, often quite developed. Horny, oval, multispiral operculum, with eccentric nucleus. Herbivorous, feeding on detritus. On sand, in seaweed, among corals, in intertidal, shallow water. About 300 species in three or more genera; ***Cerithium*** treated as one or several genera. Temperate to tropical waters, mainly Indo-Pacific.

FAMILY
PLANAXIDAE   *Pl. 31*
Clusterwinks or Grooved Snails
Principal genus: ***Planaxis*** [*ill.*]

Small to medium-sized, thick, conical, ovate shells. Large body whorl. Surface smooth or with spiral cords. Aperture lirate or ovate with notch at base of smooth, concave columella. Distinct anal canal.

Lacks umbilicus. Fibrous yellow- to rusty-brown periostracum. Thin, horny, smooth operculum. In gravel or beneath rocks, near high-tide line, in intertidal, shallow waters; some freshwater, in mangrove swamps. Many species in five or six genera. Worldwide, subtropical to tropical.

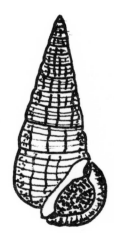

FAMILY
POTAMIDIDAE   *Pl. 31*
Telescope Shells or Mud Whelks
Principal genera: ***Cerithidea***
Telescopium
Terebralia [*ill.*]

Small to medium, thick, elongated shells, with multi-whorled, long pointed spire. Usually sculptured with rounded spiral ribs or cords; some with axial ribs. Generally brown in color. Large aperture with anterior sinus. Outer lip produced or flared. Siphonal canal weakly developed. Thin, round, horny, brown, spiral operculum with central nucleus. Herbivorous, feeding on detritus. In muddy or brackish waters near high-tide line; also in mangrove swamps or on land. A number of species in about twelve genera. Subtropical to tropical waters, especially Indo-Pacific and Panamic.

FAMILY
APORRHAIDAE   *Pl. 32*
Pelican's Foot Shells

Principal genus: ***Aporrhais*** [*ill.*]

Small thick shells, with high conical spire
and an exapnded, thickened outer lip with
long digitations. Ornamented with axial
ribs, often nodular, with tiny spiral threads.
Small, horny, brown, claw-like operculum.
Often found in fish stomachs. Shallow to
deep waters. Six species in two genera in
Atlantic and Mediterranean waters, mostly
temperate.

FAMILY
STRUTHIOLARIIDAE   *Pl. 32*
Ostrich Foot Shells

Principal genus: ***Struthiolaria*** [*ill.*]

Small, thick, ovate shells, with tall spire
and nodulose whorls and fine spiral ridges.
Large aperture with thick outer lip. Lips
and columella heavily calloused. Short
siphonal canal. Small operculum. About
seven species in two genera, nearly all in
New Zealand and Australia.

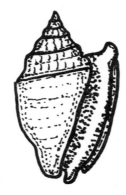

FAMILY
STROMBIDAE   *Pls. 32–36*
True Conchs

Principal genera:
Terebellum   ***Strombus*** [*ill.*]
Tibia   ***Lambis***

Mostly medium to large, thick shells with
conical, often tall, spire. Genera vary considerably in form, but all have large body
whorl. Long narrow aperture, usually
with stromboid notch through which the
eye projects. Outer lip thick, flaring, often
wing-like, sometimes with digitations.
Siphonal canal usually extended. Small,
narrow, horny, brown, claw-shaped
operculum, one edge notched or serrated;
used for locomotion, rather than to close
the aperture. ***Strombus*** moves rapidly,
with a leaping motion. Herbivorous,
feeding on algae and detritus. Juveniles of
Strombus often resemble cones. ***Terebellum***
are thin and cigar-shaped. Usually on sand
or mud, near coral reefs, in intertidal to
shallow waters. About 65 species in five
genera. Tropical waters, especially Indo-
Pacific.

FAMILY
EPITONIIDAE   *Pl. 37*
Wentletraps

Principal genera: ***Epitonium*** [*ill.*]
                     Amaea
                     Opalia

Small to medium-sized thin shells. Slender,
conical, spiral, often quite loosely coiled.
Several rounded whorls with prominent
narrow varices or costae. Mostly white,
polished; some tan to brown. Smooth,
round to ovate aperture with thick,
rounded, reflected outer lip. Usually
umbilicate. Thin, horny, dark brown,
multispiral operculum with subcentral
nucleus. Hermaphroditic. Grow very
rapidly. Carnivorous, feeding on corals,
anemones and other coelenterates. Emits
a purple fluid for protection. Usually
among rocks and corals in intertidal,
shallow waters. Several hundred species in
several genera, the ***Epitonium*** sometimes
divided into further genera. Worldwide in
temperate to tropical waters.

FAMILY

HIPPONICIDAE *Pl. 38*

Hoof Shells

Horsehoof or **Bonnet Limpets**

Principal genus: **Hipponix** [*ill.*]

Small, thick, conical, cap-shaped shells. Subcentral apex bent backward. Embryonic shells spirally coiled. Smooth or radially ribbed, sometimes with rough spiral lines. Interior smooth, with horseshoe-shaped muscle scar. Dark brown, fibrous periostracum. No operculum, but in some species a calcareous plate is secreted by the foot. Parasitic, feeding on plankton. Attached to other shells and substrate, often in clusters. Intertidal. Several species in one or two genera. Temperate to tropical waters, especially Panamic.

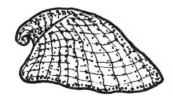

FAMILY

CAPULIDAE *Pl. 38*

Cap Limpets

Sole or principal genus: **Capulus**

Small, thin, cap-shaped shells. Small, pointed, spiral apex bent backward. Large, funnel-shaped body whorl. Rough surface, some with axial ribs or spiral lines. Very large, oval aperture with porcellaneous interior and horseshoe-shaped muscle scar. Bristly or velvety periostracum. No operculum. Hermaphroditic. Lives on filtered organisms, or parasitic, feeding mainly on mollusks, boring holes in the shells. Attached to shells or stones. A few species in one or more genera. Worldwide, mostly subtropical to tropical.

FAMILY

JANTHINIDAE *Pl. 37*

Violet Snails

Principal genus: **Janthina** [*ill.*]

Medium-sized, very thin, globose shells, with short spire and large body whorl. Extremely fine arcuate growth lines, sometimes with a few spiral grooves. Color usually pale lavender to violet. Very thin outer lip, with sinus on margin. **Recluzia** have very thin yellowish-brown periostracum. Lacks operculum. Pelagic, floating on surface upside down on a mass of mucus-coated air bubbles, usually in huge numbers. Carnivorous, feeding on jellyfish, gastropod larvae, plankton. Emits a purple fluid for protection. A few species, but with much confusion with one another, in two genera. Worldwide in temperate to tropical waters.

FAMILY

EULIMIDAE *Pl. 37*

Principal genera: **Eulima**
Balcis [*ill.*]

Tiny to small, thick, elongated, conical shells. Spire pointed, often with curved apex. Multi-whorled, whorls being somewhat convex. Smooth, glossy white surface. Ovate aperture. Some with thin pale brown operculum. Parasitic, feeding on echinoderms, starfish, sea urchins, sea cucumbers, and sand dollars, often living inside animal. Numerous species in many genera. Worldwide, Polar to tropical waters.

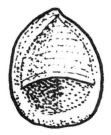

FAMILY

CALYPTRAEIDAE *Pl. 38*

Cup and Saucer

Slipper Limpets

Principal genera:
Calyptraea **Crucibulum**
Crepidula [*ill.*] **Cheilea**

Small to medium-sized, thin, conical or limpet-like shells, with an inner concave shelf or septum. Often with subcentral, somewhat spiral apex. Smooth or with radial ribs, some spiny. May have shaggy or rough periostracum. No operculum. Lives on filtered organisms. May be attached to substrate or other shells in shallow to deep water. A number of species in seven or more genera. Mainly temperate to tropical waters, especially Californian and Panamic. Family also called **CREPIDULIDAE**.

FAMILY

TRICHOTROPIDAE *Pl. 38*

Hairy Shells

Principal genus: **Trichotropis** [*ill.*]

Small, thin, turbinate, carinated shells, with tall to depressed spire. Large body whorl with strongly keeled shoulder. Large, ear-shaped aperture and flaring outer lip. Small umbilicus and siphonal canal. Often with bristly or fibrous periostracum. Horny, spiral operculum. Some hermaphroditic, first male, then female. Some in very deep waters. A number of species in ten or more genera. Worldwide in cold waters, especially Polar, N.Pacific, and Japonic waters.

FAMILY

XENOPHORIDAE   *Pls. 39–40*
Carrier Shells

Principal genera: *Xenophora* [*ill.*]
Onustus
Stellaria

Medium to large, thin, top-shaped shells, with depressed spire and concave base. Body whorl overhangs at periphery. Foreign objects usually attached to shell (see below). *Stellaria* has flattened hollow spines at edge of whorls, projecting out in long digitations around margin. Some with umbilicus, usually small, but deep in *Stellaria*. Thin, smooth, horny operculum, with concentric rings and subcentral nucleus. *Xenophora* attaches shells, pebbles or coral to its shell with a secretion from its foot; this occurs only in the early whorls of *Onustus*. Moves rapidly in a leaping motion, on sand or pebbly bottom, mostly in deep water. About 30 species in three genera. Tropical waters, mainly W.Pacific. Family also placed under Strombacea.

FAMILY

LAMELLARIIDAE   *Pl. 40*
Ear Shells

Principal genera: *Lamellaria* [*ill.*]
Velutina

Small, very thin, globose ear-shaped shells, with small, low spire. Large, smooth body whorl. Large, flaring aperture. No umbilicus. Thick periostracum. Lacks operculum. Shell usually completely covered by often colorful mantle. Hermaphroditic. Carnivorous, feeding on tunicates, ascidians, ?sponges, which the animal often resembles. Under rocks, intertidal to deep water. A number of species in seven genera. Nearly worldwide, Polar to tropical waters. Family, also called **VELUTINIDAE**, is a transitional group related to both Triviidae and Naticidae. *Velutina* also treated as separate family. Members of the genus *Sinum* are also called "ear shells".

FAMILY

TRIVIIDAE   *Pl. 41*
Sea Buttons or False Cowries

Principal genera: *Trivia* [*ill.*]
Erato

Very small to small globose or ovate shells, usually humped, with concealed spire. Transverse, spiral ribbing on dorsum of *Trivia*, extending to teeth. Surface not polished, unlike most cowries. Surface may be spotted or blotched, but not banded. Long, narrow, straight aperture. Very short siphonal canal. No periostracum or operculum. Carnivorous, feeding on tunicates, ascidians. Under rocks, in rock crevices, on coral rubble, in seaweeds, intertidal to deep waters. About 75 species in seven or more genera. Temperate to tropical waters, nearly worldwide. Once classed under Cypraeacea, later Lamellariacea, now under separate superfamily. Family also called **ERATOIDAE**.

FAMILY

CYPRAEIDAE   *Pls. 41–55*
Cowries

Sole genus: *Cypraea*

Very small to large, ovate to pyriform, often nearly cylindrical, generally with flat or slightly convex base. Spire usually hidden by large body whorl, often heavily covered by enamelled callus. Very glossy, smooth, porcellaneous surface, rarely pustulose, many very colorful, with striking patterns. Often with thick enamelled callus around margin. Long narrow aperture, usually straight, with small canals at both ends. Almost all with uniformly spaced teeth on both lips, which are rolled inward. No periostracum or operculum. Both lobes of mantle nearly cover shell, often leaving an untouched dorsal strip in pattern. Juvenile shells are olive-shaped, very thin, with sharp outer lip, projecting spire and no teeth; often have transverse bands lacking in adults. Some herbivorous, but mostly carnivorous, feeding at night on coral polyps, sponges, gorgonians and detritus. Under rocks, in corals, mostly in shallow waters. About 190 species in one genus, although some writers divide it into 30 or more genera, rather than subgenera. Mainly subtropical to tropical waters, especially Indo-Pacific.

Cypraea subgenera:

Adusta	*Ad.*	*Leporicypraea*	*Le.*
Annepona	*An.*	*Luponia*	*Lu.*
Barycypraea	*Bar.*	*Luria*	*Lur.*
Bistolida	*Bi.*	*Lyncina*	*Ly.*
Blasicura	*Bl.*	*Macrocypraea*	*Ma.*
Chelycypraea	*Ch.*	*Mauritia*	*Mau.*
Cribraria	*Cr.*	*Monetaria*	*Mo.*
Cypraea	*Cy.*	*Muracypraea*	*Mu.*
Cypraeovula	*Cyp.*	*Naria*	*Na.*
Erosaria	*Er.*	*Neobernaya*	*Ne.*
Erronea	*Err.*	*Nesiocypraea*	*Nes.*
Eustaphylaea	*Eu.*	*Notadusta*	*No.*
Guttacypraea	*Gu.*	*Notocypraea*	*Not.*
Ipsa	*Ip.*	*Nuclearia*	*Nu.*

Ornamentaria	*Or.*	*Pustularia*	*Pus.*
Ovatipsa	*Ov.*	*Ravitrona*	*Ra.*
Palmadusta	*Pal.*	*Schilderia*	*Sc.*
Paulonaria	*Pau.*	*Staphylaea*	*St.*
Ponda	*Po.*	*Talparia*	*Tal.*
Propustularia	*Pr.*	*Trona*	*Tr.*
Protacypraea	*Pro.*	*Umbilia*	*Um.*
Pseudozonaria	*Ps.*	*Zoila*	*Zo.*
Purpuradusta	*Pur.*	*Zonaria*	*Zon.*

FAMILY
OVULIDAE   *Pls. 55–56*
Egg Shells
Principal genera:
Ovula	***Cyphoma***
Volva	***Simnia***
Calpurnus	***Primovula*** [*ill.*]

Very small to medium, pear-, cowrie- or spindle-shaped shells. Smooth, usually porcellaneous, surface, mostly white to pink, often blending with its surroundings. Long, narrow aperture, broadening toward posterior. Outer lip usually thickened. Inner lip smooth and rounded. Teeth sometimes present on outer lip. Most with short canals; ***Volva*** have greatly elongated canals. Some with umbilicus. No periostracum or operculum. Mantle may cover entire dorsum. Carnivorous, feeding on coral polyps, gorgonians, ascidians. Under corals, or on host animals, usually in deep water. About 100 species in seven or more genera. Temperate to tropical waters, mainly Indo-Pacific. ***Pedicularia*** and ***Jenneria*** now included in this family, rather than in Triviidae. Family also called **AMPHIPERATIDAE.**

FAMILY
ATLANTIDAE   *Pl. 57*
Atlantas
Principal genus: ***Atlanta*** [*ill.*]

Tiny to small, very thin, fragile, discoidal shells. Usually clear to translucent white. Aperture oval to nearly triangular. Horny operculum. A pelagic heteropod. Swims upside down. Shell holds entire animal. Carnivorous, feeding on fish, worms. Several species in three genera. Temperate to tropical waters.

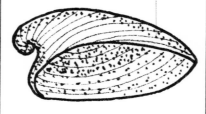

FAMILY
CARINARIIDAE   *Pl. 57*
Principal genus: ***Carinaria*** [*ill.*]

Very small to medium-sized, very thin, fragile compressed shells, with double keel and hooked spire. Clear to translucent white. Very large aperture. No operculum. A pelagic heteropod. Swims upside down. Shell, much smaller than rest of animal, carried beneath body. Carnivorous, feeding on fish, worms. A few species in three genera, one without shell. Temperate to tropical waters.

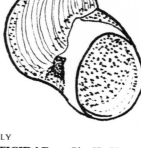

FAMILY
NATICIDAE   *Pls. 57–58*
Sand or **Moon Snails**
Principal genera:
Natica	***Lunatia***
Polinices [*ill.*]	***Sinum***

Mostly small to medium-sized globose to ovate shell with short spire and large inflated body whorl. ***Sinum*** are thin, flattened, with very large aperture. Smooth, often glossy, surface, mainly solid white to brown or with brown spots or bands. Large, semi-circular to oval aperture with sharp outer lip. Part or all of umbilicus and part of aperture often covered by large, thick callus. No siphonal canal. Periostracum usually thin and pale or yellowish-brown. ***Natica*** have thick, calcareous, grooved operculum; others have thin, translucent, horny, orange-brown operculum. Animal, much larger than shell, moves quickly with very large foot, plowing up sand in search of food. Carnivorous, feeding on bivalves by boring holes in shells. Egg capsules deposited in distinctive circular sand collar. In sand, from high-tide line to deep water. A few hundred species in several dozen genera. Worldwide, in Polar to tropical waters.

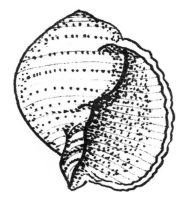

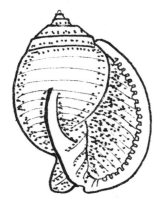

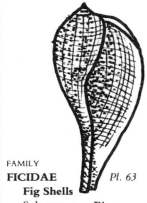

FAMILY
TONNIDAE   *Pls. 59–60*
Tun or Cask Shells

Principal genera: ***Tonna*** [ill.]
Malea
Eudolium

Medium to large, thin globose, ventricose shells, with short turbinate spire. Very large body whorl. Strong spiral cords or ridges on whorls. Large aperture with thin, crenulate or dentate outer lip, thickened in ***Malea***. Columella often with calloused parietal shield. Strong siphonal fasciole. Deep umbilicus, lacking in ***Malea***. Periostracum usually thin, flaky. No operculum except in juveniles and ***Oocorys***, a genus also considered as a separate family. Carnivorous, feeding on crustaceans, echinoderms, sea cucumbers, bivalves, fish. On sand, beyond coral reefs, generally in deep water. About 35 species in three or four genera. Temperate to tropical waters, mainly Indo-Pacific.

FAMILY
CASSIDAE   *Pls. 61–63*
Helmet Shells

Principal genera:
Cassis [ill.]   ***Morum***
Casmaria   ***Phalium***
Cypraecassis

Medium to very large, generally thick, subglobose to somewhat triangular. Short, conical spire and large body whorl. Smooth or with spiral and axial cords, some nodulose or with large knobs. Long, narrow aperture, with outer lip sometimes thickened, reflected, often dentate. Columella often denticulate or plicate, generally with large, glossy parietal shield. Siphonal notch recurved, except in ***Morum***. Small, thin, horny, brown, semicircular operculum, some with radial ribs. Carnivorous, feeding on sand dollars, sea urchins, sea biscuits. Burrow in sand, in mostly intertidal and shallow water; a few in deep water. About 60 species in seven to ten genera. Worldwide, temperate and tropical, especially Indo-Pacific and Caribbean. Family has also been known as Cassididae, a name previously assigned to a family of beetles.

FAMILY
FICIDAE   *Pl. 63*
Fig Shells

Sole genus: ***Ficus***

Medium to large, thin, fig- or pear-shaped, ventricose shells, with short spire and large body whorl. Surface has fine spiral and axial threads or cords. Large, long, wide aperture, with thin outer lip. Smooth columella and extended siphonal canal. No operculum. The two mantle lobes completely cover shell. On sand or coral rubble in shallow to deep water. About fifteen species in one genus. Tropical waters, mostly Indo-Pacific and Caribbean.

FAMILY
CYMATIIDAE   *Pls. 64–67*
Tritons or Rock Whelks

Principal genera:
Argobuccinum   ***Charonia*** [ill.]
Apollon   ***Distorsio***
Cymatium

Medium to very large, thick, solid, ovate to ventricose shells. Spire often with different-colored embryonic whorls. Decorated usually with spiral cords, often with varices, tubercles, knobs; also axial ridges. Each whorl with one or two varices, as opposed to three on the Muricidae. Porcellaneous aperture, with calloused, often dentate, outer lip and dentate inner lip. Columella plicate. Siphonal canal sometimes extended, recurved or twisted. Periostracum often thick, hairy or fibrous yellowish-brown to brown. Operculum horny, ovate, usually orange-brown, mainly with subcentral nucleus. Carnivorous, feeding on echinoderms, mollusks, worms, ascidians. On muddy sand, coral and rocks, usually near reefs, in shallow to deep water. Over 100 species in five or six genera. Temperate to tropical waters, especially Indo-Pacific. Also placed under superfamily Tonnacea.

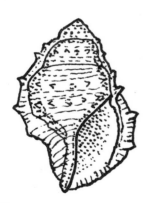

FAMILY

BURSIDAE Pl. 68
Frog Shells

Principal genus: **Bursa** [ill.]

Medium to large, thick, heavy, ovate, slightly compressed shells. Whorls with two rows of coarse, strong varices, usually nodulose. Outer lip dentate or crenulate. Columella sometimes calloused and plicate. Deep but short anal and siphonal canals, the latter deeply notched. A few with periostracum. Horny, yellowish-brown to brown operculum, with lateral or terminal nucleus. Carnivorous, some feeding on worms. On mud and sand, under rocks or in coral reefs, mostly in shallow water; some deepwater. About 50 species in perhaps six genera. Tropical waters, especially Indo-Pacific. Also placed under superfamily Tonnacea.

FAMILY

COLUBRARIIDAE Pl. 68
Dwarf or False Tritons

Principal genus: **Colubraria** [ill.]

Small to medium, thick, solid, elongate, fusiform shells. Tall spire with two embryonic whorls. Short body whorl. Prominent varices on whorls, with spiral rows of cancellate, beaded or tuberculate sculpture. Small aperture with denticulate outer lip. Large parietal callus on inner lip. Smooth or plicate columella. Siphonal canal short, open, recurved. Horny, orange-brown to brown operculum, with terminal nucleus. Under rocks, in shallow to deep water. A number of species in several genera. Warm temperate to tropical waters, mainly Indo-Pacific. Also treated as a single genus under Cymatiidae or Buccinidae.

FAMILY

MURICIDAE Pls. 69–77
Murex or Rock Shells

Genera used in this book, based on Radwin & D'Attilio (1976):

SUBFAMILY
MURICINAE

Acanthotrophon	Ac.	Murex [ill.]	Mu.
Aspella	As.	Muricanthus	Mca.
Attiliosa	At.	Naquetia	Na.
Bedeva	Be.	Nipponotrophon	Ni.
Bolinus	Bo.	Paziella	Pa.
Calotrophon	Ca.	Pazinotus	Paz.
Chicoreus	Ch.	Poirieria	Poi.
Dermomurex	De.	Prototyphis	Pr.
Ergalatax	Er.	Pterochelus	Ptc.
Haustellum	Ha.	Pterynotus	Ptn.
Hexaplex	He.	Purpurellus	Pu.
Homalocantha	Ho.	Siratus	Si.
Lataxiena	La.	Takia	Ta.
Marchia	Ma.		

SUBFAMILY
OCENEBRINAE

Ceratostoma	Ce.	Poropteron	Por.
Eupleura	Eu.	Pteropurpura	Ptp.
Hadriania	Had.	Roperia	Ro.
Jaton	Ja.	Trachypollia	Tr.
Ocenebra	Oc.	Urosalpinx	Ur.
Ocinebrina	Oci.	Xanthochorus	Xan.

SUBFAMILY
MURICOPSINAE

Bizetiella	Bi.	Murexsul	Mxl.
Evokesia	Ev.	Muricopsis	Mco.
Maxwellia	Max.	Subpterynotus	Su.
Murexiella	Mxa.	Vitularia	Vi.

SUBFAMILY
TROPHONINAE

Principal genera:

Actinotrophon	Trophon
Boreotrophon	Trophonopsis

SUBFAMILY
TYPHINAE

14 genera, but all listed in this book under **Typhis**

Small to large, generally thick, spiral shells, varying greatly in shape, with turreted whorls. Spire usually prominent. Surface sculpture often quite elaborate; strong varices, three to each whorl; many with spines, fronds, nodules. Oval or tear-shaped aperture, with lips often dentate or crenulate; sometimes with tooth for prying open bivalves. Columella usually smooth. Siphonal canal usually extended and partly closed. Large, horny, brown, oval or tear-shaped operculum, usually with anterior nucleus near margin. Produces purple pigment, once used for dye. Carnivorous, feeding on bivalves, barnacles often by drilling holes; also shrimps, sponges, algae. In sand or mud, among rocks and corals, generally in intertidal, shallow water. About 400 species in about 20 genera. Five subfamilies; principal one is Muricinae. Temperate to tropical waters worldwide, especially Indo-Pacific and Panamic.

FAMILY

CORALLIOPHILIDAE *Pls. 78–79*
Coral Shells and Turnip Shells

Principal genera: *Coralliophila*
                    Latiaxis
                    Rapa [ill.]

Small to medium-sized shells, genera quite dissimilar. *Coralliophila* are small, thick, with inflated body whorl, large purple aperture, thickened lip. Most *Latiaxis* are small to medium-sized with pronounced shoulder keels and elaborate sculpture, with spiral ridges, usually scaly or spinose. *Rapa* are medium to large, thin, turnip-shaped, with very large inflated body whorl and aperture. *Coralliophilidae* often have crenulate or dentate outer lip. Siphonal canal may be deep and curved. Umbilicus often wide and deep. Horny, dark brown operculum with lateral nucleus. Carnivorous, feeding on soft corals, hydrozoans, anemones. Burrow in corals; in rock crevices, on rocks or sea fans, in shallow to deep waters. Several hundred species in six to eight genera. Subtropical to tropical waters, especially Japonic and W. Pacific. Family also called **MAGILIDAE** and **RAPIDAE**.

FAMILY

RAPANIDAE *Pl. 79*

Principal genera: *Forreria*
                    Rapana [ill.]
                    Neorapana

Medium to large, thick, ovate shells, sharply narrowing toward anterior. Short spire, with few whorls. Inflated body whorl with prominent shoulder. Surface often has scaly or nodulose spiral ribs. Color usually tan to brown. Large aperture with flaring lip, often with tooth. Siphonal canal of *Rapana* short, *Forreria* long; large siphonal fasciole, some with scaly ribs. Usually with deep umbilicus. Large, horny operculum with lateral nucleus. In shallow water. A few species in five genera. Mostly tropical, Indo-Pacific, Japonic, and, for *Forreria*, Californian. Also treated as a subfamily, Rapaninae, of Thaididae.

FAMILY
THAIDIDAE
Pls. 80–82
Dogwinkles or Dye Shells

Principal genera:
Thais [ill.]	*Purpura*
Acanthina	*Drupa*
Neothais	*Morula*

Small to medium-sized, thick, heavy, ovate to fusiform shells, with short to medium spire. Large body whorl. Surface usually covered with spiral rows of small, rounded nodules or short spines. Lacks varices. Long, often wide, aperture. Outer lip often strongly dentate; inner lip of *Drupa* dentate. Short siphonal canal. Horny operculum with lateral nucleus. Secrete a purple fluid, used for dye, "Tyrian Purple", by the ancients. Carnivorous, feeding on worms, sea urchins, gastropods, bivalves, barnacles, coral. On rocks or corals in intertidal to shallow water. Hundreds of species in a dozen or more genera. Worldwide, mainly in tropical waters. Also placed under Muricidae, as subfamily Thaidinae. Family also called **PURPURIDAE**.

FAMILY
COLUMBARIIDAE *Pl. 82*
Pagoda Shells

Sole genus: *Columbarium*

Medium-sized, thin, fusiform shells. Tall spire with two rounded embryonic whorls. Surface has keeled whorls, either tuberculate or spiny, spines slightly upturned; covered with fine, axial lines. Very long siphonal canal. Horny, leaf-shaped operculum with terminal nucleus. In deep water. About twenty species in one genus. Mainly tropical waters, especially Indo-Pacific and South African. Also placed under Muricidae.

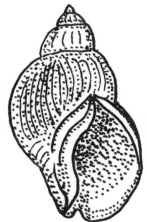

FAMILY
BUCCINIDAE   Pls. 83–86
Whelks
Principal genera:

Babylonia	*Neptunea*
Buccinum [*ill.*]	*Phos*
Cantharus	*Pisania*
Engina	*Siphonalia*

Small to large, thick shells in variable shapes, primarily ovate, fusiform. Tapering spire with pointed apex. Large body whorl. Smooth or with axial ribs and spiral cords. Aperture usually large, with notched base. Columella generally smooth. Siphonal canal usually short. Some deeply umbilicate. Often with heavy, dark periostracum. Thin, horny, ovate operculum, with apical nucleus. Carnivorous, primarily scavengers, feeding on bivalves, worms and carrion. In rocks and coral, in intertidal, shallow to deep water. Hundreds of species in several dozen genera. Mainly Arctic to temperate waters. Many genera included here should be assigned to the closely related cold-water family Neptunidae. We have followed most authors in not separating them, as much work remains to be done in properly assigning the various genera to these families.

FAMILY
COLUMBELLIDAE   Pl. 87
Dove Shells
Principal genera: ***Columbella*** [*ill.*]
                     Pyrene
                     Strombina

Small, solid shells, mostly fusiform. Usually smooth, glossy, with attractive patterns; some with fine spiral lines or axial ribs. Narrow, elongated aperture. Outer lip usually thickened, especially at center; generally denticulate or crenulate, as is columella. Short siphonal canal. No umbilicus. Some with axially striated, brown periostracum. Tiny, horny, smooth, elongated operculum. Mostly carnivorous, feeding on bivalves, crustaceans; some herbivorous, feeding on algae, detritus. Generally on sand and coral, in shallow to deep water. About 400 species in seven or more genera. Large variation in many species has led to much confusion in assigning genera and subgenera. Temperate to tropical, mainly Pacific and Panamic. Family also called **PYRENIDAE**.

FAMILY
MELONGENIDAE   Pl. 88
Principal genera: ***Volema***
                     Busycon
                     Syrinx
                     [*Ill.: **Melongena***]

Medium to very large, thick, heavy shells. Form quite variable; often pear-shaped with strongly keeled shoulder and short spire. Large, inflated body whorl. Some with axial ribs and spiral cords, often nodulose or spiny, especially on shoulder. Many are banded. Large aperture, often with flaring outer lip. Siphonal canal mainly wide and extended. Periostracum usually thick, brown. Thick, horny, claw-shaped operculum. Carnivorous, feeding on mollusks, carrion. Mostly intertidal to shallow water. A few species in three genera. Temperate to tropical waters, especially Carolinian and Caribbean.

189

NASSARIIDAE   *Pl. 89*

Dog Whelks or Basket Shells

Principal genera: *Nassarius* [ill.]
                       Bullia

Small, thick, ovate shells, with tapering, pointed spire. Surface generally cancellate; axial ribs often nodulose or beaded. Small, rounded aperture with prominent notch or fossa at base. Outer lip usually dentate or lirate inside. Parietal wall often heavily calloused. Columella sometimes denticulate. Short siphonal canal. Small, horny, ovate operculum with serrated margin and apical nucleus. Mostly carnivorous, boring into mollusks; feeding actively at night on carrion; some herbivorous, feeding on diatoms and plants. Burrow in sand or mud, in intertidal to deep waters. Many species in about fourteen genera. Worldwide, mainly subtropical to tropical waters.

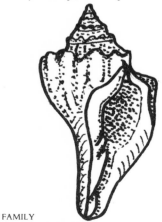

FAMILY

FASCIOLARIIDAE   *Pls. 90–92*

Tulip and Spindle Shells

Principal genera:

Fasciolaria [ill.]	*Peristernia*
Pleuroploca	*Fusinus*
Latirus	

Medium to very large, generally thick, fusiform shells. Long, pointed, multi-whorled spire. Often with nodulose whorls on spire and shoulder. Surface with axial ribs, often nodulose, and spiral threads. Ovate aperture, sometimes lirate inside. Outer lip not thickened, usually denticulate. Columella often with folds but always smooth in *Fusinus*. Extended, straight, open siphonal canal. Lacks umbilicus. Periostracum often thick, brown, flaky or fibrous. Large, thick, horny, oval or claw-shaped, operculum with spiral nucleus. Carnivorous, preying mainly on other mollusks. On sand and coral rubble, under coral rocks, in intertidal to shallow water. Many species in about eight genera. Worldwide, temperate to tropical waters. *Fusinus* also treated as a separate family, **FUSINIDAE**.

FAMILY

VOLUTIDAE   *Pls. 93–101*

Volutes

Genera used in this book, based on Weaver & duPont (1970):

Adelomelon	Ad.	*Melo*	Melo
Alcithoe	Al.	*Miomelon*	Mi.
Amoria	Am.	*Nannamoria*	Na.
Ampulla	Amp.	*Neptuneopsis*	Ne.
Arctmelon	Ar.	*Notopeplum*	Not.
Calliotectum	Ca.	*Notovoluta*	No.
Callipara	Cal.	*Odontocymbiola*	Od.
Cottonia	Co.	*Palomelon*	Pal.
Cymbiola	Cym.	*Paramoria*	Par.
Cymbiolacca	Cyl.	*Provocator*	Pr.
Cymbiolista	Cyt.	*Scaphella*	Sc.
Cymbium	Cy.	*Sigaluta*	Si.
Ericusa	Er.	*Teremachia*	Tem.
Festilyria	Fe.	*Teremelon*	Ter.
Fulgoraria	Fu.	*Ternivoluta*	Te.
Fusivoluta	Fus.	*Tractolira*	Tr.
Guivillea	Gu.	*Voluta* [ill.]	Vo.
Harpulina	Hap.	*Volutifusus*	Vof.
Harpovoluta	Har.	*Volutoconus*	Voc.
Iredalina	Ir.	*Volutocorbis*	Vol.
Livonia	Li.	*Zidona*	Zi.
Lyria	Ly.		

Medium to very large, thick, fusiform or ovate shells. *Cymbium* are cylindrical. Apex often terminated in large embryonic whorl. Often with nodulose shoulder, axial ribs and spiral threads. Many very colorful, with striking patterns. Large, elongate aperture. Columella usually calloused, with prominent folds. Horny, claw-like operculum, missing in most larger species. Mostly carnivorous, feeding on mollusks and other animals; some are scavengers. Fast-moving, most burrowing in sand, usually in deep water, but some intertidal, on sand flats. About 200 species in about 42 genera. Mainly tropical, especially Australian and W. Pacific; a very few Arctic species.

FAMILY

VOLUTOMITRIDAE   *Pl. 100*

Principal genus: *Volutomitra* [ill.]

Small to medium, fusiform shells. Tall spire, usually with embryonic nucleus of two rounded whorls. Smooth or with thin axial ribs on early whorls and fine spiral lines. Long aperture. Three or four folds on columella. Short siphonal canal. Thin periostracum. Some with small operculum. Resemble Mitridae and Volutidae, and are perhaps closely related to the former. About 25 species in four genera. Arctic to temperate waters.

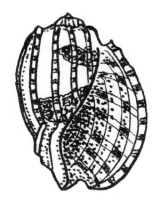

HARPIDAE   *Pls. 102–103*
Harp Shells

Principal genus: *Harpa* [*ill.*]

Medium to large, ovate shells. Short, pointed spire with two embryonic whorls. Large inflated body whorl. Prominent axial ribs or folds, forming a sharp coronate shoulder. Glossy surface, with very colorful salmon and brown scalloped patterns. Large, flaring aperture. Thickened, reflected outer lip with small anterior notch. Smooth columella with broad callus. No umbilicus, periostracum or operculum. Carnivorous, feeding on crabs and shrimps at night. Burrow in coral sands, in shallow to deep waters. About twelve species in two genera. Subtropical to tropical, especially W. Pacific and Indian Ocean.

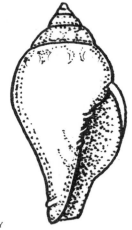

FAMILY

TURBINELLIDAE   *Pl. 103*
Chank Shells

Principal genus: *Turbinella* [*ill.*]

Large, thick, very heavy, fusiform shells, with short spire. Surface has fine spiral ridges or lines. Wide aperture. Parietal wall calloused. Concave columella with three or four strong folds. Straight, elongated siphonal canal. Narrow umbilicus. Thick, brown periostracum. Horny, claw-like operculum. Shallow to very deep water. Less than ten species, only three in *Turbinella*, in two genera. Subtropical to tropical waters. Family formerly called Xancidae.

FAMILY

OLIVIDAE   *Pls. 104–107*
Olives

Principal genera:
Oliva [*ill.*]   *Olivancillaria*
Agaronia   *Olivella*
Ancilla

Small, hard, elongate, cylindrical shells, with short, conical spire. Greatly enlarged body whorl, with channeled suture, conceals all except apical whorls. Smooth, glossy surface, often with elaborate colors and patterns. Long, narrow aperture. Upper parietal wall often with heavy callus. Several angular folds on columella. Has siphonal notch. No periostracum. Small, thin, horny operculum, lacking in *Oliva*. Two mantle-like flaps cover shell, creating glossy surface. Carnivorous, feeding on crabs, other animals, and carrion. Especially active at night. In sand, slightly below surface, in intertidal shallow water. About 60 *Oliva* and 90 other species in six or more genera. Temperate to tropical warm waters.

FAMILY

VASIDAE   *Pls. 103, 107–108*
Vase Shells

Principal genera:
Vasum [*ill.*]   *Tudicula*
Tudicla   *Afer*

Medium to large, very thick, heavy, biconic shells, usually with short spire. Large body whorl. Surface with spiral ridges and vertical ribs, with large tubercles or spines, especially at the shoulder. Long, narrow lirate aperture, with thickened, usually crenulate outer lip. Broad parietal callus. Columella calloused, with one or more folds. Medium to long siphonal canal. Thick, sometimes fibrous or scaly periostracum. Horny, claw-like operculum. Carnivorous. In sand or coral rubble, on coral reefs, mostly intertidal to shallow waters. About 20 to 30 species in seven or eight genera. Subtropical to tropical waters.

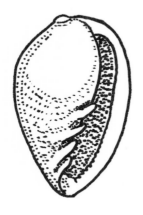

FAMILY

MARGINELLIDAE   *Pls. 108–109*
Margin or **Gem Shells**

Selected genera or subgenera:

Afrivoluta	*Af.*	*Glabella*	*Gl.*
Bullata	*Bu.*	*Marginella* [*ill.*]	*Ma.*
Closia	*Cl.*	*Persicula*	*Pe.*
Cryptospira	*Cry.*	*Prunum*	*Pru.*

Mostly very small, ovate shells. Short to medium spire, sometimes covered by callus; early whorls sometimes ribbed. Large body whorl. Very glossy, porcellaneous surface, generally with pale color. Often with large posterior calloused area. Aperture elongate, narrow, either smooth or lirate. Thick outer lip with rounded margin, sometimes denticulate. Most columellas with three to five folds. Some with siphonal notch. Very few with small operculum. Mantle covers nearly entire shell. An active carnivore. In sand and coral, mainly in intertidal, shallow water. Nearly 600 species in one or more genera; some workers propose 25 or more genera, rather than subgenera. Subtropical to tropical, especially W. Africa.

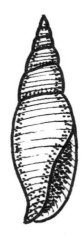

FAMILY

MITRIDAE   *Pls. 110–113*
Miters

Principal genera and subgenera:

Mitra [*ill.*]	*Mi.*	*Neocancilla*	*Neo.*
Nebularia	*Ne.*	*Scabricola*	*Sc.*
Dibaphus	*Di.*	*Swainsonia*	*Sw.*
Strigatella	*St.*	*Subcancilla*	*Su.*
Pterygia	*Pt.*	*Ziba*	*Zi.*
Imbricaria	*Im.*	*Vexillum*	*Ve.*
Cancilla	*Ca.*	*Costellaria*	*Co.*
Domiporta	*Do.*	*Pusia*	*Pu.*

Small to large, thick, elongate, ovate to fusiform shells, with high, sharply pointed spire. Smooth or with spiral grooves and axial ribs. Many very colorful, with spots or bands. Small, elongated, narrow aperture. Outer lip usually smooth; some crenulate. Columella with three or more prominent folds, uppermost being largest. Short siphonal notch. Some with very thin periostracum. Very few with small horny operculum. Has venomous gland. Carnivorous, some feeding on coral polyps, worms, small gastropods, tiny marine organisms; others are scavengers. Most burrow in sand and seaweed; under coral rocks or in coral crevices; mainly intertidal but also in very deep waters. About 500 species in eight or more genera. Worldwide in temperate to tropical waters, mainly Indo-Pacific, especially the larger, more attractive species. *Vexillum* also treated as a separate family, **VEXILLIDAE** or **COSTELLARIIDAE**.

FAMILY

CANCELLARIIDAE   *Pl. 114*
Nutmeg Shells

Principal genera: *Cancellaria* [*ill.*]
Trigonostoma

Small, thick, ovate, globose or fusiform shells with large body whorl. Surface ornament mostly strongly cancellate, with spiral and axial ribs; some with sharply angled shoulders. Usually shades of brown. Large, somewhat triangular, aperture, lirate inside. Columella strongly plicate, with light parietal callus. Some with small siphonal notch. Many umbilicate. No operculum. Herbivorous. On sand, in intertidal, shallow to relatively deep waters. A number of species in perhaps eleven genera. Mainly tropical waters, especially Panamic. Sometimes placed under superfamilies Volutacea or Mitracea, rather than its own superfamily.

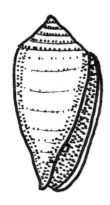

FAMILY
CONIDAE   *Pls. 115–129*
Cones

Sole or principal genus: ***Conus***

Small to large, mainly thick and heavy, conical shells. Spire high to depressed, some turreted. Large body whorl, often with coronate or nodulose shoulder. Smooth or with spiral threads or ridges, especially on spire and toward base; some faintly pustulose axially. Many with striking colors and patterns, individual species often having great variation. Elongate, narrow aperture with simple, thin, sharp lip. Smooth columella. Often with thin to very thick periostracum. Some have very small, brown, claw-like operculum with terminal nucleus. A few are quite venomous or toxoglossate, having a poison-filled radula, especially ***C.geographus***. Carnivorous, feeding primarily on worms, mollusks, fish. Usually beneath rocks, in coral crevices, in seaweeds; some burrow in sand; intertidal to deep water. About 400 species in one genera, divided by some authors into as many as 30 genera, but these are usually treated as subgenera.

FAMILY
TEREBRIDAE   *Pls. 130–131*
Augur Shells

Principal genera: ***Terebra*** [*ill.*]
                    Hastula
                    Duplicaria

Mostly small to medium–sized slender, elongate shells with high, sharply pointed spire. Many body whorls, smooth or with spiral cords or lines, often with strong axial ribs. Many colorful species, especially those in Indo-Pacific, often with bands, spots, streaks and blotches. Small, narrow aperture, pointed toward anterior, with simple, thin, sharp lip. Columella usually with single prominent fold. Short siphonal notch, usually twisted. No periostracum. Small, thin, horny, brown, narrow operculum with terminal nucleus. Carnivorous, feeding on marine worms and small invertebrates, paralyzing prey with poison-filled radula. In sand, mostly intertidal to shallow water. About 150 species, perhaps many more, in four genera. Often listed under the single genus ***Terebra***. Mostly intertidal to shallow water. Subtropical to tropical waters, especially W. Pacific.

FAMILY
TURRIDAE   *Pls. 132–133*
Turrids

Principal genera: ***Turris***
                    Polystira [*ill.*]
                    Crassispira

Small to medium–sized, mainly fusiform shells, often strongly carinated, with tall, pointed spire. Large variation in body form. Protoconch may have bulbous embryonic whorl. Most with spiral cords or threads and axial ribs. Long, narrow aperture, smooth or lirate. Slit on posterior end of outer lip ("Turrid notch"). Columella smooth or plicate. Some with parietal callus. Siphonal canal usually long and slender; some with siphonal notch. Several have a thick periostracum. Most with horny, leaf-shaped or ovate operculum with terminal nucleus. Has venom gland. Carnivorous. In sand or under coral rocks, many intertidal, but mostly deep to very deep water. At least 1,500 species, perhaps many more, with over 500 genera and sub-genera already proposed. Much work remains to be done on this very complicated, largest gastropod family. Worldwide in all waters.

SUBCLASS: OPISTHOBRANCHIA

FAMILY
PYRAMIDELLIDAE *Pl. 134*
Pyramid Shells or **Pyrams**
Principal genus: *Pyramidella* [*ill.*]

Tiny to small, elongated conic shells, with high spire and multi-whorled body. Glossy, porcellaneous; some with cancellate or spirally-grooved surface, or with axial ribbing. Mostly white. Small aperture with thin outer lip. One to three strong spiral folds on columella. Smooth, dull periostracum. Thin, horny, oval, pauci-spiral operculum, often notched, with apical nucleus. Carnivorous, some blood-suckers, feeding on worms, mollusks, sponges. On sandy or coral rubble, in intertidal to shallow waters. A few hundred species in many genera. Subtropical to tropical, mainly W. Pacific and Panamic.

FAMILY
ACTEONIDAE *Pl. 134*
Baby or **Small Bubble Shells**
Principal genera: *Acteon* [*ill.*]
Pupa

Small, thin, ovate shells, with short or concealed, multi-whorled spire. Large inflated body whorl. Surface has fine spiral threads or ribs. Long, narrow aperture, broadening toward anterior, with thin outer lip. Columella thinly calloused, with one or two folds. Some with small thin, horny, lamellate, brown operculum. Carnivorous, feeding on worms. In coral sand, in shallow to deep water. Few species in several genera. Worldwide, especially W. Pacific and Australian.

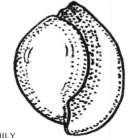

FAMILY
APLUSTRIDAE *Pl. 134*
Principal genera: *Aplustrum*
Hydatina [*ill.*]

Small to medium, very thin, fragile, globose or bulloid, with depressed spire. Large, inflated body whorl with deeply grooved suture. Smooth, glossy, or with very fine lines, often attractively banded. Very large aperture, broadening toward anterior. Very thin, sharp outer lip, extending above apex. Thin callus on columella. Thin, but tough, orange-brown periostracum. No operculum. Carnivorous, feeding on worms. On coral sand in shallow water. Very few species in three or more genera. Subtropical to tropical waters. Family also called **HYDATINIDAE.**

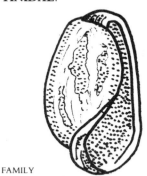

FAMILY
BULLIDAE *Pls. 134–135*
True Bubble Shells
Principal genus: *Bulla* [*ill.*]

Medium-sized, very thin, light, globose or bulloid shells with depressed spire. Large, inflated body whorl. Surface smooth, usually mottled. Very large flaring aperture, broadening toward anterior. Very thin convex lip, extending above apex. Concave columella with thin callus on parietal wall. Deep umbilicus. Carnivorous, feeding on mollusks; also herbivorous, feeding on algae. Burrows in coral sand or mud, and under seaweed, mostly intertidal to shallow water. Very few species in two or three genera. Subtropical to tropical waters.

FAMILY
ATYIDAE *Pl. 135*
Paper or **Little Bubble Shells**
Principal genera: *Atys* [*ill.*]
Haminoea

Small to medium, very thin, ovate to sub-cylindrical shells. Spire depressed, often concealed or perforated. Large body whorl. Smooth surface with very fine incised spiral lines at each end. Elongate aperture, widening toward anterior. Outer lip very thin, extending beyond apex and folding into center of spire. Concave columella with anterior fold. In sand or mud, in grasses, usually in intertidal, shallow water; also in brackish waters. Several species in three or more genera. Mainly subtropical to tropical waters. Formerly placed under Scaphandridae; *Haminoea* under Akeridae. Family also known as Haminoeidae.

FAMILY
PHILINIDAE *Pl. 135*
Principal genus: *Philene* [*ill.*]

Tiny to medium-sized, very thin, fragile, ovate shells, with depressed spire. Large, very inflated, body whorl, enclosing very small early whorls. Translucent, colorless, smooth surface, some with tiny spiral lines or punctations. Extremely large aperture with very thin, flaring outer lip, rounded below. An internal shell, completely enclosed by the reflexed mantle. Carnivorous, feeding on bivalves, using its gizzard plates. In shallow to deep water. Few species in three or more genera. Mostly subtropical to tropical, but also in Arctic waters.

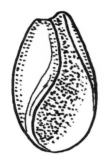

FAMILY

SCAPHANDRIDAE   *Pl. 135*
Canoe Shells

Principal genera: *Scaphander [ill.]*
                   Cylichna

Tiny to medium, thin, ovate to sub-cylindrical shells, with concealed spire. Very large body whorl, narrowing around apex. Smooth or with tiny spiral lines or punctations. White to yellowish brown. Very large aperture, broadening toward anterior. Large, thin, flaring outer lip. Some columellas with single fold. Yellowish-brown periostracum. Carnivorous, feeding on scaphopods, using gizzard plates. Shallow to very deep water. A number of species in several genera. Arctic to subtropical waters. Family also called Cylichnidae.

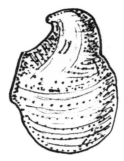

FAMILY

APLYSIIDAE   *Pl. 135*
Sea Hares

Principal genera: *Aplysia [ill.]*
                   Dolabella

Small to medium-sized, very thin, horny or calcareous, shield-like, convex shells. Apex flattened, hook-like, or with a knobbed spire. Yellowish-brown to brown. Some with periostracum. The internal shell of a large slug-like soft-bodied animal, reaching a length of 30 inches. Some have mantle glands which eject a fluid, usually purplish, when disturbed. Herbivorous, feeding on algae, seaweeds. Hermaphroditic. In rock pools, kelp beds, in intertidal to shallow waters. A few species in several genera. Worldwide, temperate to tropical waters. *Dolabella* also treated as a separate family, **DOLABELLIDAE**.

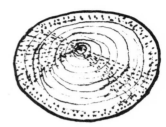

FAMILY

UMBRACULIDAE   *Pl. 135*
Umbrella Shells

Sole genus: *Umbraculum*

Small to medium, limpet-like, depressed, with subcentral nucleus. Faint radial ribbing. Underside glossy. Thin, often felt-like periostracum, extending over margin. Animal much larger than shell, which is embedded on its back. Feeds on microscopic organisms in sponges. In rock ledges or in soft substratum. Shallow to deep water. A few species in one genus. Worldwide, temperate to tropical waters.

FAMILY

CAVOLINIIDAE   *Pl. 135*
Shelled Sea Butterfly

Principal genera: *Cavolinia [ill.]*
                   Clio

Tiny to small, very thin, fragile shells. Shape quite variable: bulbous, triangular, pyramidal, cigar-shaped, conical, needle-like, but never spiral. *Cavolinia* have two fin-like projections. Pointed posterior. Translucent, usually colorless, some yellowish-brown. Pteropods, body enclosed in mantle, foot expanded to form two lateral fins. Feed on microplankton and other microscopic marine life. Pelagic, usually far offshore in deep water. A number of species in several genera. Worldwide, in Arctic to tropical waters.

FAMILY

AKERIDAE   *Pl. 135*
Papery Bubble Shells

Sole genus: *Akera*

Medium-sized, very thin, fragile, ovate to bulloid shells. Small spire with slit along suture. Surface has very fine spiral lines. Translucent, cream to buff-colored. An external shell, carried on back of animal. Hermaphroditic. Few species in one genus. In Indo-Pacific waters.

FAMILY

TYLODINIDAE   *Pl. 135*
Small Umbrella Shells

Principal genus: *Tylodina [ill.]*

Small, thin, limpet-like shells with subcentral nucleus and oval base. Faint radial ribbing. Underside glossy, with horseshoe-shaped muscle scar. Margin of shell uncalcified, rubbery. Thin periostracum, extending over margin. Feeds on microscopic organisms in sponges. Adheres to rocks with broad foot. Intertidal to deep water. A few species in several genera. Worldwide. This group also placed under Umbraculidae.

195

SUBCLASS: PULMONATA

FAMILY
AMPHIBOLIDAE *Pl. 136*
Air Breathers

Principal genus: ***Amphibola***
[*Ill.*: ***Salinator***]

Small, thin, subglobose or turbinate shells, with short, conical spire. Deep sutures on body whorl. Ovate aperture with thin outer lip. Columella may have callus. Has umbilicus. Thin, horny, subspiral operculum. Burrow in mud and sand; in salt marshes. A few species in several genera. Members of this and following three families are all air-breathers, being able to live on land.

FAMILY
MELAMPIDAE *Pl. 136*

Marsh Snails or
Air-breathing Ear Shells

Principal genera: ***Ellobium***
Melampus [*ill.*]
Cassidula

Tiny to small, somewhat thick, spiral, ovate to fusiform shells. Medium to high spire with several whorls. Surface nearly smooth. Oval aperture, pointed above, smooth or lirate inside. Columella often calloused, with one or more strong teeth. Truncate siphonal canal. Smooth, horny periostracum. Beneath driftwood, under rocks, intertidal to above the high-tide line; in salt marshes, mudbanks, mangrove swamps. A number of species in several genera. Temperate to tropical, especially W. Pacific. Family also called **ELLOBIIDAE**.

FAMILY
SIPHONARIIDAE *Pl. 136*
False Limpets or **Siphon Shells**

Principal genus: ***Siphonaria*** [*ill.*]

Small, limpet-like, depressed shells. Apex may be central or near posterior, sometimes hooked. Radial ribs. Margin may be somewhat scalloped. Glossy interior. Siphonal groove on inner right side next to horseshoe-shaped muscle scar gap. Air-breathing. Feeds on algae, detritus. Under gravel and on or under rocks near high-tide line. A number of species in a very few genera. Mainly tropical, especially Indo-Pacific.

FAMILY
TRIMUSCULIDAE *Pl. 136*
Button Shells

Sole genus: ***Trimusculus***

Small to medium, thin, limpet-like, low, conic white shells. Faint radial ribs, often crossed by concentric growth lines. Margin sometimes crenulated. Weak siphonal groove on inner right side next to horseshoe-shaped muscle scar gap. Air-breathing. On rocks, in intertidal waters. A few species in one genus. Mainly temperate to sub-tropical waters.

Class: PELECYPODA

FAMILY
SOLEMYIDAE *Pl. 137*
Awning, Veiled or **Date Clams**

Principal genus: ***Solemya*** [*ill.*]

Small to medium, thin, fragile, elongate shells, with rounded, slightly gaping ends. Equivalve; inequilateral. Smooth or with faint radial lines. External or internal ligament, behind beaks, toward posterior. Toothless hinge. Thick, glossy, brown periostracum, strongly fringed beyond margin. Some in shallow water, burrowing in sand or mud, but mostly in deep water. A very few species in two or more genera. Worldwide, mainly temperate to tropical waters.

FAMILY
NUCULIDAE *Pl. 137*
Nut Shells

Principal genera: ***Nucula*** [*ill.*]
Acila

Very small, triangular-ovate shells. Equivalve; inequilateral. Concentric growth lines. Internal ligament with narrow chondrophore. Beaks at and bent toward anterior. Hinge with two long rows of tiny transverse teeth. Inside nacreous, with crenulate inner margins. Lacks pallial sinus. Smooth, glossy, pale olive periostracum. Shallow to deep cold waters. A number of species in four genera. Worldwide, Arctic to temperate waters.

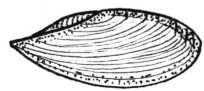

FAMILY
NUCULANIDAE   *Pl. 137*
Elongate or **Beaked Nut Clams**
Principal genera: ***Nuculana***
                     Yoldia [*ill.*]

Small, thin, elongate-triangular shells with rostrate posterior. Concentric growth lines. Ligament partially internal, with chondrophore. Hinge with two rows of tiny teeth. Inside slightly nacreous, with smooth margin. Usually with pallial sinus. Thin, glossy, greenish- to yellowish-brown periostracum. In cold, deep waters. Many species in eight or more genera. Worldwide in Arctic to temperate waters. Family also called **LEDIDAE**.

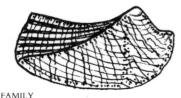

FAMILY
ARCIDAE   *Pl. 137*
Ark Shells
Principal genera:
Arca [*ill.*]   ***Anadara***
Barbatia   ***Noetia***

Small to medium, thick, trapezoidal shells, with inflated posterior and flattened cardinal area. Some with byssal gape. Some equivalve; inequilateral. Usually with strong radial ridges and fine concentric lines; often with brown zebra-like bands. External, elongate, striated ligament. Wide, inrolled or recurved beaks. Straight hinge with many small teeth in two continuous rows. Interior porcellaneous, with interior margin often strongly dentate. Lacks pallial sinus. Two adductor muscle scars, nearly equal in size. Thick, bristly, matted, brown periostracum. Attaches to substrate by a silky byssus. Often burrow or nestle in mud and sand, under stones, in dead coral. Mainly intertidal, but also shallow to deep water. Several hundred species in a few dozen genera. Worldwide, in temperate to tropical waters.

FAMILY
GLYCYMERIDIDAE   *Pl. 137*
Bittersweets or **Dog Cockles**
Principal genus: ***Glycymeris*** [*ill.*]

Thick, porcellaneous, orbicular shells with flattened cardinal area. Smooth or with radial ribs. Equivalve; equilateral. Often with brown mottling. External ligament with chevron-shaped grooves, sometimes partially in front of beaks. Beaks in center, curved inward. Arched hinge, with curved row of small chevron-shaped or transverse blunt teeth. Inner margin crenulate. Two adductor muscle scars, largest at anterior. Thin or velvety periostracum. Mainly shallow water. Many species in four or more genera. Worldwide, in temperate to tropical waters.

FAMILY
MYTILIDAE   *Pl. 138*
Mussels
Principal genera:
Mytilus [*ill.*]   ***Septifer***
Brachidontes   ***Musculus***
Ischadium   ***Lithophaga***
Perna   ***Modiolus***

Small to large, thin, elongate shells with rounded posterior. Equivalve; inequilateral. Smooth or with radial ribs and concentric growth lines. Ligament usually external. Sharp beaks at anterior. Long hinge line, sometimes with a few, very small, weak teeth behind sunken ligament. Inside nacreous. Anterior margin generally denticulate. Anterior muscle scar small, posterior muscle scar large. Periostracum usually thick brown or black, often hairy; some thin, glossy and very colorful blue or green. Some, such as **Brachidontes** and **Septifer**, have strong byssus threads; others such as **Lithophaga**, bore in clay, rock and coral; and others, such as **Modiolus** build nests. **Musculus** may live in ascidians. Edible; especially popular in Europe. On rocks, pilings, under stones, in mud or sand, often in large colonies, in intertidal water. Several hundred species in about 30 genera. Worldwide, especially in cool waters.

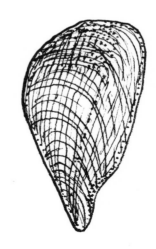

FAMILY
PINNIDAE   *Pl. 139*
Pen Shells or **Fan Mussels**
Principal genera: ***Pinna*** [*ill.*]
                     Atrina

Medium to very large, very thin, translucent, brittle, wedge-shaped shells, gaping at posterior. Smooth or with radial ribs, some scaly or spiny. Equivalve; inequilateral. Long, linear external ligament. Beaks near anterior. Toothless hinge. Thin nacreous layer on part of interior. Anterior muscle scar small, posterior muscle scar large and near center. Silky byssus at umbo; once used for weaving into fabric. Rarely with amber to black pearls. Edible. Anchors vertically in mud, sand or gravel, in shallow to deep water. A few species in three genera. Worldwide, in warm temperate to tropical waters.

197

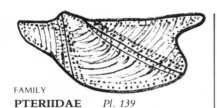

FAMILY

PTERIIDAE *Pl. 139*

Principal genera:
Pteria – Wing Oysters [*ill.*]
Pinctada – Pearl Oysters
Isognomon – Tree Oysters or
Purse Shells

Medium to large, thin, very oblique shells. **Pteria** have triangular, wing-like projections of the hinge margin. Inequivalve; left valve more convex. Concentric growth lines. **Pinctada** have scaly concentric ridges. Beaks at anterior end. Straight, elongate hinge line, with sunken ligament. Lack teeth. Hinge of **Isognomon** has several small parallel ligament grooves. Inside highly nacreous. Large posterior muscle scar nearly central; small anterior muscle scar at beak. Rough or scaly periostracum. Byssal notch in right valve. Attached to rocks, mangrove roots, in shallow water. **Pinctada** prefer muddy reefs. **Pteria** live in coral, sponges, seawhips. Many species in six genera. Worldwide in subtropical to tropical waters. **Isognomon** also treated as separate family, **ISOGNOMONIDAE.**

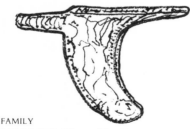

FAMILY

MALLEIDAE *Pl. 139*

Hammer Oysters

Principal genus: **Malleus** [*ill.*]

Medium to large, thick, irregular, elongate shells. Inequivalve; some with very long posterior wing, the anterior wing being shorter or absent. Margins of valves often gaping. Knob-like external ligament in deep triangular pit. Nacreous inside. One large adductor muscle scar. Strong byssal notch. A very few species in two genera. In subtropical to tropical waters, especially W. Pacific. Family also called **VULSEL-LIDAE.**

FAMILY

OSTREIDAE *Pl. 139*
Oysters

Principal genera: **Ostrea** [*ill.*]
Crassostrea
Lopha

Small to very large, usually thick shells with irregular radial ribbing. Often with lamellar surface. Inequivalve; left or lower valve is larger, thicker, quite convex; right valve is nearly flat. Inequilateral. Margins may be very deeply folded, as in **Lopha**, and sometimes denticulate. Inner margin of right valve may have small knobs. Internal ligament, located centrally in a triangular or elongated pit. Prominent beaks. Toothless, straight hinge. Inside often lustrous. Single large adductor muscle scar near center of both valves. In **Ostrea**, the muscle scar is white. The muscle scar of **Crassostrea** is colored and eccentric. Some cemented by left valve to substrate; **Lopha** attached by recurved spines. Many highly edible. On rocks, seawhips, in intertidal, shallow water; also in mangrove swamps. Many species in five or six genera. Worldwide, in temperate to tropical waters.

FAMILY

PLICATULIDAE *Pl. 140*

Kitten's Paws

Sole genus: **Plicatula**

Small, thick, irregularly triangular or fan-like shells. Prominent, broad, coarse radial ribs or folds. Inequivalve, right valve usually more convex; inequilateral. Ears small or lacking. Crenulate margins. Internal ligament. Two prominent cardinal teeth on both hinges, with long, narrow chondrophore. Single muscle scar toward posterior. Cemented by either valve, usually the right, near beak, to pebbles, coral, shells. Intertidal to shallow water. Very few species in one genus. Subtropical to tropical, mostly Panamic.

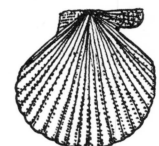

FAMILY

PECTINIDAE *Pls. 140–144*

Scallops or **Fan Shells**

Principal genera: **Amusium**
Chlamys [*ill.*]
Pecten

Small to very large fan-shaped to nearly circular shells. Mostly inequivalve; inequilateral. **Amusium:** thin, disk-shaped, slightly convex; upper (left) valve reddish, lower (right) valve near-white; small radial ribs inside. **Chlamys:** both valves convex; unequal ears; prominent radial ribs, often with scales. **Pecten:** left valve nearly flat or concave, right valve convex; ears nearly equal; broad flattened ribs. Extremely large range of colors and patterns, often remarkably bright. Internal ligament in cardinal pit beneath beaks, bordered by calcareous ridges. Lacks hinge teeth. Inside porcellaneous. One adductor muscle scar near center of valve. Byssal notch in anterior ear of right valve. Rest on right valve, either cementing it or attaching byssus to substrate, especially juveniles; adults are mostly free-swimming, propelled in jerky motion, with posterior forward, by opening and closing valves and ejecting jets of water. The muscle is an important source of food. Shallow to very deep water. Over 300 species in twelve genera. Some authors use up to 50 genera. Worldwide, temperate to tropical waters. **Amusium** also placed in separate family, **PRO-PEAMUSSIIDAE.**

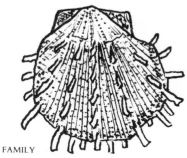

FAMILY
SPONDYLIDAE   *Pl. 145*
Thorny Oysters
Sole genus: ***Spondylus***

Medium to large, thick shells with inflated valves. Radial ribs, with large spines or larger, more convex left or lower valve, smaller spines on larger right valve, which is often foliaceous. Inequivalve; left valve with prominent ears; inequilateral. Many brightly colored, especially orange, red, purple. Mainly internal ligament in small, strong, central pit, bordered by calcareous ridges. Two prominent cardinal teeth on each short hinge; two lateral teeth in right valve. Single muscle scar on each valve. Lacks byssal notch. Cemented by right valve, at anterior margin, near beak, to substrate, usually rocks, coral or shipwrecks. Juveniles may resemble ***Chama***. Intertidal to deep water. A few dozen species in one genus, many very difficult to identify due to their great variability. Semi-tropical to tropical waters.

FAMILY
LIMIDAE   *Pl. 146*
File or **Scoop Shells**
Principal genus: ***Lima*** [*ill.*]

Thin, obliquely oblong or ovate, with longer anterior end, gaping at margins.

Has lunule. Fine radial ribs, usually with tiny, sharp, erect spines or imbricate scales. Equivalve; inequilateral. Small ears, nearly equal in size. Mostly white. Mainly internal ligament in central triangular pit, beneath beak. Straight hinge, without teeth. Single central faint adductor muscle scar. Swim like Pectinidae, though with anterior upwards, but tend to live in nests of byssal threads and rubble. In reefs, under rocks, corals, in rock crevices, usually in shallow water. Many species in several genera. Subtropical to tropical waters.

FAMILY
ANOMIIDAE   *Pl. 146*
Jingle Shells
Principal genera: ***Anomia*** [*ill.*]
                     Placuna
                     Pododesmus

Thin, translucent, irregular, generally oval shells. Inequivalve; left, or upper, valve convex; right valve flat, with byssal notch or hole, sometimes plugged, near beak, resulting in saddle-like shape; very nearly equilateral. May have rough radial lines or ribs on left valve, otherwise surface smooth. Left valve generally nacreous. Lacks hinge teeth. Two or three faint adductor muscle scars in center of left valve. Affixed permanently to substrate, usually rocks, shells, wood, by calcified byssus, except adult ***Placuna***. Intertidal to shallow water, some deep water. A number of species in five or six genera. Temperate to tropical waters.

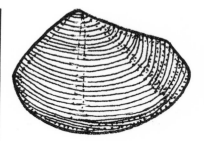

FAMILY
CRASSATELLIDAE   *Pl. 146*
Crassatellas
Principal genera: ***Crassatella***
                     Eucrassatella [*ill.*]

Very small to large, thick, heavy, triangular-ovate shells, with rounded anterior and beaked posterior. Smooth or mostly with smooth ribs, concentric striations or grooves, sometimes wavy. Equivalve or nearly so; inequilateral. Internal ligament, with pit in each valve. Large, strong, thick hinge. Two or three cardinal teeth in each valve; lateral teeth small and elongate. Lacks pallial sinus. Thick, brown periostracum. In shallow to deep water. A number of species in about eight genera. Polar to tropical waters.

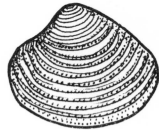

FAMILY
ASTARTIDAE   *Pl. 146*
Astartes
Principal genera: ***Astarte*** [*ill.*]

Small, thick, trigonal-ovate shells. Concentric rounded ridges and furrows. Mostly white, also inside. External ligament. Large, high, hooked beaks, pointed toward anterior. Three large hinge teeth in each valve. Lacks pallial sinus. Two adductor muscle scars, joined by pallial line. Shallow to deep water. A number of species in five genera. Mainly Arctic to cool temperate waters.

199

FAMILY

TRIGONIIDAE   *Pl. 146*

Brooch Shells or **Trigonia**

Sole genus: *Neotrigonia*

Small to medium, thick, triangular, inflated shells. Prominent scaly radial ribs. Equivalve. Short external ligament. Beaks pointed toward posterior. Large, striated, diverging hinge teeth. Inside nacreous and iridescent. Lacks pallial sinus and byssus. Very active, leaping with angulated foot. Shallow to deep water. Very few species in one genus. Only in S. Australia and Tasmania.

FAMILY

CARDITIDAE   *Pl. 146*

False-Cockles or **Cardita**

Principal genera:
Cardita [*ill.*]	*Glans*
Cardites	*Venericardia*

Small to medium, thick, obliquely triangular, rounded shells, usually inflated. Oval or heart-shaped lunule. Usually with strong radial ribs, often beaded or scaled.

Equivalve; quite inequilateral. Crenulated margins. Often with spots, mottling, small color bars, some quite colorful. External ligament. Beaks in center or toward anterior, often quite high, curved toward anterior. Thick hinge with one or two cardinal teeth, some with one or two short lateral teeth. Interior often partially flushed with color. Large posterior adductor muscle scar; anterior muscle scar elevated. Yellow to brown periostracum, sometimes hairy or velvety. Lacks pallial sinus. May be attached beneath rocks by byssus. Mostly in shallow, but also in very deep waters. Many species in sixteen or more genera. Worldwide, in all but Arctic waters.

FAMILY

GLOSSIDAE   *Pl. 147*

Principal genera: *Glossus* [*ill.*]
Meiocardia

Small to medium, thin, ovate to globose shells with inflated valves. Heart-shaped dorsal view. Large fan-shaped lunule. Equivalve; inequilateral. Smooth or with fine concentric lines. External ligament. Beaks, toward anterior end, quite prominent, inflated and strongly inrolled spirally. Thin hinge with two or three cardinal teeth; lateral teeth also well-developed. Inside white, porcellaneous. Pallial sinus small or lacking. Thin periostracum. In sand or silt, moderately deep to deep water. Very few species in two genera. Temperate to tropical waters. Family also called **ISOCARDIIDAE**.

FAMILY

LUCINIDAE   *Pl. 147*

Lucinas or **Lucines**

Principal genera:
Codakia [*ill.*]	*Lucina*
Fimbria	*Linga*

Small to large, thick, circular to ovate, convex shells. Small to large lunule. Smooth or with concentric ribs, sometimes crossed with radial ribs, forming scaly or beaded surface. Usually white. Equivalve; inequilateral. *Codakia* have smooth inner margins; *Lucina* and *Linga* have crenulated inner margins. External or partly internal ligament, set in deep groove. Small, low, nearly central beaks pointed toward anterior. Mostly with one or two small, weak cardinal teeth in each valve; lateral teeth in right valve. Lacks pallial sinus. Elongate anterior adductor muscle scar; posterior muscle scar generally rounded. Some have thin, scaly periostracum. May burrow in coral sand or mud, in shallow to deep water, but mainly intertidal. About 200 species in about 30 genera. Some temperate, but mostly subtropical to tropical. *Fimbria* also treated as a separate family, **FIMBRIIDAE**.

FAMILY

UNGULINIDAE   *Pl. 147*

Globe Shells

Principal genus: *Diplodonta* [*ill.*]

Small, thin, nearly circular, quite inflated shells. Smooth, polished surface; with concentric lines or finely granulose. Equivalve; slightly inequilateral. External ligament, elevated on platform behind beaks, sometimes extending to front of low beaks. One or two divergent cardinal teeth, sometimes singly-grooved; lateral teeth weak or missing. Inside white. Adductor muscle scars nearly equal in size. No pallial sinus. Forms nest of mud or sand cemented with mucus. On sand or mud flats, mainly intertidal, to deep water. In temperate to tropical waters. Family also called **DIPLODONTIDAE**.

FAMILY

CHAMIDAE   *Pl. 147*

Jewel Boxes or **Rock Oysters**

Genera: *Chama* [*ill.*]
           Arcinella
           Pseudochama

Small to medium, thick, irregularly rounded shells. Concentric rows of scales or foliations; **Arcinella** have radial rows of spines. Inequivalve; left (lower) valve larger, more convex and irregular; inequilateral. Often brilliantly colored in yellow, orange, pink, purple. External ligament. Spiral beaks strongly curved to right in **Chama** or left in **Pseudochama**. Thick hinge with one or two cardinal teeth in each valve. Lacks pallial sinus. Large adductor muscle scars joined by pallial line. Attached by left valve in **Chama** or right valve in **Pseudochama**, at beak, to rocks, coral, wood or shells. Some Chamas are inedible, causing dysentery. In intertidal to deep water. About 25 species in three genera. Subtropical to tropical waters.

FAMILY

CARDIIDAE   *Pls. 148–149*

Cockles or **Heart Shells**

Principal genera:

Acanthocardia	*Laevicardium*
Cardium	*Nemocardium*
Cerastoderma	*Trachycardium*
Fragum	*Vasticardium*
	[*Ill.: **Americardia**]

Small to very large, usually thin, rounded-triangular, sometimes elongate, inflated shells, some gaping at one end. Heart-shaped dorsal view. Prominent radial ribs, often scaly, spiny or knobby; some smooth and glossy. Porcellaneous, often quite colorful. Equivalve; inequilateral. Margins crenulate or dentate. Large, short, external ligament, forming a deep brown arched band behind the large, rounded beaks. Hinge plate varied in size and shape. Two small cardinal teeth, with two lateral teeth in left valve; three of each in right valve. No pallial sinus. Adductor muscle scars nearly equal in size. Periostracum varied in thickness. Leaps by means of long, angled, muscular foot. Many edible; especially valued in Europe. Usually in sand or mud from mid-tide line to deep water. About 200 species in about twenty genera. Worldwide, in most waters.

FAMILY

VENERIDAE   *Pls. 149–152*

Venus Clams

Principal genera:

Antigona	*Paphia*
Chione [*ill.*]	*Periglypta*
Dosinia	*Tapes*
Lioconcha	*Venerupis*
Mercenaria	*Venus*

Mostly medium-sized, thick, ovate or heart-shaped shells. Large lunule, often with smaller escutcheon. A great variety of concentric and/or radial sculpture, most often with rounded, concentric ribs. Porcellaneous surface, often polished; many with attractive rays, zigzag blotches and other markings. Equivalve; inequilateral. Inner margins often crenulate. Prominent external ligament, on platform, posterior to beak. Prominent beaks placed toward and pointed to anterior end. Usually with three cardinal teeth in each valve; may have weak lateral teeth. Generally with pallial sinus. Nearly equal adductor muscle scars. Lacks byssus. Burrows slightly below surface, in sand or mud, in intertidal to deep water, mostly in shallow water. Many are edible. Largest bivalve family, with over 400 species in several dozen genera. Worldwide, in most waters.

FAMILY
PETRICOLIDAE *Pl. 153*
Rock Borers or False Piddocks
Principal genus: *Petricola* [*ill.*]

Small to medium, thin, oval to elongate, inflated shells, gaping at posterior. No lunule or escutcheon. White to gray. Wrinkled or nodulose radial ribs or threads; some with concentric growth lines. Equivalve; inequilateral. Internal ligament. Beaks near anterior end. Weak, narrow hinge. Three cardinal teeth in left valve, two in right valve; no lateral teeth. Deep pallial sinus. Thin periostracum. Nestles in cavities, often boring into clay, peat, wood, limestone, dead coral. Many species in two-three genera. Temperate to tropical waters.

FAMILY
TRIDACNIDAE *Pl. 153*
Giant Clams
Genera: *Tridacna* [*ill.*]
Hippopus

Medium to extremely large, very thick, heavy, triangular-ovate shells. *Hippopus* are lozenge-shaped. Strong radial ribs, those on *Tridacna* with fluted scales; wavy growth lines. Both equilateral and strongly inequilateral. Valve edges scalloped; dentate inside in *Hippopus*. Interior porcellaneous, white. Internal ligament. Anterior part of hinge reduced in size. One cardinal tooth and one posterior lateral tooth in each valve. Adductor muscle scars at posterior. Large byssal gape in *Tridacna*; byssal gape in *Hippopus* closed in mature shells. *Tridacna* fastened by byssus to corals. Very colorful mantle. Rarely produce nonnacreous pearls. *Tridacna gigas* is largest known mollusk. In coral reefs. Six species in two genera. Only in Indo-Pacific.

FAMILY
MACTRIDAE *Pl. 153*
Surf Clams or Trough Shells
Principal genera: *Mactra* [*ill.*]
Spisula

Mostly medium to large, thin, triangular to ovate, inflated, porcellaneous shells, with somewhat gaping valves. Smooth or with concentric lines or ridges. Equivalve; inequilateral. External ligament small or lacking; mainly internal ligament beneath beaks, in chondrophore, with dark, tough resilium. Beaks, near center, bent toward anterior. A-shaped cardinal tooth in left valve, two in right valve; usually with lateral teeth. Deep, rounded pallial sinus. Buff brown or olive periostracum, usually smooth and glossy. No byssus. Usually in sand, in shallow water. Many species in about twenty genera. Worldwide, in all waters.

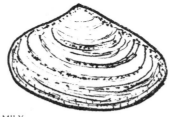

FAMILY
MESODESMATIDAE *Pl. 153*
Wedge Shells
Principal genus: *Mesodesma* [*ill.*]

Small to medium, thick, triangular or wedge-shaped, porcellaneous shells, somewhat gaping. Concentric ridges or lines. Equivalve. Ligament mainly external; internal ligament in large chondrophore; both short. Beaks pointed toward posterior. Thick, strong hinge. One cardinal tooth in each valve; lateral teeth well-developed. Has pallial sinus. Thin to thick yellowish periostracum. In sand, in shallow water. Many species is about ten genera. In mostly temperate to tropical waters.

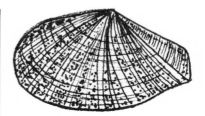

FAMILY
TELLINIDAE *Pls. 153–154*
Tellins
Principal genera: *Macoma*
Tellina [*ill.*]
Strigilla

Small to tiny, mostly thin, ovate to elongate shells, compressed laterally, with posterior end usually with ridge or slightly twisted. Concentric ridges or lines. Usually glossy, smooth, white to yellow, often with bright pink to red radial rays. Nearly equivalve; inequilateral. Smooth margins. Ligament usually external. Very small beaks. Narrow hinge plate. Two small cardinal teeth in each valve; *Tellina* also have two lateral teeth in each valve. Large, deep pallial sinus. Adductor muscle scars connected by pallial line. Burrow in sand or mud, in intertidal, shallow water. Over 200 species in about eight main genera. *Tellina* divided by some authors into many genera, rather than subgenera. Worldwide, primarily subtropical to tropical.

FAMILY
DONACIDAE *Pl. 154*
Coquina, Donax, Bean or Wedge Clams
Principal genus: *Donax* [*ill.*]

Small, solid, triangular or wedge-shaped shells; anterior longer, posterior shorter, truncated at an angle, more inflated. Fine radial ribs or lines, some with concentric growth lines; also with smooth surface.

Donax are glossy and quite variable in base color, often with rays of a second color. Many quite colorful inside. Equivalve; inequilateral. Usually with finely crenulate or denticulate internal margin. Short, arched, external ligament, on platform. Usually two cardinal teeth and one or two lateral teeth in each valve. Long deep pallial sinus. Some species edible; used for soup. Burrow near surface in sand at shore line to shallow water. About 50 species in four principal genera. Warm temperate to tropical waters.

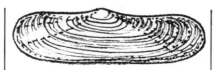

FAMILY

SOLECURTIDAE   Pl. 155

Principal genera: **Pharus**
Solecurtus
Tagelus [ill.]

Medium to large, thin, elongate–rectangular, somewhat cylindrical shells, with rounded, strongly gaping ends. Smooth; or with oblique or concentric striations. External ligament, posterior to beaks. Small beaks, usually near center. Weak, narrow hinge. Two cardinal teeth in right valve, one in left valve; no lateral teeth. Has pallial sinus. Thick, often wrinkled, periostracum. Burrow in sand and mud flats in shallow to deep water. Very few species in four or more genera. Temperate to semi–tropical waters. Also considered to be a subfamily of Psammobiidae.

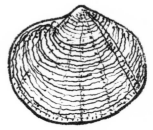

FAMILY

SEMELIDAE   Pl. 155
Semeles

Principal genera: **Semele** [ill.]
Cumingia

Small to medium, thin, ovate, rounded shells, often with ridge or slight twist of posterior. Smooth; or with concentric growth lines or ribs, often wrinkled; some with very fine radial striations, presenting a cancellate surface. Some are very bright orange, red or purple. Inside margin often tinged orange, red or purple. Equivalve; inequilateral. Ligament partially external, but mainly internal, in a long resilifer on hinge plate. Beaks in or near center. Two or three small cardinal teeth and prominent lateral teeth in both valves. Large deep, rounded pallial sinus for long siphon. Burrow in sand and mud, mainly in shallow water. Many species in seven or more genera. Mainly subtropical and tropical waters; some in temperate waters.

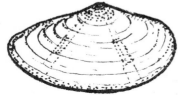

FAMILY

PSAMMOBIIDAE   Pl. 154
Sunset Shells

Principal genera: **Gari**
Sanguinolaria [ill.]

Medium-sized, thin, elongate, oval to trapezoidal shells, some gaping slightly at ends, especially posterior. Very fine radial lines and/or concentric growth lines. Some with rose or purple color. Both equivalve and inequivalve; inequilateral. Large external ligament, on platform. Small beaks. One to three weak cardinal teeth; weak lateral teeth, when present. Has large pallial sinus for very long siphon. Thick or glossy periostracum. Burrow in intertidal mud or sand, but some also deepwater. About 100 species in eight or more genera. Warm temperate to tropical waters. Family also known as **GARIDAE** or **SANGUINOLARIIDAE**.

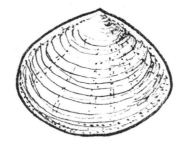

FAMILY

SCROBICULARIIDAE   Pl. 155

Principal genus: **Scrobicularia** [ill.]

Small to medium, thin, ovate to nearly circular shells. Nearly smooth, with very fine concentric growth lines. Small external ligament; large internal ligament on chondrophore. Small, low beaks. Two small cardinal teeth in right valve; **Abra** have two very small, thin lateral teeth. Large, wide pallial sinus for very long siphon. On mud, in shallow to deep waters. Few species in two genera. Arctic to temperate waters, especially W. Europe. **Abra** also placed by some authors under Semelidae; Scrobiculariidae also treated as a subfamily under Semelidae.

FAMILY

SOLENIDAE   Pl. 155

Jackknife and **True Razor Clams**

Principal genera:
Solen [ill.]   **Phaxas**
Ensis   **Siliqua**

Medium to large, thin, very much elongated, somewhat cylindrical shells with parallel sides, gaping widely at both ends. Straight or curved. **Solen** and **Ensis** have truncated ends; **Phaxas** have round ends;

Siliqua are ovate, elongate. Equivalve; inequilateral. Long, external ligament. Beaks very small; at or near anterior end in *Solen*; others may be nearer center. *Solen* have single, small cardinal tooth in both valves; others have two in left valve, one in right valve. Lateral teeth thin and very weak or lacking. *Siliqua* have a straight, vertical internal rib. Pallial sinus generally short. Thin, glossy, varnish-like periostracum. Lacks byssus. Many are edible. Burrow rapidly in sand or mud. Many species in ten or more genera. Arctic to tropical waters.

FAMILY

MYIDAE   *Pl. 155*
Soft-shelled Clams
Principal genus: *Mya* [*ill.*]

Small to large, thin, ovate to elongate, often irregular shells, some truncated at posterior, with large posterior gape. Some with a weak lunule and escutcheon. Concentric growth lines. Chalky to porcellaneous, grayish. Inequivalve, right valve more convex; inequilateral. Smooth inner margins. Some with external ligament, but mostly internal, in chondrophore in left valve with corresponding groove in right valve for long, strong siphon. Small cardinal teeth, usually one in each valve. Usually has pallial sinus. Dull, flaky periostracum. Edible. Burrow deeply in mud and sand. A number of species in Arctic to tropical waters, mainly temperate, especially W. and E. coasts of N. America.

FAMILY

CORBULIDAE   *Pl. 155*
Basket Clams
Principal genus: *Corbula* [*ill.*]

Small, thick, ovate-triangular, inflated, white shells, with angled or beaked posterior. Strong concentric ridges. Inequivalve, right valve often larger; inequilateral. Internal ligament in chondrophore in left valve. Some have one cardinal tooth in right valve. Pallial sinus small or lacking. Intertidal to shallow waters; some in brackish or fresh water. Many species in perhaps five or six genera. Mainly temperate to subtropical waters, especially Panamic.

FAMILY

HIATELLIDAE   *Pl. 155*
Giant Clams or Crypt Dwellers
Principal genera: *Hiatella* [*ill.*]
                     Panopea

Medium-sized, thin elongate-trapezoidal, often quite irregular chalky shells, gaping at both ends. Irregular, concentric furrows, creating a wrinkled surface. Equivalve; inequilateral. Strong external ligament in deep furrow. Beaks near anterior end. Thick hinge, usually lacking teeth, but some with one conical cardinal tooth in each valve. Discontinuous pallial line. Pallial sinus large and shallow, if present. Irregular adductor muscle scars, usually well-defined. Flaky periostracum. Some attached by byssus to rocks and shells. Bore in mud, or nest in kelp, rock crevices, in cool shallow to deep water. Very few species in six or more genera. Mainly Arctic to temperate, especially both northern coasts of N. America.

FAMILY

PHOLADIDAE   *Pls. 155–156*
Angel Wings or Piddock Clams
Principal genera: *Barnea* [*ill.*]
                     Zirfaea

Small to large, thin, elongate, wing-like, near-cylindrical white shells; posterior narrower, often tube-like. Anterior has wide gape, often filled by a callum in adults. Some with posterior gape. Concentric growth lines on posterior; rasp-like scales or ridges for boring on anterior. Equivalve; inequilateral. Usually has up to eight accessory valves or plates, mostly on dorsal margin. Some have a calcareous apophysis beneath the beak. Without ligament. Generally without hinge teeth. Thin, flaky, gray to black periostracum. Some are edible. Burrow in wood, peat, clay, coral, or rocks, in intertidal to shallow water. Many species in fifteen or more genera. Arctic to tropical waters.

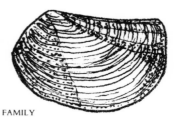

FAMILY

PANDORIDAE   *Pl. 156*
Pandoras
Sole genus: *Pandora*

Small to mostly medium, very thin white shells, with greatly variable shape, some hatchet- or fan-shaped. Left valve larger and slightly convex, right valve flat. Radial lines on right valve; left valve divided into two sections by diagonal groove. Concentric growth lines. Inequivalve. Very small beaks near anterior end. Thick dorsal margin with one to three diverging calcareous ridges or lithodesma, which support the internal ligament. Lack teeth. Inside nacreous. No pallial sinus. Usually with thin periostracum. Hermaphroditic. Generally on pebbly or shelly bottom, in intertidal to deep water. Several species in one genus. Arctic to cool tropical waters.

FAMILY

LYONSIIDAE *Pl. 156*

Glass Clams or **Paper Shells**

Principal genera: *Lyonsia* [*ill.*]
 Entodesma

Small to medium, very thin, oblong, elongate, often distorted, glassy, translucent shells. Posterior slightly gaping. Slightly inequivalve; inequilateral. Smooth, or with radial lines, often finely pustulose. Concentric growth lines or ridges. Small, internal ligament, attached to narrow ledge beneath beaks, supported by a large, calcareous lithodesma. Well-developed beaks near anterior end. Thick dorsal margin, but no hinge or teeth. Inside nacreous. Thin, yellowish periostracum with hairy, radiating wrinkles, often with entrapped sand grains covering the surface. Has small but distinct pallial sinus. Nestle in sand, gravel, mud or clay, in mainly shallow water. A few species in five or more genera. Arctic to semi-tropical, especially in cool Atlantic and Pacific waters.

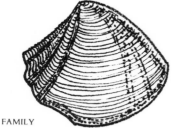

FAMILY

MYOCHAMIDAE *Pl. 156*

False Jingle Shells

Principal genera: *Myadora* [*ill.*]
 Myochama

Thin, triangular shells. Usually with concentric ridges; some with radial ridges; two or more large posterior ridges on right valve. Narrow internal ligament. Beaks pointed toward anterior. Thick hinge margin. Lack teeth, but have two tooth-like lithodesma in each valve supporting ligament. Inside nacreous. Weak adductor muscle scars. Small pallial sinus. Free or attached to shells or rocks. In mainly shallow water. Very few species in two or three genera. In Pacific waters, especially S. Australia.

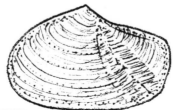

FAMILY

THRACIIDAE *Pl. 156*

Thracias

Principal genus: *Thracia* [*ill.*]

Mostly medium-sized, thin, ovate shells, some quadrate, with posterior gape. Inequivalve, right valve large and more convex. Smooth, very finely granulated or wavy. Irregular fine concentric growth lines or ridges. Porcellaneous or chalky white to grayish white. Mostly with depressed internal ligament in chondrophore in one valve; some with external ligament on both sides of beaks. Prominent central beaks; in *Thracia*, the right beak punctures the left beak. Thick dorsal margin. Lacks teeth. Inside white or slightly nacreous. Two adductor muscle scars. Strong, broad pallial sinus. Usually in deep water. Many species in about eight genera. Mostly Arctic to temperate waters.

FAMILY

CLAVAGELLIDAE *Pl. 156*

Watering Pot or **Tube Shells**

Principal genera: *Clavagella*
 Penicillus [*ill.*]

Mostly large, thin shells, with one or both very small open valves embedded at base of long, calcareous tube, terminated by a convex, perforated, fringed, calcareous disk. Pebbles, sand and small shells usually cemented to tube. Inequivalve. External ligament. No hinge teeth. The tube is secreted by the mantle of the adult. Embedded vertically in mud or sand. A few species in about four genera. Indo-Pacific waters.

FAMILY

CUSPIDARIIDAE *Pl. 156*

Dipper Shells

Principal genera: *Cuspidaria* [*ill.*]
 Cardiomya

Small, thin, globose shells, posterior with elongated, spout-like beak. Smooth surface with fine, concentric growth lines. Inequivalve. Elongate external ligament; internal ligament supported by a calcareous lithodesma. Right valve of *Cuspidaria* has a single lateral tooth. No pallial sinus. Thin periostracum. Offshore, in very deep water, up to 4,000 meters. Several species in six or more genera. Arctic to tropical, mainly E. and W. coasts of N. America.

FAMILY

VERTICORDIIDAE *Pl. 156*

Principal genera: *Euciroa* [*ill.*]
 Verticordia

Mostly small to medium, near-orbicular, thin, inflated, dull white shells. Dorsal view heart-shaped. Has lunule. Margin usually strongly crenulate. Prominent curved radial ribs, often spinose. Surface sometimes finely granular. Equivalve. Internal ligament in a large lithodesma. Large beaks pointed to anterior end. Right valve of *Verticordia* has one conical cardinal tooth; no lateral teeth. Inside nacreous. Thin pale brown periostracum. Primarily in deep water. Few species in six or more genera. Arctic to tropical waters, especially the E. and W. coasts of N. America.

205

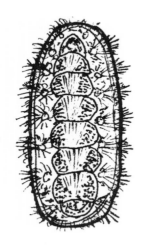

Class:
POLYPLACOPHORA

ORDER: NEOLORICATA

FAMILY

ACANTHOCHITONIDAE   *Pl. 157*
Glass-haired or Hidden-shell Chitons
Principal genera: *Acanthochitona* [*ill.*]
Cryptochiton

Small to medium, elongate narrow shells. Usually with five slits in head valve; two slits in tail valve, which also has sinus. Remainder of valves covered with flat-topped granules or pustules. Leathery girdle encircles valves; usually covered with tiny glassy spicules. All girdles have about twenty large tufts of glassy spines. Intertidal to shallow waters. Several species in two principal genera. Cold temperate to tropical waters, especially Panamic.

FAMILY
ISCHNOCHITONIDAE   *Pl. 157*
Principal genera:

Cyanoplax	*Lepidozona*
Ischnochiton [*ill.*]	*Stenoplax*
Lepidochitona	*Tonicella*

Small to medium, subovate to elongate shells. All valves have insertion plates, with smooth or faintly grooved sharp teeth. Eight or more slits in head and tail valves, one or more in other valves. Intermediate valves are divided into two areas by a diagonal rib on both sides, one having longitudinal, the other transverse ribs. End valves often have radial ribbing. Girdle usually scaly. Mostly intertidal waters. Many species in about eight or more genera. Mainly W. coast of N. America and Panamic.

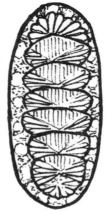

FAMILY
CALLISTOPLACIDAE   *Pl. 157*
Principal genera: *Callistochiton* [*ill.*]
Nuttallina

Small to medium, elongate to oval shells. End valves have several slits; one slit on each intermediate valve. Short, smooth insertion plates, bent inward. End valves have strong radial ribs. Intermediate valves divided into two areas by a diagonal rib on both sides, one having longitudinal, the other transverse ribs. Upper valve surface of *Nuttallina* granulose. Narrow girdle, finely scaled. Intertidal, shallow waters. Several species in a few genera. Temperate to tropical waters, especially Californian and Panamic. *Nuttallina* was formerly placed under Ischnochitonidae or Lepidochitonidae.

FAMILY
CHAETOPLEURIDAE   *Pl. 157*
Sole genus: *Chaetopleura*

Small subovate to elongate shells. Head and tail valves have radiating rows of pustules. Valves usually have several slits, as many as twelve in the head and tail valves. Insertion teeth are grooved on outer surfaces. Upper valve surfaces also have rows of pustules. Girdle is spiculose with tiny interspersed hairs or scales, often velvety in appearance. In intertidal, shallow waters. Several species in one genus. Temperate to tropical waters, especially Panamic. Was considered subfamily of Ischnochitonidae.

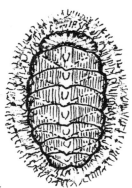

MOPALIIDAE *Pl. 157.*

Principal genera: **Amicula**
Katharina
Mopalia [*ill.*]

Medium to large, oblong to ovate shells with arch-shaped valves. Head valve has seven or more slits on insertion plates; tail valve has central sinus. **Mopalia** plates may be quite colorful, with a blue or pink color beneath. Girdle has bristles or fibrous hairs surrounded by spicules; broader at sides than at ends. **Katharina** has smooth, shiny black girdle also covering most of valves. Intertidal, shallow waters. A number of species in several genera. Mostly temperate waters, especially Aleutian and Californian.

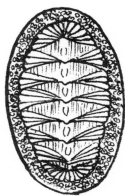

FAMILY
CHITONIDAE *Pls. 157–158.*

Principal genera:
Chiton [*ill.*]   **Tonicia**
Acanthopleura   **Rhyssoplax**

Medium to large, ovate shells. Upper valve surfaces smooth or with fine ribs. Insertion plates are slit, often deeply grooved or denticulated. **Tonicia** valves have tiny black

eye dots; head valve has seven to ten slits. **Chiton** girdle has large, imbricate scales, usually with green and black zones, underside blue-green. **Tonicia** girdle is fleshy, without scales. **Acanthopleura** has thick girdle matted with calcareous spines. Intertidal, shallow waters. Many species in several genera. In temperate to tropical waters.

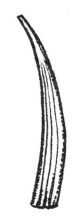

Class: SCAPHOPODA

FAMILY
DENTALIIDAE *Pl. 158*
Tusk Shells

Sole genus: **Dentalium**

Small to medium, thick, tapering, hollow, cylindrical tubes. Slightly curved, with anterior end wider. Posterior often with notch or slits, or with small terminal pipe. Surface smooth or with longitudinal ribs or lines; rarely with annular or spiral rings. Mostly white. Used by American Indians for money. Carnivorous, feeding on protozoa and foraminifera. Almost always deep water, burrowing in mud or sand with posterior exposed. Many species in one genus. Worldwide, temperate to tropical.

Class: CEPHALOPODA

FAMILY
NAUTILIDAE *Pls. 12, 158*
Sole genus: **Nautilus**

Large, thin, spirally coiled shell, with internal chambers linked by central tube or siphuncle. Surface nearly smooth, with fine growth lines and irregular reddish-brown radial stripes. Large nacreous interior. Umbilicus in all species except **Nautilus pompilius**. Edible. A carnivorous cephalopod living in very deep waters. Four or five species in one genus. W. Pacific waters only.

FAMILY
SPIRULIDAE *Pl. 158*
Ram's Horn

Sole genus: **Spirula**

Small, thin, fragile, loosely coiled, white shell, with internal chambers linked by a central tube visible externally in faint grooves. Globose aperture. A deep-water pelagic cephalopod. Very rarely collected live; commonly washed up on beaches. One species in one genus. Worldwide, subtropical to tropical.

207

Glossary of Terms

ARGONAUTIDAE   *Pl. 158*
Paper Nautilus or **Argonaut**
Sole genus: *Argonauta*

Medium to large, very thin, fragile, spirally coiled shell, laterally compressed, with nodulose double keel. Irregular, radial ridges; rows of tubercles in ***Argonauta nodusa***. No umbilicus. This pelagic cephalopod shell is actually a calcareous external egg-case. The tiny male (no larger than 5mm.) has no shell. Worldwide, in subtropical to tropical waters.

This glossary has been expanded to include not only those terms used in this publication, but also the terms most commonly used in all standard conchological works.

A

Acuminate. Pointed.

Acute. Sharply pointed.

Adductor muscle scars. The impressions left by the one or two bivalve muscles which draw the valves together.

Albino. A white or colorless form.

Algae. Small aquatic plants often found attached to shells, described as *algal growths*.

Anterior. The front end of a shell. In gastropods, the end from which the head emerges; in bivalves, the end from which the foot emerges, furthest from the ligament. The opposite of *posterior*.

Anterior canal. SEE **siphonal canal.**

Aperture. The principal or anterior opening of a gastropod.

Apex. The tip or early whorls of the gastropod spire.

Apical. At the tip or apex.

Apophysis (*pl.* apophyses). A projecting structure that supports the muscle in some gastropods. Also called **myophore**.

Arcuate. Arched or curved.

Ascidians. Sea squirts.

Auricle. The ear-like appendage of a bivalve beak, as in Pectinidae. Also called **ear**. SEE **wing**.

Axial. Longitudinal, or in the direction of the axis of the shell.

Axis. The imaginary center line of the shell, around which the whorls revolve.

B

Barnacle. A crustacean often found attached to shells.

Basal. Referring to the base or bottom of the shell.

Base. In spiral gastropods, the bottom of the shell; the extremity furthest from the apex; the last part to form. The anterior part, not including the aperture. Also, the flattened side of cowries.

Beak. The small rounded or pointed tip of a bivalve; the first part to form. Also called **umbo**.

Biconic. Shaped like two cones, base to base.

Bifid. Divided into two equal parts by a groove.

Bifurcate. Divided into two branches or parts, as in sculpture.

Bivalve. A shell with two principal valves or parts.

Body whorl. The final or largest anterior whorl of a spiral gastropod.

Brachiopod. A bivalve invertebrate (phylum Brachiopoda) resembling, but not belonging to, the Molluscan bivalves.

Brackish. Somewhat salty.

Bulloid. Bubble-shaped, as in Bullidae.

Byssal gape or **notch.** The space through which the byssus protrudes.

Byssus. A tuft of strong thread-like filaments that anchors some bivalves to other objects; secreted by the foot.

C

Calcareous. Consisting of calcium carbonate, usually of a white or chalky color.

Callum. A thin calcareous covering of the gape between valves in some bivalves.

Callosity. The state of being calloused.

Callus (*adj.* calloused). A marked thickening of calcareous material, often enamel-like, usually around the aperture, often covering the umbilicus.

Canal. A semitubular extension of the aperture lip containing the siphon, in some spiral gastropods.

Canaliculate. Longitudinally channeled or grooved.

Cancellate. The crossing of sculptural lines at right angles; latticed; reticulate. SEE **decussate**.

Cardinal teeth. The main hinge tooth or teeth of a bivalve directly beneath the beak.

Carina. A prominent sharp-edged ridge on the exterior of a whorl.

Carinate. Having a raised thin keel-like ridge.

Cartilage. SEE **ligament**.

Chitinous. Horny.

Chondrophore. A prominent internal spoon-like projection (**resilifer**) of the hinge-plate in some bivalves, which holds the internal ligament (**resilium**).

Circumpolar. For shells, found in waters surrounding the North Pole.

Columella. The central axial pillar of the spiral gastropod.

Columellar fold. A spirally wound ridge on the columella.

Columellar lip. The anterior part of the inner lip adjoining the columella, in many gastropods.

Commarginal. SEE **concentric**.

Commensal. Living together, but not parasitic.

Concave. Hollowed or rounded inward.

Concentric. Ridges or lines following the same direction as the growth lines on a bivalve. Also called **commarginal**.

Congener. Belonging to the same genus.

Conic or **conoid.** Cone-shaped.

Conspecific. Of the same species.

Convex. Arched or rounded outward.

Cord. A coarse rope-like sculptural element.

Cordate or **cordiform.** Heart-shaped.

Corneous. Horny.

Coronate. Crowned; a row or rows of short spines or tubercles on whorls of a spiral gastropod, especially at the shoulder.

Costa (*pl.* costae). Rib; a coarse, rounded sculptural element, larger than a cord; formed by a periodic thickening of the outer lip.

Costate. Rib-like.

Crenate. Having the edge notched or scalloped.

Crenulated. Having a notched or scalloped outline.

D

Deciduous. Shedding seasonally or at a stage in the life cycle.

Decollate. Apex truncated or broken off.

Decussate. Latticed; having a crossing of sculptural lines, not necessarily at right angles. *Cp.* cancellate.

Dentate. Having tooth-like projections.

Denticle. Small tooth-like projection, especially around the margin.

Denticulate(d). Finely dentate.

Depressed. Low, in proportion to the diameter.

Dextral. Right-handed. In gastropods, coiled in a spiral turning from left to right; opposite of **sinistral**. When the apex is pointed upward, the aperture is on the right side when facing the observer.

Digitation. A finger-like projection of the outer lip, as in Strombidae.

Discoidal. Disk-like; the whorls being coiled in nearly only one plane.

Divaricate. Having a surface composed of two different sets of parallel lines meeting at an angle.

Dorsal. In gastropods, the back, opposite or behind the aperture; in bivalves, toward the hinge area.

Dorsum. The back of the shell, opposite the aperture, as the hump of the shell in Cypraeidae.

E

Ear. SEE **auricle** and **wing**.

Edendate or **edentulous.** Toothless.

Emarginate. Indented or notched at the margin.

Embryonic whorls. Those whorls already formed before hatching. Also called **nuclear whorls**.

Endemic. Restricted to a particular locality or region.

Entire. Smoothly arched.

Epidermis. SEE **periostracum**.

Equilateral. Applied to bivalve shells that are symmetrical when divided from the beak to the margin into anterior and posterior halves.

Equivalve. When the two valves of a bivalve are of the same size and shape.

Escutcheon. An elongated depression behind the beaks of a bivalve, including the external ligament, if any.

F

Fasciole. A spiral band of successive growth lines on the siphonal canal of some gastropods.

Fissure. A narrow slit or cut.

Flamed. Flame-like markings.

Fold. A spirally-wound ridge on the columella.

Foliaceous or **foliose.** Consisting of thin lamellae or leaves.

Foliated. Leaf-like.

Foot. The muscular organ of the mollusk body used for locomotion.

Fossa. A groove or notch.

Fossula. A slight linear depression of the inner lip of some Cypraeidae.

Frondose. Leafy.

Fusiform or **fusoid.** Spindle-shaped; tapering toward each end.

Free valve. In attached bivalves, the valve not fixed to the attached object.

G

Gape. The opening between valves of a bivalve when closed.

Gaping. Having valves which only partially close.

Gastropod. A member of the class Gastropoda, such as a snail, slug or nudibranch, usually with a univalve shell.

Genus. A group of closely related species with common structural or phyllogenetic characteristics.

Girdle. The muscular material encircling the valves of a chiton.

Globose. Rounded or ball-shaped.

Granose or **granulate(d).** Covered with tiny grains or beads.

Growth lines. The impressed lines on the surface of a shell, parallel to the margin, caused by successive growth stages and rest periods.

H

Helical. Spirally coiled.

Heteropod. Pelagic mollusks of the superfamily Atlantacea (Syn.: Heteropoda).

Hinge. The interlocking teeth and ligament of a bivalve.

Hinge line. The dorsal margin of the bivalve, where both valves are in permanent contact.

Hinge plate. The internal surface of a bivalve, from which the hinge teeth project.

Holotype. The original specimen from which a new species is described.

Homonym. The later of two identical names given to two different species or other taxa.

I

Imbricate(d). Overlapping or shingle-like.

Imperforate. Lacking an umbilicus.

Impressed. Indented.

Inductura. A smooth shelly layer on the inner lip, often extending over much of the shell, even the exterior.

Inequilateral. Not equilateral.

Inequivalve. Not equivalve; valves of unequal size and shape.

Inflated. Swollen; usually applied to very thin shells.

Inner lip. That part of the aperture which is next to the columella.

Interspaces or **interstices.** The spaces between teeth and other raised linear surfaces.

K

Keel. A flattened ridge.

L

Labial. Referring to the lip.

Lamella (*pl.* lamellae). A thin, flat plate or scale.

Lamellate(d). Covered with thin plates or scales.

Lamina (*pl.* laminae). Lamella.

Lateral. Referring to the side.

Lateral teeth. The side teeth of a bivalve hinge, as opposed to the central **cardinal teeth**.

Left valve. The sinistral valve. On the left when the shell is placed with the posterior toward the observer and with the dorsal margin or hinge line upward.

Lenticular. Lens-shaped.

Ligament. The translucent elastic horny structure, usually internal, which joins the valves of a bivalve.

Lip. The edge of the aperture. SEE **inner lip** and **outer lip**.

Lirae. Fine lines or striae.

Lirate. Sculptured with fine incised lines.

Lithodesma. A calcareous structure reinforcing an internal ligament.

Littoral. The tidal zone between high- and low-water marks.

Lunule. In bivalves, a depressed area, usually heart-shaped, in front of the beaks.

Lyrate. Lyre-like.

M

Maculated. Spotted or splashed.

Mantle. The external fleshy membrane covering the soft parts of the shell. It secretes the shell and the periostracum.

Margin. The edge of the shell.

Mesoplax. An accessory plate of some bivalves, especially Pholadidae.

Metaplax. An elongated accessory plate of some bivalves, especially Pholadidae.

Mollusk. A member of the phyllum Mollusca; invertebrates with soft bodies, usually enclosed in or enclosing a calcareous shell.

Mouth. The aperture of a shell.

Multispiral. Having many whorls.

Muscle. The fleshy organ attaching the animal to the shell.

Myophore. SEE **apophysis.**

N

Nacre. The pearly or iridescent shell layer closest to the surface, consisting of extremely thin leaves of aragonite (calcium carbonate).

Nacreous. Pearly.

Nodose, nodulose or **nodular.** Having small knobs or tubercles.

Nomen dubium. A name without application to any known shell.

Nomen nudum. A name published without proper documentation.

Nuclear whorls. SEE **embryonic whorls.**

Nucleus. The first-formed part of the gastropod, such as its apex, or of an operculum.

O

Oblique. Slanting.

Obtuse. Blunted or rounded.

Operculate. Having an operculum.

Operculum. The horny or calcareous plate attached to the foot of some gastropods, which seals the aperture of the shell when the animal is withdrawn.

Orbicular. Circular.

Orifice. An opening.

Ornament or **ornamentation.** The relief sculpture on a shell surface, not including the growth lines.

Outer lip. The margin of an aperture furthest from the columella.

Ovate. Egg-shaped.

P

Pallial. Referring to the mantle.

Pallial line. The linear scar left by the mantle near the inner base of a bivalve.

Pallial sinus. In bivalves, a notch in the pallial line caused by the siphon.

Papillose. Covered with small nipple-like protuberances.

Paratype. One of the original group from which a new species was described.

Parietal lip. The posterior part of the inner lip in many gastropods.

Parietal shield. A shelf-like callus on the inner lip.

Parietal wall. The area within the inner lip.

Patelliform or **patellate.** Dish-shaped, as with Patellidae.

Paucispiral. Having just a few whorls in the spiral, as applied to opercula.

Pelagic. Relating to or living in open water – the oceans and seas.

Pelecypod. Former term for **bivalve**.

Penultimate whorl. The next to the last whorl of a spiral gastropod.

Periostracum. The outer hairy or fibrous covering of many shells. Also wrongly called the epidermis.

Periphery. The outermost edge of a whorl.

Peristome. The margin of the aperture of a gastropod.

Pillar. SEE **columella**.

Plate. In bivalves, a flattened calcareous structure.

Plica (*pl.* plicae). Folds or plaits; applied to the folds on the columella.

Plicate. Folded or pleated, forming ribs.

Porcelaneous. Translucent, porcelain-like.

Posterior. The apical end of a spiral gastropod; the back or siphonal end of a bivalve. The opposite of **anterior**.

Postnuclear. The whorls of a gastropod, other than the nuclear whorls.

Predatory. Preying on others for food.

Preoccupied. A name invalidated because it was used earlier for another species or other taxa.

Prodissoconch. The embryonic shell of bivalves and scaphopods, often preserved at the beak of the adult.

Produced. Elongate, as in gastropod spires.

Protoconch. The embryonic shell which becomes the initial apical whorl of a spiral gastropod.

Punctate. Dotted with minute sculptural depressions.

Pustulate. Covered with small pimples or pustules.

Pyriform. Pear-shaped.

Q

Quadrate. Rectangular, or of roughly square shape.

R

Radial. Ray-like; in bivalves, referring to the surface decoration diverging from the beak.

Radiating. Lines or rays extending outward from a point.

Radula. The lingual ribbon of gastropods, to which rows of raspy chitinous teeth are attached.

Recurved. Curved backward, as with the anterior canal.

Reflected. Turned outward or backward, as with the outer lip margin.

Resilifer. The socket-like pit on the bivalve hinge plate which holds the resilium.

Resilium. The internal ligament in the bivalve hinge.

Reticulate. SEE **cancellate**.

Rib. A relatively broad elevation of the surface.

Right valve. SEE **left valve**. The right valve is usually lowermost in the Pectinidae and uppermost in the Ostreidae.

Rostrate. Beaked at the end, as with the anterior of a bivalve.

Rostrum. A beak-like structure.

Rugose. Rough or finely wrinkled.

S

Scabrous. Rough, or covered with small raised points or patches.

Scalariform. Loosely coiled.

Scalloped. Having an undulated margin.

Scar. An impression on the interior of a bivalve left by the attachment of a muscle.

Sculpture. Ornament or ornamentation; a relief pattern on the surface of a shell.

Sedentary. Permanently attached.

Septum. A shelly concave plate or platform in the anterior end of some bivalves, or as partitioning chambers, as in Nautilidae.

Sessile. Permanently attached.

Shoulder. In gastropods, the angulation of the whorl, forming an edge of a suture.

Sinistral. Left-handed; turning from right to left. The aperture of the gastropod is on the left when facing the observer, if the apex is pointed upward.

Sinuate. Having a wavy margin.

Sinus. A deep notch, slit or indentation.

Siphon. A tubular organ of a shell through which water passes. In bivalves it is an extension of the mantle.

Siphonal canal or **groove.** A narrow tubular extension of the aperture margin through which passes the anterior siphon. Also called **anterior canal**.

Siphonal notch. A narrow slit at the end of the siphonal canal.

Socket. In bivalves, a depression in the hinge plate to receive the teeth of the opposite valve.

Spatulate. Having flattened spoon-like extensions.

Species. The subdivision of a genus, comprising a group of individuals with common specific characteristics and capable of interbreeding.

Spicule. Small prominences, usually spiny, on the girdle of a chiton.

Spinose. Having spiny or thorny protuberances.

Spire. The visible whorls of a gastropod, from the apex to, but not including, the body whorl.

Squamose or **squamous.** Scaly.

Stelliform. Star-like.

Stria. (*pl.* striae). Fine lines or furrows on a shell, indicating growth stages.

Striate. Having sculpture in the form of extremely fine lines.

Stromboid notch. A deep notch in the outer lip of the Strombidae, above the siphonal notch.

Substrate. The underlying living site of a mollusk, such as the sea floor, rocks and coral.

Sulcus (*pl.* sulci). Furrow or groove.

Sulcate(d). Furrowed or grooved.

Suture. In gastropods, the spiral line or seam joining the whorls.

Synonym. One of two or more names for the same species or other taxa, customarily the latest of these.

T

Taxodont. In bivalves, having many uniform hinge teeth.

Taxon (*pl.* taxa). Any unit in classification, such as class, superfamily, family, genus, species, subspecies, etc.

Teeth. In gastropods, the tooth-like protuberances near or in the aperture; in bivalves, the tooth-like protuberances at the hinge.

Tessellated. Having a mosaic-like coloring or appearance.

Thread. A very fine raised line on the shell surface.

Transverse. The angle of bands or lines parallel to the axis of a gastropod, at a right angle to the growth lines of a bivalve.

Trochiform. Trochus-shaped, as in Trochidae.

Truncate. Having the end sharply cut off.

Tubercle. A protuberance or knob.

Turbinate. Top-shaped, as in Turbinidae.

Turreted. High-spired, with a stepped series of whorls.

Type. SEE **holotype**.

U

Umbilicate. Having an umbilicus; navel-like.

Umbilicus. The hole or open axis within the whorls around which the gastropod coils.

Umbo (*pl.* umbones). SEE **beak**.

Undulated. Having a wavy margin.

Univalve. A mollusk with a single shell.

V

Valve. One of the halves of a bivalve, on either side of the hinge line.

Varicose. Having one or more varices.

Varix (*pl.* varices). Prominent raised ridges on the surface of the shell, formed originally at the aperture during rest periods in the shell growth.

Ventral. Referring to the margin area of a bivalve opposite to the hinge.

Ventricose. Inflated or swollen.

Volution. One of the whorls of a spiral gastropod or operculum.

W

Whorl. A complete axial turn of a spiral gastropod.

Wing. An elongate, often triangular, projection of the bivalve shell extending from the hinge area, as on Pteridae. SEE **auricle**.

Bibliography

General

Abbot, R.T. – *Kingdom of the Seashell*. Crown Publishers, Inc., New York, 1972. An illustrated compilation of many interesting subjects about and relating to seashells.

Bergeron, E. – *How to Clean Seashells*. Privately printed, 1971.

Dance, S.P. – *Rare Shells*. Faber, London and University of California Press, Los Angeles, 1969. Fascinating stories with color illustrations of some of the world's rarest shells, present and past.

Dance, S.P. – *Shell Collecting: an Illustrated History*. Faber, London and University of California Press, Los Angeles, 1966.

Dance, S.P. – *The World's Shells*. McGraw-Hill Book Co., New York, 1976. A general introduction to the classification, biology, collecting and cleaning of shells.

Feininger, A. & Emerson, W.K. – *Shells*. Viking Press, New York, 1972. Exceptional photography with an excellent text on aesthetics, as well as a selection of several hundred of the authors' favorite shells.

How to Study and Collect Shells. 4th Edition. American Malacological Society, Houston, Texas, 1972.

International Directory of Conchologists, 1978 Edition. Shell Cabinet, Falls Church, Va. An excellent source for the international exchange of shells.

Johnstone, K.Y. – *Collecting Seashells*. Grosset & Dunlap, New York, 1971. A good general introduction for the beginner.

Rice, T. – *A Catalog of Dealer's Prices for Marine Shells*. 6th Edition. Of Sea and Shore Publications, Port Gamble, Washington, 1980. Prices thousands of species based on dealers' lists, but the values are unedited.

Rice, T., ed. – *A Sheller's Directory of Clubs, Books, Periodicals and Dealers*. 6th Edition. Of Sea and Shore Publications, Port Gamble, Washington, 1978.

Stix, H. & Marguerite and Abbott, R.T. – *The Shell: Five Hundred Million Years of Inspired Design*. Harry N. Abrams, New York, 1968. The first "coffee-table" book on seashells with inspired color photographs by H. Landshoff. An abridged paperback version was published in 1977.

Worldwide: Introductions

Abbott, R.T. – *Sea Shells of the World. A Guide to the Better-Known Species*. Golden Press, N.Y., 1962. Still the best inexpensive small paperback to the most popular worldwide shells with G. and M. Sandström's rendering of 562 species. Useful as a basic checklist. Several foreign-language editions.

Abbott, R.T. – *Seashells*. Bantam Books, New York, London, Toronto, 1976. Basically, one or more shells is used as an illustration for a treatment of each family. 160 good color photographs including many of live mollusks, in this inexpensive small paperback.

Dance, S.P. – *Sea Shells*. Bantam Books, New York, London, Toronto, 1974. In this inexpensive small paperback emphasis is on a description of the families, with J. Nicholls' illustrations of a number of species.

Eisenberg, J.M. – *A Collector's Guide to Sea Shells*. The Collector's Cabinet, New York, 1971. An illustrated black-and-white paperback guide to 200 seashells, with values; the author's choices for the beginner.

Worldwide: Surveys

Dance, S., ed. – *The Collector's Encyclopedia of Seashells*. McGraw-Hill Book Co., New York, 1974. Full descriptions of over 2,000 species, 1,243 of which are illustrated in color photographs.

Lindner, G. – *Field Guide to Seashells of the World*. Van Nostrand Reinhold Co., New York, 1978. An excellent paperback guide with many listings of genera. 949 species illustrated in full-color photographs.

Melvin, A.G. – *Seashells of the World with Values*. Charles Tuttle Co., Rutland, Vt. and Tokyo, 1966. The first good guide for the collector, but now out-of-date. 1,100 species illustrated in color and rather poor supplementary black-and-white photographs, with old values.

Oliver, A.P.H. – *Guide to Shells*. Quadrangle/New York Times Book Co., 1975. Over 1,200 species described, with over 1,000 illustrated in color paintings by J. Nicholls.

Rogers, Julia E. – *The Shell Book*. Revised Edition. Charles T. Branford Co., Boston, 1951. First published in 1908, this old classic is a delightful treasury of information and trivia, but beware of the "revision", which is only an appendix correcting the obsolete names to 1951.

Wagner, R.J.L. & Abbott, R.T. – *Standard Catalog of Shells*. 3rd Edition. American Malacologists, Melbourne, Florida, 1978. An ambitious continuing loose-leaf system, presenting complete lists of species and synonyms for several families; the official list of world size records for about 1,000 species; and a list of values which unfortunately does not reflect actual dealer's prices. Occasional supplements are being issued. Also includes space for cataloging nearly 1,500 specimens, with additional pages available from the publisher.

Indo-Pacific

Allan, J. – *Australian Shells*. Revised Edition. Georgian House, Melbourne, 1959. Now out-of-date, but much fascinating reading on the many species described. Unfortunately the illustrations by the author are of poor quality and are of little help in identification.

Cernohorsky, W.O. – *Marine Shells of the Pacific.* Vol. I, 1967; Vol. II, 1972; Vol. III, 1978. Pacific Publications, Sydney. The first two volumes cover over 1,000 species, all illustrated, found from West New Guinea to the Marquesas, with emphasis on the Mitridae. The new third volume, entitled *Tropical Pacific Marine Shells,* adds over 600 species.

Cotton, B.C. – *South Australian Mollusca: I. Archaeogastropoda,* 1959; *II. Chitons,* 1964; *III. Pelecypoda,* 1961. W.L. Hawes, Adelaide.

Habe, T. – *Shells of the Western Pacific in Color.* Vol. II. Revised Edition. Hoikusha Publishing Co., Ltd., Osaka, 1968. 1457 Japonic species, not including those in Vol. I by Kira, all in full-color.

Hinton, Alan – *Guide to Australian Shells.* Robert Brown & Assoc., Pty. Ltd., Port Moresby, N.G., 1978. A concise, full-color guide illustrating 1,060 species of the principal gastropod families.

Hinton, Alan – *Shells of New Guinea and the Central Indo-Pacific.* Robert Brown & Assoc., Pty. Ltd., Port Moresby, N.G. and Jacaranda Press, Pty. Ltd., Milton, Australia, 1972. Another concise full-color guide to the principal families of gastropods, illustrating 950 species.

Kay, E. Alison – *Hawaiian Marine Shells.* Bishop Museum Press, Honolulu, 1979. Black-and-white illustrations. A comprehensive treatment with considerable taxonomic and biological information.

Kira, T. – *Shells of the Western Pacific in Color.* Vol. I. Revised Edition. Hoikusha Publishing Co., Ltd., Osaka, 1965. 1,270 Japonic species, many also found in other Indo-Pacific areas, illustrated in full-color.

Macpherson, J.H. & Gabriel, C.J. – *Marine Molluscs of Victoria.* Melbourne University Press, Parkville, Victoria, 1962. A good, well-researched book for the serious collector, with many specific locations. Line drawings only.

Kirtisinghe, P. – *Sea Shells of Sri Lanka: including forms scattered throughout the Indian and Pacific Oceans.* Charles E. Tuttle Co., Rutland, Vt. and Tokyo, Japan. 1978. A not-too-accurate guide to Singalese shells. Poor illustrations.

Moon, G.J.H. & Penniket, J.R. – *New Zealand Seashells in Colour.* A.H. & A.W. Reed, Wellington, London, Auckland, 1970. Describes 312 species in full-color.

Powell, A.W.B. – *Shells of New Zealand.* 5th Revised Edition. Whitcombe & Tombs, Ltd., Christchurch, 1976.

Salvat, B. & Rives, C. – *Coquillages de Polynesie.* Les Editions du Pacifique. Papeete, Tahiti, 1975. 450 species illustrated in full-color.

Wilson, B.R. & Gillett, K. – *Australian Shells.* A.& A. Reed, Sydney and Melbourne, 1971. The best up-to-date guide with much information about the life and habits and locations of the 600 species illustrated. Excellent full-color photographs, including many of the living animals. Does not include bivalves.

North & South America

Abbott, R.T. – *American Seashells.* 2nd Edition. Van Nostrand Rheinhold Co., New York, 1974. The up-to-date "bible" for North American seashells by the dean of American conchologists. Lists 6,500 species, illustrating over 3,000 types. A "must" for the serious collector.

Abbott, R.T. – *Seashells of North America.* Golden Press, New York, 1968. The best paperback survey of North American seashells, treating 850 species, with full-color drawings.

Abbott, R.T. – *How to Know the American Marine Shells.* Revised Edition. New American Library, 1970. An inexpensive, introductory paperback guide for the collector.

Andrews, J. – *Sea Shells of the Texas Coast.* University of Texas Press, Austin, 1971.

Bousfield, E.L. – *Canadian Atlantic Sea Shells.* National Museum of Canada, Ottawa, 1960.

Clench, W.J., ed. *Johnsonia.* – *Monographs of Marine Mollusca of the Western Atlantic.* Museum of Comparative Zoology, Cambridge, Mass.

Emerson, W.K. & Jacobson, M.K. – *The American Museum of Natural History Guide to Shells: Land, Freshwater, and Marine, from Nova Scotia to Florida.* Alfred A. Knopf, New York, 1976. An excellent handbook, available in paperback, to 800 East Coast Shells, with over 1,000 illustrations, some in color.

Humfrey, M. – *Seashells of the West Indies.* Taplinger Publishing Co., New York, 1975. Describes 650 species.

Jacobson, M.K. & Emerson, W.K. – *Shells from Cape Cod to Cape May, with special reference to the New York City Area.* Dover Publications, 1971. A excellent paperbound guide for the regional collector.

Keen, A. Myra & Cohn, E. – *Marine Molluscan Genera of Western North America: An Illustrated Key.* 2nd Edition. Stanford University Press, Stanford, Ca., 1974. The standard reference for identifying all 590 genera (not species) from Alaska to Baja California. Line drawings only.

Keen, A. Myra. – *Sea Shells of Tropical West America: Marine Mollusks from Baja California to Peru.* 2nd Edition. Stanford University Press, Stanford, Ca., 1971. The "bible" for Panamic seashells. Lists 3,325 species, with over 4,000 illustrations. Another "must" for the serious collector.

McLean, J.H. – *Marine Shells of Southern California.* Los Angeles County Museum of Natural History, Los Angeles, 1969.

Morris, P.A. – *A Field Guide to Shells of the Atlantic and Gulf Coasts and the West Indies.* Houghton Mifflin Co., Boston, 1973.

Morris, P.A. – *A Field Guide to the Shells of the Pacific Coast, Hawaii and the Gulf of California.* 2nd Edition. Houghton Mifflin Co., Boston, 1966.

Rice, T. – *Marine Shells of the Pacific Northwest.* Of Sea and Shore Publications, Port Gamble, Washington, 1972. 254 species illustrated in full-color.

Rios, E. de C. – *Brazilian Seashells.* Museu Oceanografico de Rio Grande, Brazil, and R. Petit, N. Myrtle Beach, S.C., 1970.

Rios, E. de C. – *Brazilian Marine Mollusks.* 1976. Catalogs 1,330 species with over 1,250 illustrations.

Warmke, G.L. & Abbott, R.T. – *Caribbean Seashells: A Guide to the Marine Mollusks of Puerto Rico and other West Indian Islands, Bermuda and the Lower Florida Keys.* Dover Publications, Inc., New York, reprint, 1975, of 1961 publication. An excellent paperback for the collector, with special emphasis on the shells of Puerto Rico.

Europe

Bouchet, P. – *Seashells of Western Europe.* American Malacologists, Melbourne, Florida, 1980. Illustrates about 200 species, including a number of living mollusks, in full-color.

Dautzenberg, P. – *Des Coquilles des Côtes de France.* Librarie du Muséum, Paris, 1913.

Lellak, J. – *Shells of Great Britain and Europe.* Hamlyn Publishing Group Ltd., London and New York, 1975. Only 101 seashells, illustrated by Alena Čepická.

McMillan, Nora F. – *British Shells.* Frederick Warne & Co., London, reprint, 1968.

Parenzen, P. – *Carta d'Identita delle Conchiglia del Mediterraneo. Vol. I: Gastropoda,* 1970. *Vol. II, Parts 1 and 2: Bivalvia,* 1974 & 1976. Bios Taras, Taranto, Italy. Line drawings only, but a thorough treatment.

Tebble, N. – *British Bivalve Seashells.* British Museum (Natural History), London, 1966.

Africa

Barnard, K.H. – *A Beginner's Guide to South African Shells.* Maskew Miller, Ltd., Cape Town, 1953.

Kennelly, D.H. – *Marine Shells of Southern Africa.* 3rd Edition. Books of Africa Printery, Ltd., Cape Town, 1973.

Kensley, B. – *Sea-shells of Southern Africa: Gastropods.* Maskew Miller, Ltd., Cape Town, 1973.

Nickles, M. – *Mollusques Testacés Marins de la Côte Occidentale d'Afrique.* Paul Lechevalier, Paris, 1950. Now out-of-date. Line drawings only.

Spry, J.F. – *The Sea Shells of Dar es Salaam* (East Africa). *Part I: Gastropoda,* 1961; *Part II: Pelecypoda,* 1964. Tanganyika Society, Dar es Salaam.

Monographs on Seashell Families

Burgess, C.M. – *The Living Cowries.* A.S. Barnes & Co., South Brunswick, N.J., 1970. The "bible" on this most popular family, with all known species fully treated. Excellent full-color photographs. For an updating, use Walls & Taylor.

Indo-Pacific Mollusca: Monographs of the Marine Mollusks of the Tropical Western Pacific and Indian Oceans. R.T. Abbott, ed. Delaware Museum of Natural History, Greenville, Delaware, 1959 to 1976. Professional studies of a number of families and genera.

Monographs of Marine Mollusca. R.T. Abbot, ed. A continuation of *Indo-Pacific Mollusca.* American Malacologists, Melbourne, Florida, 1978–.

Marsh, J.A. & Rippingale, O.H. – *Cone Shells of the World.* 3rd Edition. Jacaranda Press Pty. Ltd., Brisbane, Australia, 1974. Superseded for the most part by Wall's monograph.

Radwin, G.E. & D'Attilio, A. – *Murex Shells of the World.* Stanford University Press, Stanford, Cal., 1976. The most up-to-date authoritative work on this family, treating 390 species in great detail and in full-color. Only a few Trophons are included.

Walls, J.G. – *Cone Shells: A Synopsis of the Living Conidae.* T.F.H. Publications, Inc., Neptune City, N.J., 1979. The latest book on this family. Many of the author's conclusions have been questioned, but it is the best reference to Conidae to date.

Walls, J.G. & Taylor, J. – *Cowries.* 2nd Edition. T.F.H. Publications, Inc., Neptune City, N.J., 1979. A handy guide for the collector. Illustrates 187 species in full-color.

Weaver, C.S. & du Pont, J.E. – *Living Volutes.* Delaware Museum of Natural History, Greenville, Delaware, 1976. The standard text on this attractive family. All species fully described and illustrated in full-color.

Zeigler, R.F. & Porreca, H.C. – *Olive Shells of the World.* Zeigler & Porreca, W. Henrietta, N.Y., 1969. This survey, though not too thorough, is the only one available. Full-color illustrations.

Systematics and Physiology

Hyman, L.H. – *The Invertebrates, Vol. 6. Mollusca I.* McGraw-Hill Book Co., New York, 1967.

Moore, R.C., ed. – *Treatise on Invertebrate Paleontology. Part I: Mollusca I (Scaphopoda-Archaeogastropoda),* 1960–1964, *N. (Bivalvia),* 1969. Geological Society of America, and University of Kansas Press.

Purchon, R.D. – *The Biology of the Mollusca.* 2nd Edition. Pergamon Press, Oxford and New York, 1977.

Societies

Thiele, J. – *Handbuch der Systematischen Weichtierkunde.* Jena, 1929.

Wilbur, K.M. & Yonge, C.M. – *Physiology of Mollusca.* Vol. I: Classification and Structure. Academic Press, New York, 1964.

Periodicals

Hawaiian Shell News – Illustrated monthly newsletter, edited by S. Lillico, published by Hawaiian Malacological Society, P.O. Box 10391, Honolulu, Hawaii, 96816.

La Conchiglia – Magazine, bimonthly, edited by K.Nicolay, published by La Conchiglia, via C.Federici 1, Rome, Italy, 00147. Editions in Italian and English.

Of Sea and Shore – Quarterly magazine, edited by Tom Rice, published by Of Sea and Shore Publications, P.O. Box 33, Port Gamble, Washington, 98364.

Shell Collector – Quarterly magazine, edited by K.Anders, published by Shell Collector Publications, P.O. Box 14633, Ft. Lauderdale, Florida, 33302.

The following are the principal national malacological organizations. For the address of the current corresponding secretary and information about membership, meetings and publications, contact the curator of seashells or invertebrates at any of the corresponding national or regional natural history museums listed overleaf or in the city listed below.

Australia	Malacological Society of Australia, Sydney
Belgium	Fondation Conchyliogique Belgique, Rhose-Saint-Genèse
	Société Belge de Malacologie, Brussels
Brazil	Sociedade Brasileira de Malacologia, Juiz de Flora
France	Société Française de Malacologie, Paris
	Centre Française de Malacologie sur la Côte d'Azur, Nice
Germany	Deutsche Malakozoologische Gesellschaft, Frankfurt/Main
Great Britain	Conchological Society of Great Britain and Ireland, London
Hawaii	Hawaiian Malacological Society, Honolulu
Israel	Israel Malacological Society, Haifa
Italy	Unione Malacologia Italiana, Milan
Japan	Malacological Society of Japan, Tokyo
Netherlands	Nederlandse Malacologische Vereniging, Amsterdam
New Zealand	New Zealand Shell Club, Auckland
Philippines	Association of Philippine Shell Collectors, Manila
South Africa	Conchological Society of Southern Africa, Cape Town
Switzerland	Unitas Malacologica Europaea, Basel
United States	American Malacological Union, c/o P.O. Box 394, Wrightsville Beach, N.C. 28480 The society publishes an updated list of the many local and regional shell clubs both in the United States and worldwide in its publication *"How to Collect Shells"*.
	Conchologists of America, c/o Sally Jo Gray, 3943 Cornell Way, Eugene, Oregon 97405
	Western Society of Malacologists, c/o Mrs Carol C. Skoglund, 3846 E. Highland Ave., Phoenix, Arizona 85018

Museums

The following museums have large collections of seashells, most with extensive exhibits open to the public.

Australia	South Australian Museum, Adelaide, S. Australia	**South Africa**	South African Museum of Natural History, Cape Town
	Tasmanian Museum, Hobart, Tasmania	**Spain**	Museo Nacional de Ciencias Naturales, Madrid
	National Museum of Victoria, Melbourne, Victoria	**Sweden**	Naturhistoriska Riksmuseet, Stockholm
	Australian Museum, Sydney, N.S.W.	**Switzerland**	Musée d'Histoire Naturelle, Geneva
Austria	Kaiserlich Museum, Vienna		
Belgium	Institut Royal des Sciences Naturelles de Belgique, Brussels	**UNITED STATES**	
		California	Natural History Museum, Los Angeles
	Musée Royal de l'Afrique Centrale, Tervueren		Natural History Museum, San Diego
England	British Museum (Natural History), London		California Academy of Sciences, San Francisco
	National Museum of Wales, Cardiff, Wales	**Delaware**	Delaware Museum of Natural History, Greenville
France	Musée National d'Histoire Naturelle, Paris	**Florida**	Beal–Maltbie Shell Museum, Winter Park
	Musée d'Histoire Naturelle, Bordeaux	**Hawaii**	Bernice P. Bishop Museum, Honolulu
Germany	Naturmuseum Senckenberg, Frankfurt/Main	**Illinois**	Field Museum of Natural History, Chicago
	Zoological Museum, East Berlin	**Massachusetts**	Museum of Comparative Zoology, Harvard University, Cambridge
Italy	Museo di Zoologia, Rome		
	Museo Civico di Storia Naturale, Venice	**Michigan**	Museum of Zoology, University of Michigan, Ann Arbor
Japan	National Science Museum, Tokyo	**New York**	American Museum of Natural History, New York
Netherlands	Zoologisch Museum, Amsterdam		
	Rijksmuseum van Natuurlijke Historie, Leiden	**Pennsylvania**	Academy of Natural Sciences, Philadelphia
New Zealand	Auckland Institute and Museum, Auckland	**Washington, D.C.**	U.S. National Museum, Smithsonian Institution

Acknowledgements

All of the photographs were taken with a 35mm Nikon-F camera with a Micro-Nikkor-P lens, generally set at f22 with a one-second exposure. A copy stand was used with four fixed and two moveable 50-watt reflector spots with diffusion filters. Kodachrome 40 Type A Film was used for plates 1–12 and Kodak Ektachrome 50 Tungsten Professional Film for plates 13–158. Except for plates 1–12, I have attempted to blend the modern scientific illustration with the effect of the softer, more aesthetically appealing watercolor plate of the early nineteenth century.

I would like to thank William E. Old for his continual encouragement and tireless help throughout the production of this book, in keeping me abreast of the numerous changes in classification and nomenclature, in correcting so many of my attributions, in editing the entire manuscript, and for his valued friendship for nearly ten years.

Robert and Dorothy Janowsky gave their time most generously in assisting in identifications and valuations. I would also like to thank several other dealers who have supplied me with a full set of their 1978 to 1980 price lists: Kirk Anders, Richard M. Kurz, Robert Morrison and Carol Skoglund.

My thanks are extended to Mae Lackner and Lorraine Wipperman for their many hours of work in typing the preliminary lists of species and compiling many of the valuations.

I am most grateful to the many professional malacologists listed in the bibliography from whose works I drew so freely, especially R. Tucker Abbott and A. Myra Keen.

Above all, I wish to express my gratitude to my wife, Betty, who allowed my collection to take over our dining room and the preparation of this book to consume nearly two years of an otherwise blessed marriage.

Index

This index includes, as well as the 2,600 species illustrated in this book, listings of over 2,400 additional species, nearly all with current valuations (in dollars).

Valuations are based upon condition, size and location date. They are the average range of prices currently quoted by shell dealers for selected individual specimens. Their buying prices may be quite a bit lower, especially for quantities of common shells. Imperfect specimens ("seconds"), juveniles, beach or dead specimens, and acid-cleaned or polished shells are often worth considerably less. Insufficient locality data also affects the value, but to a lesser degree. World–record–size specimens may be worth many times more, as are rarer colors, albino or melanistic specimens, and especially sinistral examples of normally dextral shells. The value of a rare or recently discovered species may decrease significantly if additional specimens are discovered and offered for sale.

Page numbers in **bold** refer to the illustrations. Synonyms are not referred to in bold.

220

223

OLIVANCILLARIA – *Continued*
vesica Gm. (2.–3.), **125**
Olive, 7, 191; **122–5**
OLIVELLA, 191
altatae Burch & Campbell PAN. (1.–2.)
anazora Duclos (.50–.75), **125**
aureocincta Cpr. PAN. (1.)
biplicata Sow. (.35–.50), **125**
dama Wood (.35–.50), **125**
fletcherae Berry PAN. (.50–.75)
floralia Duclos FLA.-W.I.; BRAZIL (1.)
gracilis Brod & Sow. (1.50–2.50), **125**
morrisoni Olsson PAN. (.75)
mutica Say. N.C.-FLA.-W.I. (.50)
nivea Gm. FLA.-W.I.; BRAZIL (.75)
pedroana Conrad ORE.-BAJA CAL. (.50)
pulchella Duclos (.75–1.), **125**
pusilla Marrat FLA. (.75)
semistriata Gray PAN. (.50–1.)
sphoni Burch & Campbell PAN. (1.–1.50)
tergina Duclos PAN. (.50–1.)
volutella Lam. (.35–.50), **125**
zanoeta Duclos (.75–1.), **125**
zonalis Lam. PAN. (.50)
OLIVIDAE, 26, 191; **122–5**
ONCHIDIATA, 26
ONITHOCHITON hirasei Pilsbry (.75–1.), **176**
neglectus Rochebrune N.Z. (1.50)
ONUSTUS, 184 (*see also* ***XENOPHORA***)
OOCORYS, 186
bartschi Rehder S.E.FLA.-G.of MEX. (75.–100.)
OOCORYTHIDAE, 25
OPALIA, 182
crenata L. FLA.-BRAZIL; E.ATL. (2.)
diadema Sow. PAN. (1.)
evicta de Boury ALASKA-BAJA CAL. (1.50)
exoleura Dall PAN. (3.)
funiculata Carpenter (1.–2.), **55**
insculpta Carpenter, **55**
nitida Kuroda JAPAN (2.)
OPEATOSTOMA pseudodon Burrow (1.–2.), **109**
OPISTHOBRANCHIA, 26, 194–5
ORBITESTELLIDAE, 25
ORECTOSPIRA, 180
tectiformis Watson (4.–6.), **47**
ORECTOSPIRIDAE, 25, 180; **47**
Oriental clam, **169**
Ormer, 177; **30**
OSTREA, 198
angelica Rochebrune (1.–1.50), **157**
cristagalli L. (2.–5.), **157**
cucullata Born. (1.–1.50), **157**
folium L. W.PAC. (2.)
hyotis L. (.50–1.), **157**
imbricata Menke (1.–1.50), **157**
iridescens Hanley PAN. (3.)
lurida Cpr. (.50–.75), **157**
megodon Hanley (1.50–2.), **157**
palmula Cpr. PAN. (.50)
OSTREACEA, 28
OSTREIDAE, 28, 198; **157**
Ostrich foot, 182; **50**
OTOPLEURA
mitralis Adams W.PAC. (.75)
OVULA, 185
costellatum Lam. (12.50–20.), **73**
ishibashii Kuroda JAPAN-TAI. (30.–40.)
ovum L. (1.–1.50), **73**
OVULIDAE, 25, 185; **73–4**
OXYNOACEA, 26
OXYNOE
panamensis Pils. & Olsson PAN. (1.50)
OXYNOIDAE, 26
OXYSTELE sinensis Gm. (.50–1.), **37**
tabularis Krauss (.50–1.), **37**
"tigrina" (.50–1.), **37**
Oyster, 198
Oyster borer, **99**
Oyster drill, **88**

PACHYSIPHONARIA lessoni Blainville (.75), **154**
Pagoda shell, 188–9
Painted lady, **44**
PANDORA, 204
arcuata Sow. (1.50–2.50), **174**
cornuta C.B.Adams PAN. (3.50)
gouldiana Dall (1.–1.50), **174**
grandis Dall ALASKA-ORE. (3.)
trilineata Say. N.C.-FLA.-TEXAS (1.)
uncifera Pils. & Lowe PAN. (1.50)
PANDORACEA, 29
PANDORIDAE, 29, 204; **174**
PANOPEA, 204
PANOPEA – *Continued*
generosa Gould ALASKA-G.of CAL. (2.50–4.)
zelandica Q. & G. (3.–5.), **173**
Paper bubble, **153**
Paper nautilus, 208; **27**, **176**
Paper scallop, **158**
Paper shell, 194, 205
Papery bubble shells, 195
PAPHIA, 201
amabilis Phil. JAPAN-TAI. (.50)
euglypta Philippi (.75–1.), **169**
exarata Philippi (.75–1.), **169**
japonica Deshayes (.50–.75), **169**
schnelliana Dunker (1.–1.50), **169**
sulcosa Philippi (1.–1.50), **169**
undulata Born. (.75–1.), **169**
PAPYRIDEA
aspersa Sow. PAN. (1.50–2.)
crockeri Hertlein & Strong (3.–5.), **167**
soleniformis Brug. (1.50–2.50), **167**
PARAMETARIA dupontii Kiener (.50–.75), **105**
macrostoma Reeve PAN. (5.)
PARAPHOLAS californica Conrad (2.–3.), **173**
PARVAMUSSIUM caducum Smith (1.50–3.), **158**
PARASITA, 26
PARICOPLAX
crocina Reeve S.AUST. (4.)
PATELLA, 178
aenea Gmelin CHILE (1.50)
argentata Sow., **34**
aspera Lam. W.EUR.-MED. (.75–1.)
barbara L. (1.50–2.50), **33**
caerulea L. (.75–1.), **33**
cochlear Born. (1.50–2.50), **33**
compressa L. (2.–3.50), **33**
concolor Krauss S.AFR. (1.)
depressa Pennant W.EUR. (.75)
ferruginea Gm. MED. (1.50–3.)
granatina L. (2.50–3.50), **33**
granularis L. (1.50), **33**
laticostata Blain. W.AUST. (1.50)
longicosta Lam. (1.50–2.), **34**
lusitanica Gm. W.EUR.-MED. (.35–.50)
maxima Orbigny, **34**
miniata Born. (2.–3.50), **34**
natalensis Krauss W.-S.AFR. (.50–1.)
nigrolineata Reeve JAPAN (.50)
oculus Born. (1.50), **34**
plumbea Lam. W.AFR. (1.50)
safiana Lam. (.75–1.), **34**
stellaeformis Reeve JAPAN (1.)
tabularis Krauss (2.–5.), **34**
variabilis Krauss S.AFR. (1.)
vulgata L. (.75–1.), **34**
PATELLACEA, 25
PATELLIDAE, 25, 178; **33–5**
PATIONIGERA deaurata Gm. (2.–3.), **34**
Pea-pod shell, **156**
Pearl oyster, 198; **157**
Pearl shell, **41**
PECTEN, 7, 198
See also ***AMUSIUM, AEQUIPECTEN, ARGOPECTEN, CHLAMYS, DECATOPECTEN, LYROPECTEN, PLACOPECTEN,*** for duplicate listings of ***PECTINIDAE*** described in this book. All other species are grouped below for convenience.
alba Tate AUST. (1.50)
albicans Schröter (.75–1.), **158**
antillarum Récluz FLA.-W.I. (2.–5.)
aspera Sow. (.75–1.), **158**
aurantiacus Adams & Reeve (7.50–15.; Select colors – 20.–30.), **158**
benedicti Verrill & Bush FLA.-G.of MEX. (2.–5.)
biolleyi Hert. & Strong BAJA CAL.-ECU. (2.)
camerella Berry BAJA CAL. (1.50–3.)
caroli Iredale (1.–1.50), **158**
caurinus Gould (3.–5.), **162**
chazeliei Dautz. FLA.-G.of MEX.-W.I.-BRAZIL (7.50)
cumingii Reeve AUST. (1.50–2.50)
corallinoides Orb. W.AFR. (40.–50.)
delicatula Hutton N.Z. (4.)
diegensis Dall (15.–25.), **159**
empressae Kuroda & Habe JAPAN (5.)
flabellum Gm. (1.50–2.50), **159**
flexuosus Poli E.ATL.-MED. (5.–10.)
fulvicostata Adams & Reeve W.AUST. (1.–2.)
funebris Reeve AUST. (1.–2.)
glaber L. (1.–1.50; Yellow – 3.–5.), **159**
glaber mytilene, **159**
hyalinus Poli MED. (5.–10.)
incantata Hert. GALÁP. (12.50)
inflexus Poli (3.–5.), **159**
PECTEN – *Continued*
jacobeus L. (2.–5.), **162**
larvatus Reeve W.PAC. (1.–3.)
langfordi D., B. & R. HAW. – syn. for *P.noduliferum* Sow. (I-P) (40.–60.)
linki Dall W.I. (5.)
lischkei Dunker (3.–5.), **160**
lividus Lam. AUST. (2.)
lowei Hert. CAL.-ECU. (1.50–2.50)
luculentum Reeve (3.–5.), **160**
machrochericola Habe JAPAN (2.50)
maximus L. (1.50–3.), **162**
meridionalis Tate (2.–3.), **160**
meridionalis fumata Reeve, **160**
mildredae Bayer FLA.-G.of MEX. (40.–75.)
miles Reeve INDON. (75.)
multisquamata Dunker FLA.-W.I. (60.–75.)
multistriata Poli MED.-W.AFR. (6.–10.)
nivea L. W.EUR. (25.–45.)
novaezelandiae Reeve (1.–2.), **160**
pallium L. (.75–2.), **161**
patriae Doello-Jurado, **160**
pauciplicatum Iredale, **161**
pernomus Hert. BAJA CAL.-ECU. (5.)
perulus Olsson PAN.-PERU (1.–2.50)
phrygium Dall MASS.-FLA.-G.of MEX.-W.I. (20.–35.)
plica L. I-P (1.–2.)
pourtalesianum Dall FLA.-G.of MEX.-W.I. (2.)
preissiana Ire. W.AUST. (2.)
proteus Lightfoot (2.–4.), **161**
puncticulatus Dunker W.PAC. (1.50–3.)
pyxidatus Born. W.PAC. (1.50–3.)
radula L. (1.–2.), **161**
rastellum Lam. (20.–30.), **161**
raveneli Dall (1.–3.; Orange – 5.–7.50), **161**
rushenbergeri Tryon PER.G. (2.)
scabricostatus Lam. (1.–2.), **161**
sericeus Hinds (5.–7.50), **162**
sinensis Sow. (2.–3.), **161**
speciosa Reeve (15.–30.), **161**
strangei Reeve AUST. (1.–2.)
superbus Sow. (25.–40.), **161**
thaanumi D., B. & R. W.PAC. (30.–40.)
tranquebaricus Gm. IND.OC.-W.PAC. (1.50–2.)
tricarinata Anton, **158**
tumbezensis Orbigny (2.–4.), **162**
velero Hert. G.of CAL.-PERU (3.–6.)
vesiculosus Dunker (2.50–4.), **162**
vogdesi Arnold (2.50–5.), **162**
wardiana Ire. W.PAC. (2.–5.)
yessoensis Jay (2.–5.), **162**
zelandiae Gray N.Z. (2.50)
ziczac L. (1.50–5.; Orange, red – 15.–20.), **162**
PECTINACEA, 28
PECTINIDAE, 12, 28, 198; **158–62**
PECTINODONTA orientalis Schepman (.35–.50), **35**
rhyssa Dall JAPAN (.35–.50)
PEDICULARIA, 185
californica Newcomb (1.–1.50), **59**
PEDIPES
unisulcatus Cooper CAL.-G.of CAL. (.35)
Pelagic mollusks, 13
PELECYPODA, 28, 196–205
Pelecypods, 12
Pelican's foot, 182; **50**
PENICILLUS, 205
giganteus Sow. (10.–25.), **174**
penis L. (7.50–10.), **174**
strangulatum Chenu (7.50–15.), **174**
PENION adusta Philippi (2.–3.), **103**
grandis Gray AUST. (5.)
mandarina Duclos (3.–5.), **103**
maxima Tryon (4.–6.), **103**
oligostira Tate (3.–5.), **103**
sulcatus Lam. N.Z. (3.50)
PENITELLA penita Conrad (1.–1.50), **173**
Pen shell, 197; **157**
PERIGLYPTA, 201
edmondsoni Dall (1.–1.50), **169**
listeri Gray (1.–1.50), **169**
multicostata Sow. (1.50–2.50), **169**
puerpura L. (1.–1.50), **169**
reticulata L. (1.–1.50), **169**
PERINGIA
ulvae Pennant MED. (.75)
PERIPLOMA
planiusculum Sow. PAN. (D–1.)
PERIPLOMATIDAE, 29
PERISTERNIA, 190
australiensis Reeve (1.00), **109**
chlorostoma Sow. HAW. (.35–.50)
PERISTERNIA – *Continued*
fastigium Reeve (3.00), **109**
"incarnata" Kiener (1.00), **109**
leucothea Melvill S.AFR. (3.)
nassatula Lam. (1.00), **109**
nassoides Reeve IND.OC. (2.50)
rhodostoma Dunker, **109**
Periwinkle, 180; **36**, **46**
PERNA, 197
canaliculata Gm. (.50–1.), **156**
chemnitziana Orbigny, **157**
viridis L. (1.–1.50), **156**
PEROTROCHUS, **177**
PERRONA – *see* ***CLAVATULA***
PETALOCONCHUS, 181
macrophragma Cpr. PAN. (1.–1.50)
varians Orbigny (2.–3.), **48**
PETRICOLA, 202
denticulatum Sow. PAN. (1.–2.)
lucasana Hert. & Strong PAN. (3.)
parallela Pilsbry (1.–1.50), **170**
pholadiformis Lam. (1.–2.), **171**
PETRICOLIDAE, 28, 202; **171**
PHACOIDES – *see* ***LUCINA***
PHACOSOMA
coerulea Reeve AUST. (1.)
PHALIUM, 186
areola L. (1.50–3.), **80**
bandatum Iredale (1.50–3.), **80**
bisulcatum Schubert & Wagner (.75–1.50), **80**
bisulcatum booleyi Sow., **80**
bisulcatum diuturna, **80**
bisulcatum pila Reeve, **80**
canaliculata Brug. (1.50–2.50), **80**
cicatricosum Gm. (2.–4.), **80**
decussatum L. (.75–1.), **80**
faurotis Jousseaume (2.–3.), **80**
flammiferum Röd., **81**
glabratum Dunker (2.–3.), 80
glabratum angasi Iredale, **80**
glabratum bulla Habe, 80
glaucum L. (1.50–3.), **81**
granulatum Born. (2.–4.), 81
granulatum centriquadratum Val. (.75–1.50), **81**
granulatum inflatum Shaw, **81**
granulatum undulatum Gm. (2.–3.), **81**
iheringi Carcelles BRAZIL (5.–12.50)
inornatum Pilsbry (1.50–2.), **81**
labiatum Perry (2.–3.), 81
labiatum iredalei Bayer, **81**
persimilis Kira, **80**
pfeifferi Hidalgo, **80**
pyrum Lam. (1.50–3.), **81**
saburon Brug. (2.50–4.), **81**
semigranosum Lam. (2.–3.), **81**
strigatum Gm. (.75–1.50), **81**
thomsoni Brazier (3.–4.), **81**
umbilicatum Pease HAW. (35.)
whitworthi Abbott W.AUST. (35.–45.)
PHANOZESTA semitorta Kuroda & Habe (1.50–2.50), **84**
PHARUS, 203
legumen L. W.EUR.-MED. (1.50)
PHASIANELLA, 179
aethiopicus Philippi (.75–1.), **44**
australis Gm. (1.50–3.50), **44**
kochi Philippi (.75–1.), **44**
ventricosus Swainson (1.50–2.), **44**
PHASIANELLIDAE, 25, 179; **44**
PHAXAS, 203
Pheasant shell, 179; **44**
PHENACOLEPADIDAE, 25
PHENACOVOLVA angasi Reeve (3.50–5.), **74**
birostris L. (1.–2.50), **74**
brevirostris Schumacher, **74**
carpenteri Dunker JAPAN (1.–1.50)
fusula Cate & Azuma JAPAN (5.)
longirostrata Sow. (7.50–10.), **74**
philippinarium Sow. W.PAC. (5.)
rosea Adams (1.–1.50), **74**
rosea nectarea Ire. AUST. (2.–5.)
saturnalia Cate & Azuma JAPAN (3.)
PHILBERTIA
doris Dall PAN. (1.50)
PHILENE, 194
kurodai Habe (2.00), **153**
PHILINACEA, 26
PHILINE
aperta L. NORTH SEA-MED. (1.50)
hayashii Habe JAPAN (7.50)
PHILINIDAE, 26, 194; **153**
PHILIPPIA, 180
hybrida L. (1.50), **47**
krebsii Mörch N.C.-FLA.-BRAZIL (3.–5.)
lutea Lam. (2.50), **47**
radiata Röd. (.50–1.), **47**
PHILOBRYIDAE, 28
PHOLADACEA, 28
PHOLADIDEA
quadra Sow. PAN. (4.–5.)